lesbian
potentiality &
feminist media
in the 1970s

A CAMERA OBSCURA BOOK

lesbian potentiality & feminist media in the 1970s

rox samer

DUKE UNIVERSITY PRESS DURHAM & LONDON 2022

© 2022 Duke University Press
All rights reserved
Project editor: Annie Lubinsky
Designed by Aimee C. Harrison
Typeset in Portrait Text Regular &
Clash Display (Indian Type Foundry)
by Westchester Publishing Services

Library of Congress Cataloging-in-Publication Data
Names: Samer, Rox, [date] author.
Title: Lesbian potentiality and feminist media in the
1970s / Rox Samer.
Other titles: Camera obscura book (Duke University
Press)
Description: Durham : Duke University Press, 2022. |
Series: A camera obscura book | Includes
bibliographical references and index.
Identifiers: LCCN 2021026131 (print) | LCCN 2021026132
(ebook)
ISBN 9781478015383 (hardcover)
ISBN 9781478018025 (paperback)
ISBN 9781478022640 (ebook)
Subjects: LCSH: Feminism and motion pictures. |
Feminism in literature. | Lesbians in literature. |
Science fiction—History and criticism. | Feminism—
History—20th century. | Feminist theory. | Lesbian
feminist theory. | BISAC: SOCIAL SCIENCE / Media
Studies | SOCIAL SCIENCE / Feminism & Feminist
Theory
Classification: LCC PN1995.9.W6 S264 2022 (print) |
LCC PN1995.9.W6 (ebook) | DDC 791.43/6526643—
dc23/eng/20211021
LC recordavailableathttps:/ /lccn.loc.gov/2021026131
LC ebookrec ordavailableathttps:/ /lccn.loc.gov
/2021026132

Cover art: Stills from *Fever Dream* (Chick Strand, dir.,
1979).

For all my mentors
with boundless gratitude

contents

acknowledgments

Lesbian Potentiality and Feminist Media in the 1970s was written over the course of many presents, some now long past if but in a flash of historical time. I am forever grateful for my many mentors and coconspirators along this journey.

Much of this book's writing was supported by the collegial friendships of my fellow Clark University faculty. Hugh Manon, Gohar Siddiqui, and Soren Sorensen mentored me as the newest Screen faculty and did so with care that far exceeds what is professionally asked of them. I am grateful for Stephen DiRado's, Kristina Wilson's, and the rest of the Department of Visual and Performing Arts's enthusiastic support. Chris Ruble, our resource librarian, hunted down films and made clips for my classes so I could devote substantial time to writing. Chris also helped me secure many of the images printed here. Jessa Loomis joined me on hikes and New England adventures and helped me articulate the project in broader terms. I am honored to be a member of the queer cabal with Liz Blake and Bob Tobin.

I began the project that became this book at the University of Southern California's (USC) School of Cinematic Arts under the direction of Kara Keeling. I do not exaggerate when I say Kara taught me how to think. All that follows is indebted to the rigor and tenacity of thought Kara modeled for and demanded of me. Jack Halberstam, Aniko Imre, and Henry Jenkins served on my PhD committee, and I carried their encouragement and questions with me through the revision and expansion of this manuscript. Laura Isabel Serna directed an invaluable interdisciplinary graduate writing group.

My fellow graduate students got me through the PhD. micha cárdenas and Raffi Sarkissian became family. Branden Buehler, Sonia Misra, Tom Sapsford, and Rosanne Sia remain great supports. Lara Bradshaw, Umayyah Cable, Jennifer DeClue, Feng-Mei Heberer, Alison Kozberg, and Luci Marzola gave critical feedback on early chapter drafts.

During my time as a graduate student I was blessed with the guidance of informal mentors at USC and elsewhere, including Alex Juhasz, Chuck Kleinhans, Julia Lesage, and Bill Whittington. Chuck, I miss our long conversations on your and Julia's porch. I am thankful for Alex's, Bill's, and Julia's enduring mentorship, as I am that of my undergraduate mentor, Monica McTighe, without whom I may never have aspired to scholarly life, and that of Russell Shitabata, who has encouraged my intellectual curiosity since I was a teen and who, alongside Anne McGrail and Allie Shitabata, continues to teach me about many subjects.

The research presented here would have been impossible without the aid of many archives, libraries, librarians, and archivists. Special thanks to Linda Long and Special Collections at the University of Oregon; Joanne Donovan and Diana Carey at the Arthur and Elizabeth Schlesinger Library on the History of Women in America at Harvard University; Maida Goodwin and Kate Long at the Sophia Smith Collection at Smith College; May Haduong and Cassie Blake at the Academy Film Archive; Todd Wiener at the UCLA Film and Television Archive; and Meghann Matwichuk at the University of Delaware. I am forever grateful for a trip to the Lesbian Herstory Archives, which, among other things, enabled my chance meeting of Beth Capper, who in turn informed me of the British Film Institute's print of *We're Alive*. Thanks to Steve Tollervey, who made my jetlagged trip to the BFI basement a delight and kept me from freezing with tea and a portable heater.

I am indebted to those I interviewed over the course of my research, including Amanda Bankier, JEB, Christine Choy, Ariel Dougherty, Mary Lee Farmer, Jeanne Gomoll, Sharon Karp, Julie Phillips, Francis Reid, Jeff Smith, and Cathy Zheutlin. I owe much to Alexis Lothian, without whom I might have never made it to WisCon.

Many of the ideas and arguments advanced in the pages to follow were formulated in conversations with colleagues at conferences and in the correspondence that grew out of such meetings. Thanks especially to B. Bradburd, Nick Davis, Victor Fan, Jack Gieseking, Laura Horak, Kei Kaimana, Cáel M.

Keegan, Jen Malkowski, Quinn Miller, Candace Moore, Teddy Pozo, Erica Rand, Eliza Steinbock, and Greg Youmans, whose friendships have grown my heart and mind in tandem. Thank you to Victoria Hesford and Teddy Pozo for inviting me to your classes to share my research.

Elizabeth Ault, my editor, has encouraged and challenged me from the start of our collaboration. Two anonymous readers gave generous and concrete feedback that shaped the manuscript indelibly. In August 2020, Nick Davis and Laura Horak enthusiastically workshopped the revised manuscript with me over Zoom, helping me ease the book into its final form. Patricia White's warm welcoming of the manuscript into the Camera Obscura book series gave me confidence and renewed my enthusiasm.

Rachel Corbman read the manuscript not long before it went to press. More than one footnote has been expanded thanks to her vast knowledge and wisdom. And amid a global pandemic, Rachel has given lesbian potentiality new meaning and resonance to this author.

"Cat Chat" or "The Rulers of Catscadia," a tight-knit evolving group of decades-long friends, their partners, and their cats, including Ari Chadwick-Saund, Adam Chimeo, Katie Cissel, Kristina Moravec, Raffi Sarkissian, Ash Tiedtke, Kingsley, Tonks, and Toby, has played no small part in making life livable. Thank you for your love, friends. Without my mom, Sally Marie, this book would not be possible, and without Zoe Samer, my comrade from the start, the journey to and through this writing would have been lonely indeed.

A huge thanks to the dance instructors, therapists, stylists, baristas, and grocers whose labor supported the research and writing of this book. Atsuko Okatsuka got me dancing again in graduate school, and Danny Dolan danced me through the final stages of book revision and formatting—in a pandemic and via Instagram, no less.

The final thanks go to Amelie, Elio, Buffy, Beanie, and Artie, whose companionship has brought me much joy. To Elio, who was here but briefly: I miss you dearly. To Amelie, who has been here from the beginning: you are my everything. Thank you for writing this with me.

introduction
living in the lesbian's former future:
a media historiography of imagination
for when the present is past

/lezbiən/

Lesbian. The first syllable of the word always feels like molasses. Pressing my tongue into the roof of my mouth before dragging it down and back in a movement that seems almost imperceptibly slower than it ought to, the first syllable is swallowed by the second and third as time returns to its conventional speed. I have gotten more than enough practice, tasted many a spoonful of lavender molasses, writing a book on lesbian existence and feminist media in the 1970s. "Lesbian existence," as opposed to the more clinical "lesbianism," Adrienne Rich writes, "suggests both the fact of the historical presence of lesbians and our continuing creation of the meaning of that existence."[1] The work that went into creating this meaning by the time Rich's essay was published in 1980 was no small matter. More than a simple identity category, the lesbian was taken up by scores of feminists in their activism, scholarship, and creative and cultural work in broad attempts at reimagining gender and sexual existence.[2]

It is my contention that the lesbian sign achieved its most robust work in feminist media and feminist media cultures of the second half of the 1970s. During the height of cultural feminism in the United States and Canada, lesbian feminism—the set of political praxes valuing women's emotional and erotic connection with one another as central to the overthrowing of patriarchy—flourished alongside feminist presses, bookstores, record labels, film distributors, and visual art and video collectives. Feminist art, literature, music, and films circulated through feminist communities, encouraging the mass-imagination of what being lesbian might entail and could come to mean. This project turns specifically to feminist experimental and documentary film and video and feminist science fiction (SF) literature, as the two facilitated this work of imagination in an exceptional manner. Feminist experimental and documentary films and videos of the 1970s introduced diverse audiences to the lives of others, past, present, and future, at once making familiar what was previously unknowable to most, from lesbian lovemaking to women's prison experiences, and defamiliarizing the all too well known—namely, heterosexuality and the everyday exploitation of women. Likewise, 1970s feminist SF literature transported readers to entirely other times and places, envisioning what life may be like under different societal conditions and, in turn, making the limitations of the here and now more apparent. Across these texts, the lesbian sign—sometimes spoken, sometimes written, other times connoted, coded, or inferred—enabled the imagination of how women might live and love differently. Due to widespread feminist interest in seeing women's cinema and the formation of feminist SF fandom as a counterpublic, this cultural work of creating the meaning of lesbian existence was undertaken not by a select and elite few but by thousands—in post-screening discussions and the pages of fanzines, at SF conventions and women's prison video workshops. Approaching the history of lesbian feminism by way of feminist media and feminist media cultures opens up the 1970s lesbian sign and expands our conception of what counts as lesbian feminism.

In the early 1970s, feminists naming themselves lesbian feminists reclaimed the anachronistic and diagnostic "Lesbian" (often with a capitalized "L," harking back to Sappho's ancient island of Lesbos) to become visible, thinkable, and imaginable as women-loving women.[3] Contrary to psychoanalysts, who claimed women's sexual desire for other women to be symptomatic of their desire for male power in a patriarchal world, lesbian feminists insisted that lesbians sought one another out for sex, romance, friendship, and antipatriarchal comradery.[4] Rather than gaining power, in reorienting themselves toward fellow women, they often lost the social and economic protections of the family and heterosexual partnership. *Sappho Was a Right-On Woman: A Liberated View of Lesbianism* (1972), one of the first book-length statements on lesbian feminism, signaled this with its dedication to "those who have suffered for their sexual preference, most especially to Sandy, who committed suicide, to Cam, who died of alcoholism, and to Lydia, who was murdered; and to all who are working to create a future for Lesbians."[5] In *Sappho*, Radicalesbians and lovers Sidney Abbott and Barbara Love detail the joys of gaining a gay consciousness and living an openly (capital "L") Lesbian life dedicated to women's liberation.[6] They write that they and their lesbian feminist peers are contributing to the "new set of values based on an appreciation of both the differences and the common humanity existing between individuals and groups" being developed by coterminous social movements.[7] In changing societal attitudes, *Sappho*'s authors hoped Lesbians (and, implicitly, all sexual, gender, and racial minorities) could "become most ordinary people,"[8] modeling a theoretical move that would characterize much of identity politics for the following decades.

Come the 1990s, queer theorists would start to question the use of the lesbian sign.[9] Aims at normalcy had seemingly calcified the lesbian sign into something not especially interested in a potential world wherein people could love, fuck, reproduce, and otherwise live differently. Instead, those operating under the lesbian sign, like many operating under the gay sign, often appeared more invested in carving out a place within the unjust world around them in which white cisgender monogamous lesbians and gay men would be tolerated.[10] During the 1990s, lesbians became a niche market that corporations such as Absolut and Subaru could cater to without risking the loss of their broader straight market.[11] As early as 1991, Judith Butler predicted that the gay and lesbian signs would cease to produce the erotic practices so long enabled by their very instability.[12] In another act of reclamation, the "queer" of queer activism, queer culture, and queer theory became an attempt to keep such gender and sexual possibilities open.[13]

Despite the prevalence of normalizing rhetoric such as Abbott and Love's, "lesbian," for much of the 1970s, maintained an amorphous shape. How and why one became a lesbian and even what being a lesbian entailed varied greatly from person to person. For some women, it was a political decision, a way to free themselves from heterosexual society's prescribed gender roles.[14] For others, it enabled them to express and pursue sexual desires that they had been repressing for years.[15] Often, however, it was not so simple. Instead, as the lesbian historian Amy Kesselman points out, "As the idea of love between

3

women emerged in the women's movement, many women looked critically at the limitations they had imposed on their relationships with women and opened themselves to sexual feelings towards each other."[16] Like much feminist thinking, these conscious decisions "challenge[d] the mystifications and silence that often made it difficult for women to experience or pursue pleasure" and revealed "the power of the women's liberation movement to enable women with a range of sexual experiences to reconfirm, reconfigure, or change their sexual desires."[17] This reconfiguration extended from sex to all aspects of social life. By the mid-'70s, feminists who had not identified as lesbians just years before were organizing, cohabitating, corresponding, making art, making love, working, and raising animals and children in ways previously unimaginable—all under the sign of "lesbian."

What "lesbian" in the 1970s signified included these tangible and immediate possibilities, but it also signaled something more: the potential that gendered and sexual life could and would someday be substantially different, that heteropatriarchy may topple, and that women would be the ones to topple it. The eradication of sexism, misogyny, and homophobia would not simply mean a world where lesbian existence was normalized—where lesbians, too, could get married, make babies, and achieve the privileges of white middle-class domesticity. In the absence of compulsory heterosexuality—the ideological presumption, shared by most feminists, of men and women's innate attraction[18]—society itself would be entirely reconfigured. And in such a lesbian future, the continued creation of the meaning of lesbian existence would not cease but would look, sound, and feel entirely different than it did in the 1970s present.

In naming this felt sense, this signification of futurity, lesbian potentiality, I draw from Italian philosopher Giorgio Agamben's essay "On Potentiality," in which he argues that Aristotle's concept—potentiality—is integral to understanding human struggles for survival and expression. Potentiality refers to when a person has the faculty to do something, whether or not they ever in fact do it. It is a mode of existence defined by just such a privation— the sensation of a faculty ironically present most palpably in its absence. Potentiality is political, Agamben argues, because it serves as a constant threat and is most keenly felt where power exerts itself.[19] But it also flourishes when freedom is fought for, during moments of revolution and resistance. Agamben's primary example is poet Anna Akhmatova's recounting of the origins of her *Requiem* collection about Stalin's Great Purge of the Communist Party in the 1930s. Standing outside the Leningrad prison, awaiting news of her son arrested on political grounds, Akhmatova is asked by another woman who recognizes her, "Can you speak of this?" "Akhmatova," Agamben writes, "was silent for a moment and then, without knowing how or why, found an answer to the question: 'Yes,' she said, 'I can.'"[20] This "I can" is about more than Akhmatova's abilities as a poet to skillfully represent her and others' adversity through language. Agamben explains, "For everyone a moment comes in which she or he must utter this 'I can,' which does not refer to any certainty or specific capacity but is nevertheless, absolutely demanding. Beyond all faculties, this 'I can' does not mean anything—yet it marks what is, for each of us, perhaps the hardest and bitterest experience possible: the experience of potentiality."[21] For countless feminists in the 1970s, lesbian existence was that formidable force shining a light on the way to a better future.

In bringing together many women of disparate backgrounds, both physically and virtually (in instances of written, audio cassette, or video cassette correspondence), feminist media not only offered representations of lesbian potentiality but facilitated experiences of it. There is a scene near the end of Joanna Russ's science fiction novel *The Female Man* (1975) in which the protagonist Joanna describes acting on her fantasies about her friend Laur as tantamount to creating her own reality—"an impossible project." After kneeling behind Laur's chair as she reads, Joanna kisses Laur's neck and then over her ear and cheek to her mouth, knowing that at any second Laur will rebuke her and "the world will be itself again." Except Laur kisses her back. In this moment, reality for Joanna is torn wide open, and she tells the reader, "If this is possible, anything is possible."[22] Such experiences of potentiality were incredibly common in the 1970s due to lesbian feminism's growing luster. In Russ's novel, Joanna and Laur eventually get stoned and make "awkward, self-conscious love," but "nothing that happened afterward," Joanna tells us, "was as important to me (in an unhuman way) as that first, awful wrench of the mind."[23] In the 1970s, feminist film and video and feminist SF literature provided many such lesbian "kisses" across the United States and Canada, engendering entire feminist media cultures. And while I, over the four chapters of this book, explore the awkward "lovemaking" that followed—feminist audiences' and fans' excited delineation of certain possibilities, sometimes to the neglect of others—it is also important to identify the potentiality of these first, awful wrenches of the mind.

In turning to the lesbian realities created by these feminist media cultures and the media they circulated, I flash a light on a history of lesbian existence that "could have been but was not."[24] Not only had "lesbian" in the late 1970s yet to cohere into what the sign would come to mean to Butler and other queer scholars writing in the 1990s and 2000s; it also pointed toward lesbian

5

futures that queer politics and queer studies have conveniently forgotten in favor of their own, lesbian futures that would not come to be but whose sensation on the horizon was nonetheless crucial to so many. The Lesbian, under the purview of potentiality, becomes the mode of existence of a certain privation—a heuristic for illuminating the contingency of history.

Potential Interventions

As a historical concept that roughly aligns with a period in the United States and Canada previously identified as the height of cultural feminism (between radical feminism of the late 1960s and early 1970s and the dissolution of the "second wave" in the early 1980s),[25] lesbian potentiality distinguishes a function of the lesbian sign missed by sweeping feminist histories attendant exclusively to activism and scholarly theory. Like Greg Youmans's *Word Is Out* (2011), Kristen Hogan's *The Feminist Bookstore Movement* (2016), and Cait McKinney's *Information Activism* (2020), this study of lesbian potentiality takes the cultural work of cultural feminism seriously.[26] Characterizations of cultural feminism as a means of seeking refuge from male supremacy miss the forms of creative thinking cultural texts and their media cultures enabled.[27] Lesbian potentiality also points to the diffuse work the lesbian did across cultural spheres not always aligned or completely in sync with the feminist political coterie named lesbian feminism. It reveals how the creation of the meaning of lesbian existence in the 1970s was not confined to the work of activist leaders or scholars but undertaken by countless people of many genders and sexualities through the production, distribution, exhibition, and reception of feminist media.

Rarely have 1970s feminist film and video and feminist SF literature been studied together.[28] This is no doubt partially due to the fact that the two media cultures themselves hardly ever intersected or overlapped. Science fiction film in the 1970s was largely the stuff of New Hollywood and either blockbuster or extremely low-budget exploitation special effects, its feminism the celebration of a few strong female characters and the creative reading of camp fans.[29] As video became an increasingly domestic medium, women began recording their favorite SF television series—most notably, *Star Trek* reruns—and remixing them to craft texts more to their liking, erotically and politically.[30] Meanwhile, robust feminist media cultures burgeoned separately around experimental and documentary film and video and SF literature—the queer progeny of lesbian potentiality and each medium/genre. In studying these two feminist media cultures here, I allow the two to bump

6

up against each other, the variance in lesbian potentiality's work across each materializing in the gaps and the breadth and wealth of the imagination of lesbian existence cumulating through their conjunction.

As a historiographical concept, lesbian potentiality provides feminist, queer, and transgender media studies with a way of connecting potentialities past and present that neither obfuscates nor reifies their differences. It is a method of illuminating social movement history that also attends to its privations—the what was *and* the what could have been. "The here and now" might at times *feel* like "a prison house," but that need not mean casting it away in favor of idealized pasts or futures yet unknown.[31] There are historiographical alternatives to simply converting past potentialities into a resource in the service of our imagined future. As I explain over the course of this introduction, the queer aesthetics of the past do not contain the map to queer futures. We may be of a future, but we are not living in a lesbian feminist future, nor shall we ever have the opportunity. This does not mean that the potentialities of the past are not worth thinking with, not worth understanding in the context of the quagmires of their own presents even as we also pursue the project of confronting the challenges of our own time. Lesbian potentiality as historiographical methodology means not losing the historical subject in favor of either the contemporary or the futural. Only in doing as much might we, in turn, recognize ourselves as historical subjects, acknowledging that our own work in the pursuit of potentiality will look, sound, and feel totally different from that of the unknowable potentialities to come.

Attuned to the contingency of history, one discerns that lesbian existence (or what I call, building on Agamben, "being lesbian") might have led to not-being lesbian—which is not to say to heterosexuality, bisexuality, or androgyny, but to a not-lesbian that exceeded late twentieth-century understandings of gender and sexuality. Rich supplements her term "lesbian existence" with "lesbian continuum," which she uses to name the range of emotional and political bonds between and among women occluded by the most common understandings of "lesbianism."[32] In the not-being lesbian that might have followed being lesbian, the lesbian continuum could have extended beyond woman identification, letting go of compulsory heterosexuality's part-and-parcel cisnormativity. Rather than being extended, however, the lesbian continuum was cut short. This project, as I explain, does not offer yet another history of the women's movement's failure. But "LGBT," "LGBTQIA," or any such identitarian appellation—however expansive—is not an extension of the lesbian continuum. For this very reason, in every conference presentation and campus lecture I still feel the weight of "lesbian" on my tongue. Perhaps I should not admit this. Perhaps it is poor advertising, as they say.

Cunnilingus jokes notwithstanding, the problem is not purely physiological. In that stalling of the oratory metronome, history has taken hold. This book works against a guiding impulse of queer studies: its rejection of the possibility of women's and gay liberation thinking in concert with queerness. This working against takes work. Kadji Amin contends that *queer*—unlike *gay* or *lesbian* or *feminist*—appears slick, almost infinitely mobile, and unbound from any particular identity, historical context, set of objects, or methods because of its historical stickiness. Its emergence in the US scene of the 1990s has ensured that "*only certain* forms of nonnormativity, *only particular* sex acts seem to attach to it."[33] In an attempt to distinguish itself from gay and lesbian studies before it, a field very much the product of 1960s and '70s social movements, queer studies of the 1990s declared a primary interest in the discursive production of sexual identities, a project cast as at odds with the essentialisms of cultural feminism and gay liberation. Guided by Eve Kosofsky Sedgwick's contention that the closet served as the structuring metaphor of twentieth-century sexualities,[34] queer scholars interested in historiography and theories of temporality have returned time and again to the pre-Stonewall period, to eras more or less long before US gay and lesbian cultures "came out" en masse,[35] seeing in the liberation movement era's speaking of homosexuality—its "reverse discourse"—an erasure of nonnormative genders and sexualities' problematizing of hetero-homo and male-female binaries.[36] Critiquing lesbian feminists who lamented the relative invisibility of lesbian sexuality before women's liberation, Jack Halberstam claims that attending to discourses of sexual acts and desires uncovers "sexual scenes and sexual practices and pleasurable identifications that are often rendered invisible by the homosexual-heterosexual continuum."[37] In *Cruising Utopia*, José Esteban Muñoz both narrowly and amorphously limits his study to "a historically specific nexus of cultural production before, around, and slightly after the Stonewall rebellion of 1969."[38] Shortly after 1969, it is implied, utopian feelings sufficient for a critical methodology that looks backward to enact a queer future dissipate. A too-close past, the 1970s and its liberation movements are not queer enough to get us to the queerness that is not yet here.

Within queer studies, the lesbian feminist has served as a figure particularly deserving of derision. The lesbian feminist, as Sara Ahmed has so eloquently explained, "is without question a killjoy figure; so often coming up as being anti, antisex, antifun; antilife. The investment in her misery needs to be understood as just that: an investment."[39] This investment is shared by heteropatriarchy and queer studies. As the movement for women's liberation grew increasingly visible to the broader public, cisgender straight male misogynists regularly derided lesbian feminists for being humorless, a pain, and a bore. Sadly, such charges have been taken up more recently, if more artfully, by others. "In some queer literatures," Ahmed writes, "lesbian feminism itself appears as a miserable scene that we had to get through, or pass through, before we could embrace the happier possibility of becoming queer."[40] For this reason, queer historiographies that do address lesbian feminism—and, drawing on the metaphors of queer studies' affective turn, think about what it feels like to "touch" this era from the present—foreground the bad feelings of such lesbian feminist contact. In *Time Binds*, Elizabeth Freeman describes the gravitational pull that "lesbian" exerts on "queer" as a form of "temporal drag."[41] Whereas the queer gets to be performative and deviant in the name of a radical future, the lesbian feminist is constantly cast as an anachronistic drag. And in an attempt to hold on to the historical feeling of the lesbian, to not cut it loose as much of queer studies would have her, Freeman transforms lesbian feminist temporal drag into a queer methodology of historiographical media analysis, a way of "connecting queer performativity to disavowed political histories."[42] Freeman's case in point is Elisabeth Subrin's experimental video *Shulie* (1997), a shot-by-shot remake of a 1967 documentary about the radical feminist Shulamith Firestone. As Victoria Hesford points out, Firestone, though an influential thinker to a range of 1970s feminisms, neither openly identified as a lesbian nor had much to say about lesbians or lesbian feminism.[43] Her exemplary lesbian drag, in fact, a lesbian precursor, Freeman yet again situates the moment of queer political possibility prior to the emergence of lesbian feminism in the 1970s.

In *Feeling Women's Liberation*, Hesford explores how feminism's concern with its own history and the queer desire for history have passed each other like ships in the night, leaving each other "untouched and often unnoticed by the other."[44] For Hesford, much like myself, the lesbian feminist 1970s would make a logical site for such an encounter. Hesford takes it upon herself to theorize why this has not come to pass. She compellingly claims that "instead of approaching the archive [of 1970s feminisms] as an array of rhetorical materials that sought to persuade and enact a new political constituency and world into being, it has instead largely been read as evidence of specific and coherent theoretical and ideological standpoints, which are then defended or criticized in a more knowing present."[45] The deep entanglement of feminism and lesbian existence at this time and the mass media's perception of their coconstitution are integral to this process. If in the nineteenth and early twentieth centuries the lesbian was a ghost that haunted popular and "high" culture, threatening to disrupt the bland homogeneity of heterosexual society, "the feminist-as-lesbian," Hesford argues, became a ghost of women's liberation, haunting the present so forcefully that we can see neither how she was produced nor how she might interest us.[46] First conjured by dyke-baiting antifeminists and anti-lesbian feminists but ironically kept afloat by queer studies' attempts to distinguish itself from the social movements that immediately preceded it, the feminist-as-lesbian has become an image memory, distorting how the women's movement is remembered and felt today.[47] Her spectrality shields how 1970s feminisms challenged postwar American heteropatriarchal hegemony, even as her hypervisibility serves as a constant reminder of the endurance of gender and sexual oppression.[48] Studying the feminist-as-lesbian's emergence in the year 1970, Hesford makes a case for folding her back into the ongoing elaboration of feminist symbolic space so that she becomes "a sign of the possibilities—unrealized as well as realized—of women's liberation."[49]

Lesbian Potentiality and Feminist Media in the 1970s is in many ways a response to Hesford's call. It follows the feminist-as-lesbian through the archives of two feminist media cultures, studying the plentiful and at times surprising and less recognizable forms through which she takes shape. Whereas Hesford focuses her attention on the emergence of the feminist-as-lesbian across mass-media stories and early feminist theory published in the year 1970, this book lifts the record player stylus and places it on the 1974-79 period to follow the dissemination of lesbian potentiality through diverse discourses within the movement, as well as at various intersections between the women's movement and preexisting media cultures. It dives squarely into the fray—that messy temporal territory so carefully avoided by earlier queer scholars. It does so believing that, if one wishes to understand the queerness of lesbian existence, the threat the feminist-as-lesbian posed to heteropatriarchy in the 1970s, one needs to look to her influence—the breadth of thinking, imagining, organizing, and community building the lesbian sign made possible.

A Short History of Lesbian Potentiality

Lesbian potentiality permeates radical feminist theory of the early 1970s, and it is partially responsible for the development of lesbian separatism in the years immediately thereafter. One early statement of lesbian potentiality, widely cited and well circulated through the women's movement, was Anne

Koedt's "The Myth of the Vaginal Orgasm." First delivered in 1968 and then published in 1970, Koedt's essay offered feminists, by way of lesbian sexuality, a sort of collective "we can." In the essay, Koedt extends radical feminist claims about male supremacy to the sexual sphere and argues that straight men (whom today we would also identify as cisgender) have controlled the dialogue about sex to sustain the fulfillment of their own sexual pleasure and maintain their social dominance of (again, cisgender) women.[50] She outlines scientific studies on female sexual pleasure, which conclude that cisgender women experience climax predominantly through the clitoris, rather than the vagina, as Freud and others had previously claimed.[51] With this knowledge, she writes, straight cisgender men could become sexually expendable, since whom cisgender women receive sexual pleasure from becomes divorceable from their partners' sexes. This is Koedt's "we can" moment. Cis women can satisfy one another sexually, which may even be more desirable, Koedt claims, as they (unlike cis women and men under patriarchy) are also able to relate to one another "on a full, human basis."[52] Although incredibly limited in its articulation of what produces sexual pleasure, Koedt's essay is important because it supplements critiques of the structural oppression of cis women with the proposal of an alternative that considers their pleasure paramount.[53] She concludes the essay by arguing that this knowledge could change society profoundly: "The establishment of clitoral orgasm as fact would threaten the heterosexual institution. For it would indicate that sexual pleasure was obtainable from either men or women, thus making heterosexuality not an absolute but an option. It would thus open up the whole question of human sexual relationships beyond the confines of the present male-female role system."[54] In this way, though initially articulated in relation to cisgender women's sexual freedom, lesbian potentiality, for Koedt, would inevitably expand to the imagination of a more equitable sexual future in which everyone would be bisexual, androgynous, and freer.

For Koedt and many other radical feminists in the early 1970s, lesbian potentiality existed first and foremost as a refusal of heteropatriarchy's insistent exertion of its own potentiality. According to Agamben, while other animals have the specific potentiality to do this or that, humans are the only creatures with the potentiality to not-do, the only ones capable of their own impotentiality, and thus freedom, as they have the power of refusal.[55] Being lesbian, for many radical feminists, meant refusing (at least temporarily) the heterosexuality integral to male supremacy. "The lesbian," as Hesford explains, "became a figure that provided a form for thinking women's liberation as the freeing of women from the obliged affections and affective obligations of the 'sex-caste system.'"[56] Because of this, radical feminists expressed lesbian fantasies for women's liberation and did so with a surprisingly projective and creative force.

"The Woman Identified Woman" (1970), written by the Radicalesbians (of which Abbott and Love were members), offers another notorious example of one such fantasy.[57] The manifesto was first distributed as part of a "Lavender Menace" zap action at the Second Congress to Unite Women. As Alice Echols and Dana R. Shugar have chronicled in great detail, its authors' primary goal was to create a space for lesbians within radical feminism by articulating lesbian existence in their terms.[58] With it, the Radicalesbians position the lesbian as the vanguard of feminism for having already gone through the "torturous journey" of "the liberation of the self."[59] What begins as a personal necessity (coming out, finding other women like them, and so on), they write, becomes political as lesbians are forced to confront the limitations placed on them in being female and are driven to question the world around them. Though it might take them decades, lesbians inevitably reject the self-hatred and guilt they have learned and replace it with self-love and, in turn, the love of all women. In doing so, the Radicalesbians argue, lesbians have all already gone through the process of challenging patriarchy and heterosexism and thus have years of insight to offer radical feminists, who had only recently begun to argue for the transformation of gendered society. In fact, men's labeling of certain women "lesbians" or "dykes," the Radicalesbians claim, is exactly what allows men to define "women" as those who "get fucked by men" and thus as existing under the "male grid of role definitions."[60] They offer "woman identified woman" as a way to open and extend possibilities for sisterly commitment and solidarity across the "sexist" and "male supremacist" categories of "homosexual" and "heterosexual." Instead of trying to change men, which, they claim, preoccupies too much of feminists' energy, they will change themselves, and they will do so together. As women-identified women, they will "create a new sense of self" through which they will "achieve maximum autonomy in human expression."[61] The lesbian potentiality of becoming "woman-identified" radiated across feminism in the following decade. It was women-identified women with whom Audre Lorde in 1978 claimed that she had found others "brave enough to risk sharing the erotic's electrical charge" and "pursue genuine change within [their] world" together.[62] And it was woman-identification that Rich in 1980 claimed to be a specifically lesbian "source of energy" that could challenge the falseness, hypocrisy, and hysteria of compulsory heterosexuality and lead to the liberation of all women.[63]

Introduction

However, under radical feminism this potentiality was repeatedly curbed or redirected so that the sexuality of such lesbian potentiality was left behind. One can see this most clearly in the speeches of women's movement figurehead Ti-Grace Atkinson that circulated through the movement for years before being published in *Amazon Odyssey* in 1974. For Atkinson, lesbian potentiality was strategic. In her speeches she defines lesbian existence as a "commitment, by choice, full-time, of one woman to others of her class."[64] She extends this with the analogy, "Lesbianism is to feminism what the Communist Party was to the trade-union movement."[65] Thus, for Atkinson and other "political lesbians" of her ilk, lesbian potentiality's value lay in its class solidarity, and commitment to lesbianism will bring women together to work toward revolution. It had little to do with sexual desire or romance between women or even how same-sex relationships could change the oppressive social structures of straight romantic partnership.

Politicized this way, lesbian potentiality did not share potentiality's most exciting characteristics, nor could it perform its full political function. According to Agamben, experiences of potentiality are dependent on knowledge or ability. Unlike *generic potentiality*, which is what we mean when we say a child has the potential to become a great artist or leader, *existing potentiality*, such as that of the architect to build or the poet to write, means that, unlike the child, the architect or poet need not suffer an alteration but instead already is potential.[66] For Atkinson and other "political lesbians," lesbian potentiality was a generic potentiality. It did not precipitate from the lived experiences and knowledges of lesbians in the present. Such a radical feminist approach to lesbian existence becomes a temporal problem, the lesbian existing almost outside of time itself and therefore not truly existing as anything more than a concept. By remaking the lesbian into a figure for feminism "both Koedt and Atkinson invest[ed] her with a futurity that is also, at the same time, an attempt to free her from her own historicity."[67] In "Compulsory Heterosexuality and Lesbian Existence," Rich writes about these and other likeminded feminists' assumptions that, in a world of equality, everyone would be bisexual: "Such a notion blurs and sentimentalizes the actualities within which women have experienced sexuality; it is the old liberal leap across the tasks and struggles of here and now, the continuing process of sexual definition which will generate its own possibilities and choices."[68] Radical feminists in the early 1970s conveniently ignored that, for many, sex between women and the romantic and kinship structures of lesbian partnership or communal living were not merely stepping stones toward more equitable relations with men but desirable in and of themselves for both the present and foreseeable future. In doing so, radical feminists delimited lesbian potentiality's political function, as lesbian existence served but one purpose, losing all possibility of continued instigation thereafter.

Within a year of the writing of these radical feminist lesbian imaginings, lesbian separatism emerged as a lived political practice. Taking radical feminists' calls for women to unite together as a class seriously, separatists believed that, by segmenting themselves off from heterosexual society either by moving to "lesbian lands" outside metropolitan centers or creating women-only collectives within cities, they could direct the entirety of their energy toward one another and, in doing so, foster new ways for women to be in the world.[69] The initial goal for most separatists was to create safe spaces where women could escape the physical, sexual, and social violence they regularly experienced as a result of misogyny.[70] As Carol Anne Douglas writes in *off our backs* (1974), her call for a feminist nation, "Such a free society for women could provide the greatest possible opportunity for women to develop themselves, their relationships with each other, and their own politics and culture."[71] In such separatist spaces, many believed they would finally be able to shed their patriarchal conditioning and create new definitions of womanhood that did not hinge on their relation to men.[72] The Killer Dykes articulated this vision most forcefully in a 1971 poem, the last three stanzas of which read:

> You don't have much time to reform anyway
> The Killer Dykes have already set the date
> > when at the stroke of midnight
> > we'll change all you back into pumpkins
> > or maybe into welcome mats for our sisters; and then
>
> > take over Clark St. for the lesbians
> > take over the world for the lesbians
> > rename it Isle of Lesbos
> > drop Isle
> > for our world will no longer be an island
> > we'll unite with our sisters all over the galaxy
>
> > and turn you all into fertilizer
> > so your masculinity-proving fertilization
> > all your sexist shit
> > can be put to good use.[73]

Whether they put it mildly, as in the case of Douglas's careful argument for the benefits of a feminist nation, or forcefully, as exemplified by the Killer

Dykes' angry but broad ("sisters all over the galaxy") poetic charge, many lesbian feminists in the early 1970s believed that separatism was necessary to spark revolution. Invested in love as well as comradery among women, separatists saw lesbian potentiality as more than temporarily withholding sexual access from the oppressors. Lesbian existence provided the starting point for eradicating misogyny, sexism, and homophobia. Separatism thus expanded the temporality of radical feminism's lesbian potentiality, valuing the present tense nature of same-sex romantic, sexual, and kinship relations while also looking ahead to the futures that its sociality and politics could make possible. As lesbian separatists created the collectives and lesbian lands where women might gain the experience, knowledge, and skills necessary to create meaningful structural change, they sought to transform lesbian potentiality from generic into existing potentiality.

This is apparent in the example of the Washington, DC, collective the Furies. Founded in the spring of 1971, the Furies initially consisted of twelve white women age eighteen to twenty-eight of working-class, middle-class, and upper-middle-class backgrounds (including Ginny Berson, Joan E. Biren [JEB], Rita Mae Brown, and Charlotte Bunch) who chose to break away from the DC Women's Liberation Movement to escape homophobia within the organization and create lesbian leadership for the women's movement.[74] Although young and white, nearly all of the Furies had experience organizing against racial discrimination and for the New Left.[75] And while they did believe sexism to "be the root of all other oppressions," they were also inspired by the Black Panther Party and the Weathermen to contribute to radical groups' incitement of a global revolution for all.[76] Moreover, in the pages of the nationally distributed newspaper they edited together, *The Furies*, they advocated for feminist theories by women of color, working-class women, and lesbians: "Feminist ideology must be created by those with the greatest stake in the male system or it will be reformist and sell less privileged ones down the river."[77] In *The Furies*, they also theorized what they put into practice in their collective in the hope that sharing what they learned from the experience would help eradicate all oppression of women in the future. In a 1972 memo to the rest of the collective, Bunch described her vision of fifty years out in which the United States has dissolved completely, its various regions being run by different minority groups, including "A Federation of Feminist States" governed by a lesbian feminist party. It is then, she claims, that lesbian feminism, still separatist and still implicitly white, would be able to build alliances with racial minority and gay male groups.[78] Lesbian potentiality, for the Furies, would deliver women's freedom. However, it would

15

also eventually lead to a complete restructuring of society in which new ways of relating to others would have been made possible. Lesbian existence would continue; however, it would no longer call for divisions but would flourish within a reconfigured field of relationality.

To build toward this future in the present, the Furies, like many other lesbian feminists, believed that all women should become lesbians. As Berson wrote in the editorial for the first issue of *The Furies*, "Lesbianism is not a matter of sexual preference, but rather one of political choice which every woman must take if she is to become woman-identified and thereby end male supremacy."[79] For Berson and her cohort, unlike Atkinson, however, this was more than dogma. For them, it meant the immediate rejection of traditional middle-class family structures in favor of experimenting with new models of collective living. The Furies created "a kind of laboratory where each member tried to overcome patterns of behavior that reflected both her class status and her internalized hatred of women."[80] As Anne M. Valk documents, they pooled their wages, redistributed their resources to correct for past class and heterosexual privileges, and shared all possessions and responsibilities, including, for some time, the care for three children from members' past heterosexual relationships.[81] Coletta Reid detailed in an article published in June–July 1972, "In addition to working on political projects, [they] tried to get in better physical and mental condition."[82] One of their members taught the others karate, and together they formed weekly study groups devoted to researching how past revolutions took meaningful action.[83] Through their community outreach projects (which included self-defense and mechanical skills workshops, political theory discussion groups, poetry readings, and film screenings) and their publication of *The Furies*, the collective shared what its members learned through separatism with the women's movement at large.[84]

With each of these endeavors, the Furies acted on the sense of potentiality that their lesbian existence granted them and sought to make possible what they felt themselves to be collectively capable of. After the collective disbanded, its members continued to put out *The Furies*. While the collective living/working setup did not turn out to be sustainable for the twelve of them, the Furies remained committed to leading by example. Alongside their theoretical essays and personal accounts of collective living they published articles on lesbian history; poetry; strength training and martial arts exercises; directions and diagrams for how to relieve a "lesbian headache" through massage; and JEB's beautiful photography of the Furies and other DC lesbian feminists organizing, playing sports, and embracing. The fifth issue of *The Furies* included a full two-page newspaper spread of such photographs. Atop the black-and-white collage of women chopping wood, climbing trees without shirts on, playing softball, talking in a garden, and straddling each other in a park, the playful title reads, "Come Outside (On a Queer Day You Can See Forever)."[85] Here and elsewhere, the Furies used humor and affection, alongside abstract thinking and more practical survival skill sets, to articulate their very felt, embodied sense that in confronting their own oppression and building their own worlds they might contribute meaningfully to the kinds of changes society so desperately needed.

The Furies anticipated Muñoz's claims for queerness as a horizon. In *Cruising Utopia*, Muñoz describes queer aesthetics as providing audiences and readers affective access to queer futures.[86] Through quotidian images of indeterminacy, gesture, and performativity, gay men's poetry and performances from the decade before Stonewall, such as Frank O'Hara's "Having a Coke with You" (1966) and Amiri Baraka's *The Toilet* (1964), Muñoz claims, make queer futures palpable as if present. Queerness, as this potentiality for Muñoz, exists in a perpetual futurity that enables those of us in the present to "dream and enact new and better pleasures, other ways of being in the world, and ultimately new worlds."[87] Muñoz draws on Agamben in his theorization of queerness as potentiality, but he does not address the evolving nature of potentiality by way of impotentiality. Potentiality, for Agamben, is defined by its simultaneous impotentiality. Agamben quotes Aristotle, who writes: "A thing is said to be potential if, when the act of which it is said to be potential is realized, there will be nothing impotential."[88] This, Agamben explains, means more than possibility's ruling out of impossibility. Instead, with true potentiality, the potentiality to not-be no longer lags behind actuality but "passes fully into it as such."[89] Potentiality, by way of impotentiality, is thus not annulled in actuality but both destroyed and preserved; it "survives actuality and, in this way, gives itself to itself."[90] Lesbian potentiality is the mode of existence of just such a privation. While radical feminism's thinking of lesbian existence as heterosexual impotentiality meant a temporary refusal of male sexual supremacy, lesbian impotentiality meant a commitment to rethinking lesbian sex, romance, and collective living with social change. In the metaphor of queer horizon, as lesbian feminists brought new ways of being into the world, lesbian (im)potentiality would reilluminate the same sky but with slightly different colors, the rosy pinks of yesterday's future lesbian morphing into the swirling pumpkin oranges and violet blues of today's.

While lesbian potentiality for radical feminist theory was more akin to what Agamben describes as generic potentiality, and lesbian separatism tried to convert this generic potentiality into something more, many feminist cultural texts of the second half of the 1970s consign the lesbian with an existing potentiality. Through the imagination of what could be and what such alternatives might look, sound, and feel like, the lesbian potentiality of feminist film and video and feminist SF literature maintain Agamben's defining characteristic of potentiality: impotentiality or the potentiality to not do, to not pass into actuality or to preserve itself when it does do so.[91] Put another way, these cultural texts engender new space-times from which women might love and live differently than they do in the present but also suggest that the lesbian existence they envision need not come to be, or stay as it is should it come to be. Being lesbian does not demarcate who lesbians are once and for all or even who they are for now. Their lesbians are the lesbians who could be but are not. Their potentiality is such that they give themselves to themselves so that their imagination might continue. These texts conceive of the temporality of lesbian potentiality differently from the theory and praxis before them, not situating the past, present, and future as distinct, successive moments but, in varying ways, coexisting, co-constituted temporalities. As a result, audiences get to live in time differently and experience lesbian (im)potentiality in a manner inaccessible via activism proper and only gestured to by feminist theory.

Lesbian feminist SF literature of the 1970s juxtaposes heterosexual pasts and presents with potential lesbian futures, using the genre's temporal flexibility to narrativize the meeting of different temporalities and, in turn, provoke questions about their desirability. Russ's "When It Changed" (1972) and *The Female Man* (1975), James Tiptree, Jr.'s "Houston, Houston, Do You Read?" (1976), Suzy McKee Charnas's *Motherlines* (1978), and Sally Miller Gearhart's *The Wanderground* (1978) depict women's societies or worlds that have either left men behind or lost the male half of the species through natural disaster or war. The narrative conflict of these stories occurs when these societies contact remnants of heteropatriarchal pasts. Characters from pasts more like our own present cannot believe what they find in the future. Sex has become completely divorced from reproduction. Women (they do usually hold on to this gendered designation, if also ridding it of its contemporary connotations) have developed entirely unrecognizable erotic networks, as their romantic, sexual, and kinship ties disentangle and rebraid themselves in unpredictable patterns. Over decades or centuries of such processes, what it means to be a woman and what defines the human have radically altered. Like "women identified women," these fictional folks from the future have created new senses of self. These stories thus work backward, in a way, as they explore lesbian potentiality in actuality, otherwise impossible, and lesbian potentiality gets extended in multiple directions across time.

Counterintuitively, these stories do not grant readers full access to these new ways of living. The stories perform what Ursula K. Le Guin calls science fiction's "thought-experiment" heuristic, as readers travel to these futures and experience what it could mean to be born into those bodies that today would most likely be assigned female at birth under totally different social conditions.[92] However, more often than not, readers are situated alongside a protagonist who occupies a liminal position on the border of past, present, and future societies. Readers, like the stories' protagonists, may find the future they travel to appealing but are also unclear about whether they belong, experiencing a sort of ambivalence about any desire for such a lesbian feminist future. These are not lesbian feminism's futures. They are not predictive, and yet in their accounting for the process of (im)potentiality, their fictionalized constituents continue to work toward more equitable futures and, in doing so, come to resemble 1970s lesbians less and less.

"Houston, Houston, Do You Read?"—Tiptree's Hugo and Nebula award-winning novella (and the last the author would publish before his name would be revealed as one of two pseudonyms of sixty-one-year-old Alice B. Sheldon)—takes place approximately three hundred years in Earth's future after an epidemic put an end to the reproduction of infants with XY chromosomes more than two hundred years earlier. Earth's population has drastically declined to two million, and its exclusively XX chromosomal inhabitants have developed the means to reproduce the human species through cloning. Each person refers to those of their same genotype as "sisters," and they each typically give birth to two "sister" or clone babies (after becoming pregnant through a form of in vitro) during their teenage years to contribute to the growth of the population. They all write journals, and they keep a central library of each genotype's memoirs. Every ten years they read their "book" from start to finish, learning from those who shared their genes and lived before them, noting similarities in personalities, health risks, and interests but also tracking the unique contributions of each person as someone not solely defined by her genetic makeup. No longer autonomous individuals, humans have come to understand themselves through their "sisters" and their collective histories. They continue to evolve as a society and culture, the books of older clones becoming increasingly "unrealistic," by which they mean they cannot imagine living as they did then. In this future, sisterhood serves not as a solution but as a starting point. The human has become lesbian, but their potentiality as such is renewed, as these humans-as-lesbians continue

19

to build toward an even better world for those to come. Humanity might be free of compulsory heterosexuality, but they do not assume human struggle to be extinct.

As readers, we are not privy to this information immediately but come to learn it piece by piece as the story's male protagonist puts the clues together. "Houston, Houston" is narrated by a physicist, Dr. Orren Lorimer, one of three twentieth-century astronauts to have traveled by accident to this future. Unknown to the reader, and even to Lorimer, the story is his verbal recollection to the crew of the spaceship *Gloria* after they have given him and Major Norman "Dave" Davis and Captain Bernhard "Bud" Geirr, the two other male crew members of the broken-down 1970s spaceship *Sunbird*, a tell-all drug. After spending months with these three men, the *Gloria* crew remain uncertain as to whether they ought to take them back to Earth and drug them to observe their uninhibited speech and behavior and thus learn their true nature—or so Lorimer suspects once he discovers he has been drugged. Much of the story is focused on the past: Lorimer's thoughts about his, Bud's, and Dave's rescue and time aboard the *Gloria*, as well as about his time aboard the *Sunbird* and his life on Earth before that. All his memories and observations, which move in and out of the relative past and present tenses, are not happening in his head, as he thinks, but, in fact, are being narrated to his hosts aboard *Gloria*. Situated this way, we (like Judy Paris, Judy Dakar, Lady Blue Parks, Connie Morelos, and Andy Kay) are Lorimer's audience. Like these twenty-third-century crew members, we analyze how Lorimer thinks. Unlike to them, however, he is relatively familiar to us as someone from a time similar to our own. And like him, we exist in a near state of privation when it comes to knowledge of the future down on Earth. As readers we pick up clues in the *Gloria* crew's language and rely on Lorimer's thoughts and reflections to figure out what is going on and what we think of it.

Lorimer thus serves as a very particular conduit between the present as past and the future as present. Forming a link between the two times, he is also constantly locating himself somewhere between the sexes on board. Aboard the *Sunbird* he was always the odd man out—the scientist, not the astronaut, and thus the smallest, least athletic, and nerdiest of the group. He inadvertently tells his observers that he has never felt like a normal guy, and the story opens with a memory of being bullied into using the girls' bathroom in junior high. While Lorimer, like his two compatriots, was married with children, he does not express the same attitude of male supremacy toward the crew of the *Gloria* as Bud and Dave do. He is attracted to the crew and watches them touch one another, wondering what they do in their quarters together at night, but he is also friendly with them, especially the two "sister" Judys, in a way that he is not with Bud and Dave. When he figures out that all "sisters" are clones and says, contrary to their fear, that he is not offended, the Judys tell Lorimer that they think of him as "more hu—more like us."[93] The members of the *Gloria*'s crew are willing to share with Lorimer information about how they live on Earth and why they have organized life in this way, because they consider him different from the others. Unlike Bud and Dave, Lorimer makes a life among them aboard *Gloria*, twentieth-century patriarchy having not served him well as a not particularly masculine man.

Through drugging the men and observing their behavior, the crew of *Gloria* receive a rich history lesson, as the misogyny, homophobia, and transphobia of the past are enacted before them. Tension between Bud and Dave and the *Gloria* crew builds, and Bud's frustration with living under a woman's command culminates in his sexual assault of Judy Paris, an act inconceivable in the reality of this future. When Bud first makes his advances, Lorimer tries to warn the crew of what he expects will happen. They do not heed his warnings and say that Judys can take care of themselves; instead, they observe the event like anthropologists, filming them and collecting Bud's sperm as a sample. Andy (who is named for his clone line's taking of androgens, a.k.a. testosterone, and has been passing as a cis man to deflect the suspicions of Bud and Dave as to what awaits them down on Earth) is the only crew member to try to help Judy. When Bud hits Andy, Lorimer finally reveals the secret, yelling at Bud to stop hitting him because "he" is really a "she" like all the others. Bud rages about the subservience he expects to encounter when they land and belittles Andy as a "bull dyke" incapable of pleasing the female population as he will, starting now with Judy Paris. While shockingly little is done to stop Bud, the story soon ends with each of the three cis men being administered an antidote for the drug, which, Lorimer tells the reader, "tastes cool going down, something like peace and freedom . . . [o]r death,"[94] suggesting that all three are being terminated. This ending might read like a separatist out-and-out rejection of half of the species as inherently misogynist and domineering. Interestingly, Sheldon, after Tiptree's outing, felt the need to assuage readers upset by the implication that assassinating men was the solution to women's problems.[95]

While what we do know about the ways these humans in the future live generates a certain level of curiosity, at the end of the novella we, along with Lorimer, are still in the dark. As readers we can only begin to guess what we may have in common with those living down on Earth. Theirs is not 1970s lesbian feminism's future. These future lesbians are not separatists, and they are not simply creating lesbian lands. For one, their restructuring of society is global (governments and capitalism no longer exist). Still, theirs is *a* lesbian feminist future, and this future's concern for Lorimer as a feminine man, inclusion of transgender Andy, and hinting at thousands of ways to be human expand the gendered bonds of the lesbian continuum. While drafting "Houston, Houston," Tiptree would write quite polemically in letters to feminist fanzines that he believed a ratio of fewer men to women would be productive to correcting many social woes. For this, the self-presenting male feminist received criticism from men and women alike, the former accusing him of reverse sexism and the latter castigating him for binary thinking.[96] However, this proposal's fictionalization in "Houston, Houston" reveals that the creative exercise of envisioning a world without twentieth-century men facilitated the imagination of more genders, not fewer, and opened the potential for more to come.

Due to the substantial economic barriers women filmmakers faced in the 1970s, as well as feminist critiques of the patriarchal dangers of narrative cinema, feminist film and video was typically short, experimental, or documentary, rather than long-form fiction. As a result, lesbian potentiality in these films is not so much narrativized as connoted through cinematography, editing, and music. Lesbian feminist classics such as Jan Oxenberg's *Home Movie* (1972) and *A Comedy in Six Unnatural Acts* (1975) and Barbara Hammer's *Dyketactics* (1974), *Superdyke* (1975), and *Women I Love* (1976) bring audiences into lesbian domestic and communal spaces and, through their various formal means and structures, explore what being lesbian felt like to their out lesbian filmmakers. Each of these films also gestures toward "how it could be," the sense of potentiality that accompanied everyday lesbian existence. In Oxenberg's autobiographical *Home Movie*, this sense of potentiality rushes in with the film's pivot from Oxenberg's past as a teenage lesbian cheerleader to her present as a member in Los Angeles's lesbian feminist community, pictured through the crosscutting of documentary protest footage and a lesbian football game in which she is no longer on the sidelines but part of the team. As the footage of Oxenberg as a cheerleader winds down through slow motion, her voiceover states, "All the time I was doing this kind of thing, you know, 'Rah, Rah, Jim Smith, he's our man,' there was this secret place inside of me that really knew what was best for me, that was building my real self this whole time, and maintaining my real feelings. It just feels really good now to have broken through the façade." A slow piano chord ushers in the

22

first shot of grown-up Oxenberg, now dressed in a Lavender Menace T-shirt and throwing the football. The piano's tempo picks up, and soon Oxenberg is lost in a lesbian huddle, a close-up tracking embracing arms. The camera pulls back as the group breaks apart, and, intercut with the slow-motion game in which whole bodies become entangled, legs wrapping around waists and faces nuzzling into bottoms, are quick black-and-white shots from women's and gay liberation actions. On the soundtrack, folk artist Debra Quinn sings, "We are not alone, we are together, we are together, we have each other, so don't tell us what to be // We are not helpless, we are women, we are women, and we're not waiting any longer to be free, to be free, to be free." It is not only Oxenberg's closeted childhood that is now past but also a politics of seeking acceptance. This pack of Brown and white lesbians are rolling, grabbing, caressing, and laughing their way into a lesbian future defined by freedom. The film ends mid-action. The football game is not over; nor is the process of creating the meaning of lesbian existence. Just as there are no clear teams, scores, or clock, when, where, and with whom being lesbian might lead is entirely up for grabs. A sense of something else being possible leads these lesbians here, and the feeling has not dissipated. It continues to move and to motivate, reaching out to other ways of being, if not an end zone.

Films such as Oxenberg's did more than capture or document the feeling of potentiality so keen for so many lesbians at this time; they created such an experience for viewers, adapting it to cinematic form and externalizing what was often quite internal and therefore unverifiable. But moments of lesbian (im)potentiality were not confined to the screens of out lesbian filmmakers. In 1979, the Los Angeles–based experimental and ethnographic documentary filmmaker Chick Strand made two films that, I argue, offer two of the most poignant affectations of lesbian potentiality. In the first, *Cartoon le Mousse* (1979), lesbian potentiality is more generic, proffering a refusal of heterosexuality, not unlike Atkinson's and Koedt's from the start of the decade. The film contrasts lesbian subjects with heteronormative structures of desire through the juxtaposition of imagery and sound. However, in *Cartoon le Mousse* and even more so in *Fever Dream* (1979), lesbian potentiality's refusal of heterosexuality is imbued with an eroticism and playfulness absent from both the desexualized (Atkinson) and hypersexualized (Koedt) writing of their feminist theory counterparts. The films are not prescriptive of a properly lesbian form of sexuality. Instead, with just the faintest suggestion of what could be or could come to be, these films' lesbian potentiality maintains that it could not come to be. In doing so, they ask those they engage to think about whether they offer desirable alternatives and for whom.

Cartoon le Mousse can also be understood as a project of re-vision. In 1972, Rich called for a feminist critique of literature to study how women have lived and how language has trapped them so that they might "begin to see—and therefore live—afresh."[97] Whereas Oxenberg did as much with the home movie format, looking back at herself as a child and teenager and at how her parents pictured her before offering a vision of her lesbian adulthood and what could come, Strand takes on the sensual pleasures of Hollywood cinema. Through the crafting of two distinct parts of her film—one remixed footage and one original photography—Strand contrasts the banal terror of seventy years of heteropatriarchal cinema with a brief and murky glimpse at the lesbian cinema that could come to stand in its place. The film begins with a woman walking onto a stage and announcing to her audience, of which the viewer is a part, first in English and then in French, that the theater is "proud to present a re-enactment of defective facsimiles and counterfeits." These defective facsimiles and counterfeits turn out to be found animated and live footage from Classical Hollywood, which Strand remixes in the first, longer portion of the film. The montage's black-and-white images dwell on empty spaces. Combined with eerie organ music, which at times mixes with voice-overs, lyrics, and sound effects, these empty spaces appear as if those of a haunted house, and their various "scenes" are given titles such as "Rituals Involving the Meditation of Pure Light Trapped in a Ridiculous Image" or "Variation on a Bourgeois Living Room in which the Shadow Woman Hangs Herself." Domesticity, on- and off-screen, Strand suggests, has never been safe for women; it has always been a horror. This first half of the film ends with a series of violent images: an animated rabbit swinging by a brook and singing "Someday My Prince Will Come" explodes as the film cuts to a thunderstorm; a big fish consumes a school of smaller fish; back inside, drapes catch on fire. A music cue, not totally unlike that in *Home Movie*, ushers in a distinct second passage of the film, which consists of original black-and-white footage of women undressing and caressing each other shot by Strand at her home in Tujunga Valley, just north of Los Angeles.

On the other side of bourgeois heteropatriarchy, for Strand, are not men and women cohabitating on more equal terms, as Koedt or Atkinson would have it, but sensual lesbian existence. Re-vision includes "the challenge and promise of a whole new psychic geography to be explored."[98] It can be difficult and dangerous, Rich cautions, to try to find "language and images for a consciousness we are just coming into."[99] The first passage of the film consists largely of long shots of empty spaces with animated creatures and few other figures inhabiting the frame, suggesting that women, if not Woman, in Hollywood were nowhere to be found.[100] The second, meanwhile, is shot in extreme close-up, and barely discernible bodies, which are nonetheless present and coded as both female and feminine, fill the frame. A separate instrumental track, more relaxed but still a bit strange, runs over this footage. It is not austere and forceful like that of the first passage but sensual and passionate. Due to the proximity of the figures and the lack of lighting other than backlighting, one can tell little more about who they are. Their ages and races, even how many there are, are all unclear. One cannot tell exactly what they are doing, but it is apparent that they are close and touching. On occasion, long hair falls down across the frame, the horizontality to their positions evoking lovemaking.

From behind the lights, across the 180-degree line from the camera, must appear a well-lit lesbian scene, but this is not what Strand films. Instead, she offers viewers an experience of lesbian potentiality without letting them cross with the lesbians into their actuality. That Rich was right in her caution about the difficulty of re-vision is attested to in the struggles of lesbian separatists to create sustainable new ways of living, and it offers one account for why Tiptree let neither Lorimer nor the reader see what those aboard *Gloria* did in their quarters at night. But that they did things is not a question, and here Strand eroticizes this unknowing knowing through her striking cinematography. Darkness and shadows are important figures of potentiality for Agamben and for Aristotle before him. The potentiality of sight is located in darkness.[101] Sight is as dependent on its privation as its actualization in light. Through filming lesbian existence in silhouette, Strand's film shows viewers what they cannot see. Exactly who and what being lesbian might entail is kept ambiguous in its nonbeing. However, such nonbeing is not the same as nonexistence. Strand's potential lesbians exist in a space-time on the borders of present and future, visible and close enough to touch but also, paradoxically, unseeable and out of reach.

Strand devoted an entire seven-minute film to this sort of lesbian filmmaking that same year with *Fever Dream*, in which she filmed two lesbian friends massaging each other's nude bodies and then kissing in the rain. Described by Strand in an interview with the documentary film scholar Irina Leimbacher as "a dream I once had," *Fever Dream*, if still not explicit in that it does not show genital sexual contact, is more elaborate in its representation of lesbian erotics.[102] The film is again shot in black and white and extreme close-up but this time with significantly less contrast and more extended shots, which allows viewers to become familiar with its two performers' torsos, backsides, and hands. Most of the film is framed so that the

25

women's faces are off-screen, and the camera instead follows their hands as they massage each other's bodies with oil, squeezing, caressing, and teasing each other's breasts, bottoms, stomachs, and shoulders. The extreme close-ups make it sometimes unclear as to which body parts are being massaged—the fleshiness and wetness of the image itself becoming erotic regardless (see figures I.1–I.3). As in *Cartoon le Mousse*, these two women at times appear to be facing each other. At other times, however, they approach each other from behind, above, and below. The lyrical editing, which is accompanied by a haunting soundtrack that conjoins George Crumb's "Voice of the Whale" with an Indonesian lullaby, gongs, and spacy tape effects, moves viewers from position to position in a rhythmic fashion that is neither rushed nor drawn out. In the last minute of the film, the two appear in a medium close-up for the first time. Now largely obscured by a thick wall of rain, rather than an extreme close-up, the two face each other, framed from the neck up (see figure I.4). The woman with shorter hair moves her head down, nearly out of the frame, so that she appears to be mouthing the other's breasts. After a while, the woman with longer hair moves her lover's head up. The two kiss each other deeply, and the film cuts to black. Across the film, the two women remain unperturbed by outside forces. They are instead enveloped in each other's bodies. For viewers, they are both there, in front of us on the screen, and thus in a way here with us, but also, because of the film's minimalist set and lighting, nowhere. Whereas for Muñoz, avant-garde performances of queer citizenship in the 1960s contain "an anticipatory illumination of a queer world, a sign of an actually existing queer reality," Strand's lesbians exist almost as if outside of time itself.[103] The darkness that surrounds them is not that of a dimly lit domicile. Rather, they cannot be located spatially or temporally. Their image does not signify the same certainty of their possibility to be in the future. Like Muñoz's queers, these lesbians prompt us to imagine, but the sort of lesbian existence we might imagine with or through their representation is less directed. If being lesbian has become fuller and more fleshed out than it was in *Cartoon le Mousse*, it nonetheless names a mode of existence that is both potential and impotential at once.

Strand's films have never been written about in lesbian media contexts, as they were made by a filmmaker who did not openly identify as lesbian and held only a tangential relationship to the women's movement.[104] Literally dark and difficult to discern, they were not taken up by early gay and lesbian cinema studies scholars interested first and foremost in matters of visibility and identification. In the decades since, queer media studies has come to question such paradigms, demonstrating that they fail to account for the

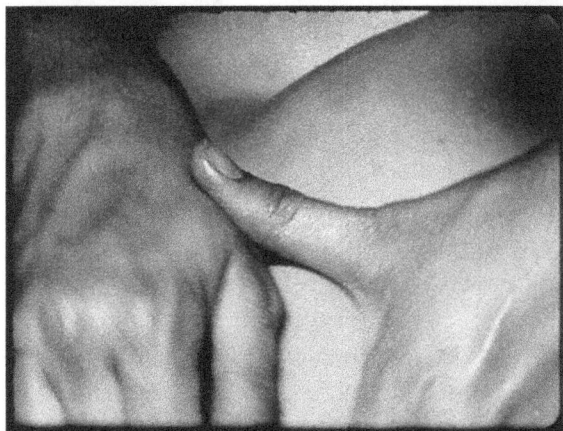

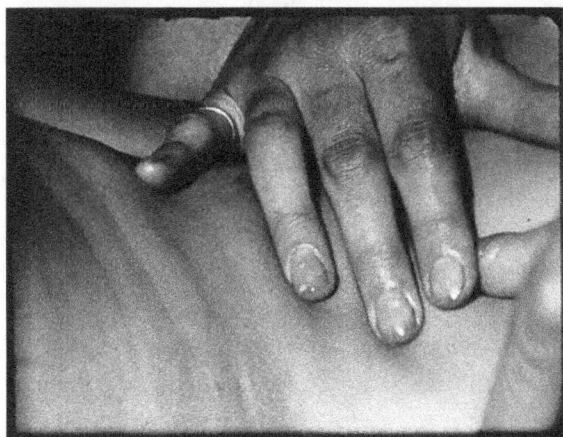

I.1–I.3 Close-up massaging in *Fever Dream* (Chick Strand, dir., 1979). Images courtesy of the Strand Family Estate and the Academy Film Archive.

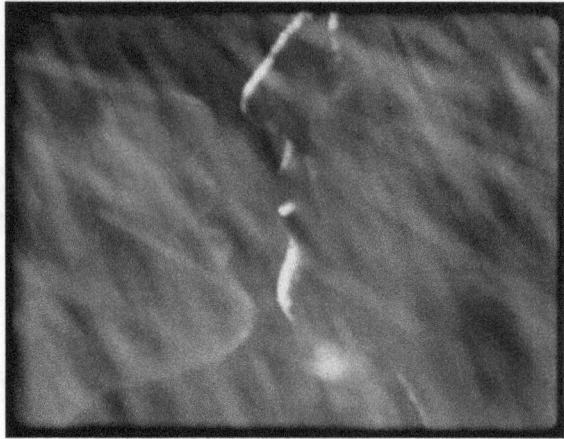

I.4 Just before the kiss and cut to black in *Fever Dream* (Chick Strand, dir., 1979). Image courtesy of the Strand Family Estate and the Academy Film Archive.

varied ways in which queer people participate in cinema's structures of desire and arguing that they can even be destructive, as they often concede to hegemonic notions of gender and sexuality.[105] Significantly, the creative and critical forms of lesbian spectatorship so rich in Classical Hollywood did not disappear with gay liberation. When asked about the sexual politics of *Fever Dream*, Strand rather frustratingly but also knowingly turned over the work to her audience: "You know I have no message for you. None. Unless you want to make it up. Unless you want to. But it's not my message to you, it's the message you get out of it." When pressed by Leimbacher, "So giving the responsibility to . . . ," Strand interjected, "the viewer. Or giving the gift to the viewer."[106] In taking seriously such a gift and analyzing the work of a lesbian film not made by an out lesbian filmmaker but nonetheless made and circulated when lesbian existence was on so many people's minds, I reveal lesbian representation in the 1970s to have been about more than visibility in a positivist sense. Attempts in the 1970s to represent queer women's sexualities across media did more than simply ask their viewers to identify with their lesbian characters or celebrate the lives of particular identitarian subjects. While occasionally ontological, lesbian representation was also epistemological, interested not only in what "lesbian" was but also in thinking through what "lesbian" could *do* to divert and subvert patriarchy and heterosexism. More than mere negation, "becoming lesbian," for many feminists, precipitated "a welcome and joyful expansion of their sexual and emotional vocabularies."[107] Both of these films and these SF stories suggest

28

that such an expansion need not end there but could continue to extend with the imagination of new ways of being lesbian.

In the Archives of Lesbian Potentiality

This process of potentiality was not limited to that of the filmmaker or author. Because of feminist interest in feminist media, literature, and culture, stories such as Tiptree's and films like Strand's moved through feminist communities where their visions were taken up by audiences who articulated their own in response. While this project is invested in the imagining that creative texts uniquely made possible, the book that follows is more interested in how such lesbian potentiality circulated through the women's movement, engendering new media cultures in the process. As a result, this is a necessarily archival project.

I occasionally take up a more theoretical queer studies conception of archives, curating my own collection of cultural texts constructing the subject in question.[108] More often, however, I am interested in sharing research conducted in physical archives, including institutional archives (the Arthur and Elizabeth Schlesinger Library on the History of Women in America at Harvard University; the Sophia Smith Collection at Smith College; Special Collections at the University of Oregon; the Academy of Motion Picture Arts and Sciences Film Archive; the Getty Research Institute; and the British Film Institute); noninstitutional archives (Lesbian Herstory Archives); and, on a few occasions, collections still located in participants' basements and attics. In the 1990s, queer theories of the archive were partly motivated by a distrust of institutions, whose acquisition of feminist and queer collections were feared to threaten the end of community-based collections or the straightening of history.[109] Like Kate Eichhorn, I have found this not, in fact, to have been the case, and like Regina Kunzel, Rachel Corbman, and other queer historians, I believe this more theoretical queer conception of the archive could only be strengthened by periodical tethering to material collections and institutions.[110] In the mid-1990s and early 2000s, dozens of feminist collections from the 1970s were taken in by institutions such those listed earlier. This archival turn in feminism, as Eichhorn names it, has moved scholars beyond clichéd generational debates.[111] Earlier generations' feminisms have not been hurled into a scrap heap, as straight cisgender feminists such as Susan Faludi would have us believe, but have been preserved at no small cost in dollars or labor.[112] Far from serving as the dutiful daughters straight cis

29

feminists envision, researchers of younger generations, such as Eichhorn, Corbman, and I, have become active agents in such archives. How we thumb through a collection's files and receive what we find can, in fact, be quite divergent and queer. In short, the millennial archival turn has finally facilitated the meeting of feminism's concern with its own history and the queer desire for history.

In this tête-à-tête, feminist archives become plentiful sites of potentiality, lesbian and queer and yet unnamable. They produce "a space to imagine an encounter that otherwise may have remained unimaginable."[113] Like a 1970s reader of a feminist SF novel or novella or a 1970s viewer of a feminist experimental film, an archival researcher occupies many space-times at once. Poring over manuscripts, correspondence, photographs, and videos, often for many hours at a time and many days in a row, one is both of one's own time and of the past, getting lost in dramas now long over and enraptured by visions of futures that never came to be. In some cases, these queer archival trysts are invited. As early as 1979, Sheldon had decided to donate materials to an archive someday and, attempting to dissuade a concerned correspondent, the author wrote, "So relent; think of that far-off PhD candidate, reverently fingering your yellowed pages with green furry fingers, and feeling you live again in the facets of her huge nocturnal eyes."[114] This archival proximity, for many feminist, queer, and trans scholars, carries an affective dimension, as one does not simply gather information about the past but becomes caught up emotionally in the physical touch of historical matter.[115] More than forty years later, my green furry fingers and huge nocturnal eyes have made many trips to visit Sheldon's papers in the University of Oregon's Special Collections, first as, yes, a doctoral candidate, and later as a postdoctoral scholar, assistant professor, and documentary filmmaker.[116] Each time I leave more convinced of such collections' importance to those feminist and queer historiographies that are also transgender historiographies.

The force of lesbian potentiality and its stakes for working-class and poor women, closeted lesbians, lesbians of color, and trans and gender-nonconforming people—lesbian, out, and otherwise—became apparent when I turned away from writings of women's movement figureheads and canonical representations of lesbian existence and delved into the imaginative archives of feminist film and video organizations and feminist SF fandom. In these archives, "lesbian" attaches itself to the strangest of bedfellows, literal and figurative. Hesford argues that central to queer studies' production of the feminist-as-lesbian ghost was her figuring as whiteness.[117] Racism remains a problem in both movements for, and in theories of, gender and sexual

30

liberation. This is a point lost in queer studies scholarship that capitalizes on feminist historians' writing about the women's movement as a white middle-class project and naturalizes it exclusively as such, suggesting, in contrast, that the lessons of intra-movement racism have been fully learned by later generations of scholars and activists. As historian Maylei Blackwell and sociologist Becky Thompson make clear in their histories of women of color and multiracial feminisms, the histories cited by queer studies in its dismissal of lesbian feminism are histories of hegemonic feminism that ignore the centrality of women of color to the women's movement in the 1970s, as well as contributions of white antiracist feminists.[118] Queer studies' production of the figure of the feminist-as-lesbian has simultaneously produced women's liberation as a cisgender women's movement. Trans men and women, including trans lesbians, were active lesbian feminists and contributors to lesbian feminist cultures, including lesbian separatist spaces, as Finn Enke, Emma Heaney, and Cristan Williams demonstrate.[119] As Enke notes, the transphobic and white-supremacist tidying of social movement histories often go hand in hand, so that, among other things, feminism might pass as a coherent subject.[120] That many queer and trans scholars do not know about such transfeminist histories is a result of a few transphobic feminists, who, because of their celebrity, have come to dominate the popular discourse about the 1970s.[121] Contrary to those who reference the transphobic famed members of the movement time and again, extending their platform even in criticizing it, gender-nonconformity in 1970s feminisms abounded. That "lesbian," "feminist," and "women's" appear insufficient at marking this is partially a result of the challenges trans existence poses to historical records and archiving.[122] It is also largely a result of the discursive work of queer studies' feminist-as-lesbian ghost.

Rather than further theorizing the hold such a past and its ghosts might have on such a present, my project pursues the past potentialities located in less familiar archives of lesbian existence, exposing ideas and imaginations contemporary feminist, queer, and trans media studies may want to imagine within the ongoing project of forging freer futures. The four chapters that follow accompany lesbian potentiality through the archives of feminist film and video and feminist science fiction. In these archives, lesbian potentiality meets the potentiality of these media, engendering new media cultures and extending the process of (im)potentiality.

Chapter 1 looks to the labor of feminist film and video distributors and feminist audiences that put lesbian potentiality into movement. At the 1975 Conference of Feminist Film and Video Organizations in New York City, feminist media workers gathered to discuss how they might use film and video to change a society that they identified as heterosexist, classist, racist, ageist, and imperialist.[123] The answer lay partially in building a feminist media network through which feminist media could circulate and resources on distribution and exhibition could be shared. The chapter focuses on the National Women's Film Circuit (NWFC) and International Videoletters, two projects that emerged from the conference (and its "sister conference," the Feminist Eye Conference in Los Angeles), both of which were run by lesbian feminist media workers. As NWFC packages and International Videoletters traveled to dozens of locations, the two projects circulated the lesbian impressions of their organizers and initiated a series of intimate intellectual exchanges between US feminist communities unique to film and video. In watching and discussing feminist films and videos together, feminist spectators perceived differently together and were moved to think and feel more expansively. The individual's perception of lesbian potentiality—that internal sense that gendered and sexual life could and would someday be substantially different—gained momentum through the virtual creation of such a world within and among local feminist communities.

Chapter 2 focuses on a specific subset of documentaries that circulated through this feminist media network: feminist prison documentaries. In these documentaries, made in collaboration with lesbian feminist media workers (who took cameras into prisons under the auspices of documenting the supposed success of prison reform or as a part of the feminist-led arts programs made possible by such reforms), Black feminist theorizing of the prison-industrial complex, its racialized and gendered violences, these violences' histories, and their future abolition took on an embodied audiovisual form. Lesbian potentiality radiates out from those in front of the camera, connecting those before the camera and those behind it, as well as those in the audience, and giving their freedom dreams of futures without prisons affective force. In many 1970s "women's prisons," lesbian relationships were forbidden, and physical expressions of affection could be written up as homosexual activity, which, in turn, might lead to increased harassment, denial of parole, or nonconsensual psychiatric "treatment."[124] Lesbian existence is barely named across this small cohort of feminist prison documentaries. However, the looks, smiles, and fleeting touches between prisoners pictured often appear as if the stuff of lesbian fan fiction, connoting romantic love and sexual attraction, if not naming them outright. These intimacies around which the lesbian sign hovered are not minor, as they are inseparable from the era's fight to abolish the racist neoliberal carceral state. For those imprisoned in

32

the few "women's prisons," cisnormative segregation, spun as a matter of prisoner safety, often meant increased isolation from the public and thus greater vulnerability to abuse, including sexual violence. These documentaries contextualize lesbian potentiality as integral to the fugitive freedom dreaming and Black feminist love politics of 1970s Black feminist theory.

Chapter 3 turns to the formation of feminist science fiction fandom as a counterpublic, documenting how feminist SF writers and fans took the potentiality of the genre and made it their own. Individuals dipped in and out of feminist fandom, but the counterpublic was sustained through the regular circulation of fanzines (soon supplemented by feminist SF conventions and feminist spaces at more general conventions and, eventually, online activity). In the pages of these fanzines, as well as in the pages of the SF literature they discussed, lesbian potentiality fused with that of the genre as a whole, their collective visions of feminist futures often centering lesbian existence. Feminist SF authors and fans claimed the genre for 1970s women but also for those folks of future genders who would continue to reconfigure social life. WisCon, the international feminist SF convention, first convened in 1977 and—as of 2020—continues to meet annually. The chapter focuses on how feminist SF fans questioned, critiqued, and parodied the processes of community formation to allow, ironically, feminist SF fandom's institutionalization. I demonstrate how, through blending practices common to lesbian feminist activism and SF fandom, complete with a specifically feminist sense of humor, feminist SF fans renewed their commitments to thinking through differences over the decades and welcoming new participants as they moved from fanzines to conventions and online spaces.

Chapter 4 examines the life, work, and influence of one very special feminist SF author, James Tiptree, Jr./Alice B. Sheldon. Studying Tip/Alli (as the author would sign SF fandom letters after being outed in *Locus* in January 1977) necessitates a rewrite of the family drama around trans inclusion in feminist genealogy as a science fiction. In studying how Tip/Alli did gender across Sheldon's life, Tiptree's epistolary relationships, and Tip/Alli's reckoning with feminism, queerness, and fandom after coming out, Tip/Alli teaches us that the story of gender in the 1970s was not so simple or straightforward. This era does not belong to transphobic feminists, and trans and queer scholars should not cede it to them. That Sheldon would claim "Lesbian" late in life in conversation with both cisgender and transgender lesbian feminist authors supports my argument that in the late 1970s "Lesbian" signified something far more nebulous and dynamic than it has come to signify in more recent decades. Its potentiality, for Sheldon and

33

others, included exploring gender in ways that may look nonbinary or trans-masculine to us today. In writing this story of Tip/Alli and the author's influence on younger science fiction authors and fans, including via the two prizes created in the author's name, I delineate one especially generative line of descent from 1970s feminisms to twenty-first-century transfeminism.

Here, as well as in the book's epilogue on an early progeny of these two feminist media cultures—*Born in Flames* (Lizzie Borden, dir., 1983)—I model how we might rethink intergenerational relationality without rejecting it outright. Holding on to Rich while adapting and expanding on her models for lesbian feminist genealogy is central to this project. As noted earlier, Rich describes lesbian existence as that which "suggests both the fact of the historical presence of lesbians and our continuing creation of the meaning of that existence." In her reading of Rich's 1980 essay, Hesford shifts the "our" of "our continuing creation of the meaning of [lesbian] existence" from the implied "lesbians" to "feminists," writing immediately after quoting the line above, "It is up to us as feminists to articulate and make connections between different women in different times and spaces."[125] This fits with Rich's own theorizing of the lesbian continuum, but it also shifts the meaning of the possessive pronoun in a fashion that facilitates the extension of Rich's work to the present. In my chapter on Tip/Alli and the epilogue that follows, I underscore the necessity of such a shift. I contend that the liberating reimagination celebrated in Rich's essay continues, but to see it in the arguably expansive shift from "lesbians" to "feminists," one must be open to linking the freedom of women (trans and cis), nonbinary people, trans men, and folks of other—including future—genders. The writing of feminist historiography need not stall in the face of trans existence. Trans existence does not erase, replace, or diminish cis lesbian existence. In the 1970s, those who did not conform to sexual and gender norms were working to find a vocabulary that fit, just as many are doing now. Often that was "lesbian" and "woman-identification."[126] At other times, it was a more amorphous constellation of words, images, and affects that orbited "lesbian" and "woman identification." Not only were trans people there all along, but we also continue to augment the forms of imagination that lesbian existence in the 1970s made possible.

Temporal Asymmetry

As a nonbinary queer scholar whose lovers have included people of many genders, I find that my embarrassing struggle to speak another generation's word stems not solely from the questionable applicability of the term for myself.

Instead, it arises from my awareness that, while we are living in the lesbian's former future, this future—our present—is not the future that 1970s lesbian feminists imagined (or, more accurately, it is not one of the futures they imagined). That such futures did not come to pass does not mark past social movements' failure. Studies that want to dismiss social movements' histories and radical imaginations for not sufficiently altering society's basic structures seemingly forget what Morgan Bassichis, Alexander Lee, and Dean Spade remind us in *Captive Genders*: "There are two major features of the second half of the twentieth century that shaped the context in which the queer and trans movement developed: (1) the active resistance and challenge by radical movement to state violence, and subsequent systematic backlash, and (2) the massive turmoil and transformation of the global economy."[127] Systemic backlash and neoliberalism have been displaced onto the critical limitations of earlier movements, whose histories are then written as tales of moral failure. I briefly explore the effects of the systemic backlash of the New Right and the rise of neoliberalism on feminist media, feminist media cultures, and lesbian potentiality in the book's epilogue. Doing as much bears witness to the breadth of the forces with which 1970s movements were contending, and within and against which social movements continue to work, at the time of this book's writing.

Lesbian Potentiality and Feminist Media in the 1970s offers a media historiography of imagination for when the present is past. That the 1970s drag for some and not for others is due to the contingency of history and the asymmetry of temporal modes.[128] Just as the future remains uncertain to those of us in the present—an anxiety that, as Kara Keeling demonstrates, motivates corporate formulations of future scenarios in addition to stimulating radical imagination[129]—the past held many potentialities, its former futures including the forging of not-lesbian futures that would eclipse the era's often exclusionary lesbian lands. I am thus asking something odd of you in our reconsideration of the history of 1970s feminisms: that we think not only about what was but also about what Agamben articulated as the contingency of the past—namely, the mutual existence of what happened and what did not happen, or what could have not been but was and what could have been but was not.[130] Such attempts at thinking about history in a contingent fashion, Agamben writes, have been tempered by the irrevocability of the past or the unrealizability of the past's potentiality; by conditioned necessity or the belief that something cannot both be and not be; and by retroactive influence of future events' predictions.[131] The difficulty for historians and philosophers of history to think outside of such frameworks has caused history to have been written as a matter of will, which overrides contingency or potentiality by emphasizing agency in action and actuality.[132] Queer studies has described lesbian feminism from the perspective of Nietzschean "counterwill," angry that what was done cannot be undone and thus stuck with the resentful declaration of "what was." In doing so, it ironically joins those who would rather not see this past differently, including those who are proud of how the New Right contained the era's radicalism and transphobic feminists nostalgic for the time's "simple" essentialisms. In acknowledging that the past could have been different, we can better see the potentiality of our own present. Lesbians, young and old, remain integral members of ongoing movements for social change. But the moment of the Lesbian as the privileged sign for the toppling of heteropatriarchy, the eradication of misogyny and homophobia, and the evolution of gender and sexual existence has closed. The ease with which "queer" itself is now being thrown in with "lesbian," "gay," and "bisexual" in movements toward inclusion within the institutions of marriage, military, and the prison-industrial complex suggests that the queer is likely hot on the former's bare heels. However, the potentiality that binds even as it exceeds these names remains open to renewal.

Past, present, and future are not clearly demarcated partitions of time. They are in constant movement in relation to one another, being invoked by a historian located in time and read by a reader who, in turn, inhabits a slightly different temporal location (or many, upon rereading). In each case, the past is a former present (as well as a former future), and the future is a future present. How we affectively relate to former presents, now past, is going to constantly change (as is the "we" invoked and the "former presents," which include "our" present). Rather than linger on the theorizing of one period's relationality to another, the interdisciplinary methodology of potentiality proffered by the current study is intended to model an approach to social movement histories that can be adapted for future historical studies, including historical studies of former futures. In attending to the imaginations of past movements, we make more apparent the potentiality of our own present. The self-knowledge gleaned in this revised re-vision need not demand the survival of one's identity as its reward. "We" are fighting for a freer future, just as "they" were, but what this ultimately means is sparking change in the present. Like Keeling, I do not believe utopia can be mapped through the poetic knowledge of imagination.[133] Nothing is more precarious than futurity. But that does not mean imagination is not imperative. In the face of activist burnout, factional divisiveness, and everyday futility and resignation, the imagination can be that force which is most clarifying, most sustaining. Imagining with others, this project proposes, can only grow more radiant if extended from those one currently organizes with, in person and online, to include those who came before and imagined futures now past.

I invite readers to engage with *this* historiography of the Lesbian's former futures as they imagine their own futures for today. The Lesbian might get left behind in the process, our tongues turning to other namings of freedom and desire, but that need not mean potentiality is lost. It is regenerated, transformed for futures when our present is past.

feminist media in movement
the national women's film circuit
& international videoletters

The demand to make lesbian visible, whether as ammunition for anti-homophobic campaigns or as figures for identification, renders lesbian static, makes lesbian into (an) image, and forestalls any examination of lesbian within context. —AMY VILLAREJO, *Lesbian Rule*

This is why we're doing this, why we've chosen to distribute films: because we think they can not only start discussion, not only educate and inform people, but really move people. —JOAN E. BIREN, "Moonforce Media Interview"

During the early 1970s, dozens of feminist media organizations sprang up across the United States and Canada—as well as in Mexico, Australia, the United Kingdom, France, Germany, Chile, and elsewhere—to meet the media-making desires of their local feminist communities. Many of these organizations were video collectives, documenting women's movement protests and feminist cultural events, oftentimes for local public television or closed-circuit university networks. Other feminist media organizations were devoted to providing women with access to film and video equipment and instruction.[1] A few began to amass small collections of women's films to distribute, but most rented films for their screenings directly from filmmakers.[2] Each of these organizations operated independently, serving their local feminist communities as they saw fit. Initially, even Women Make Movies—founded in 1972 and now an international women's film distributor—was first and foremost committed to activist film production and the community workshops of its Chelsea Picture Station.[3] Before long, however, many of its participants began expressing the desire to connect with others doing similar work. By building a feminist media network, these women envisioned they might reduce excess labor in programming and distribution and generate ideas among feminist communities. In 1975, Women Make Movies and Frances Reid and Cathy Zheutlin (who would soon form Iris Films) organized two conferences—the Conference of Feminist Film and Video Organizations in New York City and the Feminist Eye Conference in Los Angeles (LA)—to begin building such a network.[4] Through the "connectedness" these conferences provided, feminist media workers were able to "do complementary work, learn from eachother [sic], and avoid duplication." This, as they reflected afterward, gave them "a larger perspective" and allowed them to develop "new ideas that [they]'d have taken longer to get to, if [they]'d remained isolated."[5]

To record their ideas and keep them going, the women at the New York conference drafted and signed "An Ongoing Manifesto" (sometimes cited as "Womanifesto"), which they then circulated among their contacts working in women's media.[6] In the document they declared their commitment to feminist control of the entire film and video production, distribution, and exhibition process. They wrote, "We do not accept the existing power structure and we are committed to changing it by the content and structure of our images and by the ways we relate to each other in our work and with our audience." They saw this politicized media practice as "part of the larger movement of women dedicated to changing society by struggling against oppression as it manifests itself in sexism, heterosexism, classism, racism, ageism, and imperialism."[7] The (wo)manifesto circulated widely among feminist filmmakers and film scholars through its publication in the feminist film journal *Women and Film*.[8] It was also mailed to those feminist media workers registered for the Feminist Eye Conference the following month in LA with the hope that the values and ideas expressed in the manifesto would be discussed, expanded, and criticized in the spirit of the "'on-going' nature" in which the manifesto was conceived.[9]

Two projects emerged directly from these feminist media conferences with the goal of continuing this ongoing work of changing society by way of media and feminist media worker-and-audience relations: the National Women's Film Circuit (NWFC [1975–80]), a distribution system that circulated preconstituted packages of multigeneric feminist films through as wide a nontheatrical feminist US market as possible, and International Videoletters (1975–77), a realist documentary video "monthly feminist exchange of news, issues, events" between US feminist communities with international aspirations.[10] This chapter offers a history of these two brief but imaginative projects. Drawing on correspondence, videos, records, and ephemera now located in the collections of three of the feminist media workers involved in one or more of these projects, as well as oral histories with six of the projects' participants, I explore how the distribution and exhibition of feminist media recrafted feminist relationality both between and among women located in the women's movement's metropolitan and college town hubs and those of suburban, rural, and imprisoned women's communities. As NWFC packages and International Videoletters traveled not just to New York and LA but also to Tucson, Rochester, and dozens of other locations, the two projects initiated a series of intimate intellectual exchanges between US feminist communities largely impossible through other forms of political organization.[11] In watching feminist films and videos together, often pursuant to lively discussion, audiences participated in nothing less than the temporary construction of an alternative reality. For two hours at a time, feminist spectators perceived differently together and were moved to think and feel more expansively. This labor of reception was done *with* those on the screen and those behind the screen image's cameras (who, in the case of the videoletters, might the following month be the ones in the audience themselves). Both intellectual and embodied, this affectivity put lesbian potentiality in movement. Lesbian potentiality was not merely a matter of any given film or package of film or videos' representation of lesbian existence. It included but also exceeded both representation and programming. The individual's felt sense that gendered and sexual life would someday be substantially different—that in a future beyond compulsory heterosexuality, society would be entirely reconfigured—gained force and momentum through the virtual creation of a social world among (and, through circulation, between) local feminist communities.

This conceptualization of feminist film and video exhibition as a site of feminist world making demands a rethinking of the stakes of the "realist/formalist debate" in feminist film theory of the 1970s. At this time, British feminist film theorists writing in *Screen* and American feminist film theorists writing in *Camera Obscura* wrestled with the question of what feminism's relationship to cinema should be.[12] Most saw their roles as feminist theorists as one of deconstructing and demystifying the workings of cinema when it came to images of women, and they championed those films they saw as doing the work of cinematic deconstruction, too.[13] These formalist film theorists were dismissive of realist documentaries and other feminist films that did not centralize the problem of film language or make an attempt to elaborate a new syntax and "speak" the female body differently.[14] Most significant, in accepting "the apparent denotation of the sign," feminist realist documentaries denied "any awareness of the intervention, the mediation of the cinematic apparatus."[15] As a result, feminist formalist film theorists could not conceive of realist documentary film spectators as anything more than passive consumers of such films' knowledge. In their view, the transparent "windows on the world" these documentaries provided differed little from those of Classical Hollywood narrative fiction films, appealing to spectators through the verisimilitude of the screen world and character identification. Their pleasures therefore corroborated spectators' identification with the entire cinematic institution, an institution feminist formalist film theorists saw as responsible for the oppression of women through its production of twentieth-century society "Woman."[16] While realist documentaries were immensely popular with feminist audiences, including NWFC and International Videoletter audiences, and other feminist film scholars argued for their value as consciousness-raising tools and took the genre and its aesthetics seriously, this discourse remains rather unfairly characterized as a debate.[17] The legacy of 1970s film feminisms too often is formalism.

However, just as methodological and theoretical developments in cinema and media studies, including phenomenology, have challenged the rule of psychoanalysis and semiotics (which did not so much undergird such formalist analyses as subsume them), so might newer theories guide a reconsideration of the work of realist feminist documentaries of the 1970s, such as International Videoletters, and the distribution and exhibition efforts that enabled their reception. Throughout this chapter, I rely on the insights of phenomenological film and media theorists, who have demonstrated spectatorship to be more than a mental or psychic encounter with the screen, in turn allowing for richer theorization of the film and video experience.[18] Media address the body, and spectatorship is at times best framed as an exchange between two bodies—that of the viewer and that of the film or video. This is certainly the case when it comes to the reception of feminist media in the 1970s. Feminist audiences attended NWFC and International Videoletter screenings not simply to see and celebrate the work of feminist filmmakers but to interact with women located elsewhere, who now, if temporarily and ephemerally, appeared before them. Contrary to formalist theorists' claims, the fact that these images were constructed was not lost on audiences. Just as scholars were not paralyzed into passivity (and thus able to write the critiques that they did), more general feminist audiences were also able to analyze what appeared before them. Furthermore, this analysis, often practiced collectively in post-screening discussions, did not detract from what was also a highly sensorial and affective spectatorial endeavor. Certain films and videos, what Laura U. Marks terms "haptic cinema," defy body-and-mind boundaries, asking their viewers to think with their skin.[19] In the case of International Videoletters, such intellectual exchanges between human and video bodies were intensified by an immediacy, eroticism, and epistolary address particular to documentary video.

In naming as "lesbian feminist affectivity" this labor of feminist viewers, performed in concert with one another, as well as with the women on-screen and those who made their images, I purposefully delineate the centrality of desire to the practices of 1970s feminist media workers and viewers. By the mid-'70s, the guiding question for many formalist theorists was: "Is it possible for the woman to express her own desires?"[20] As the editors of *Jump Cut*'s 1981 special section "Lesbians and Film" first articulated, and queer film theorists would go on to elaborate, there is a heterocentrism to this framework.[21] Not only does it presume the female subject to be straight (and, in the process, ironically flatten "women" to "woman" in a manner not unlike the patriarchal structures it was critiquing), but its making a puzzle of women's desire refuses to listen to or learn from those women who, due to their positioning outside of heterosexuality, already have had to navigate cinema's oppressive structures of desire to identify and articulate their own. The NWFC and International Videoletter audiences were not made up exclusively of lesbians; nor were their films and videos predominantly about lesbian existence. However, both projects were led by lesbian feminists and bear the mark of what, following Amy Villarejo, we might label their "lesbian impressions."[22] These films and videos circulated the lesbian sign through a variety of contexts. It was a lesbian seeking to change sexist, heterosexist, classist, racist, ageist, imperialist society that set this media in movement and, in turn, moved people. In pursuing the lesbian impression of feminist media workers, we discover in the labor of their audiences not only women's desire for other women and lesbians' desire for visibility, but the desire of many

43

feminists—across identities, locations, and political ideologies—to come together through media and create the world anew. We discover lesbian potentiality at work.

Iris Films and the Formation of the NWFC

The idea for the National Women's Film Circuit first took shape in February 1975 at the Conference of Feminist Film and Video Organizations in New York. It was there that Frances Reid and Cathy Zheutlin met Joan E. Biren (JEB). Reid and Zheutlin, who were both from LA, had a few years of experience working in film production, and they had recently become friends after walking off the set of a misogynist Hollywood film director together.[23] Biren, meanwhile, was from Washington, DC. A former member of the lesbian separatist collective the Furies (the photographer for the newspaper's "Queer Day" photo spread), she was rather well known for her expulsion from the group in 1972.[24] Biren had been supporting herself for the previous few years as a freelance photographer, documenting the women's movement for the Washington *Blade, Post*, and *Star*, as well as *off our backs* and *Ms.* The three hit it off, and when they reunited a month later at the Feminist Eye Conference in LA, they; Reid's partner, Liz Stevens; and Biren's partner, Mary Lee Farmer, formed Iris Films. Seeking to contribute to the growing feminist media network through both production and distribution, the five women imagined that their company would broadly serve the US women's movement while offering a specifically lesbian perspective. Reid and Zheutlin brought filmmaking experience to the group, while Biren and Farmer contributed extensive organizing experience.[25] In forming Iris Films, they put the "Ongoing Manifesto" Biren, Reid, and Zheutlin had signed into practice, connecting feminist communities, beginning with their own on each coast and, soon, hundreds of others. In the process, they democratized the interactions of feminist media workers and their audiences.

From the start, this bicoastal collective work proved to be less than easy. Not only was long-distance communication challenging, but the women of "Iris West" (Reid, Stevens, and Zheutlin in LA) and "Iris East" (Biren and Farmer in DC) also barely knew one another and had to quickly develop methods of rectifying as much. Long-distance phone calls were expensive and letters were limiting, so the group soon began to supplement these more traditional forms of communication with audiotapes that they mailed back and forth with their letters. These tapes allowed them to communicate more thoroughly and provided a more personal way to get to know one another.

44

On these tapes, now located among Biren's papers at Smith College, digitized and available to those with the desire to listen, the Irises (as they came to call themselves) gossip about Zheutlin's lovers and their and their friends' cats; talk through local politics; wish one another well when one of them was sick; and sing one another "Happy Birthday." On the few occasions when all five were able to meet in person, they also taped their discussions. They made their first tape at the Feminist Eye Conference in LA, where they initially met as an organization. This first tape records the group brainstorming about what women could use most in terms of a new film organization and how just such a bicoastal endeavor would work.[26] On the tape Reid and Zheutlin express an interest in returning to production and describe a few ideas about films they want to make as Iris Films, including a women's music film with Olivia Records and a documentary about lesbian mothers, who, like Stevens, were currently facing unprecedented challenges in custody battles. In the tapes they made over the following weeks, however, they would eventually agree to hold off on film production and prioritize the formation of a lesbian feminist distribution system.

While committed to organizing the NWFC as a specifically lesbian project, in following the spirit of the (wo)manifesto the Irises agreed that it was important to reach diverse feminist audiences and saw the fight against misogyny and homophobia as part of a wider array of freedom struggles. In the packages they would circulate as the NWFC, then, they would program lesbian films alongside feminist films on other subjects. It was important to the Irises that they get a sense of the range of feminist films being made before selecting the dozen or so that they would distribute through their first circuit packages. Among them, the five women were familiar with a number of such films. However, they decided to organize a festival at the end of August 1975 to survey those that might be hiding away in drawers, never having been seen by anyone other than the filmmakers' friends or, perhaps, the classes for which they made the films.[27] In May 1975, Iris Films put out a call for films to be screened at the festival and considered for national distribution, writing: "Dear Sister Filmmaker, Films communicating women's ideas and feelings are being made, but, unfortunately, not enough people are seeing them. While the need to define and expand women's culture is greater every day, commercial distributors either reject or neglect films made by women that express the realities of our lives and visions."[28] Iris Films would fill this void with its NWFC. To be considered for distribution along the circuit, films had to be screened at the festival. The Irises wanted to make it easy for filmmakers, especially those who had never submitted a film to a festival before. Submission to the festival therefore did not include an entry fee, and all submitted films would be programmed with a few restrictions. For one, the Irises could accept only films made on 16 mm film. Second, believing "women-controlled media [to be] vital to ending sexist oppression," the Irises would program films produced by women and men together only when "the women ha[d] had substantial control of the production." Finally, although unclear as to how, exactly, they would make such determinations, the Irises concluded their festival call by insisting they would not distribute films that were "sexist, classist, or racist."[29]

While they waited for submissions to come in, the Irises began planning other details for the fall, such as routes, schedules, and budgets. This took a lot of coordination between Iris West and Iris East. The two halves of the collective split the responsibilities and continued to share their work via the postal service. They reached out to contacts in various cities across the country, asking them to serve as local producers of the circuit, and they tried to figure out the finances for the operation, including their budgets for shipping prints, paying projectionists, and renting spaces and projectors in the various cities; admission costs; and how to split the filmmakers' pay. Iris Films had yet to incorporate as a nonprofit or receive any grants, and the five financed the operation themselves. For this reason, one pair of their audiotapes was dedicated to each coast's detailing of personal finances so they might all gain a clearer sense of how much capital they had to work with and how much they would need to raise.[30] Making such decisions over audiotape led to an acknowledgment of class differences within the collective, which meant varying means in terms of contributing both time and money. Tensions often ran high in these tapes, and they only escalated as the group came to realize that they did not share the same attitudes toward many of their decisions. For example, East advocated for as wide a circuit as possible, while West thought it perhaps best to begin in cities closer to their two home bases in case of emergencies. The two halves also took varying approaches to their audiotapes. East processed their thoughts on the business matters at hand before recording their conclusions, while West used the tapes to process their thinking, which made for disorganized and long-winded tapes. While these choices reflected differences between East and West Coast feminist cultures, they were also largely a result of the fact that Iris West was made up of three people, instead of a sole couple, and arguably needed more time to process meeting content.[31]

These frequent disagreements led to bigger questions about the ideal ways to run their feminist collective, such as how to balance valuing democratic decision making and equality with the reality of needing to make quick decisions as the festival approached, as well as how to balance responsibilities when two members were inherently more involved in festival planning by virtue of living in the festival city. Biren and Farmer worked with friends who were law students at Georgetown University to find an auditorium for the festival. They spent much of their summer prescreening hundreds of festival submissions whenever they could in Biren's living room, sometimes with friends or their softball team.[32] At one point, Reid and Stevens entertained the idea of not coming out to the festival at all. They would be sacrificing their vacation time as a couple, and flying across the country was more expensive than the camping trip they had been planning before Iris was formed. Throughout these discussions, which happened over letters, audiotapes, and occasional scheduled phone calls, each of the Irises tried to speak as individuals so as to be responsible to one another as equals. However, disagreements between the two couples, with Zheutlin awkwardly in the middle, kept arising.[33] Ultimately, the five were able to make a number of important agreements about the NWFC. They concluded that the price of tickets should vary from town to town. Relatedly, they agreed that many decisions, including whether or not screenings should be "for women only," ought to be left to local circuit producers, who would better know their community's expectations for such events.

The DC Festival of the NWFC ran August 22–26, 1975, with two to four programs a day, together screening approximately one hundred films by more than seventy women.[34] All of the films had been made over the preceding six years across the United States, England, Canada, and Australia, and many were being screened for the first time anywhere.[35] Iris Films held audience discussions after each premiere and collected surveys on all of the films. The festival schedule included a header that read: "These films were made by women. They examine the world we all live in. They analyze the situation of women in this world. They imagine a different world and inspire us with their vision. These films are part of a process of changing the world. The process continues as you use the films."[36] Iris valued women's work as underpaid and underrepresented and sought to make it more accessible to those who would appreciate it most. They also understood these films as serving a range of functions beyond visibility or positivity. In watching these feminist films, they hoped, audiences would analyze contemporary society and imagine alternatives, both together in the discussions afterward and outside the theater in their everyday lives. Lesbian potentiality was not envisioned as the property of any one film. Instead, it was part of a process that began

47

with a group of films and continued in the imagination, analysis, and action of audiences.

Festival reviewers quickly picked up on this dual functionality of feminist films as instigating both imagination and analysis. In her review for the DC underground newspaper *Grass Roots*, Beth Stone describes the premiere as "powerful." Four of the six films she profiles were documentaries of varying subjects and styles that would end up in circuit packages: Kathleen Shannon's *Would I Ever Like to Work* (1974), a participatory film about a mother on welfare that was made as a part of the "Working Mothers" series of the National Film Board of Canada's Studio D; Cambridge Documentary Films' *Taking Our Bodies Back: The Women's Health Movement* (1974), one of many women's health documentaries made at this time, in this case documenting the injustices of for-profit medicine and a few of the alternatives beginning to be developed; Sally Barrett-Page's *Like a Rose* (1975), a prison documentary that focuses on the experiences of two white women serving twenty-five-year sentences in the Missouri State Correctional Center for Women; and Donna Deitch's *Woman to Woman* (1975), a film about women's experiences in the workforce, which Stone liked for its "free-flowing raps [that] glide between hookers, housewives, mothers and friends."[37] These documentaries, Stone claims, were the best of the festival, as they offered "life experiences" that audiences could "draw upon for insight into [their] own lives and for direction and incentive in [their] attempts to change the world."[38] Meanwhile, in a review for the women's art and culture journal *Sibyl-Child*, Pat Dowell predicts the popularity of Barbara Hammer and Jan Oxenberg's lesbian experimental and documentary films, claiming the seven Hammer films and two Oxenberg films screened offered audiences a "new dispensation" in women's art for "women moving confidently and joyfully into a new culture."[39] While Dowell contrasts this to an "old dispensation" that examines women's oppression, indicating a progression that she wishes for women's cinema, she considers the programming of both kinds of films together to be a strong point of their exhibition.[40] Regardless of which films they favored, reviewers identified the strength of the festival as its facilitation of the analysis of feminist films with a range of subjects, modes, and styles alongside one another, a practice that the NWFC would continue on a smaller scale with its packages.

Festival reviewers also saw this process extending from the minds of individual viewers during the screenings to entire audiences in the discussions afterward. Stone wrote, "Much of the festival's excitement came from audience participation," elaborating that the "discussion forums enhanced our experiences by allowing us to share our responses to the visual messages."[41] Having attended every screening, Dowell similarly wrote, "I felt like I was settled in for a long campaign, and it was worth it, not only for the films I saw but for the experience of the festival itself, which was organized along principles different from those I have come to expect in film events."[42] She describes the discussions after the screenings as "quite stimulating, providing an energetic exchange of ideas."[43] She commends Biren and Farmer for providing time at the end of the festival for self-critique. "Their responsive attitude toward the audience was precisely what made this festival special beyond the films themselves," she writes, adding that the audiences' participation in discussions of the films and the festival "indicated that an audience will respond just as intelligently as they are treated."[44] In her conclusion, Dowell predicts that what the future film circuit will offer feminist audiences is "real participation," a right, she notes, too often denied to commercial and even museum and university film audiences.[45]

After the DC festival, Iris Films split into two independent organizations. Negotiating decision making between LA and DC had become too complicated, and their method of mailing cassettes of their meetings back and forth, although innovative, caused delays. At the festival, Iris West and Iris East learned that they had a difficult time making decisions even in person, and they came to the conclusion that their recurring disagreements about how to run the company were irresolvable.[46] Iris West would retain the name Iris Films and go on to distribute women's films, as well as to produce their own documentary about lesbian mothers, *In the Best Interests of the Children* (1977). In addition to their own films and those of Hammer and Oxenberg, Iris distributed *We're Alive* (1974), "a production of solidarity and love" made over the course of an eight-month weekly video workshop at the California Institute for Women and produced with the UCLA Women's Film Workshop; the Santa Cruz Women's Media Collective's *Wishfulfilming* (1973), a black-and-white "docu-drama about a women's film collective making a movie [that] explores new ideas about non-hierarchal work, and visions of a society based on needs, not profit"; Lois Tupper's dramatic short film *Our Little Munchkin Here* (1975), about female adolescence; and Linda Klosky's animated short film *And Then There Were* (1973), about deforestation.[47] Biren and Farmer, meanwhile, formed the nonprofit Moonforce Media and continued the work of the NWFC. Reid, Stevens, and Zheutlin briefly entertained running a separate California circuit, feeling responsible to the West Coast producers they had worked with in preparation for the NWFC.[48] Before long, however, they introduced Moonforce Media

49

to their West Coast contacts, and Zheutlin produced the circuit the two times it traveled to LA.

Moonforce Media and the Implementation of the NWFC

Putting the principles of the (wo)manifesto into practice, Moonforce Media radicalized feminist film distribution. Like many other feminist film distributors, Moonforce Media held nonexclusive contracts with filmmakers, meaning it was but one company to distribute their films. Unsurprisingly, Iris's initial distribution offerings overlapped with Moonforce's, both groups having been privy to feminist audiences' preferences at the festival. In 1975, Women Make Movies was still dividing its energy among filmmaking, film distribution, and film education, and Moonforce distributed its productions *Livia Makes Some Changes* (1974) and *Healthcaring: From Our End of the Speculum* (1976). In 1979, *Camera Obscura* published questionnaires it sent to alternative distribution companies specializing in films by women. Iris Films and Women Make Movies are among those companies that, *Camera Obscura* reports, "were formed in order to distribute work they felt ought to be seen or must be seen" and, in so doing, "anticipated some audience interests and [grew] as a result of their foresight."[49] *Camera Obscura* claims that the "essential differences" between such distribution companies were few.[50] Moonforce Media (which was not sent the survey, did not complete it, or did not have its survey published) did differ from Iris Films, Women Make Movies, and others like it in a few key ways. Unlike Iris Films and Women Make Movies, Moonforce Media did not rent out individual films. Instead, it curated packages of five or six short films, intended to represent the range of recent feminist filmmaking, and collaborated with local circuit "producers" in their exhibition. In addition to more popular titles available through Iris Films, Women Make Movies, and other feminist film distributors, Moonforce Media distributed films that were otherwise unavailable, such as Sharon Madden's *Friends* (1976); that could be rented only directly from their individual filmmakers, such as Deitch's *Woman to Woman*; or had to be acquired from a foreign institution, such as Shannon's National Film Board of Canada project *Would I Ever Like to Work*.

Former organizers and now established feminist cultural workers (Biren by way of her photography and Farmer by way of the women's bookstore she managed in DC), Biren and Farmer reached out to their women's movement contacts across the country, and the NWFC eventually traveled to nearly fifty different locations, including big cities and small towns in every geographical region from the South to the Pacific Northwest.[51] The NWFC screenings were produced by cinema clubs, women's community centers, lesbian task forces, unions, women's studies departments and student associations, the National Organization for Women, women's bookstores, production companies, music stores, and restaurants.[52] As the circuit made its way to each of its destinations, its films' many feminisms ventured forth as well. Collected and projected together, the Californian lesbians of Hammer's and Oxenberg's films commingled with the "hookers, housewives, mothers and friends" of Deitch's *Woman to Woman* and the New York and New England women's health advocates in Women Make Movies' *Healthcaring* and Cambridge Documentary Films' *Taking Our Bodies Back*. Meanwhile, in the women's centers, college auditoriums, and union halls where these packages played, each of these filmic subjects came face to face, so to speak, with factory workers in Minnesota, southern dykes, Indigenous and Chicana women in New Mexico, and feminists and lesbians of various sorts all over.

While nontheatrical exhibition was typical of much women's movement media at this time, the range of local producers with whom Moonforce partnered was possible only due to the company's unique method of combining distribution, programming, and exhibition support.[53] Its packages, as small collections of women's recent work, provided nonmedia workers and those outside metropolitan and college town hubs with greater access to feminist media by making it easier to program entire evenings of feminist films. Most feminist films at this time were shorts, lasting between three and forty-five minutes. The circuit did the work of packaging a selection of films that could fill two hours and cover a range of subjects and styles in the process. Whereas Reid and Zheutlin had expressed reservations on early Iris audiotapes about women with little experience exhibiting NWFC packages,[54] Biren and Farmer, as self-taught media workers themselves, were confident about women's abilities to learn on the spot. Each package included a detailed set of instructions about how to organize and run a film screening for those local producers doing as much for the first time.[55] Among other things, these producers' notes recommended screen sizes for audiences of different sizes and taught producers how to select the best projector for their space. Because of these efforts, women across the United States with little film experience were able to access feminist films while gaining media skills of their own.

After their split from Iris Films, Biren and Farmer remained committed to serving the women's movement as a lesbian feminist organization.[56] However, what Moonforce Media's lesbian feminist programming would include and how it would facilitate its audiences' engagement with it does not fit scholarly

51

framings of lesbian feminist media and politics. Like Iris Films, Moonforce Media programmed the earliest films made by "out" lesbian filmmakers, the same films that, Dowell argued, offered audiences a "new dispensation" in women's art: the autobiographical experimental and documentary films of Hammer and Oxenberg. Their films were some of Iris and Moonforce's "highest-profile" titles.[57] Queer cinema and media studies scholars have attributed the popularity of Hammer's and Oxenberg's films to their having met young, white, middle-class lesbians' desires for representation. Their films celebrated women's love for one another, and lesbian feminists, Richard Dyer and Michelle Citron tell us, celebrated them in turn.[58] Without refuting such claims, looking to this enthusiastic reception of lesbian feminist film within the context of the simultaneous radicalizing of feminist film distribution and exhibition reveals that narrative to be but one piece of the picture— one that, in affirming visibility as paramount, in turn renders lesbian static.

The process of lesbian potentiality—the analysis of the contemporary organization of social life paired with the imagination of future possibilities both immediate and on the horizon—was integral to Biren and Farmer's lesbian impression on the NWFC. As Biren told a Feminist Radio Network interviewer, each of the films they selected for distribution included both a "critique of the society that we're living in now" and "a vision of how that might change in such a way to make that society better for us all to live in."[59] Recognizing that any given film could do only so much, Moonforce Media envisioned audiences gaining greater insight from thinking about each package's films together. Their programming of assorted films alongside one another was about more than reaching wide feminist audiences. Each package was made up of five or six films, including both fiction films and documentaries, as well as films that covered a range of feminist issues, from women's health care and imprisonment to sexuality. Lesbian feminist film programming, under Moonforce Media's tutelage, was not separatist, and it aspired to intersectionality. The address of Moonforce's programming did not presume a singular shared identity among any individual audience or across the geographically disparate circuit audiences. Biren and Farmer highlighted women's sexuality as a topic of discussion for feminist film audiences—an apt choice considering the centrality of desire and pleasure to burgeoning feminist film theory. But, unlike writing in *Screen* and *Camera Obscura*, Biren and Farmer did not presume viewers to be straight, and they explicitly sought to address issues of race and class simultaneously. They were unable to program films by or about lesbians of color or working-class lesbians, as no such films had been submitted to the DC festival for consideration. However, they

52

did program the white, middle-class lesbian films of Hammer and Oxenberg alongside documentaries that featured women of color and centralized issues of race and class in accessing health care, parenting, and the workforce, hoping audiences would do the work of drawing connections across this disparate content in their post-screening discussions. As a result, Moonforce Media held a much different attitude toward spectators than did formalist film theorists. Unlike their counterparts in academia, Biren and Farmer saw feminist viewers as active, arguing that they were as "important a part of the process as the filmmaker, the producer of [the] local showing or the organizers of the circuit nationally."[60] According to Moonforce Media, it was precisely because of the active engagement of viewers that feminist film could serve as a site of critical analysis and social change.[61]

Immediately after the DC festival, Biren and Farmer organized and began to advertise the circuit's first two packages.[62] At the festival they had collected approximately one thousand surveys, which they then used to make their selections for these packages, balancing the festival's most popular titles with others that also met their criteria for vision/critique. The fliers for the circuit announced that the films were drawn "from over 100 festival entries—the best in feminist filmmaking today" or declared them "6 of the nation's best feminist films" (see figures 1.1–1.2). [63] In an article published alongside the "*Camera Obscura* Questionnaire on Alternative Film Distribution," Freude Bartlett, who ran the Serious Business Company out of Oakland, California, wrote that "distribution is synonymous with marketing," and "'alternative distribution' is a misnomer albeit a handy one."[64] Film distribution, whether done by a Hollywood distributor or a feminist collective, in her opinion, is "essentially a mail-order business."[65] While it is obvious that Moonforce's fliers advertising the quality of NWFC films were intended to get people in seats (whether those were actual theater or classroom seats or diner booths and bookstore couches), unlike for Hollywood distributors and some, but certainly not all, feminist distributors, making money was not the goal. Moonforce Media was never a lucrative endeavor. Biren and Farmer did not rent out their films at a cost. Whoever wanted to produce a NWFC screening could. Biren and Farmer simply asked producers to charge whatever minimal admission fee seemed fit for their town to cover the costs of screenings (shipping fees, projector, screen, space rental). Producers could keep 10 percent of the gross receipts from ticket sales as compensation after these costs had been covered. Not every screening made a profit, but 40 percent of whatever profits Moonforce did make went back to the filmmakers; they used the rest to maintain the operation.[66] Biren and Farmer supported themselves through

OVEN PRODUCTIONS, CWRU WOMEN'S CENTER, & MOONFORCE MEDIA PRESENT

6 OF THE NATION'S BEST

FEMINIST FILMS

Like A Rose—a moving personal portrait of two women in prison
Fear—one woman's struggle with a rapist
A Foot In The Clouds—an amazing drama in which two women with different self definitions learn from each other

The Emerging Woman—a powerful documentary of the history of women in the U.S.
And Then There Were . . . —delightful mosaic animation
Dyketactics—sensual exploration of women loving women

MAY 20 & 21   8:30 PM

SCHMITT AUD. – CWRU

TICKETS: $2.00   FREE CHILDCARE BY RESERVATION   CALL 371-1697

1.1–1.2 Flyers for Moonforce Media's National Women's Film Circuit. Joan E. Biren Papers, Sophia Smith Collection, Smith College Special Collections, Northampton, Massachusetts.

their photography and bookstore management, respectively. For them, as was the case for many other feminist media workers at this time, Moonforce Media was always a voluntary labor of love.[67] With the minimal profits they made over the following three years, they were able to put together another festival in spring 1978 and, from its submissions, a third and fourth package of films.[68]

To encourage the active engagement of audiences they believed to be integral to the process of analysis and imagination via film, Biren and Farmer included a set of discussion questions with each package and followed the

54

FIRST AREA SHOWING

SELECTIONS FROM OVER 100 FESTIVAL ENTRIES — THE BEST IN FEMINIST FILMMAKING TODAY

NATIONAL WOMEN'S FILM CIRCUIT

WOMAN TO WOM— AN By Donna Deitch (48 min.—1975) ❧ **LIVIA MAKES SOME CHANGES** By Malanaphy Sandys & Weaver of Women Make Movies, Inc. (7 min.—1974) ❧ **OUR LITTLE MUNCHKIN HERE** By Lois Tupper (10 min.—1975) **HOME MOVIE** By Jan Oxenberg (12 min.—1972)❧ **MENSES** By Barbara Hammer (4 min. 1974) ❧ **TAKING OUR BODIES BACK: THE WOMENS HEALTH MOVEMENT** By Cambridge Documentary Films, Inc. (33 min.—1974)

SAT. MARCH 13, YWCA, DURHAM, TIMES: 1:30pm, 6pm/ SUN. MARCH 14, UNC UNION, C.H., 6 & 9pm $2

The Circuit is a project of Moonforce Media, Inc.

discussions audiences had around the country through the questionnaires that they asked each local circuit producer to fill out. Of the Women's Film Project's *Emerging Woman* (1974), a documentary about the history of the women's movement, Moonforce suggested that local producers ask, "What lessons can be drawn from [the film] as to the effectiveness of separatist vs. coalition politics and reformist vs. radical politics? What do you feel can be done to unite within one political movement women of different races and classes?"[69] For Barrett-Page's *Like a Rose* prison documentary, they encouraged

55

audiences to discuss what women outside of prison can do to help women on the inside. When it came to Hammer's personal experimental *Women I Love* (1976), Moonforce asked viewers to compare their own daydreams about past lovers with those in the film before discussing how the filmmaker's style affected the tone and emotional quality of the film and whether such explicit representations of lesbian sexuality could help to dispel homophobic prejudices both inside and outside the women's movement.[70] Alongside these discussion guides, they provided a list of resources for those interested in learning more about any particular subject covered by the films. Biren and Farmer put together these packages, complete with films, instructions for producers, and recommended discussion questions, in a way that made sense to them, but they also knew that each circuit location's audience would bring its own passions and perspectives to the screenings and the following discussions.

Both Annette Kuhn and E. Ann Kaplan, who published two of the first book-length studies of women's cinema (in 1982 and 1983, respectively), claim that alternative film distribution's primary function in the 1960s and '70s was to help political filmmakers direct their films toward specific audiences and delimit interpretations.[71] This fit with formalist film theory's attribution of power and agency to the screen and its authors and formalism's corresponding depreciation of spectators. For Kaplan, this was further exacerbated by what she considered "the culminating contradiction"—namely, "that filmmakers whose whole purpose was to change people's ways of seeing, believing, and behaving have only been able to reach an audience committed to their values."[72] Not only are such claims highly pessimistic, but they misinterpret feminist audiences (and radical audiences more broadly), seeing them in monolithic terms. In actual practice, feminist film distribution is revealed to be much more than a mere "mail order business" serving ideologically indistinguishable consumers.[73] Yes, the feminist media workers who ran these companies and the audiences who showed up for their screenings shared a commitment, broadly speaking, to feminism and to women's media. But the late 1970s was a period of "mass mobilization among antiracist women—both straight and lesbian."[74] Many US feminists of color were organizing along racial/ethnic lines.[75] As Chela Sandoval notes, moving between and among ideological positionings, US feminists of color often appeared as "the mobile (yet ever-present in their 'absence') members" of the women's and gay liberation movements.[76] What audiences' feminisms entailed—what each individual viewer, as well as each location's audience as a whole, brought to these screenings—and the critical thinking they did together in their discussions afterward varied greatly. Deeply familiar with the women's movement, Biren and Farmer did not merely "plac[e] films before audiences."[77] They selected films with a wide range of critiques and visions, taught women how to run film screenings, and put together discussion guides precisely to encourage critical engagement within feminist communities.

Lesbian Feminist Affectivity's Ephemera

Following Bartlett, Kaplan, and Kuhn, one could read Moonforce Media's questionnaires and Biren and Farmer's responses to their recurring critiques with later programming as the company's attempts to "capitalize" on its audiences' labor. Instead, before turning to International Videoletters, the second project to come out of the 1975 feminist media conferences, I conclude my study of the NWFC by arguing that there is more to learn if we approach these questionnaires as archives of lesbian feminist affectivity. The questionnaires index the anecdotal, as local producers record their impressions of different audiences' responses to the films. Handwritten, usually immediately after a screening, they relay fleeting moments of reception, often in incomplete sentences. Now located among Biren's papers at Smith College, the questionnaires offer ephemeral evidence of the ways in which feminist audiences thought through the realities that appeared before them on-screen, which, in turn, informed how they negotiated related issues and ideas in their own communities.[78] Affectivity, Kara Keeling explains, is a form of labor that "does not yet register in the economic sense as labor."[79] While affect generally describes the emotions and sensations a subject experiences when moving through the world, affectivity is the cognitive processing of those affects. Seeing cinematic perception as a process employed by twentieth-century subjects when engaging with images both inside the movie theater and outside in the material world, Keeling argues that affectivity is central to a subject's survival of reality as well as reality's (re)production.[80] This invites a rethinking of feminist reception of realist documentaries and feminist media more broadly.

Understood as affectivity, the reception of feminist media in the 1970s becomes less a matter of "reading," wherein one either does or does not possess the proper tools of analysis (training in psychoanalytic and semiotic theory), than a form of labor that draws on a wide range of knowledge, including knowledge gleaned through the body and its sensations inside the theater (or, as in the case with the NWFC, more often in a women's center or bookstore) and out (including the home, the workplace, the local feminist community) and includes imagination alongside critique. Feminist archives, like

57

those at Smith College, are plentiful sites of potentiality. Reading Moonforce Media's questionnaires as themselves archives of lesbian feminist affectivity gives us a sense of the work that feminist media *did* within and across US feminist locations. In investing not only their time and money but also their affect and labor in the reception of feminist film, NWFC audiences contributed to the reproduction of late twentieth-century reality. By participating in a process of critique that extended beyond the films before them to the society in which they lived, and, through these same films, imagining a better world, feminist audiences created a world in which such a process, previously impossible, became possible. Lesbian potentiality was not only actualized but also renewed and absconded with as audiences left screenings and moved through their various social worlds.

Often in the South or more rural areas, film circuit producers used their questionnaires to highlight the importance of media and culture in sustaining local lesbian communities. In these places, the existence of lesbian groups was tenuous and dependent upon the ongoing organizing efforts of a few committed women. In October 1977 in New Orleans, for example, the package that included Deitch's *Woman to Woman*, Women Make Movies' *Livia Makes Some Changes*, Tupper's *Our Little Munchkin Here*, Oxenberg's *Home Movie*, Hammer's *Menses*, and Cambridge Documentary Films' *Taking Our Bodies Back* was programmed twice—once for a lesbian group and once at an arts center—gathering a total of only forty-eight spectators.[81] In her questionnaire, Casey, the local producer, draws a number of contrasts between the "dyke" and "liberal art center" audiences before making a case for the former's need for more film programming such as the NWFC. Casey writes that the dyke audience was not amused by *Livia Makes Some Changes* (a docudrama about a stay-at-home mother returning to the workforce), while the liberal art center audience thought it was "cute." The dyke audience found Hammer's menstruation film *Menses* "comic," while the liberals were "horrified" by the blood. Both audiences, however, loved Oxenberg's *Home Movie*, the dykes getting "really rowdy" during its screening and the liberals "chuckl[ing] heavily." Casey concludes that, although the low attendance could be discouraging to Moonforce, she thinks it is important that the film circuit keep coming—and quickly, too, as "the dyke South needs to get films that are current, not 4 years later."[82] The producer from Athens, Georgia, similarly wrote, "The women's community was very excited about the films and want to see another package!"[83] She elaborates that, while having seventy people in attendance might not seem "worth it" to Moonforce, for the Athens women's community the circuit could prove vital in helping to sustain the growing local lesbian activity, which, she notes, had just expanded to include a regular meeting group and newsletter. The producer from Mama Peaches Restaurant in Chicago expressed similar sentiments, writing that such events provided the struggling Chicago women's community with integral moments of strength.[84] In their encouragement of discussion, NWFC screenings bridged the cinematic and the social. The enthusiastic responses of lesbian and feminist audiences were the result not just of personal engagements with films—experiences of identification, say—but also of shared encounters with the women on the screen, which facilitated further encounters with one another locally.

In other cases, the reception of the NWFC exceeded any coherent sense of a local community, lesbian, feminist, or otherwise, as hundreds of people brought a wide range of perspectives and debates to discussions. In January 1976, 850 people in Minneapolis–St. Paul also saw the package comprising *Woman to Woman, Livia Makes Some Changes, Our Little Munchkin Here, Home Movie, Menses,* and *Taking Our Bodies Back* over five screenings in the course of a weekend.[85] Kathleen Laughlin, the local producer, notes in her questionnaire that the films drew rather mixed audiences, including fewer lesbians and more men then she had expected, as well as plenty of students and factory workers and increasingly racially diverse audiences each night, suggesting that word of mouth after the first couple of screenings had been responsible for bringing more people of color to the program.[86] Laughlin makes a number of notes about the general reactions that each film garnered, as well as a few pointed audience critiques that stood out to her—such as one woman telling her afterward that she and her friends thought *Taking Our Bodies Back* was a downer for the program to end on, especially due to what they found to be its simplified takes on childbirth and abortion, which surprised Laughlin. She then exclaims, "But who can ever speak for a 'whole audience's' reaction?!"[87] Apart from a few particularly small audiences, circuit locations typically brought in audiences of one hundred to three hundred spectators across two or three screenings. Producers reflected on the challenges of recording such audiences' responses (in Lexington, Kentucky, the audience is described as including everyone from "grandmothers to local leaping lesbians").[88] They often noted where local interest seemed particularly acute. Sue Hyde in St. Louis mentioned that much of the 161 person audience there had firsthand experience with the Tipton, Missouri, prison of *Like a Rose,* which made for a productive discussion of the film.[89] In moments such as these, it becomes apparent that the multigeneric programming of NWFC packages led to varied localized engagements.

Across the questionnaires, however, a few common threads can be identified. Notably, although Moonforce included only one explicitly lesbian film in each package (Jan Oxenberg's *Home Movie*, Barbara Hammer's *Dyketactics* or *Women I Love*, or Christina Mohana's *Ninja*), these films regularly provoked the strongest reactions. A few producer questionnaires note that people walked out of screenings after these films were shown, and in a couple of places, the packages were censored after local politicians learned of their lesbian content.[90] Everywhere that it did show and for those audience members who did stay, however, Oxenberg's *Home Movie* (1972)—an autobiographical documentary about lesbian childhood and finding community in the women's movement in LA—appears to have been enthusiastically received.[91] Comments in producers' questionnaires suggest that many lesbians found Oxenberg's story of growing up gay with an otherwise "typical" (i.e., white, middle-class American) childhood relatable. Many audience members, lesbian and non-lesbian, found her tale of becoming a cheerleader to spend more time with other girls charming. And quite a few found the film's conclusion, which cuts together footage of a lesbian football game turned erotic tumbling pile and that of a Gay Pride march to a Debra Quinn song declaring "we are together" and "we're not waiting any longer to be free," to be a hopeful indicator of what was to come (see figures 1.3–1.4). *Home Movie*'s lesbian potentiality, in short, shone bright. The producer in Makawao, Hawaii, wrote, "Many comments on seeing the usually macho, murderous game of football played lovingly. Everyone felt the glow from this one."[92] Meanwhile, the producer in Norman, Oklahoma, wrote, "The Darling of them all! Never has slow motion football been so acclaimed—also, I think a few women got the message that lesbians are everywhere and it's OK."[93] Such reflections indicate a consistency in NWFC audiences' reception of Oxenberg's film, and they narrativize, if ever so fleetingly, the cognitive processing of affects that individual viewers navigated in discussions afterward together.

Meanwhile, the same questionnaires suggest that Hammer's films, including *Menses* (1974) but more so *Dyketactics* (1974) and *Women I Love*, garnered the greatest debate and controversy. A common theme in their circuit reception seems to have been discussions about what constitutes lesbian existence and how it ought to be filmed. The NWFC audiences constantly debated whether women's love or their sexual desire for one another ought to take precedence. And yet, oddly enough, they could not come to a consensus on which of these Hammer's films offer. Some found *Dyketactics*, which both Hammer and Moonforce Media advertised as a "lesbian commercial," too pornographic, while others thought the sex was too clinical and not sexy enough.[94] Straight viewers in Albuquerque, meanwhile, loved it.[95] *Women I Love*, a highly experimental film that cuts together footage of time spent with past lovers with stop-motion animation of yonic plants and vegetables, was "too abstract" for the Student Association for Women in Normal, Illinois (see figures 1.5–1.6).[96] At the premiere of the third and fourth packages at the Ontario Theater in Washington, DC, where individuals got their own questionnaires, a number of audience members commented on how exciting they found *Women I Love*'s use of experimental techniques and wrote that they made interesting connections between the film's various subjects. A few, however, noted that they wanted to see more of the relationships in the film, and one person wrote, "Little redeeming values [*sic*] except perhaps the vegetables."[97] Hammer's films, typically taken as indicative of lesbian separatist ideology, are not solely the result of a politics and practice in these questionnaires but are, in fact, productive of a discourse regarding lesbian sexuality, romance, and culture. Some of the more resistant responses to Hammer's films are clearly indicative of ideological battles going on within the women's movement at the time.[98] The National Organization for Women in DC, for example, declared the women's movement was not "ready 'for that film' yet," echoing the organization's long-expressed sentiments of reticence when it came to affiliations between the women's movement and lesbian existence.[99] When discussing the future of the circuit in Amarillo, Texas, the producer commented that while she was relatively comfortable showing *Home Movie* because she thought it "reache[d] gay and straight women," she would be uncomfortable showing *Women I Love*, as it was "made for lesbians" and she did not think it would reach straight women at all.[100] That heteropatriarchy may topple, and that women would be the ones to topple it, was threatening not only to men but to many straight feminists set on women's innate attraction to men, and such critiques of Hammer's films can be seen as a defensive attempt to contain lesbian potentiality through identitarian language that divides and separates—in this case, straight women from lesbians.

Still, other questionnaires indicate the profound strangeness for all audiences to get to see lesbian existence on-screen. Oxenberg's and Hammer's films did not receive the same critiques of didacticism that more "straight" documentaries in NWFC packages did. In fact, whether positively or negatively received, the lesbian films were often singled out as offering something that all audiences—gay, straight, women-only, or mixed—had never encountered

61

1.3–1.4 "We're not waiting any longer to be free" in *Home Movie* (Jan Oxenberg, dir., 1972). Screen grabs.

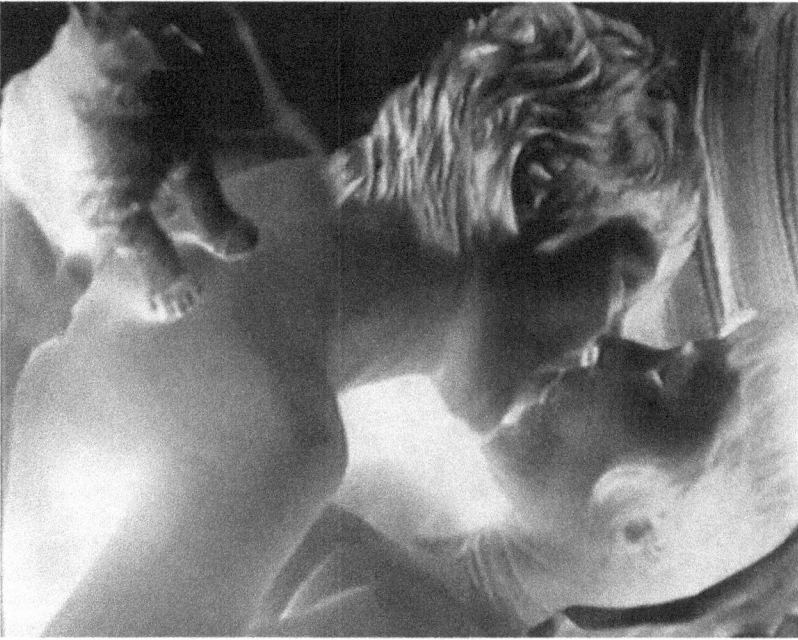

1.5 Lesbian lovers in *Women I Love* (Barbara Hammer, dir., 1976). Screen grab.

before. To some's chagrin and others' pleasure, these lesbian films, through Moonforce's radicalization of feminist film distribution, put lesbian potentiality into movement. What gendered and sexual life might look, sound, and feel like outside, beyond, or after compulsory heterosexuality became a question for many—lesbian-identified and not—to ponder together.

These films' NWFC reception, the ephemeral evidence of their audiences' lesbian feminist affectivity, demonstrates the dynamic and dialogical nature of lesbian feminist film and media. Gay and lesbian film scholars writing in the 1980s were quick to draw on Hammer's own writing about her films and to make connections between her ideas in filming them and the essentializing and romanticizing ideology of much cultural feminism, so much so that it has become practically reflexive for queer film scholars to do so since.[101] Greg Youmans complicates Hammer's relationship to essentialism and lesbian separatism. By looking to trans and genderqueer media artists' returns to Hammer's early oeuvre and by highlighting the sexiness and humor they find there, Youmans makes the case for a more performative reading of *Dyketactics*, *Menses*, and *Women I Love*.[102] Youmans also cites Hammer as saying she never insisted on women-only screenings.[103] That said, as these

63

1.6 Artichoke in *Women I Love* (Barbara Hammer, dir., 1976). Screen grab.

NWFC questionnaires reveal, the work of lesbian feminist cinema did not end with the political program of either its filmmakers or its distributors but continued through the labor of its audiences.

The questionnaires suggest that, while Hammer's and Oxenberg's films were cherished as the first made by "out" lesbian filmmakers, their representations of "lesbian" were never taken as the final say in the matter of lesbian sexuality, romance, or politics. As Biren recently reflected, "Sometimes this is the first time lesbians look each other in the eye, when they get in here and see a Jan Oxenberg film, and it's incredibly validating and incredibly exciting because they get that reflection of themselves in the film and then they get the community that they live in. . . . All kinds of things spring from that."[104] These films offered feminist communities a starting point, an initiation of lesbian possibilities to be taken up and extended in reception. The directions such discussions traversed were varied and intense. This is often captured in dizzying reflections of local producers in their questionnaires. Of *Dyke-tactics*, the Albuquerque producer wrote: "'a beautiful film of humans loving humans' 'filth' 'it's about time we were out of the closet' 'I don't want anyone to know what my lover and I do' 'there's more to us than just our sexuality' 'beautiful'" (see figures 1.7–1.8). [105] In a certain regard, these short strings of words and phrases tell us very little about the post-screening discussions. Their anecdotal and ephemeral evidence allow those of us in the present to catch but a glimpse. At the same time, they bear the trace of NWFC audiences' lesbian feminist affectivity, the intensity of feminist spectators' engagement with one another and with the women who appeared onscreen.

For those viewers who were attracted to NWFC screenings because of the lesbian impression of their programmers, part of what the packages enabled in terms of imagination was a future lesbian cinema different from the one presented before them. At the bottom of their questionnaires, Moonforce Media asked producers whether they thought the circuit should return to their town; if so, how often; and "What do people want to see?" One recurring and resounding answer to this last question was that audiences wanted to see more films by and about women of color. They wanted more films about Black, Latina, and Indigenous women, and they wanted them to be lesbian films and fun films, rather than just the few fairly serious documentaries in the packages that did address women of color's lives. The producer of the Albuquerque screenings in January 1976 writes, "There were no real criticisms of the films until the Saturday night all women's show. These were aimed primarily at 'The Emerging Woman' and 'Dyketactics.' Many women felt that once more Chicana and Native American women were ignored."[106] Furthermore, the producer elaborates, audiences did not appreciate how the politics of Black families received less careful attention than that of white families in *The Emerging Woman*. Because of this, she concludes, "Many women will not come back to another showing."[107] However, when the NWFC returned to Albuquerque in 1977, this time with the *Woman to Woman, Home Movie*, and *Menses* package, the same producer noted that those who had resented *Emerging Woman* and *Dyketactics* appreciated Deitch's film, which humorously drew connections among the lives of working women of different classes and races, including suburban housewives, sex workers, imprisoned women, a lesbian psychologist, and a telephone operator.[108] Audiences in Athens, Georgia, concurred; the local producer wrote of *Woman to Woman*, "People liked seeing Chicanas and Black women as well as the usual whites."[109] While any given film it programmed might hit or miss with different audiences, Moonforce Media, by packaging divergent films together and taking audience feedback into consideration in its ongoing programming, sustained the imagination of future lesbian cinemas.

The history of lesbian cinema, as it is typically written by way of filmmaker and representation in the most mimetic sense, appears to be exclusively white

65

402 Clarke Rd SW (4)
NM 87105 EM 9

Where responses differ for different showings, please indicate. Please feel free to use as many additional pages as you need or any other format to let us know as much as possible about what happened. Thanks.

1. What was the overall reaction to the showing? *positive and exciting, the straight audiences loved dyketactics.*

2. Was the showing time ____ about right, _X_ too long, ____ too short?

3. Was the number of films (6) _X_ about right, _X_ too many, ____ too few?

4. Was the mixture of different kinds good? (Comment) *yes, seemed to appeal to most people, the different lengths of the films was was also good.*

5. Was the order in which they were shown good? (Suggestions) *yes*

6. How about disscussion breaks? How many were there? *2* . Was this _X_ about right, _X_ too many, ____ too few? Did they seem to fall in the right places? *yes*

Which films were most talked about? *Emerging Woman, Dyketactics, Like a Rose*

7. Did you experience any technical difficulties either in setting up for or in running the films? (Please explain) *no, projector was not working as well as it should have*

8. How many womanhours were put in to produce the Circuit in your city? *~80 hrs*

9. What was the biggest "up" of being a producer? *"having it over w/" womans only discussion discussion.*

10. What was the biggest "bummer" of being a producer? *"A Foot in the Clouds"*

11. What one thing can you think of that would most improve attendance at future Circuit showings? *more attention to publicity. Inclusion of films that deal w/ the "emerging woman" that lives west of the mississippi.*

12. Are you willing to produce the Circuit again in about six months? _X_ Yes. ____ No.

13. What would you most like to see us (Moonforce) do differently about the Circuit next time around? *in a nutshell — include all feminist films in subsequent packages. - Have only 2 reels for purposes of providing discussion breaks*

-more-

ı. What should be kept the same? _information to producers, variety of films_
free communication between ~~to~~ we and thee .

15. Based on the discussions, please give us a general idea of how most people felt
about each film:

THE EMERGING WOMAN _Well thought of, ~~but is an~~ ~~rather~~ ~~optimistic at~~_
~~first cost~~ _charisma ~~~~ engendered fine discussion_

AND THEN THERE WERE _"loved it" "isn't ~~~~ wonderful what they can ~~do~~ do_
w/ bits of cardboard" "fine environmental film"

DYKETACTICS _"a beautiful film of humans loving humans" "filth" "it's about_
time we were out of the closet" "I don't want anyone to know what my lover
and I do" "there's more to us than just our sexuality" "beautiful"

LIKE A ROSE _Touched folks deeply once they figured out what was_
going on — did not realize that here were 2 dykes doing
something other than making love.

FEAR _"ritual is something to be careful of" "bad technically" "it was nice to_
see the woman win" "perpetuated racist myths"

A FOOT IN THE CLOUDS _no ~~distinct~~ discussion_

16. We hope you will use the remaining space to tell us whatever else we forgot to ask.
Like should we plan to bring the Circuit back to your city? How often should the Circuit
come to your city? What do people want to see? Is it working?

at this time we feel the circuit should come not more than 2
times a year to Albuquerque.

1.7–1.8 Albuquerque NWFC questionnaire. Joan E. Biren Papers, SSC-MS-00587,
Sophia Smith Collection, Smith College Special Collections, Northampton,
Massachusetts.

and middle class until the 1980s, when Michelle Parkerson's short films debuted. However, NWFC reception demonstrates that its audiences' aspirations were otherwise from the start. In the discussions that followed NWFC screenings, lesbians of color courageously practiced what Audre Lorde called the "transformation of silence into language and action."[110] As early as the first white lesbian films' releases, these women demanded lesbian of color films. In the face of the specifically white middle-class lesbian feminist reality placed before them, working-class lesbians and lesbians of color articulated their own, refusing to remain silent. This was not just a call for inclusion or a plea for visibility or positivity in any simple sense. Rather, as the Albuquerque producer's comments suggest, post-screening discussions explored how articulations of white women's sexualities often pathologized those of Black women in the process. In such cases, NWFC lesbian affectivity meant a collective examination of the very structures of lesbian visibility. Neither the films in and of themselves nor filmmakers' testimonies on their own could ever reveal as much. Secondary materials are primary to the study of the work these lesbian films did across US feminist communities. Presentations of anecdotal and ephemeral evidence, such as those the NWFC post-screening questionnaires offer, José Esteban Muñoz writes, "[grant] entrance and access to those who have been locked out of official histories and, for that matter, 'material reality.'"[111] When one reads the NWFC producers' anecdotes about local audiences' discussions, the history of lesbian cinema is revealed to be less white than previously thought. More than that, these anecdotes provide evidence of a movement of women for whom attending feminist film screenings was part of a broader project of making sense of, critiquing, and imagining otherwise racist and classist (as well as sexist and homophobic) late twentieth-century reality.

Biren and Farmer kept track of and engaged with audiences' recurring criticisms in their programming of later packages. The two were not involved in production and could only distribute films that were produced and submitted for consideration. One common critique of their first two packages that they felt confident in meeting with the third and fourth packages was audiences' desires for "slicker" women's films. As Patricia Zimmermann has documented, by the 1970s amateur film discourse had for some time articulated Hollywood narrative style as "a natural, filmmaking version of common sense."[112] This amateur and early professional work of feminist filmmakers on 16 mm stock did not meet all of their audiences' aesthetic expectations, which likewise were derived from the films they typically saw in theaters. As the producer in Cleveland put it, some audience members attended NWFC screenings expecting "to see professional Hollywood-type films that had been made by women."[113] Furthermore, producers often noted that audience members were disappointed in the technical quality of the films, especially considering they had been advertised as some of the "best" feminist films. While Biren and Farmer would continue to see their packaging system as a way to feature the work of new feminist filmmakers, as well as that of those who were more experienced, the NWFC's later packages did include more technically sophisticated films. As Biren and Farmer told a Feminist Radio Network interviewer just before the DC premiere of the third and fourth packages, "These two packages of films really, from end-to-end, are just gorgeous, well-made films."[114]

Due to the scale and budget of their organization, however, Biren and Farmer could not meet all the requests of local circuit producers, filmmakers, or audiences. Moonforce Media, much to the disappointment of a number of interested fledgling feminist filmmakers who inquired about Super 8 film and video, distributed only 16 mm films. They were dependent on NWFC producers to find projectors and projectionists in each of the circuit's locations, and Biren and Farmer believed that combining 8 mm, Super 8, and video formats within packages with 16 mm film would lead to too many complications.[115] Similarly, Moonforce could not meet the requests it received for international screenings. Most of these requests were from feminist groups in Canada, but some hailed from as far away as Hong Kong.[116] To each of these, Biren and Farmer wrote back that they would love to distribute internationally but could not risk the delays and expenses of shipping the films to these places.[117] The farthest the circuit traveled was to Makawao, Hawaii. Although interest in the NWFC never waned, Biren and Farmer struggled financially and were never able to afford to hire additional employees. When the couple broke up in 1980, the circuit came to an end as well.[118] In the 1980s, Women Make Movies further developed its distribution wing, and as a feminist media organization with a better eye for business, it would continue to forge long-distance relations with feminists across the country and around the globe.[119] However, nothing quite like the NWFC would ever replace it. Thanks to Moonforce Media, women isolated in rural areas were able to meet and connect with one another through NWFC screenings. Feminist audiences all over the United States, not just those in LA, New York, and other metropolitan centers, were given the opportunity to analyze these packages' films in relation to one another and, in doing so, articulate their realities in relation to not just one reality but to the many realities placed before them. Through the programming and distribution of Moonforce Media,

69

lesbian feminist cinema in the late 1970s served as a site not only of visibility and validation but also of moving political contestation.

International Videoletters

The NWFC was not the only project to come out of the 1975 conferences as a part of the participants' effort to build a feminist media network. The idea for the International Videoletters project—most commonly advertised as "a monthly feminist exchange of news, issues, events" (and with VIDEOLETTERS in all caps)—was first conceived at the New York Conference of Feminist Film and Video Organizations, and the first videoletters crafted for the project were screened at the Feminist Eye Conference in LA the following month.[120] Each videoletter ran for approximately thirty minutes (the length of half-inch reel-to-reel videotapes). Videoletters covered local protests and organizing efforts, lectures, art exhibits, concerts, and theater performances. Some videoletters focused on a single issue or event, but most videoletters served as compilations of sorts so that on each videoletter, as well as among videoletters and between videoletters and audiences, various feminisms commingled. Shortly after the Feminist Eye Conference, Carol Clement, a lesbian feminist graphic artist based in New York who was affiliated with Women Make Movies (and, at the time, the partner of Ariel Dougherty, one of the organization's cofounders), designed the substantive logo that would adorn International Videoletters fliers.[121] The logo pictures outer space, framed as if on a television screen and rendered in a horizontally streaky fashion that recalls the medium's iconic low-quality images. A shooting star and wayward planet hover in the background. Front and center is Earth, whose continents have been reshaped into a handheld camera labeled "INTERNATIONAL." Just below, "VIDEOLETTERS," in large three-dimensional letters, with a Venus symbol for the "O," spins out of orbit, protruding from the TV screen (see figure 1.9). Either above or below this half-page logo, fliers announced which "constellation"—that is, which set of participating cities—would be screening their letters next. By naming these groupings of cities "constellations" in the correspondence with one another, feminist media workers imagined a network connecting them that was vast, bright, and otherworldly.[122] And advertised this way, International Videoletters offered feminist communities across the Anglophone world, if not the galaxy, access to one another and their activities through videotaped correspondence.

International Videoletters was conceived by American, Canadian, and Australian feminist media workers at the New York conference as a solution

L.A./Chicago/D.C./N.Y.C.

a bi-monthly women's information exchange

INTERNATIONAL VIDEOLETTERS #1
showing

Wed., April 16, 1975 8pm at Women's Interarts Center 549 W 52nd St

in conjunction with the Women's Video Festival

$1

International VIDEOLETTERS is an experimental project developed at the Conference of Feminist Film and Video Organizations, in February, in New York City. As a result of the Feminist Eye conference in late March in Los Angeles, the project will expand to include 9 cities. For more information about the VIDEOLETTERS call: (212) 929-6477.

Women Make Movies/Open Video/Women's Video Project/WIC-Video

1.9 International Videoletters flyer. Arthur and Elizabeth Schlesinger Library on the History of Women in America, Radcliffe Institute for Advanced Study, Harvard University, Cambridge, Massachusetts.

to feminist communities' feelings of isolation. The feminist press reported factual details of protests and events, but it provided neither the immediacy nor the intimacy feminists craved. Film and video could provide audiences with a more sensory experience of other communities' activities, and, as conference participants with experience working in video production and public access television pointed out, video was quick, easy, and cheap, meaning it could do so with an immediacy that film could not.[123] The Sony Portapack camera, they explained, was light enough to be used by a two-person crew, and its recordings could be played back right away.[124] Thus, by writing one another letters through the medium of half-inch video (which, like Iris's audiotapes, they mailed after producing), the feminist media workers who gathered at the New York conference imagined they might "increase awareness of what is happening in other places; develop a feeling of closeness among women in different cities; encourage the growth and participation of an interested audience; and record and preserve women's history and culture."[125] If NWFC packages were collections shaped by the lesbian impressions of their distributors, their questionnaires providing ephemeral evidence of the lesbian feminist affectivity of their audiences, International Videoletters employed video's potential for amateur archiving.[126] They recorded the lesbian impressions of feminist media workers and, through their distribution and exhibition, created an affective, intimate, and at times explicitly erotic network among geographically disparate women. With each constellation's mailing of videotapes, lesbian potentiality was renewed.

A decade before videocassette recorders became commonplace in middle-class homes, making amateur archiving largely a domestic matter, feminist media workers archived their own lives and experiences as members of the women's movement and did so for one another.[127] They joined activists who since the mid-1960s had been using video as "a tool of media access (in terms of production and distribution) and an access medium (in terms of reception)."[128] In small cities, videoletter production was usually taken on by a single organization, while videoletters from large cities were often produced by coalitions of organizations. In New York City, five groups—Women Make Movies, Open Video, Video Commune, the Women's Interarts Center, and Lesbians Organized for Video Experience—made videoletters together. By the time of the Feminist Eye Conference in late March 1975, women in New York, Chicago, DC, and LA had all made videoletters. The Feminist Eye opened with a screening of the Women Make Movies' Chelsea Picture Station short film *Fear* (Jean Shaw, dir., 1973) and the notorious neorealist pro-labor *Salt of the Earth*, made by blacklisted Hollywood producers in

1954, followed by the International Videoletters premiere.[129] After this initial screening, five more cities joined the project. The nine cities organized into three "constellations" of three cities apiece, with which they would exchange their half-hour-long tapes before sending their package of three tapes on to the other constellations.[130] Over the next two years, an estimated twenty-seven organizations from seventeen communities made and circulated videoletters and organized screenings for their local feminist communities.[131] Some cities formed new constellations, while others joined existing constellations, and some contributed but one or two videoletters and held only sporadic screenings.[132] The project never achieved the international reach for which it had hoped. Coordinating the video technology and costs of shipping with "sister organizations" in Canada, Australia, and the United Kingdom proved challenging.[133] Ultimately, only a few Canadian letters were produced. Nonetheless, through the project's archiving of feminist activities, feminists across the United States were able, as one Spectra Feminist Media flier advertised, to "meet some interesting women."[134]

Other than running approximately thirty minutes and being realist in the broadest sense, the videoletters were not standardized in terms of either content or style. In addition to local protests and organizing efforts, lectures, art exhibits, concerts, and theater performances, they sometimes covered—very much in the vein of a letter—more mundane subjects, such as weather, but did so through methods that took advantage of their audiovisual format. For example, the women of the Tucson Feminist Media Collective showed their constellation their summer heatwave by recording themselves frying an egg on the sidewalk, much to the chagrin of a local policeman.[135] The women who produced the videoletters were trying, as Dougherty articulated in a letter to the Bay Area's Just Us Video Collective, to "find new forms for communication and new ways of expressing ideas."[136] Just Us was interested in expanding videoletters into a more regular feminist news service, but, as Dougherty explained on behalf of the New York City organizations, many were worried that much of what made the project special—namely, the space its flexibility created for creativity—would wither with standardization.[137] Frances Reid of Iris Films produced videoletters with others in LA and concurred, saying, "For a lot of people, it was a chance to experiment with something and, hopefully, in a safe environment where you're sending this out to other women who are trying to do the same thing."[138] Screenings would typically conclude with a discussion of the screened videoletters and the production of a feedback tape, which would be sent back through the constellation.[139] While feminist realist documentaries of the first half of

73

the decade "came out of the same ethos as the consciousness-raising groups [of the time] and had the same goals," International Videoletters adapted the very process of consciousness-raising in their distribution and exhibition.[140] And the videoletters were crafted with an attention to the potential of realist documentary, their producers knowing that they were not simply recording and representing the reality of life around them but creatively and actively shaping it through its production, distribution, and exhibition for equally invested others.

The videoletters varied greatly in their use of narrative (or lack thereof). Often documenting a series of events on a relatively short length of tape, some videoletter producers experimented with ways of connecting each segment for viewers. In one LA letter, two guides (Susan Mogul and Pam McDonald) whisk viewers through a tour of the Woman's Building but do so in an almost Georges Méliès–like fashion, popping up in different costumes, sometimes together, sometimes apart, "transport[ing] [viewers] through time and space" so that they might experience feminist art workshops and exhibitions hosted over a number of weeks.[141] In other videoletters, however, spectators are left to do the work of connecting the moving parts. One videoletter by Berkeley's Just Us Video Collective compiles footage of three women's cultural events in the Bay Area—Margie Adams recording her first album; a comedic theatrical performance by Lilitheatre; and Holly Near, Meg Christian, Cris Williamson, and Margie Adams's "Women on Wheels" concert in February 1976—and cuts the footage of all three together after just the briefest of introductions. Others still took the opportunity to document contemporary feminist activism to tell a history of local coalitions. In the first videoletter from Washington, DC, the Spectra Feminist Media Project documents its local celebration of International Women's Day. The videoletter focuses on the Coalition of Labor Women and the Central Labor Council of Washington's demonstrations, interviewing participants and filming speakers who connect the present concerns of race and gender discrimination in the workplace and the long history of female leaders in the labor movement. Spanning the almost science-fictional to the travelogue and the historical, International Videoletter narratives diverged greatly. None, however, appear to have positioned spectators as passive consumers; each narrative instead invited audiences to participate in the meaning-making process.

In addition to narrative, International Videoletter producers experimented with editing, cinematography, and sound. Although all were shot in a fairly realist "run and gun" fashion due to their documentation of live events, the variety of techniques and styles that the videoletters use show their producers' interest in form and craft. This craftwork is only the more impressive when done in camera, as was the case with Spectra's International Women's Day videoletter. The video begins with establishing shots of the protest before taking viewers into the fray. Taken from a balcony, these early shots offer viewers a sense of the scope and setting of the event. A dramatic low-angle shot of the US Capitol Building's dome is followed by a high-angle shot of those marching below (see figure 1.10).[142] The audio, also recorded from the balcony, faintly captures the protesters singing what sounds like a version of the African American protest song "We Shall Not Be Moved." The camera then moves to the same level as the protesters, where it remains for the rest of the video. Both keen to capture the activities happening around them and aware of the little tape they had to work with, the Spectra women behind the camera made deliberate and creative cuts, crafting a montage of the day as it played out. The video ends with a series of excerpts of speeches made before a crowd at a podium. In this sequence, the camera alternates between steady shots of the speakers and pans of the crowd, huddled tightly now that it has begun to snow. Sometimes one can hear the Spectra women kibitzing. As a white male speaker for the Central Labor Council drones on, one woman whispers to another, "Do we want this?" The camera stays on him a few more seconds and then cuts away. The tape ends with the speech of a cheerful representative from the Coalition of Black Trade Unionists (see figure 1.11). She opens by joking, "This is the first time the Coalition of Black Trade Unionists has made a speech in the snow." She tells the crowd that President Gerald Ford predicts national unemployment rates will rise to 10 percent by July and states that in most cities the rates for Black people's unemployment have already passed this. "Today," she declares, "women and Blacks are facing the most economic crisis of any Americans." The camera pans the crowd one last time, then the videoletter abruptly ends (see figure 1.12), the Spectra women having run out of tape. How much they were able to capture from the day's events (as well as the attention they brought to shaping its content thematically and focusing on issues of labor) is formidable, as are the methods they used to do so, all to transport International Women's Day, Washington, DC, to women around the world.

Made within local feminist communities and exhibited for others, videoletters put localized feminisms in correspondence—or, as we might say more colloquially, in touch. The women of the Spectra Feminist Media Project introduced themselves to the women in their constellation and those of these other International Videoletter constellations not as individuals but by way of the environment in which they worked and in relation to those

75

1.10–1.12 Spectra Feminist Media Project's "International Women's Day" International Videoletter, 1975. Screen grabs. Long Beach Museum of Art Video Archive, Getty Research Institute, Los Angeles.

they saw as doing important feminist work around their city. When Deborah George of Spectra sent the International Women's Day videoletter to New York City, the Washington, DC, audience had just watched a videoletter from New York that included footage of its own International Women's Day march. George scribbled a quick note to Dougherty: "I think the contrast betw. the 2 cities is interesting to see."[143] Through such juxtapositions of similar content, shot and edited through varied methods, feminist media workers and their audiences were able to see, hear, and feel the differences between their local feminist communities and those elsewhere.

In making International Videoletters, 1970s feminist media workers recognized what early psychoanalytic and semiotic feminist film theory overlooked and feminist phenomenological film theory has since revealed: that cinema is a dialogical space of exchange between two bodies—the spectator and the film. In fact, it was obvious to feminist media workers that there was always the potential for exchange among nearly infinite numbers of bodies, if one counted the bodies of those who collectively produced the film, the

77

many viewers these producers met through the circulation of the film body in distribution, and the dynamic of exchanges between viewers in any single given site of exhibition.

Laura U. Marks has argued that, with the medium of video (as opposed to film), the bodily exchange of viewer and text can take on a particularly haptic quality, as video's electronic texture demands that the viewer's body becomes more involved in the process of seeing.[144] Video's denial of depth of vision and multiplication of surface, Marks claims, lends the medium an eroticism that is much different from that of the mastery of optical visuality. The eroticism of this haptic visuality, she writes, "puts into question cinema's illusion of representing reality, by pushing the viewer's look back to the surface of the image" and "enables an embodied perception, the viewer responding to the video as to another body and to the screen as another skin."[145] Marks takes the experimental video art of Sadie Benning and Seoungho Cho as exemplary of haptic visuality. The tiny cars, Hershey's Kisses, and birthday-cake candles Benning uses to tell personal stories of teenage lesbian love with their lo-fi Pixelvision camera become eroticized through the attention paid to their surfaces, which are both detailed and incomplete in their graininess. We can similarly ask how early video's haptic visuality lent a certain subtle eroticism to the many bodily exchanges of the videoletters project.

Each videoletter includes moments in which the three-dimensionality of a protest, concert, or art exhibit are lost in a flat close-up or even a long shot of protesters, who appear right there at the surface of the screen. In the Woman's Building videoletter, the artwork created in the building's workshops and displayed in its exhibitions is rendered in black and white, grainy flatness, creating a sensorily unrealistic but nonetheless sensual encounter for viewers. Furthermore, the videoletter's transitions, its transportations through "time and space"—that is, between different Woman's Building workshops and exhibitions—are often disorienting, each cut wrenching the viewer's mind and body. After an interview with Sheila de Bretteville at an Eileen Gray exhibit opening, the videoletter abruptly cuts to a set of mechanical teeth of indeterminate scale munching. The camera then slowly zooms out and reveals these teeth to be part of a large installation piece with a giant plush heart behind it (see figures 1.13–1.14). For a moment, however, figure and ground are completely indistinguishable. According to Marks, such haptic images are erotic because of the particular kind of intersubjective relationship they construct between viewer and video in which viewers surrender their sense of separateness from the image.[146]

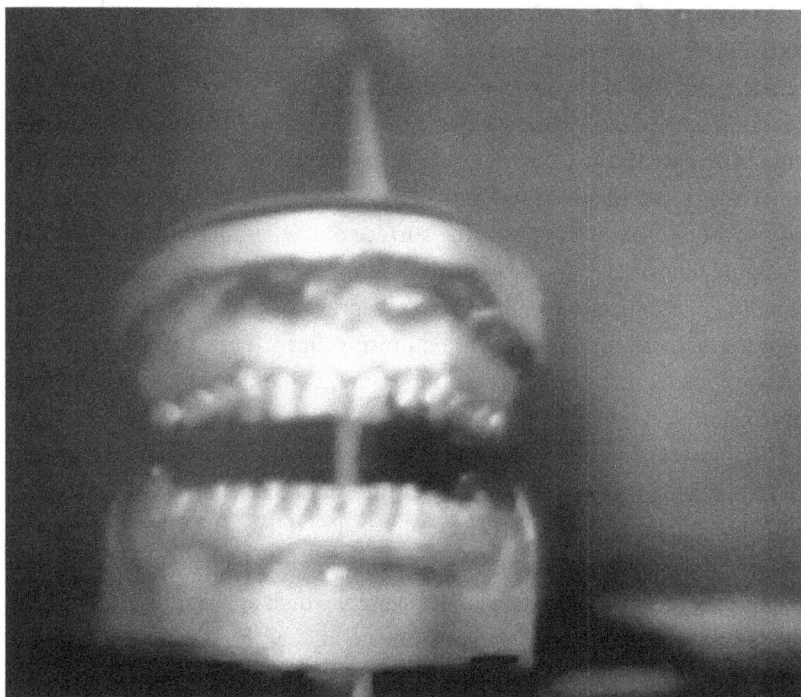

1.13–1.14 Teeth munching in Feminist Studio Workshop's "Woman's Building" International Videoletter, 1975. Screen grabs. Long Beach Museum of Art Video Archive, Getty Research Institute, Los Angeles.

In the case of the haptic images of International Videoletters, where, due to the exhibition context, one can be fairly certain that most spectators remained aware of their own sense of self, Jennifer Barker's complication of Marks is appreciated. Barker explains that in this mutuality of screen and viewer, which Marks likens to an erotic embrace, we do not so much lose ourselves in the image as feel as if we exist "both 'here'—at the surface of our own body—and 'there'—at the surface of the film [or video]'s body—in the same moment."[147] In the grainy black-and-white images of the Woman's Building's art installations and other haptic images of the International Videoletters, the commingling of feminisms that I argue is characteristic of many 1970s feminist media reception contexts took on an almost physical dimension.

The Spectra Feminist Media flier that enticed spectators by inviting them to "meet some interesting women via International Feminist Videoletters" emphasized the project's perceived physicality. Here, the DC organization eschewed the project's typical intergalactic, cerebral logo for a more anthropomorphic and intimate image. The sketch, which appeared just under the flier's flirtatious invitation, depicts nine people, each wearing a Suffragist-style sash to show they represent different cities, passionately conversing (see figure 1.15). There are only slim gaps between the figures' bodies, as some lean back to back and others casually embrace. "San Francisco" has an arm around "Rochester's" shoulders. "Rochester," meanwhile, looks down sheepishly as "Los Angeles" also reaches out to caress the upstate city's stomach. International Videoletters is pictured as offering feminist communities the intra-movement intimacy that so many desired.

While most of the existing videoletters contain moments of haptic visuality, they also all make use of particularly documentary gazes, which give them an additional eroticism that I would like to claim as lesbian. To be clear, none of these videoletters are about lesbian existence or even women's sexuality. Many of the women who made videoletters were lesbians, as were many of the women who appeared in them. They document lesbian impressions of the activities of local feminist communities. These impressions' power, however, quite often resides in the erotic views of women's bodies that they provide to feminist audiences. The flirtatious representations of International Videoletters in the Spectra Media flier could thus indicate not only the proximity and felt intimacy the project provided but also the eroticism particular to the documentary mode, which, as Villarejo writes, arguably "has less in common with popular narrative cinema and more in common with the gazes one permits or denies oneself in daily encounters

1.15 Spectra Feminist Media "Meet Some Interesting Women" flyer. Arthur and Elizabeth Schlesinger Library on the History of Women in America, Radcliffe Institute for Advanced Study, Harvard University, Cambridge, Massachusetts.

with people and their bodies."[148] And it is by working to restore context to the production and circulation of such lesbian documentary gazes that, Villarejo contends, we might move beyond visibility as the static and singular value of lesbian desire and "open lesbian to a dense and uneven complex of perception and expression, labor and production, consumption and reception, bodily and sexual practices, habits of mind and reading, class differentiations and racialized positions, industrial effects, national locations, movement and stasis, and hence organizations of time and space."[149] International Videoletters, as a documentary project that experimented with "new forms for communication and new ways of expressing ideas" and circulated through the women's movement to "develop a feeling of closeness among women in different cities," preserves a rare archive of the mobility and agility of 1970s lesbian desire. Here, it becomes apparent that the romantic and sexual desire women expressed and explored during women's and gay liberation cannot be siphoned off from the feminist desire to connect and communicate with politically like-minded others across geographies.

In the Just Us Video Collective's "Women in the Arts" videoletter, which cuts together footage from three different Bay Area women's cultural events, the feminist desire for intra-movement intimacy is met with a lesbian documentary gaze whose haptic visuality delivers an anticarceral argument compounded with lesbian feminist joy and pleasure. Stationed in the audience of a theatrical performance and a musical performance, after being guided through a music studio as Margie Adams and her band record a song, we take in the videoletter's three performances in ways quite similar to (and yet distinctly different from) how we might if we attended each in person. We watch Adams's hands as they move methodically down the keyboard and back up again during a solo. When the rest of the band joins in and the camera zooms back out, we see Adams smile and possibly even feel interpellated when she exclaims to her bandmates, "Yeah! That's nice." By the last segment of the video, however, our looking has become even more intense, if only because, unlike in narrative cinema, we have yet to receive a reverse shot. In the Woman's Building video our guides moved us between artists and artworks and often addressed the camera directly, but here we stare long and hard at the procession of female performers before us, and our gaze remains uninterrupted. In the last segment, after Cris Williamson completes a song at the piano, Holly Near's sister and the tour's signer, the actor Timothy Near, comes to the front of the stage and delivers a monologue about sign language before teaching the audience how to sign the chorus of Holly's song "You've Got Me Flying." While ostensibly about sign language, her monologue provides an analysis of a few key signs, which, with her emphatic delivery, offers an embodied critique of heteropatriarchy and the prison system. And videoletter viewers who have been looking hard are made to listen.

Speaking to the power of sign language and its "very direct images," Timothy's choice of examples and bodily emphasis of certain signs clue original audience members and, later, videoletter audiences to the fact that she is doing more than providing information; she is making arguments. Timothy contrasts the sign for "prison," which involves putting one's hands before one's face, with the sign for "free," in which one moves one's hands out from in front of one's body, opening one's self rather than shutting one's self in, making the perhaps obvious point that prison and freedom are opposites. Timothy then, however, tells the audiences that she finds it quite interesting that the sign for "safe" uses the same movement away from the body as that for "free," making the argument, through implication and physically communicated conviction, that to be free one must also feel safe.[150] She further implies that not only is freedom the antithesis of prison; safety is, too (see figures 1.16 and 1.17). The audience applauds, and Timothy's knowing nod suggests that she at least feels as if she has gotten her points across. Timothy then tells the crowd that she is "especially interested in signing to music" and "*especially* [she exaggerates the sign this second time] interested in signing the songs that happen up here [on women's music stages], because they are so full of images, like 'evening kisses' and 'morning smiles' or 'thunder' and 'lightning' and 'shooting stars' or 'unicorn,'" demonstrating each with coy, warm, knowing looks on her face. Timothy explains that she often takes liberties with signing, which she calls "creative signing."[151] For example, in her sister Holly's song "You've Got Me Flying," she takes "flying" to mean "flying" in the literal sense but also to mean "flying," as in jumping for joy, as well as "power" and "courage" or "sisterhood" and thus translates interchangeably as such. As Timothy signs each of these different interpretations, she moves not just her hands but her entire body as reinforcement of their significance—a lightness accompanying the joyful sign, a solidity for the power and courage signs, and an openness for that of sisterhood. And, again, she receives cheers from the unseen concert crowd.

Videoletter spectators, while not there for the live performance, gained access to an extra intimate exchange with Timothy and her body through the video body. Positioned at the front of the audience by two cameras cross dissolved live with a switcher, videoletter spectators constantly look up at Timothy and are occasionally brought in close to her face or hands through one of the two cinematographers' zoom. Considered exemplary of

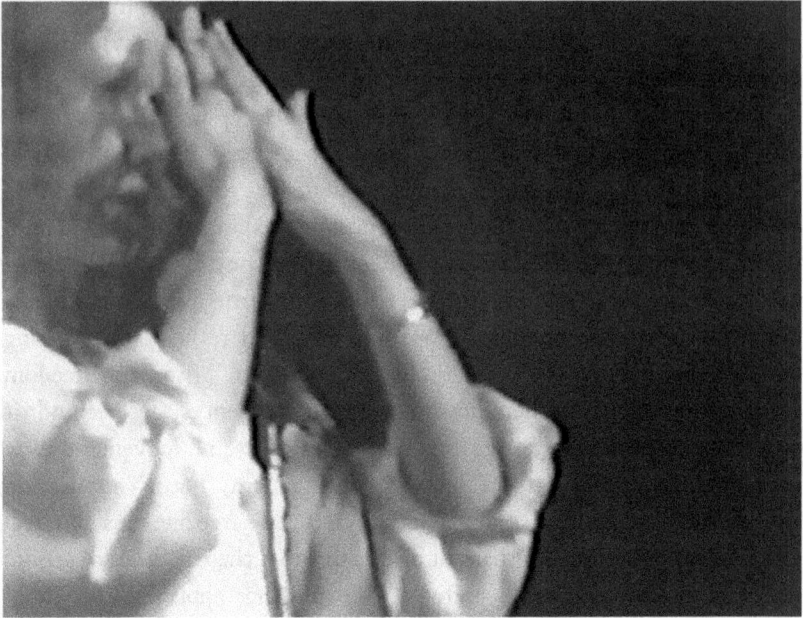

1.16 Timothy Near signing "prison" in Just Us International Videoletter, 1976. Screen grab. Arthur and Elizabeth Schlesinger Library on the History of Women in America, Radcliffe Institute for Advanced Study, Harvard University, Cambridge, Massachusetts.

the "affection-image" by Gilles Deleuze, close-ups have the power to tear the image away from the background, which becomes "any space whatever," and arrest the viewer. While the concert audience likely found it difficult to forget where they were—no matter how enamored they were with Timothy, they were aware of the others around them and tethered to their specific spot in the crowd—the Just Us Collective's zoom isolates Timothy against the black background behind her. Like Strand's lesbians in *Fever Dream*, Timothy in close-up appears as if nowhere. Like Strand's lesbians, she is close enough to touch and yet out of reach. The haptic visuality of her video rendering gives her a texture different from lesbians on 16 mm film, but the intimacy is nonetheless remarkably similar. Unlike Strand's lesbians, Timothy signs and speaks. Against the flat black background of the videoletter, she is speaking to those feminist audiences who have gathered to watch the correspondence of feminist geographies and, in turn, found themselves face to face with her.

During Timothy's ten-minute performance, her face serves as an important site for viewers' emotional and intellectual engagement. Nick Davis,

1.17 Timothy Near signing "safe" in Just Us International Videoletter, 1976. Screen grab. Arthur and Elizabeth Schlesinger Library on the History of Women in America, Radcliffe Institute for Advanced Study, Harvard University, Cambridge, Massachusetts.

drawing on Deleuze (and on Deleuze's writing with Félix Guattari), has contended that in films where virtual, if not actual, lesbians appear, the face in close-up serves "a potent but not prescriptive venue of lesbian signification," politically and erotically.[152] After signing "You've Got Me Flying," wherein she is pictured in a rare wide shot with all of the musicians and singers onstage, Timothy teaches the crowd the sign for "sisterhood" (see figures 1.18–1.19). She details how she has had to make up the sign, as there was no existing sign for it. She chose to combine the "sister" and "together" signs but not without further intervention. The sign for "sister," she explains with a controlled flatness in her voice and the slightest of eye rolls, comes from that of "girl," which in turn involves a movement mimicking the tying of a bonnet. In signing "sisterhood," however, she ends the sign by raising that of "together" above her head, "because it adds a little 'umpf' [she pumps her arms up] and because women hold up half the sky." She, the band, and the audience then sing part of the song again, this time with everyone signing together.

1.18–1.19 Timothy Near teaching the sign for "sisterhood" in Just Us International Videoletter, 1976. Screen grabs. Arthur and Elizabeth Schlesinger Library on the History of Women in America, Radcliffe Institute for Advanced Study, Harvard University, Cambridge, Massachusetts.

Impossible to include in a purely audio format, this videoletter privileges its audiences with an otherwise inaccessible element of recorded women's music culture. Some International Videoletter viewers gathered to learn of feminist efforts in the Bay Area. Others may have showed up to "meet some interesting women." They all, in turn, got to take in Timothy's charismatic face, including her many smiles, eye rolls, and other fleeting movements of her mouth and eyes while also hearing her points about the unfreedom of prison and constraints of patriarchal language, spoken and signed, which held ramifications and relevance far beyond Timothy's northern California setting. The lesbian gaze met intersectional feminist politics, and in the minds and bodies of feminist video audiences the two affectively intertwined. Timothy's performance was likely quite powerful in person. In documenting it on videotape and in close-up, the International Videoletters project sent lesbian potentiality—the sensation of a future on the horizon not only beyond patriarchy and its compulsory heterosexuality but beyond compulsory able-bodiedness and beyond prisons—soaring across its feminist constellations.[153]

Realistically Nearly Nonextant

Between 1975 and 1977, dozens of videoletters were made by feminist media workers from tens of communities across the United States and Canada. Today, only twelve videoletters are known to still exist.[154] Like the National Women's Circuit, the International Videoletters project came to a close within a few years when economic hardship and the difficulties of long-distance communication grew too severe. While videoletters archived feminist communities' activities for one another, because they were also created on the spot for immediate distribution they were never formally gathered for preservation. Each city made but a few copies of each tape, and most met the fate of the whims of those with whom they landed last. Considering that the cities themselves were the authors, few personal identifying markers traveled with them. It is by chance that many of the remaining videoletters made their way into institutional archives, each having landed in the hands of otherwise well-known feminist activists and artists, such as Susan Mogul and Ariel Dougherty, whose collections were eventually acquired, respectively, by the Getty Research Institute and Harvard University's Arthur and Elizabeth Schlesinger Library on the History of Women in America. There they lie, awaiting analysis of the lesbian potentiality in movement they themselves archive (as well as, I hope, further analyses), but they might

87

not have made it there to begin with. The particularities of the project—the speed with which the videoletters were made; the unusual routes of constellated cities through which they were distributed, and the unregulated manner in which they circulated—might normalize the nonextant nature of most videoletters. However, International Videoletters was but one project of a broader body of realist documentary that flourished in the 1970s, only to be superseded by more avant-garde fare as a result of formalist feminist theory's influence on alternative media distribution.

Following the recession of the 1970s and the US government's defunding of the arts in the 1980s, feminist and other radical film and video distributors were forced to prioritize stable markets to stay in business. With the collapse of small distributors such as Moonforce Media, Women Make Movies took the lead in feminist film distribution. Those at its helm were quick to identify higher education as their most stable and lucrative market.[155] When compared with women's groups and activist nonprofits, college and university departments and libraries had consistent and sizeable budgets with which they could regularly rent or buy prints and videos. Thus, in an ironic self-fulfillment of their own criticism of alternative film distribution, formalist theorists delimited what was circulated and for whom, college and university faculty being most interested in those formalist films analyzed in *Screen* and *Camera Obscura*. Alexandra Juhasz makes this point most succinctly when she writes, "Due to the insidious economic relationship between film scholarship and alternative film distribution, many of these films [realist feminist and queer documentaries of the 1970s and '80s] are lost for reevaluation."[156] Juhasz recounts searching for *Self-Health* (1974) after reading Julia Lesage's 1978 essay on the film (a rare example of a 1970s feminist film theory championing realist documentary) and being unable to rent it, the feminist distribution companies that once carried it no longer in business and the film now unlocatable. While feminist theorists of the 1970s saw little value in such realist documentaries, feminists, AIDS activists, and others continued to make them well into the 1990s but too often did so without knowledge of those who worked in similar modes before them. Juhasz is not afraid to name this erasure a result of intellectually obfuscated classism and racism: "The word *naïve* regularly accompanied the critique of feminist documentaries that recorded real women talking about their lives and issues in real time. *Naïve* means 'If they knew better, they wouldn't do this.' The 'they' here are most often producers of color, poor people, less educated people, some women."[157] Juhasz and Lesage have shown how realist documentaries served as urgent and necessary consciousness-raising tools within activist communities. Meanwhile, my analysis of International Videoletters and the NWFC here elaborates on the affective dimension of this labor on the part of feminist audiences in the 1970s, the distribution and exhibition of realist films and videos (often alongside more formalist films) providing the much-desired intimacy between geographically disparate feminist communities. That this work is limited in its ability to extend across time and connect feminist audiences past and present, due to shifting emphases in alternative media distribution, marks a severe loss.

The circulation of lesbian potentiality was stopped short in part by neoliberalism, including the neoliberal university and academic feminism. However, in a perhaps not-so-strange twist of fate, lesbian potentiality was captured and preserved, like a lightning bug in a jar, by quite similar forces decades later. In *The Archival Turn in Feminism*, Kate Eichhorn writes, "As neoliberal restructuring rendered anti-economic endeavors increasingly untenable, the archive was adopted as a viable and even necessary means to legitimate forms of knowledge and cultural production in the present." The archive, Eichhorn claims, "restore[s] to us what is routinely taken away under neoliberalism—not history itself but rather the ability to understand the conditions of our everyday lives longitudinally and, more important, the conviction that we might, once again, be *agents* of change in time and history."[158] The lesbian potentiality of 1970s feminist media cultures shines—if not brightly, then at least dimly—through the boxes of feminist media workers that have made their way into institutional archives over the past two decades. No longer speeding through feminist communities on scant resources, it restlessly waits in these collections for those who have the interest and means to make their way to meet it.

The repercussions of this archival history are significant when it comes to feminist media made by those who were most vulnerable. In the next chapter, I turn to the production of feminist prison documentaries in the 1970s, the first evidence of which I encountered under the faint glow of lesbian potentiality in the very same boxes as the NWFC and International Video-letters records and correspondence. These films and videos, if made under the auspices of serving the institutional purposes of prison reform, provided imprisoned women (and those of other genders incarcerated at "women's prisons"), most of whom were poor and Black or Brown, with platforms for the theorization of gendered and racialized life under the neoliberal carceral state. Through the analysis of these documentaries, we see how high-stakes 1970s feminist media cultures' fashioning of new realities was for those for whom freedom often seemed furthest off.

89

producing freedom
1970s feminist documentary
& women's prison activism

Feminist documentary filmmaking is a cinematic genre congruent with a political movement . . . In the late 1960s and early 1970s in the United States, women's consciousness-raising groups, reading groups, and task-oriented groups were emerging from and often superseded the organizations of the antiwar New Left. Women who had learned film-making in the antiwar movement and previously 'uncommitted' women filmmakers began to make self-consciously Feminist films, and other women began to learn filmmaking specifically to contribute to the movement. The films these people made came out of the same ethos as the consciousness-raising groups and had the same goals.—JULIA LESAGE, "The Political Aesthetics of Feminist Documentary Film"

The "Women on Wheels" concert documented in the Just Us "Women in the Arts" videoletter was one of nine concerts performed over the course of the first two weeks of February 1976 across California as part of a consciousness-raising (CR) effort about women in prison. Timothy Near's signed "direct image" analysis of the symbiosis of freedom and safety and their antithesis, the prison system, served as part of a broader initiative, organized by lesbian feminist prison activists, to educate Californian feminists about the inhumane treatment of imprisoned women and the unjust social and legal circumstances that landed certain women (i.e., poor women and women of color and few others) in prison time and again. The ninth concert was performed at the California Institute for Women (CIW). Each of the eight concerts leading up to the CIW concert was followed by a workshop on women and prison led by Karlene Faith, who, as the lead organizer of the Santa Cruz Women's Prison Project (1972–76), provided those imprisoned at CIW with university-level courses, cultural workshops, and artistic performances. Faith started her "Women on Wheels" workshops by screening *We're Alive* (1974), a forty-minute documentary made by the CIW Video Workshop with the Women's Film Workshop of the University of California, Los Angeles (UCLA) about women's prison experiences. In a few of the tour cities, those who had participated in the film's production two years earlier, now out on parole, joined Faith in leading discussions of the film.[1] At these screenings and others around the United States, *We're Alive*'s cohort of 1970s feminist prison documentaries introduced feminist audiences to crucial critiques of the racist prison-industrial complex (i.e., the economic, social, and political structures enabling the expansion of the prison system); the misogyny, sexism, and homophobia experienced by those imprisoned in "women's prisons"; and the work these very women (and all those imprisoned at such institutions) were doing to envision and create a livable life for themselves and others like them. Considering that those imprisoned at "women's prisons" were neglected by movements for both prison abolition and prison reform in favor of those incarcerated at "men's prisons" (with the exception of a few individual women), this cinematic production of freedom dreams, this Black feminist love politics via film and video, issued for and with the women's movement constituted an important site of Black feminist theory.

This chapter offers close textual analyses of three understudied and nearly nonextant feminist prison documentaries of the 1970s: *Songs, Skits, Poetry, and Prison Life* (the women of the Bedford Hills Correctional Facility for Women and Women Make Movies [1974]), *We're Alive* (CIW Video Workshop with the UCLA Women's Film Workshop [1974]), and *Inside Women Inside* (Christine Choy and Cynthia Maurizio and Third World Newsreel [1978]). Each of these documentaries was made under the auspices of either feminist filmmakers documenting the success of prison reform at "women's prisons" or as a part of a feminist-led arts program made possible by such reforms. These pretenses made such filming possible, but the resulting films offered excruciatingly critical perspectives on the racist systems that landed certain women behind bars more often than others and the sexist mistreatment of imprisoned women, while also conveying quite affectively the ways those imprisoned at "women's prisons" sustained and supported one another and providing glimpses into the worlds forged in the face of such inscrutable violence. These documentaries counter the prison system's attempts to deny prisoners freedom by insisting on their freedom to imagine a world beyond prisons. In doing this political work together with and for social movement audiences, imprisoned women refused prison's demands for gender-conforming passivity. The very production of these documentaries is erotic in Audre Lorde's sense of the word, as the films both powerfully depict and are the result of women sharing physical, emotional, and intellectual joy with one another.[2] Committed to one another's freedom and the freedom of future women, all participants can be situated along Adrienne Rich's lesbian continuum.[3] And in making imprisoned women (and others imprisoned at "women's prisons")—once invisible to movements for racial justice and gender justice alike—visible and heard, they document the loving looks and expressions of affection uncontainable by the prison system, despite its relentless homophobic and transphobic attempts at as much.[4] Lesbian potentiality, the sense that gendered and sexual life could and would someday be substantially different, connects those before and behind the camera and those in the audience. And if lesbian potentiality is to renew itself through impotentiality, these films contend, prisons, as primary institutions of racial and gendered violence, must in the process be abolished.

Feminist documentary filmmaker and film scholar Alexandra Juhasz claims that film and patriarchy share the project of objectifying women, making victims of them, while video and feminism produce women as subjects.[5] While I do not subscribe wholeheartedly to the tautological elements of Juhasz's argument, I would concede that it is no accident that the gleam of lesbian potentiality is brightest in *Songs* (made entirely on video) and *We're Alive* (made largely on video). These two documentaries' haptic images resemble those of Margie Adams and Timothy Near in the Just Us Video Collective's "Women in the Arts" videoletter. But all three of these documentaries, including *Inside Women Inside* (made on film), demonstrate feminist collective documentary's potential to reverse the prisonlike victimization of the classic documentary scene. In its place stands a body of Black anticarceral feminist theory that situates women's imprisonment as both a racial violence that extends enslavement into the twentieth century and a gendered violence that punishes those who have violated society's gender norms.

Each of these documentaries was produced by Brown and white women, as well as Black women, and often their testimony speaks to experiences shared by all those imprisoned at "women's prisons." But together and individually they produce Black feminist theory. Theirs is a Black feminist theory that, like that of their contemporaries, the Combahee River Collective, contends that freedom for Black women would mean freedom for all, as Black women's freedom "would necessitate the destruction of all systems of oppression."[6] Here such a Black feminist theory takes advantage of its audiovisual form, addressing both its critiques of the present and visions for the future from one set of embodied subjects to another.

Anticarceral Feminism

From September 9 to 13, 1971, the country was shaken by news of the Attica Rebellion. Two weeks prior, the Black radical leader George Jackson had been killed in an attempted prison break in California. Tensions around the State of New York's lackluster attempts at prison reform were already high, and when news of Jackson's death reached upstate, one thousand of the roughly two thousand people imprisoned at the Attica Correctional Facility organized a rebellion, taking control of the prison yard and taking thirty-nine security guards and prison personnel hostage. The prisoners made thirty-three demands, and for four days they negotiated with Commissioner of Corrections Russell G. Oswald, who eventually agreed to twenty-eight of them, "thus recognizing the overall legitimacy of the grievances."[7] However, before negotiations could resolve peacefully, Governor Nelson Rockefeller ordered the retaking of the prison, and state troopers, National Guardsmen, and prison guards invaded the prison yard. They killed thirty-three prisoners and eleven security guards and injured more than eighty others. Much of the rebellion and the government's response was documented by news crews and broadcast around the country. When Rockefeller aborted Oswald's negotiations in favor of violence, Americans—who, in no small part thanks to television, were becoming increasingly aware of the excesses of US violence in Vietnam—witnessed the possibility of such horrors on US soil and learned that such acts of mass murder were but one form of violence enacted regularly in US prisons.

In the immediate aftermath of the Attica Rebellion, prisons around the United States escalated efforts at prison reform, spurred on by the advocacy of local anticarceral activists and prisoner rights advocacy groups. For those imprisoned at "men's prisons," this often meant improvements in living and working conditions; greater access to educational and vocational training and expansion of work release programs; more consistent and caring medical treatment; and closer attention to the needs of various prisoner constituencies, including non-English-speakers and queer people. Such reforms had substantial ramifications for prisoners' daily lives, and while they were implemented with the goal of quelling prisoner rebellions, they also oftentimes unwittingly strengthened the development of prisoners' political consciousnesses and supported anticarceral activism and thought. As the criminal justice scholars Phyllis Jo Baunach and Thomas Murton reported in 1973, "Increased use of volunteers in the prison has enabled inmates to maintain communications with the free world."[8] In more direct conversation with those active in social movements of the time, poor prisoners and prisoners of color understood themselves more and more as political prisoners.[9] While most had not been arrested for acts of politicized resistance, through the expansion of available reading materials (including greater access to the writing of political prisoners), as well as increased educational opportunities with volunteers and greater freedom in correspondence, people arrested for economically motivated crimes came to see their imprisonment as the result of a political system set up by an unjust society to maintain racial, ethnic, and class hierarchies and power dynamics. Prison newsletters, typically published by anticarceral collectives on the outside in collaboration with those imprisoned on the inside, and documentaries made by filmmakers foregrounding prisoners' ideas through interviews, such as *Teach Our Children* (Christine Choy and Sue Robeson [1972]) and *Attica* (Cinda Firestone [1974]), brought this message of the political nature of all imprisonment to the public.

Whereas prison reform at Attica and other "men's prisons" often meant substantive change in prisoners' living and working conditions and communications with the outside world, "women's prisons" received only the faintest of trickle-down reform. In these institutions, the shift from more custodial approaches to imprisonment to reform-based approaches was much belated and often half-hearted. New vocational training and additional educational opportunities were minimal, at best, and often very nearly completely absent, fluctuating according to their custody-oriented wardens' whims. College-level programs in prison increased at this time fifteen-fold, but, other than the Santa Cruz Women's Prison Project at CIW, which was the first of its kind, no new college-level programs were implemented in "women's prisons."[10] Instead, it was presumed that the "training" those imprisoned at women's prisons got in domestic tasks such as cleaning, cooking, and sewing through their work at the prison was enough. According to prison administrators, these prisoners could expect to receive jobs performing such tasks, and such tasks exclusively, outside of prison. Aspirations for any position demanding greater education or more advanced skills were deemed unrealistic. But it was not solely that these prison administrators were serving as agents of dystopian practicality. Their job was to ensure little possibility for female prisoners and to sustain "women's prisons" through recidivism.

Prison administrators' denial of college-level courses, vocational training, and other reform measures was but one more entry in a history of sexist approaches to incarceration. The emphasis on domestic labor was more than a devaluation of women and "women's work." It was part of the prison system's attempts to reform those incarcerated at "women's prisons" along gendered lines. Those incarcerated at "women's prisons" had long been seen not only as having violated the law but also as having violated gender norms in doing so and were therefore expected to learn gender conformity as a part of their prison experience.[11] At many prisons, one of the responsibilities of female prison guards and other prison personnel was to demonstrate proper (cisgender, straight) femininity in behavior, verbal expression, and dress, founded on white—specifically, Anglo-Saxon—middle-class paradigms.[12] As Alison Griffiths documents, "women's prisons" did not even receive film exhibition as a recreation option in the 1910s when "men's prisons" did, cinema being considered at the time a working-class corruptor of sex and gender, and its effects on women who had already demonstrated an aptitude for "unfeminine" behavior were not to be taken lightly.[13] This was only affirmed for administrators at the Bedford Hills Reformatory in 1920 when the cancellation of a scheduled film screening led to a rebellion and prison escape.[14] Long before the 1970s, when anticarceral and prisoner rights activism transformed "men's prisons" under the aegis of prison reform, the resources and attention given to prisoners at different institutions was far from equal.

In the 1970s, this anxiety about gender-nonconformity and women's criminality grew, taking on new dimensions as a result of antifeminist reactionism. In 1975, the publication of the criminologist Freda Adler's *Sisters in Crime* seemingly affirmed the fears of those who argued that the expansion of women's rights and what was commonly called "gender roles" would, among other things, initiate a "female crime wave."[15] If women were to be as free as men, what would stop them from committing violent crimes like men? What would prevent them from committing violent crimes against men? "The phenomenon of female criminality," Adler writes in her book's prologue, "is but one wave in this rising tide of female assertiveness—a wave which

95

has not yet crested and may even be seeking its level uncomfortably close to the high-water mark set by male violence."[16] Drawing direct parallels between "women's lib" and crime, Adler claims, "In the same way that women are demanding equal opportunity in fields of legitimate endeavor, a similar number of determined women are forcing their way into the world of major crimes."[17] While Adler later wrote a follow-up piece and gave interviews explaining that most women were incarcerated for committing nonviolent crimes, motivated by economic disparity, her initial analysis was taken up by the mainstream media as support for commonsense logics about gender, crime, and the threat of social movements to that status quo.[18] This gender-deviant prisoner, so easily imagined by many (and quite often pictured as lesbian), dominated the American imagination in the 1970s—as evidenced by the wave of popular women's prison exploitation films, such as *Women in Cages* (1971), *The Big Bird Cage* (1972), and *Caged Heat* (1974)—and delayed analysis of the "feminization of poverty," which was causing an actual increase in women's imprisonment.[19] Adler concludes her study, "It is not at all inconceivable that a female Attica could occur at any one of a number of institutions." While she seems to see this as a good thing, she naively believes that such an event would "upset the traditional applecart of benign neglect which has ruled the field of female corrections in the past."[20] Uprisings at "women's prisons" would grow increasingly common across the 1970s as those incarcerated there fought for reform measures equal to those being implemented in "men's prisons" and protested violence particular to their circumstances, including a prison culture where sexual assault at the hands of guards was so common it was almost pedestrian. However, these uprisings, including the rebellion at Bedford Hills in August 1974, the rebellion at the North Carolina Correctional Center for Women (NCCCW) in June 1975, and the rebellion at CIW of Christmas 1975, failed to generate widespread activist mobilization as Attica had.[21]

During the 1970s, the lack of attention and care given by prison administrators and state officials to those incarcerated at "women's prisons" such as Bedford Hills, NCCCW, and CIW was only echoed and exacerbated by the lack of attention and care of anticarceral and prisoner rights activists. As Victoria Law writes, "While male prisoners gained political consciousness and enjoyed support from outside groups and individuals, these same groups and individuals ignored the female prison population with the exceptions of a few well-known political prisoners such as Angela Davis and Assata Shakur."[22] Imprisoned women were damned if they did and damned if they didn't: further rebellion led to being cast even more as gender deviants, while failing to resist the conditions of their imprisonment (or acting in ways that did not register publicly as resistance) labeled them passive and apolitical.[23] As early as 1972, the Black feminist critic Michele Wallace noted that "since the battle of Attica, a lot of artists have been making a mad dash for the prisons, that is, the men's prisons. The feeling seems to be that political prisoners can only be male."[24] Wallace argues that while it may be true that most—or, at least, many—imprisoned Black and Latino men are political prisoners, all imprisoned Black women definitely are:

> Let's face it, women go to prison for one reason—men. If a woman decides that she doesn't want to be tied down, doesn't want to do anything in particular, just wants to bum around for a while, she will end up in a mental institution if she's white, and in a jail if she's black. A woman can never afford to be so unclear about what she wants to do because if she doesn't know, there is a man that will know for her, and, eleven times out of ten, that ain't good.[25]

Wallace, alongside her mother, the visual artist Faith Ringgold, briefly ran Art Without Walls, which brought workshops on art, poetry, dance, yoga, and rap to the Women's House of Detention in New York City. Art Without Walls was a rare early reform program at a "women's prison." In the 1970s, however, things slowly began to change for those incarcerated in "women's prisons" as anticarceral feminists such as Wallace and Ringgold gained the attention of the women's movement. Greater numbers of feminist organizers and artists, many of whom had been unfamiliar with prisons and prisoner rights matters, started working with those incarcerated at "women's prisons" and advocating for reform measures—before prison administrators, local criminal justice systems, and the state—on their behalf.

Anticarceral feminists found a stronghold in the women's movement in the mid-1970s when organizing around a series of cases in which women were being tried for killing their or others' rapists in self-defense. In 1974, Joan (pronounced "Jo-Ann" and often misspelled "Joann" by journalists and scholars) Little, a Black woman doing time in Beaufort County Jail in North Carolina for burglary and larceny, was charged with murder for killing a white male jail guard who forced her into oral sex by holding an icepick to her head. She eventually gained control of the icepick and defended herself with it before fleeing the jail. The jury found Little not guilty, and she became the first woman in the United States to be acquitted for using deadly violence to protect herself from sexual violence, setting a precedent for future cases.[26] A month after Little's jailbreak, Inez García, a Latina living in Soledad,

97

California, was sexually assaulted by two men, who then called and threatened to kill her if she told anyone about the assault. When she went after them with a rifle, she found them beating her roommate. One threw a knife at García, and she shot him. Demonstrating no remorse, García was initially found guilty of second-degree murder and sentenced to five years to life at CIW. In March 1977, the sentence was overturned on appeal.[27] In May 1973, a full year before Little's and García's arrests, Yvonne Wanrow, an Indigenous woman from Spokane, Washington, was found guilty of second-degree murder by an all-white jury for shooting a known child rapist who had broken into her home in an attempt to assault her child. Wanrow's appeals lasted much longer than Little's and García's, and she eventually accepted a plea bargain, which reduced her crime to manslaughter in self-defense. She was sentenced to five years of probation.[28] Last, in February 1976, Dessie Woods, a Black activist and practicing Muslim from Georgia, was found guilty of manslaughter for killing her and a friend's sexual assailant with his own gun. After seeing how much press the Little and García cases had generated, Woods's judge issued a court order that substantially curtailed demonstrations and media at the courthouse.[29] Woods was imprisoned for six years before being released. During that time, she kept prisoner rights activists apprised of her abuse at the hands of prison guards, theorizing the specificity of her experience—in court, in prison—as specifically that of a Black woman.[30] Through these four women's stories, the women's movement at large began to see criminal justice and imprisonment as feminist issues. As Emily L. Thuma writes in *All Our Trials*, her history of 1970s anticarceral feminist grassroots organizing, "The breadth and efficacy of these four campaigns were made possible by the extent to which each woman's story of violation and resistance came to symbolically represent multiple and intersecting struggles for racial, gender, and economic justice."[31] Because of Little, García, Wanrow, and Woods, more people began to see women—especially poor women of color who dared in a white-supremacist patriarchy to defend themselves and those closest to them—as political prisoners.

These women's stories were picked up by both liberal feminist journals such as *Ms.* (which published an article by Angela Davis on the Joan Little case and put Inez García on the cover of the May 1975 issue) and radical feminist journals such as *off our backs* (which, because of its ongoing coverage of these female prisoners and the challenges of "women's prisons," was listed as a prisoner rights resource in anti-prison pamphlets' suggested reading lists).[32] The interest these women's stories generated within the women's movement led to the formation and funding of their defense funds, as well as the foundation of organizations dedicated to supporting imprisoned women, such as the Through the Looking Glass collective of Seattle and Women Free Women in Prison of New York City. White and Jewish lesbian feminists often took the lead in organizing women's prison collectives and serving on imprisoned women's legal defense teams.[33] Both Through the Looking Glass and Women Free Women in Prison also produced women's prison newsletters—*Through the Looking Glass: A Women and Children Prison Newsletter* (1976–86) and *No More Cages: A Bi-monthly Women's Prison Newsletter* (1979–85). These newsletters were envisioned as a means to link women inside and outside of prison.[34] In the "Statement of Purposes" they published at the front of every issue of *No More Cages*, Women Free Women in Prison states that it came to publishing the newsletter having become aware that "women in prison are positioned dangerously at the intersection of a complex system of multiple oppressions." Its editors explain that, although they are lesbian feminists, they "did not go into the prisons exclusively for the women's movement." Instead, they "went into the prisons for the women themselves, because their oppression overwhelmed us and screamed for action."[35] Both *Through the Looking Glass* and *No More Cages* were a way to generate and support such actions and get imprisoned women's voices heard by those working in many movements.

Feminist documentaries were yet another method raising the consciousness of the women's movement around "women's prisons." In their case they did the work of literally making imprisoned women (and others imprisoned at "women's prisons") visible and heard.[36] Due to the circumstances and parameters of their production, the formal properties of film and video, and their methods of distribution and contexts of reception, how they raised consciousnesses differed greatly from their sibling media of women's prison newsletters. Like the feminist science fiction fanzines of this book's next chapter, the prison newsletters, through their written address of and circulation among others with similar concerns, created a counterpublic, constituting the imagined world of anticarceral feminism, which "fostered life-supporting relationships and alternatives to the dominant political culture that systematically devalued and excluded those deemed criminally other."[37] Many of their entries, including the artwork and poetry of prisoners, could be understood as what Robin D. G. Kelley calls "freedom dreams," instances of Black radical imagination, works of poetic knowledge that simultaneously compel the reliving of horrors and the envisioning of a new society.[38] As Angela Davis contended in 1971 from her cell in the Marin County jail, ever since the beginning of chattel slavery Black women have played a pivotal role in

99

"developing and sharpening the thrust towards freedom."[39] In the 1970s, this included the development of Black feminism, which redefined the very source of theory, expanding "the definition of who constitutes a theorist, the voice of authority speaking for black women, to include poets, blues singers, storytellers, painters, mothers, preachers, and teachers."[40] Imprisoned Black feminist theorists sometimes wrote, as Davis, Woods, and other contributors to prison newsletters did. They also made documentaries, producing freedom dreams on 16 mm film, video, or some combination of the two. In documentaries such as *Songs, Skits, Poetry, and Prison Life, We're Alive,* and *Inside Women Inside,* Black feminist accounts of the prison-industrial complex and its racialized and gendered violence and visions of its future abolition took on an embodied audiovisual form and, distributed by feminist film distributors, drew lesbian feminist affectivity to the gendered politics of anti-Black racism.

Here I analyze *Songs, We're Alive,* and *Inside Women Inside* for the freedom dreams they produce. This approach rejects the critiques of realist documentary proffered by 1970s feminist formalist film scholars, deriding such documentaries for presenting the women and worlds they depict as transparent reality rather than formally marking the mediation of the cinematic apparatus. I would argue that those making these feminist prison documentaries thought critically and creatively about form, purposefully crafting themselves and their peers as subjects, much as those who made International Videoletters did. And I take these documentary media makers' use of form seriously, drawing attention, through formal analysis, to the techniques, tactics, and strategies by which imprisoned women and their collaborators on the outside produced audiovisual Black feminist theory. That said, I would also contend that those who reify form as the sole site of political intervention for leftist filmmakers ultimately take a classist and racist position, casting aside the films and videos made by those for whom the resources and time necessary to make the most formally inventive media are unavailable (as well as by those who find realist cinema more politically compelling). As Julia Lesage writes in a rare early defense of feminist realist documentaries, "If the Feminist filmmakers deliberately used a traditional 'realist' documentary structure, it is because they saw making these films as an urgent public act and wished to . . . bring Feminist analysis to many women it might otherwise never reach."[41] Davis notoriously wrote her article "Reflections on the Black Woman's Role in the Community of Slaves" for *Black Scholar* with only materials she had access to in jail. For the imprisoned producers of feminist prison documentaries, taking advantage of the resources at hand meant picking up the few handheld cameras and minimal sync sound equipment allowed in the prison, which, especially under the circumstances, lent themselves to interviews that, when cut together, constructed a collectively authored work of theory.

Rehabilitation as Twentieth-Century Enslavement

Both *Songs* and *We're Alive* were made as a part of arts programming at their respective prisons—the Bedford Hills Correctional Facility for Women (formerly Reformatory) in Westchester County, just north of New York City, and the California Institute for Women, sixty miles east of Los Angeles. *Songs* was made over the course of a three-month weekly workshop on video production taught by Ariel Dougherty, a cofounder of Women Make Movies.[42] *We're Alive*, meanwhile, was the culmination of a six-month weekly workshop at CIW led by the Women's Film Workshop of UCLA.[43] In each case, imprisoned women (and quite possibly others imprisoned at these "women's prisons") gained technical, creative, and organizational skills, learning how to operate cameras, record sound, and, in the case of *We're Alive*, structure a documentary.[44] As a voice-over announces at the start of *We're Alive*, "This film was made by women inside and women outside working together. Every Sunday for six months we met in a classroom at the prison where we planned the film and photographed it on videotape. Everyone operated the camera, and the songs were written, performed, and recorded by women inside." This agency of planning and photographing a film was more than a matter of vocational training, of gaining skills they might use on release. Interviewing and filming one another presented a rare opportunity for such prisoners to testify to their experiences of incarceration and the unjust economic and social structures that landed them there. Likewise, while *Inside Women Inside* was not made as part of an educational or vocational training program, its filmmakers, Christine Choy and Cynthia Maurizio of the recently renamed Third World Newsreel (previously simply Newsreel), gained access to the NCCCW, the Correctional Institute for Women at Rikers Island, and Elmhurst General Hospital in Queens under the auspices of documenting the improvements to "women's prisons" in the post-Attica reform era, all the while hoping to actually document imprisoned women's experiences of the prison-industrial complex.[45] These films vary in length, structure, focus of their analysis, and tone, but they share the thesis that prisons, far from rehabilitating prisoners as they claim to, serve as a modern-day form of enslavement wherein the freedom of poor Black people is not only restricted

101

but its very hope is routinely quashed. In the face of such repression, the activity of making documentaries defied gendered expectations of apolitical resignation.

Before I move into my analysis of the documentaries, I should note that I shift between referring to the people who made and appeared in them as "prisoners," "imprisoned women," and "those imprisoned at Bedford Hills" or "those imprisoned at 'women's prisons.'" None of these terms is ideal. Using the label "prisoners" or the more descriptive "those imprisoned at" risks reducing their identity to their status under the carceral state, reinforcing its ideology, which converts those incarcerated for breaking the law into beings known as "criminals." Often the documentaries, and those in them, refer to themselves as "the women at (or of)" a given prison, as in the title card for *Songs*, which describes the documentary as "a selection from Productions made by the WOMEN at Bedford Hills Correctional Facility" (original formatting). However, considering the cissexism of the prison system, whereby prisoners are typically segregated by their sex as assigned at birth, it is important to hold open the possibility that not all of these documentary subjects are women. As the historian Regina Kunzel notes, drawing on accounts from Bedford Hills, "The practices and preferences of prison butches in the 1950s, 1960s, and 1970s suggest that the boundary between butch identity and what would later come to be called transgender identity was fluid."[46] I have tried to be especially careful on the rare occasion when gender-nonconformity does seem to be deliberately marked, as in the case in *Songs* when two musicians, named Trent and Robbie, perform for the camera, and Robbie sings of the love of a "Papa" for a "Mama."

That being said, a name cannot be taken as a clear signifier of gender identity. As Quinlan Miller points out, when dealing with historical materials it is worth noting that any person may be untransitioned.[47] Most people who appear in these films, however, do so anonymously. They are named neither verbally nor via title cards, perhaps in an effort to blur the line between visibility and invisibility for safety's sake. Denied most subjects' names, I cannot use their names in place of pronouns, as Miller does, and while Miller, who studies sitcoms of the 1950s and '60s, can move between a series of gender-neutral descriptors ("actor," "comedian," "performer"), the gender-neutral term most common to my milieu ("prisoner"), as outlined earlier, has its own limitations. I at times use more gender-neutral terms such as "imprisoned people," but exclusively doing so, I worry, obfuscates the gendered arguments they themselves are making about the differences of their experiences from those of those incarcerated at "men's prisons." As Kelley writes, Black radical feminists are too often rendered invisible by a "gender-neutral conception of the black community [which] presumes that freedom for black people as a whole will result in freedom for black women."[48] My hope in making this caveat is that when I use these subjects' own words, such as "women," they can be heard with a capaciousness that refuses the cissexism of the system that naturalizes such usages.

In *Songs*, interviews with prisoners are intercut with theatrical and musical performances and poetry readings. In their interviews, the women of Bedford Hills serve as both interviewees and interviewers. In doing so, they are able to provide information that is likely unfamiliar to viewers who lack prison experience, such as the unfair and absurd rules by which parole and furlough are determined and the incompetence of the training programs intended to prepare the women for employment when they are released. However, interviewing one another also provides more affective clues into what they themselves think and feel about the unjust system in which they are trapped. In the interview that opens the video, two Black women seated at desks ask each other about their experiences at Bedford Hills. The answers they provide do not say much, but the looks they direct at each other and toward those behind the camera suggest a great deal. The woman facing the camera begins by asking the other, "Do you feel like being in here has helped you?" The other answers, "No, I don't." The first then asks what she plans to do when she gets out, how long her parole will be, and whether she likes the Bedford Hills facilities. To this last question, the second woman answers, "I do not like them very much," and, uncomfortable, turns and looks at those videotaping the interview, before looking away again and laughing (see figure 2.1). When she asks her companion the same questions, the second interviewee says she "hates it," too, and the segment ends with the two nearly rolling out of their seats in a fit of laughter that is echoed off-screen by those behind the camera. From the start of the documentary, then, viewers—via almost entirely nonverbal clues, untranscribable and therefore possible only in film or video—are being clued in to the solidarity that these women have built in their shared experience of prison life.

The gravity of such moments of laughter and solidarity gains contextualization alongside the interviews that more elaborately articulate the myth of rehabilitation through imprisonment. In one such interview, a Black prisoner describes to her white prisoner interviewer the shock of entering prison, only to find herself in a place that deprives all those incarcerated of even their most basic freedoms. If prison is supposed to rehabilitate you into

2.1 Solidarity through laughter in *Songs, Skits, Poetry, and Prison Life* (the Women of the Bedford Hills Correctional Facility For Women/Women Make Movies, 1974). Screen grab. Arthur and Elizabeth Schlesinger Library on the History of Women in America, Radcliffe Institute for Advanced Study, Harvard University, Cambridge, Massachusetts.

society—to "help you," as the documentary's very first interviewer put it—then its methods make no sense, this Black prisoner explains. Referring to the contemporary era of liberation movements and their influence on American culture, she states, "This life we are living now is something of freedom. Everyone talks of freedom, even teenagers. Everything is free: sex free, home free, live free. You know?" As she explains, "And to begin to learn this in the streets and then be taken away from it . . ." The camera zooms from a medium shot of the two of them, seated side by side, from the waist up, a map of Africa on the wall hovering between them (see figure 2.2), to a close-up of the interviewee talking. Inside prison, cut off from the outside world where freedom is expounded (as signified visually by the map of Africa, a sign of Black nationalism and liberation), she explains, everything must be approved by administrators. There is no freedom in prison, and without the agency to make choices, their preparedness for the outside world is doomed to failure. For those entering prison for the first time, she says, discovering this

2.2 "This life we are living now is something of freedom" in *Songs, Skits, Poetry, and Prison Life* (the Women of the Bedford Hills Correctional Facility for Women/Women Make Movies, 1974). Screen grab. Arthur and Elizabeth Schlesinger Library on the History of Women in America, Radcliffe Institute for Advanced Study, Harvard University, Cambridge, Massachusetts.

can really "hit [you] below the belt." When her white interviewer becomes her interviewee, the white prisoner elaborates on this testimony: "You're supposed to come in here for what they call 'rehabilitation,' and yet they have no real training program. . . . They throw you in the caf[eteria] or the industry or the laundry, and then, when it's time for you to be paroled, they say 'find yourself a job.' They expect you to have a job to go out to, but yet they don't let you go out [and] see if you can find one unless your family can afford furlough for you." While work release programs were becoming increasingly common in "men's prisons," the same was not true for those imprisoned in "women's prisons." This is a point that the women of Bedford Hills would continue to make time and again, all the way up to 1978, when they filed a class action suit for such gender discrimination.[49] In *Songs*, they argue, contrary to its claims otherwise, the US prison system deprives women, especially poor women (i.e., those whose families cannot "afford furlough"), the chance to integrate into society upon release.

105

We're Alive's critique of the myth of rehabilitation is articulated most strongly in its section on recidivism. The bulk of *We're Alive*, a forty-minute documentary bookended by color film montages of women on the outside (in offices, salons, schools, strip clubs, retirement homes, and so on at the start of the documentary and participating in protests, unionizing, and engaging with feminist friends at the end), is devoted to video interviews shot in black and white between prisoners inside CIW. The video footage is itself organized by a series of title cards that include facts and figures related to women's incarceration. The title card for the section on recidivism reads, "70 per cent [*sic*] who leave CIW come back." In most of the interviews, the CIW women appear in handheld medium shots and close-ups, cut together with a few tracking shots and pans, which reveal them to be seated in a large circle, much like that of a consciousness-raising (CR) group. Soon after the title card on recidivism, a Black woman with sunglasses and expressive hands explains to the camera and for those seated around the circle that the work of the prison is quite the opposite of rehabilitation. Rather than helping one grow and gain skills, she says, "The state brings you in here and all of a sudden you're totally dependent on the state, you know, for everything. If they don't cook your meals and open that door for you to eat, you'd sit in your room and wait and wait and wait for food. . . . If they didn't do all these things for you, then, you know, you'd never get them done." The camera zooms in on her hands, which subtly but firmly punctuate her words with their small gestures. Her right hand, the more emphatic, leaves the frame, and the camera stays on her left, where her thumb and forefinger press circles as she explains that this provision at the hands of the state is a form of conditioning: "And I think that subconsciously they gear your mind towards having it all the time. You don't have to worry about your meals, because someone over there's gonna cook. You don't have worry about clean sheets on your bed, you don't have to worry about anything. Consequently, it makes you dependent on the state." As the camera zooms back out and slowly tracks up her body from her hands to her face, this Black woman sets the stakes of such dependence and the recidivism it encourages through the gendered personification of the state, generating laughter in acknowledgment of the truth of her characterization from off-screen: "She's just a great big-armed mother [laughs with others laughing off-screen]. And there's really no warmth from her, there's no sincerity, there's nothing, you know. And they totally destroy a person" (see figures 2.3–2.4). In these interviews, Black women theorize the structural racism of the prison-industrial complex, whereby they, in Lorde's words, were never meant to survive.[50] Instead, the

2.3–2.4 The state is a "big-armed mother" in *We're Alive* (the CIW Video Workshop with the Women's Film Workshop of UCLA/Joint Productions, 1974). Screen grabs. Images courtesy of UCLA Film & Television Archive.

carceral state is set up to encourage the relentless incarceration of Black women, men, and other folks. Making this analysis on video with a cast and crew of similarly situated others contextualizes these imprisoned Black women's arguments as that of a community thinking and working to create change for themselves and others like them.

This community of imprisoned people includes poor white people who—less at risk of fatal violence at the hands of police and safe from threats of anti-Black racism (among other things, prisons actively recruited guards from within the Ku Klux Klan at this time)—similarly received little to no rehabilitation or help getting back on their feet after being incarcerated.[51] The *We're Alive* interview with the Black woman on "the big-armed mother" of the carceral state is followed by two interviews with white women about recidivism. In the first, a middle-age white woman wearing glasses admits that "if [she] were out on the streets, [she] would be taking drugs"; instead, she has been working on her music and writing songs. When someone off-screen points out that she will eventually get out of prison and a second asks what she will do then, she confesses, while smiling and laughing nervously, "I'm afraid. To tell you the truth, I'm really kind of scared." She, like so many other poor women, has been locked up for a nonviolent drug-related offense. While in prison, she has been denied access to drugs but has not received the support, psychological or economic, she will need to continue to live drug-free once she is out, making it likely that she will face arrest and incarceration yet again. In the interview that follows, a white woman in her twenties speaks to the comparative usefulness of the Santa Cruz Women's Prison Project's workshops, of which this video's production was a part. She is not, however, speaking to the usefulness of learning skills that will help her fellow imprisoned women gain employment and thus avoid recidivism themselves, as envisioned under the new reform measures that made such workshops possible. Rather, she states, "The workshops have come in, and they've given me a reason to know what's wrong." She elaborates, "All I knew was something was wrong, but I couldn't identify it. And getting together with women and realizing some word called sisterhood has helped." Once cut off from the outside world, those imprisoned at "women's prisons," through the reform programs initiated by anticarceral feminists, were able to participate like their free peers in consciousness-raising and use CR to collectively theorize their gendered experiences of the prison-industrial complex and carceral state.

We're Alive is both the result of CR and models a form of CR through editing, drawing attention to similarities in the women of CIW's experiences of incarceration and the myth of rehabilitation. However, its editing also makes clear that these women's encounters with police, judges and juries, prison boards, and guards vary greatly. Racism, and anti-Black racism in particular, creates conditions under which poor Black women and other women of color are not only more likely to end up in prison, but once they are incarcerated, they face greater harassment and policing from prison personnel than white women do and are less likely to serve the shorter side of their sentence. One Black prisoner tells a story about guards not allowing her and her friends to move dining room tables so they can all sit together, as the white women do, and threatening punishment when she pointed out the discrepancy. This same prisoner explains later, "There's more whites in the United States than there are Blacks. But if you take the percentage as far as Blacks in prisons and whites in prisons, I feel that the majority would be Black compared to the percent Black in California." Meanwhile, the prison board, which determines how much of the sentence any given prisoner will serve, is all white. A white prisoner explains an unfair policy the board recently instituted that says "crimes which have any violence, a lot of which carry a six month minimum . . . that these people will do three years or more. For various crimes involving violence. That is flat out illegal. They legally can't say that, but they do, and they make us do the hard time." Someone off-screen asks, "What's the composition of the board?" Someone else off-screen answers, "Just white." The video cuts to a Black woman who asks for confirmation, "Just white?" And the camera pans to a second Black woman, who confirms, "Ain't no Mexicans, ain't no Blacks, ain't no pinks, ain't no greens, ain't nothing but them whiteys up there to talk to you like you're a dog shit in a garbage can." In moments such as this, these injustices of incarceration are theorized as forms of further racial injustice.

The critique of the myth of rehabilitation—that prison does more harm than help, as the second *Songs* interviewee puts it—gains its most explicit antiracist inflection in *Inside Women Inside*. Echoing the women at Bedford Hills, who speak to the lack of freedom inside, and the *We're Alive* women, who argue that such stifling of freedom in fact makes one dependent on the carceral state, an unseen prisoner early on in *Inside Women Inside* declares in voice-over, "You're told when to eat, when to sleep, when to get up, when to do this, when to do that. And the people here tell you that it's not so bad . . . that they rehabilitate you, but I don't believe it, because they treat us like we're dogs." Much of the film focuses on the work that these incarcerated women are required to do. Various interviewees speak to the heavy manual labor they do for no pay. Some are pictured seated in a cell or behind

109

a sewing machine, while others remain unseen. Together they form a collective acousmêtre of sorts, their authority affirmed in the play between visibility and invisibility.[52] This testimony is interspersed with and carried over across an elaborate montage of these same women working at sewing machines, carrying heavy boxes up and down stairs, and doing laundry en masse. The familiarity of having Black people do manual labor for no pay is not lost on the prisoners of these "women's prisons," and this is made clear for viewers in a voice-over in which a woman declares, "This is like reverting back to slavery days. Instead of bringing us from Africa, they're bringing us from Harlem and the Bronx, but it's all the same game." Choy and Maurizio's film, unlike *Songs* and *We're Alive*, visits not one but three prisons and includes interviews with both prisoners and prison personnel (which I address later). However, in editing *Inside Women Inside*, Choy and Maurizio chose to center this last Black woman's voice. It is her testimony, bookending the film and woven throughout, that makes the political stakes of the other imprisoned women's testimony particularly clear.

Two minutes into the film, it is this Black woman's voice that takes us out of the stark, peopleless shots that open the film and into the talking-head interviews. Not totally unlike the beginning of Chick Strand's *Cartoon le Mousse* of the following year, the film opens with a montage of empty interior spaces cut to an anxious Iannis Xenakis soundtrack. Chiaroscuro shadows cast the bars of the windows on the walls and floors. Ominously, grilled doors slide closed with no sign of human interference. This place, the film tells us, is a cage. The film's first interview, featuring (yet unpictured) the young Black woman Choy and Maurizio chose to center, comes in via voice-over, speaking to a felt sense of the myth of rehabilitation: "You don't get to feeling like you're being reformed. You get to feeling you're being oppressed." The camera pans and zooms in on a prison door slamming, then makes a number of similar quick hand zooms on a series of stills of a young Black woman being photographed with her booking number. In voice-over one hears: "There's no telling what I might do to get free. There's no telling what I might do just to be treated like a human." The film finally takes us into the interview itself, where this woman, now seen sporting a headband and nose ring, elaborates for the camera: "To have an officer call you a bitch and know you can get written up and thrown in the bin for 'insubordination.' To be talked to any way and you can't protest. And if you do, your protest doesn't go anywhere but right on in a little circle. It's a vicious circle where you can never win. No matter how much you love, you lose love. You know? You lose that feeling after a while. You get to feeling like a caged animal." As the camera slowly zooms in

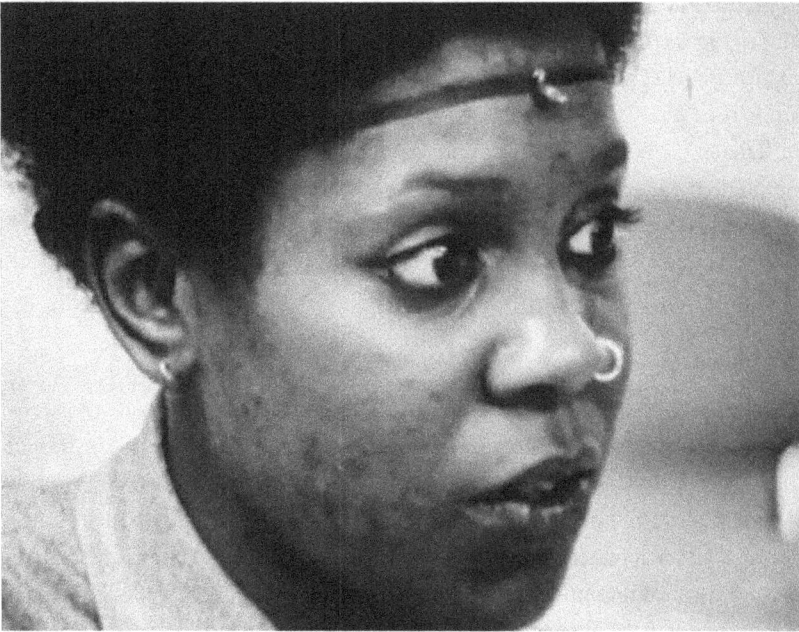

2.5 "No matter how much you love, you lose love" in *Inside Women Inside* (Christine Choy and Cynthia Maurizio/Third World Newsreel, 1978). Screen grab.

on her face, she pauses for clarity and emphasis between sentences and even between a few words or clauses: "No matter how much you love [pause], you lose love [pause]. You know? [pause]" (see figure 2.5). While the earlier shots of empty prison yards and hallways contextualize the testimonies to come, later close-ups such as this one isolate their speaker, individualizing (as evidenced not just in her words but also in their expression, including her pauses and facial expressions) while, counterintuitively, also expanding her testimony as exemplary of the many others like her who, shut behind bars, do not have the opportunity to share their experiences with others outside. These close-ups are not universalizing, as Greg Youmans claims the close-ups are in *Word Is Out* (1978), the quintessential gay liberal documentary re-leased theatrically and on TV that same year.[53] Nor does *Inside Women Inside* (or any of these women's prison films) share what Damon R. Young describes as *Word Is Out*'s "optimistic estimation," whereby the individualization paradoxically central to such a close-up's universalizing work is expected to level differences (between subjects on-screen or between these subjects on-screen and those in the audience).[54] Instead, more akin to the close-up on

III

the light-skinned Mignon Dupree near the end of Julie Dash's short fiction film *Illusions* (1982)—which, Nick Davis writes, "does everything possible to ensure we 'see' and indeed 'recognize' Mignon [as Black]"[55]—*Inside Women Inside* uses close-ups such as this to signify the particularities of subjects' experiences while also crosscutting them with those of other prisoners to eloquently theorize the anti-Black violence of imprisonment, its history in chattel slavery, and its enduring emotional and psychological effects on Black women.

Crosscutting as Consciousness-raising

Quite often the interviews of *Songs* and *We're Alive* are recognizable visually as the result of consciousness-raising-like settings. The video workshop at CIW was but one workshop in which these women participated (alongside "Women and the Law," "Radical Psychology," "Politics: US Institutions and Political Consciousness," and "Women in Society," to name but a few), where, as the white woman in the recidivism section noted, women developed their means of identifying and theorizing what "was wrong."[56] In these workshops, just as in the CR circles of the Combahee River Collective and other feminist groups outside prison, the women of CIW "began to recognize the commonality of our experiences and, from that sharing and growing consciousness, to build a politics" that they believed might change their lives and end their oppression.[57] *We're Alive* cuts among close-ups of individual speakers in a number of actual CR circles, reconstituting them, through editing, as members of one large CR circle. Crosscutting in each of these feminist prison documentaries itself constitutes a form of CR, crafting a collective form of theorizing through the building of different prisoners' thoughts and reflections. In a social movement milieu that cast imprisoned women as apolitical, listening to the testimony of only a few well-known female political prisoners, this method of editing many unnamed women's words together spoke back in force. Though they may not use the same, explicit political terminology as, say, Bobby Seale in Newsreel's *Bobby Seale* (1968) or Huey P. Newton and Eldridge Cleaver in the group's *Black Panther* (1968), these documentaries' masses of women—all speaking together from their shared, while also distinguishable, experiences of the prison-industrial complex—articulate how imprisoned Black women and poor women, much like their more celebrated male compatriots, are political prisoners of the same carceral state. Significant to their understanding of themselves as political prisoners, they clarify, is the uniqueness of "women's prisons," including the treatment they receive from prison administrators as a result of social attitudes toward women's criminality.

Inside Women Inside expands this methodology of crosscutting as CR, evident in *Songs* and *We're Alive*, to cut together the testimony of women at three different prisons, as well as interviews with both prisoners and prison personnel. By crosscutting among interviews with prison superintendents, psychiatrists, and other prison administrators and those with imprisoned women, which directly contrast or otherwise critically complicate the versions of imprisoned life being offered by prison personnel, *Inside Women Inside* models imprisoned women's resistance, delegitimizing prison authorities' authority in favor of prisoners' own. In one scene, an interview with the Elmhurst facility psychiatrist is crosscut with interviews with two separate women behind bars, each of whom is all too familiar with prison psychiatrists' control over her and her fellow prisoners' lives. The camera tilts down from a reproduction of a Renoir painting of a mother and daughter to a close-up of a white male psychiatrist seated below it; as the camera slowly zooms out, he calmly describes his responsibility to evaluate the women's mental health and determine their fitness to stand trial. The film then cuts to an older prisoner behind bars who gives poignancy to the psychiatrist's seemingly benign words, expressing anger that she was not allowed to testify—"to defend [her]self"—and was sentenced to death by electric chair. When asked by an interviewer behind the camera whether she saw a psychiatrist, she answers, "Yes, ma'am. I went about three times. . . . I told him I didn't want to see him no more, because I wasn't crazy." The film returns to the psychiatrist, who, now situated in a long shot between the American and New York City flags and beneath the Renoir, tells those behind the camera that women in prison are subject to much stress, making medication "very important." The film then cuts to a younger Black woman who, also literally behind bars, provides a series of counterexamples regarding the abuse of medication in "women's prisons," both her own and those of others she knows (see figures 2.6–2.7). Here prison's denial of freedom is extended to the very substances these women are intended to consume. The second woman speaks to being put on medication without being told what it is and says she knows a number of people in prison with her who, despite "not [being] crazy," are plied with so many drugs that they are rarely conscious. Similar experiences are shared in the CR circles of *We're Alive*, but here we are not asked to take imprisoned women's testimony about prison personnel for granted. Instead, the film's use of crosscutting as a CR technique—its dialectical relay of prisoners and prison personnel crafted in postproduction—transforms the basic grammar

113

2.6–2.7 Crosscutting as consciousness raising in *Inside Women Inside* (Christine Choy and Cynthia Maurizio/Third World Newsreel, 1978). Screen grabs.

of the realist documentary film (talking head interviews) to craft arguments that in turn rely on the labor of feminist audiences in reception.

Another feminist prison documentary that uses this crosscutting as CR technique is *Like a Rose* (1975), a twenty-minute black-and-white film made by Sally Barrett-Page with the "Prisoners and Staff of the State Correctional Center for Women at Tipton" that circulated through the National Women's Film Circuit (NWFC). Like *Songs*, *We're Alive*, and *Inside Women Inside*, *Like a Rose* debunks the myth of rehabilitation, meditating on the boredom of imprisonment and the very limited opportunities for education and self-growth. Unlike the three documentaries discussed at greater length across this chapter, *Like a Rose* cannot be understood as a work of Black feminist theory, as it focuses nearly exclusively on the experiences of two white women, Carolyn Dillard and Peggy Russell, contrasting their lives inside and outside of prison, the differences between which appear arguably ever starker, considering the white, middle-class iconography of their outside. As one contributor to the women's studies journal *Frontiers* wrote about the film, "Without attempting a blatant exposé of the prison system, the film's personal approach towards its subject implicitly states the insensitivity of this system in meeting the needs of the inmates. By focusing on the lives of two women living in prison, *Like a Rose* reveals the pain, the indignities, and the human waste endured by women behind bars."[58] Dillard's and Russell's combined experiences form a synecdoche for women's experiences in prison—or, at least, that of those at Tipton. The film features far fewer close-ups than the three films discussed earlier. Much of the film is a single medium long two-shot of Dillard and Russell seated on a bed, hinting at their being lovers (see figure 2.8)—or, as the *Frontiers* author writes, having "develop[ed] emotional support for each other."[59] The film does not weave Dillard and Russell into a tapestry of prison life. In the few shots in which they are pictured outside their cell, they appear quite literally in stark relief before or beside the Black and Brown bodies of the other prisoners around them. After Dillard and Russell explain the limited vocational and educational opportunities provided by the prison, Dillard is pictured teaching a young Black woman to read (see figure 2.9). After the two read a passage from a book, Dillard helping the younger woman sound out the challenging words, the two talk about how learning to read ought to help her secure a job as a social worker, as she would like to when she gets out. The scene is constructed traditionally, with wide shots of the two seated beside each other opening and closing the scene and close-ups of each of them reading or helping the other read in the middle. Dillard is cast as a philanthropic

2.8 Carolyn Dillard and Peggy Russell in *Like A Rose* (Sally Barrett-Page, dir., 1975). Screen grab.

white woman, while the very work that prisons are supposed to be doing through educational and vocational training is seen as being done by prisoners themselves.

Like Choy and Maurizio, Barrett-Page interviewed prison personnel as a part of gaining access to the women inside. And like *Inside Women Inside*, *Like a Rose* contrasts its prisoners' testimony with that of a prison staff member. Through its crosscutting between Dillard's and Russell's testimony and that of one particular administrator, the film brings to light the very particularly gendered nature of prison reform. In the final scene, constructed as such in postproduction, an unnamed white administrator of the Missouri State Correctional Center for Women, sitting behind a desk in an office in a medium shot, tells the camera, "The staff is a very compassionate staff, but in the last couple of years, in the new concept of prison reform, it has been difficult to turn ourselves around from custody and to treatment, and this is what I think prisons/corrections is all about." As she speaks, the film cuts to a sign in the prison office that reads, "The State Correctional Center for Women's responsibility is to return the female ex-offender to community

2.9 Carolyn Dillard teaching a young Black woman to read in *Like A Rose* (Sally Barrett-Page, dir., 1975). Screen grab.

status as successful wives, mothers and productive employees." The benign nature of "reform" or "rehabilitation," as opposed to "custody," is called into question. Not only has the falsity of the sign's claim already been revealed in Dillard's and Russell's critique of the lack of educational and vocational training provided at the prison, but the ideological stakes of this rehabilitation has been exposed. The work of correcting gender-nonconformity, on the agenda of "women's prisons" for nearly a century, is reframed as an element of prison reform, alongside vocational training. As we return to the staff member behind the desk, she elaborates that, despite its "very compassionate staff," the Missouri State Correctional Center for Women has found it challenging to rehabilitate its resistant charges. The women resent staff, the administrator explains, for taking away their freedom and act out. The film soon cuts to a series of still photographs of isolated women, frozen in medium or long shots, looking dejected or disconnected, and Russell counters in a voice-over, "In all institutions, I believe, there is a breakdown in communication between staff and inmates, because there is no woman-to-woman conversation. In fact, an inmate really has nowhere to go if she is

117

in trouble." Almost as if to demonstrate the lack of communication between staff and inmates, the film ends by continuing this shot/reverse-shot-like montage between the administrator and Dillard and Russell. The film cuts back to the administrator, and she articulates the gender-conforming goals of the prison in her own words: "We must discipline the women. We must try to make them into ladies and to situate them to go back into society as productive citizens." To this, Dillard, through the film's editing, responds, "Some of the very same things that make survival possible in here are the opposite of what you need to get along out there." The administrator claims the prisoners simply do not know how to structure their time productively, and Dillard speaks to her desire to take college courses, like those in "men's prisons" do, and being denied the opportunity. As the film continues this back and forth, it becomes clear that the staff and prisoners do not simply provide two different perspectives on the rehabilitation offered by the prison as it moves from a more custody-based approach to a rehabilitation-based approach under prison reform. Instead, rehabilitation-based approaches to women's incarceration have simply reframed punishment for gender deviancy, making learning gender-conformity an educational matter.

Freedom Dreams

In producing these films, those imprisoned at "women's prisons" resisted the conditions of their rehabilitation. By participating in the video production workshops that resulted in *Songs* and *We're Alive* or speaking to the filmmakers admitted into their institutions, as in *Inside Women Inside* and *Like a Rose*, imprisoned women and those of other genders imprisoned at these same institutions defied the cisnormative and heteronormative gender roles central to their rehabilitation, which would demand passivity and resignation of them. Correspondence between those inside "women's prisons" and those outside was closely monitored, and *off our backs*, *Through the Looking Glass*, *No More Cages*, and other lesbian feminist publications were routinely banned out of fear they would inspire rebellion.[60] Speaking up, if only to a visitor with a camera or tape recorder, in such circumstances was an act of resistance. As Stephen Dillon writes in his study of fugitive life in the social movements of the 1960s and '70s, "The knowledge produced by the prisoner exposes a truth about the United States that cannot be accessed from elsewhere."[61] Dillon names writing and art as "sites for the creation of alternative epistemologies that the neoliberal-carceral state continually worked to erase and expunge from the knowable."[62] Documentaries made by those imprisoned at "women's prisons" are another such site. In producing knowledge of the gendered form of anti-Black racism of "women's prisons," those who made *Songs, We're Alive,* and *Inside Women Inside* refused their invisibility and erasure.

Much of the content of these documentaries could be found in either the published writings of better-known prisoners or in the contributions of prisoners to the women's prison newsletters *Through the Looking Glass* and *No More Cages.* What the documentaries uniquely offered was a dialogical exchange between both minds and bodies, as those on-screen reached out to those in the audience through the erotic embrace of haptic black-and-white film or video. Far from strictly realistic, in that they are shot in black and white and the mise-en-scène (i.e., faces behind bars before a dark cell or faces surrounded by the plain walls of a prison classroom) and electronic texture of their early video capture denies depth of vision and the perspective or illusionism central to visual theories of realist space, they nonetheless provide sites of exchange among feminist bodies—on the screen and off.[63] In their mobile camerawork, tracking from hands to faces, and hand zooms, moving in more and more tightly on their Black subjects' faces as they speak, they tap into the additional eroticism particular to the documentary mode, wherein one takes in people's bodies in a fashion akin to daily life.[64] In the cases of *Songs* and *We're Alive,* the looks of spectators align not with those of women on the outside looking in but those of the inside looking at one another. While *Through the Looking Glass* and *No More Cages* and the writings of Angela Davis and others circulated among those already invested—or, at least, proactively interested—in women's imprisonment, *Songs, We're Alive,* and *Inside Women Inside,* due to feminist film and video distributors' circulation of them through the women's movement (*Songs* circulated as a New York City International Videoletter), reached a great number of spectators with little to no knowledge of such matters. Just a few years before written theory such as the Combahee River Collective's "A Black Feminist Statement" (drafted by the organization in 1977 and published and circulated widely in 1979) and *This Bridge Called My Back: Writings by Radical Women of Color* (1981) would radically reorient second-wave feminism and center women of color's voices in the movement, these documentaries introduced feminist audiences across the United States to an embodied audiovisual form of Black feminist theory.

Those who produced these documentaries also produced an especially affective form of Black feminist freedom dreams. Freedom dreams name how Black intellectuals, activists, and artists have imagined life after revolution. Kelley identifies them in the poetic knowledge produced by the emancipatory language of W. E. B. Du Bois, Aimé Césaire, Audre Lorde, Angela Davis, and the Combahee River Collective. Central to Kelley's conceptualization of these writers' freedom dreams is the influence of the social movements around them. Social movements "do what great poetry always does"—namely, "transports us to another place, compel[s] us to relive horrors and, more importantly, enable[s] us to imagine a new society."[65] As Kara Keeling carefully clarifies in *Queer Times, Black Futures*, freedom dreams do not provide a map to utopia but hold the potential to spark change in the present (whether that present is the same present in which the dreams were imagined or another present of their later circulation).[66] Meanwhile, Dillon, in writing about the writing and art of fugitives in the 1960s and '70s, including Shakur and Davis, builds on Kelley, distinguishing between "neoliberal freedom" and "fugitive freedom." The freedom of the freedom dreams produced by feminist prison documentaries in the 1970s entails the latter: "not contingent, but infinitely expansive, open, and always already taking flight."[67] When their subjects describe the discovery of the lack of freedom in prison "hit[ing] below the belt" or personify the prison as a "great big-armed mother," they are not simply explaining the immediate effect of administrative procedures. They are also speaking to the prison's broader attempts to frame freedom as a matter of regulation and discipline, something deniable to those who have broken society's laws for citizenry; they are describing the very work of the neoliberal carceral state to "control, manage, and capture the notions of freedom produced by the left by rendering them unthinkable and impossible."[68] Lesbian potentiality and its multigendered valences were part of this. A young white woman in *We're Alive* speaks to prison personnel who are interrogating her as someone they perceive as straight (due to her marital status and gender presentation) but who nonetheless has maintained a series of sexual relations with other women in prison, concluding: "And I think maybe one of the things prison started to do for a while was limit my conception of what's possible."

In monitoring and policing incarcerated women's sexual relations, prison administrators worked to deny prisoners the experience of lesbian potentiality. They sought to prohibit that sense of anything being possible that Joanna experienced while kissing Laur for the first time in *The Female Man*. And yet, while their subjects might remain behind bars, this sense of possibility breaks free through these documentaries. Surrounding, bookending, and infusing these documentaries' critiques are fleeting dreams of freedom to come, as well as—counter to the prison-industrial complex's best attempts—evidence of fugitive freedom found.

Freedom dreams—gleaming with lesbian potentiality, if not out and out representations of lesbian existence and perceivable only through something akin to what in the first chapter I termed "lesbian feminist affectivity"—are strewn like stars across *Songs*' twenty minutes. As the video's title announces, *Songs* crosscuts its interviews with songs, skits, and poetry, written and performed by women at the Bedford Hills facility, which not only offer additional forms for articulating its subjects' experiences of law enforcement and imprisonment but also, through their creative means, document how these women care for one another and create community.[69] Doing as much is freedom dreaming, believing that there is a life worth living for and creating that life against all odds. It is a part of the Black feminist tradition of freedom dreaming that Jennifer C. Nash names Black feminist love politics, in which personal forms of love, including romantic love, are transformed into a collective theory of justice oriented toward a yet unknown future.[70] The political community created through Black feminist love politics "eschews the wounded subject that lies at the heart of identity politics. In its place, it crafts a collectivity marked by 'communal affect,' a utopian, visionary, future-oriented community held together by affiliation and 'public feeling' rather than an imagined—or enforced—sameness."[71] While each of these documentaries does the important work of theorizing anticarceral feminism, making clear how prisons concentrate the devaluation of women under heteropatriarchy and the punishment of those who violate gender norms while also compounding the anti-Black racism of white supremacy, they do so with a utopianism that insists it need not and will not always be this way. At times they practice a form of intersectionality that Nash is wary of in its presentism, juridical orientation, and seeming acceptance of identity categories as fixed and knowable. But in their heterogeneity, shifting among temporalities and crafting of new forms of relationality through their circulation of affect, they also evince a postintersectional futurity of the sort Nash champions. And the charge of lesbian potentiality that courses through their freedom dreams, which includes a tinge of romance but is not subsumed by it, is central to their Black feminist love politics. What binds the women on-screen is not only their experiences as imprisoned women but their vision for a future in which not only they as individual prisoners but all today nameable as Black women are free.

We're Alive and *Inside Women Inside* save their freedom dreams for their conclusions, pointing to their visions of the future at their ends to make the stakes of their preceding theorizing of the present violence of the prison-industrial complex more poignant. *Songs*, however, weaves its freedom dreams throughout. There is rarely a shot in which spectators are not being invited to join the future-oriented community pictured on-screen. This is in large part due to the prevalence of songs, skits, and poetry, as the film's title suggests. The viewer watching and listening, unfamiliar with such prison experiences, is not simply told what the demolition of the prison-industrial complex would look like. Instead, through these highly affective performances, they receive a sense of the kinds of freedoms that would replace the neoliberal carceral state's regulation of freedom and unfreedom—that is, kinds of freedoms that, despite its best efforts, the prison-industrial complex cannot quash. After the opening interview of *Songs* (which, if you remember, concluded in laughter), a short montage of footage from events to come, cut to Billie Holiday's "God Bless the Child," brings us to the first poem of the video. As Holiday's voice fades away, a single performer comes into view in a medium close-up. She adjusts her collar, looking up past the camera quickly, and says, "I am kinda cute, huh," which again garners laughter from the direction of her off-screen look. She then reads Robert Bersohn's poem "The Dignity of Labor," which contrasts the supposed benefits of labor with the presumed detriments of leisure. As she reads the closing line, she looks up at the camera, making the wit of the poem's closure—"But give me leisure every time"—a flirty poignancy. Each of the documentary video's performances, staged for the camera, offers similar small resistances, enacted with imprisoned others, to the structures delimiting its subjects' time and labor. Lesbian potentiality is not solely the property of those imprisoned women who partake in love and sex with other women inside prison. It lives in the varied exchanges among women on-screen, between the women on-screen and those behind the camera, and between all of these women and the audiences watching and listening in women's movement screenings across the United States. It exists in the simultaneous impotentiality of these moments—in the fact that such virtual relationality between inside and outside might not become actual and that they could change when they do.

Freedom dreaming and the lesbian potentiality of are not simply crosscut in *Songs* with more sober critiques of the prison system. Instead, the two are inseparable parts of the same project. This is seen in a skit titled "In Court," which parodies the racism of the trial process. In it, a white male judge (played by a Black prisoner) sentences a Black woman to seventeen years for armed robbery and assault, though little evidence has been presented against her. The district attorney is seen regularly playing to the judge's prejudices, and the digs made at the judge by the defense lawyer suggest that white people, unable to distinguish among different Black people, are happy to send any Black person to prison for any given crime. When the prisoner playing the bailiff swears in the woman playing the defendant, the two stand close and make considerable eye contact; later, when the defendant is sentenced to seventeen years in prison, she buries her obviously fake crying in the bailiff actor's chest (see figure 2.10). If not explicitly lesbian in that they are neither sexually explicit nor narrativized through voice-over or a framing interview as part of a romance, this intimacy and the joy it generates (seen most obviously in the big smile of the actor playing the bailiff, arms wrapped around the actor playing the defendant) is an index of the forms of fugitive freedom crafted by those imprisoned at "women's prisons." They both show and do not show what love looks like for these two and those around them. As is the case with the future women and Andy aboard the spaceship *Gloria* in James Tiptree, Jr.'s "Houston, Houston, Do You Read?" we do not know what happens when they are alone. But we do not need to. Not knowing holds open the signification of such an embrace, such a laugh, and what is even meant if we are to label them "lesbian." Both powerfully depicting and the result of women (and others imprisoned at "women's prisons") sharing physical, emotional, and intellectual joy with one another, these moments are erotic.[72] Their eroticism and its fugitivity also continue, infiltrating the women's movement through the documentary's distribution (via International Videoletters).

Central to these films' overturning of the traditional documentary dynamic, wherein documentary subjects are captured and contained by an outside filmmaker, is that these prisoners, in filming themselves, consign to themselves an existing potentiality. The future in which racist and sexist discrimination does not exist, in which the prison system does not exist, exists as a potential in these prisoners' love for one another. The songs of *Songs* exemplify this. Music and singing are integral to these imprisoned people's day-to-day survival, and songs appear throughout the video at a greater frequency than any other sort of performance. In one scene, the Black prisoner who earlier spoke of being shocked at the prison's denial of prisoners' agency interviews two Black prisoners, Trent and Robbie, who are also musicians. Trent and Robbie each jockey for the camera's attention— "Wait, I ain't said nothing yet"; "Put it back on me"—before telling their fellow prisoner interviewer and cameraperson that over the previous couple months they taught themselves to play, respectively, the saxophone and the guitar. As Robbie puts it, they have chosen to "utilize the time" in prison to learn these instruments. In watching and listening to their performance of

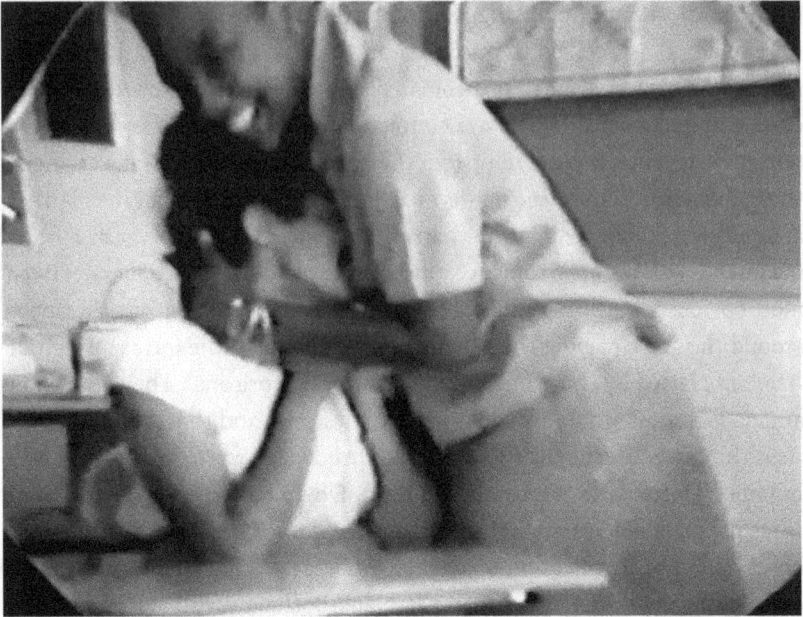

2.10 Bailiff and Defendant embrace in "In Court" skit in *Songs, Skits, Poetry, and Prison Life* (Women of the Bedford Hills Correctional Facility For Women/Women Make Movies, 1974). Screen grab. Arthur and Elizabeth Schlesinger Library on the History of Women in America, Radcliffe Institute for Advanced Study, Harvard University, Cambridge, Massachusetts.

"Deep Elem Blues," it becomes apparent that what Trent and Robbie have gained is more than a skill. In a song sung by a "Papa" to a "Mama," Robbie's vocal delivery, together with Robbie's guitar and Trent's saxophone, not only impresses on the viewer the distress and sadness of imprisonment but also illuminates the bonds forged therein.[73] The final shot of the performance reveals a small audience of fellow prisoners, but much of the performance and the interviews before it are shot in tight medium close-ups, the scene's lined background of narrow prison windows compressed with the foreground of the performers' faces and the whole frame becoming electronically textured surface (see figures 2.11 and 2.12). As Trent and Robbie vie for the camera's attention and answer their interviewer's questions, they are teased, whistled at, and cheered on from off-screen. For Giorgio Agamben, the realm of the aesthetic, of creation and creativity, is an especially vital sphere for potentiality and its coconstituting impotentiality. According to Agamben, painters, poets, and architects exist in a mode of privation. The painter may paint or

2.11 Trent performing in *Songs, Skits, Poetry, and Prison Life* (Women of the Bedford Hills Correctional Facility for Women/Women Make Movies, 1974). Screen grab. Arthur and Elizabeth Schlesinger Library on the History of Women in America, Radcliffe Institute for Advanced Study, Harvard University, Cambridge, Massachusetts.

not paint, but their faculty or power to paint is constant, and this is no small matter.[74] As musicians and performers, and now as filmmakers, those who made *Songs* are seizing their potentiality and, in owning it, indicating the open-ended nature of what is to come, of what they and others like them could and might do.

Sex remains off-screen and "off-scene."[75] These documentaries are not part of the post–Production Code era's bringing on-scene what was previously off/obscene. In women's prison exploitation films of the 1970s, "the women's prison became virtually synonymous with lesbianism of an overtly sexualized and threatening sort."[76] And while Judith Mayne, Jack Halberstam, and Chris Holmlund have read these films against the grain for their feminist and queer spectatorial pleasures,[77] this is not what I mean by the lesbian potentiality of these documentaries' Black feminist love politics. Instead, the actual sex of the fugitive freedom dreams crafted by those imprisoned at "women's prions" together—the what could come to be, which includes even as it eclipses sex—materializes in the tension between the

125

2.12 Robbie performing in *Songs, Skits, Poetry, and Prison Life* (Women of the Bedford Hills Correctional Facility for Women/Women Make Movies, 1974). Screen grab. Arthur and Elizabeth Schlesinger Library on the History of Women in America, Radcliffe Institute for Advanced Study, Harvard University, Cambridge, Massachusetts.

on-scene and off-scene. There is clearly love here, and it is a collective love located in affects that cannot be contained to one couple or sets of couples (or broader or otherwise configured romantic, sexual, and imprisoned kinship networks). Instead, it radiates out to all those involved in the production of the documentary and those in its eventual audiences. But because of its audiovisual documentary form (unlike the written theory Nash analyzes), this love indubitably includes the sexual and the romantic in the dynamics between subject and camera and screen and spectator.

Such sexual screen dynamics are perhaps most evident in *Songs'* a cappella numbers. In one, six women stand in a semicircle in the classroom and perform the Drifters' "There Goes My Baby." As they sing, "There goes my baby, movin' on down the line; Wonder where, wonder where, wonder where she is bound," the woman farthest to the left shimmies forward and then back again, making eyes at someone off-screen (see figure 2.13). As the group croons together, "I broke her heart and made her cry; Now I'm alone, so all alone; What can I do, what can I do," they sway left and then right. Their exchanges of smiles and looks both on-screen and with those off-screen indicate they are singing for one another as much as with one another. The eroticism of both the documentary gaze and the haptic images of black-and-white video mean that spectators of *Songs* become involved and entangled in the bodily exchange of performer, audience, and screen. Again, while nothing in this documentary is named "lesbian," its images and sounds in both the context of its production and its reception and the labor of all those involved, including its distribution by lesbian feminist media workers, ignites the process of lesbian potentiality. What are most clearly recognizable as signs of lesbian desire—the flirtatious looks between women before and behind the camera—are inseparable from the film's issuing of freedom dreams, its Black feminist love politics, and the desires of feminist audiences to come together through media and create the world anew.

Songs brings viewers in with a scene of comradery and leaves us with another. In its final minutes, *Songs* returns to the setup from the first interview; this time, the second interviewer is being interviewed by a different Black woman. Although they are interviewing each other presumably for this completed video (as well as to give those behind the camera—including, perhaps, the first interviewer—practice operating the equipment, as this was a video workshop), the two prisoners' interest in each other is preeminent. When asked whether she is married, the interviewer-turned-interviewee answers that she is not. When asked why not, she answers, "I can't find nobody to marry me," and the two double over in laughter. The interviewee then takes the microphone and asks her interviewer, "What do you plan to do when you get out of here, Alberta Stokes?" Alberta answers, "I plan on taking care of the kids staying in my house." The interviewer-turned-interviewee-turned-interviewer asks Alberta how many kids she has, and she answers that she has two. The interviewer then asks her whether she is married, to which she answers, "No." When asked why not, Alberta answers, "Because there's no husband for me." Her interviewer presses her again, flirtatiously cajoling, "Why not? You're not that bad looking." Alberta raises her hands as if to indicate uncertainty but then declares, "They're all washed up." The two collapse into laughter, and the video ends. Prison media scholars have noted how common it is for prison documentaries to "end up reinforcing and reproducing the carceral regime rather than undoing it: ideas of individual responsibility; the prison as a response to crime; the criminal as dangerous (and as black)."[78] As I hope my analysis has made clear, this was not the case with *Songs* (or *We're Alive* or *Inside Women Inside*). Such critiques only make clearer the significance of these moments when signs of love, affection,

127

2.13 Shimmying in *Songs, Skits, Poetry, and Prison Life* (Women of the Bedford Hills Correctional Facility for Women/Women Make Movies, 1974). Screen grab. Arthur and Elizabeth Schlesinger Library on the History of Women in America, Radcliffe Institute for Advanced Study, Harvard University, Cambridge, Massachusetts.

community, and desire—so formidably opposed by prison administrations—manage to escape.

At the start of this chapter, I said I did not fully agree with the tautology of Juhasz's claim that film objectifies women and makes victims of them, much as patriarchy does, while video, like feminism, produces women as subjects. Still, I conceded that the gleam of lesbian potentiality is brighter in *Songs* and *We're Alive* than *Inside Women Inside*, and this is because, like Juhasz's prison videos, their production was more collaborative, such fugitive on- and offscreen, on- and off-scene tensions being impossible without a crew (as well as a cast) of prisoners.

The counterexample, *Like a Rose*, meanwhile, is nearly, if not completely, devoid of lesbian potentiality. The NWFC audiences read the film's subjects, Dillard and Russell, as lesbian. As the Albuquerque producer wrote about *Like a Rose*, "[The film] touched folks deeply once they figured out what was going on—did not [initially] realize that there were 2 dykes doing something other than making love" (see figures 1.7–1.8).[79] But their isolating two-shot

fails to attribute the same fugitive freedom to their love, and lesbian potentiality is minimized even as Dillard and Russell are arguably not the only
dykes pictured. There is one scene in *Like a Rose* in which Black women joyfully fill the screen, dancing arm in arm. If it were not for the relative clarity
of the image and depth of field, due to being shot on film, the scene could
almost be a scene out of *Songs*. Prisoners sway in pairs, and the camera zooms
in on a couple, one member of which is wearing a white turtleneck and dark
jeans and the other a black halter-top and light-colored cut-off jeans. They
rock in toward each other and then out before the one in the turtleneck
rocks past the other, their gently clasped hands seemingly never breaking
as they twist into a new configuration, the zooming camera emphasizing
their proximity to each other through close-up even as it creates distance,
as, unlike the *Songs* performers, they act as if they are totally unaware of its
presence. In place of any direct address of the camera by these dancers or
the audio of an interview with them, Russell's voice-over is brought in. She
begins by explaining the importance of Saturday night dances at Tipton,
which are "supposed to be a great treat." The film cuts to two older Black
women sitting at the edge of the dance floor. One puts an arm around the
shoulders of the other, and they both sway in their seats. Russell tells us
the Saturday night dance is "a great event when you're first new at Tipton."
The film cuts among a few pairs on the dance floor, including Dillard, who is
seen dancing enthusiastically with one of the previously seated Black women.
But as the camera zooms out from one particularly intimate Black couple,
dancing cheek to cheek, their bodies entwined as they sway more slowly
(see figure 2.14), revealing another nearby dancing similarly closely, Russell's
voice-over returns, declaring, "Fewer and fewer girls go up to these Saturday night dances. . . . The longer you're at Tipton, the less you enter into
these so-called social activities, because they only make you sadder. You are
seeking, searching for something that isn't there." Whether one accepts this
as truth depends on whether one understands the voice-over as function-
ing as a form of anchorage—that is, determining the meaning of the image
with which it is paired, or whether one is open to relay, identifying a dis-
sonance between the intimacies on-screen and the despairing voice-over on
the soundtrack.[80] In either case, access to what the Black women who pre-
dominate the dance floor think and feel is denied. The film continues the
carceral regime, as its white speaking subjects and white filmmaker reinforce
the unfreedom of the neoliberal carceral state. *Like a Rose* ends awkwardly,
determined to go out on a hopeful note that rings hollow. Dillard exasperatedly says that one can "keep trying and keep pushing [for reform, for work

129

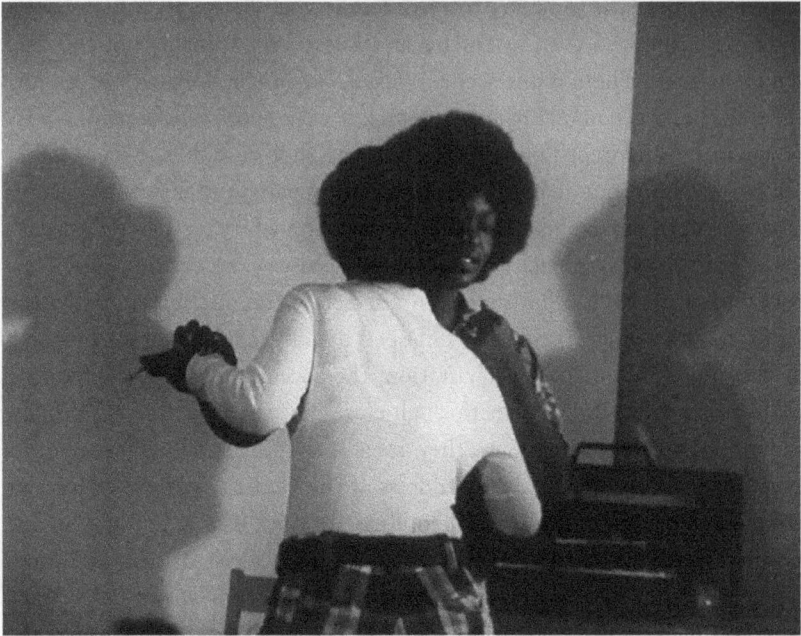

2.14 Dancing cheek-to-cheek in *Like a Rose* (Sally Barrett-Page, dir., 1975). Screen grab.

and vocational opportunities], but for how long?" Russell responds, placing a placating hand on the younger woman's knee: "Well, the idea is don't give up, baby, because we always come out smelling like a rose." Dillard stares despondently into space, nodding as if in agreement, while also clearly distracted by the heavy thoughts she shared but seconds before. The carceral state's emphasizing of individual responsibility is underscored, and thoughts of all others who are incarcerated are left behind.

Songs, *We're Alive*, and *Inside Women Inside*, in contrast, leave spectators with their own, uniquely cinematic freedom dreams. *Songs* sends us off with laughter, the fugitive freedom these women have found together taking flight before our very eyes, leaving flirtatious teasing and laughter in its place. *Inside Women Inside* returns us to similarly stark images that it began with, but this time the same woman who brought us into the film with her critique of rehabilitation as oppression tells us that, against all odds, she is fighting inside and when she gets out she is going to continue to fight on the outside:

> Now when I get out of here, they're going to have a big fight. . . . If we stand together and we ask for vocational training, we'll get a school. But

if we put ourselves into the school, we can do something. If we put ourselves into what we want, we can get it. Because I'm going to get mine. Now any sister who wants to fight with me can come on and get it with me. But if she don't start fighting, I'll see her on the way back, 'cause I'm not staying back there with her. I'm going to fight, because this can't go on. It's a mad race. It's never been known in history that a race has been known to stay down for so long, especially if they got people in it like me, because I'm not going to stay down.

In its final moments, the film freezes on her face, but her monologue continues: "Because I'm very proud. I'm a very proud Black woman." Even as she speaks for herself and has clearly been selected for focus by Choy and Maurizio because of her strong personality, she makes clear that her incarceration cannot be disentangled from that of others like her. This is the woman who earlier told us that, in prison, "no matter how much you love, you lose love. . . . You lose that feeling after a while. You get to feeling like a caged animal." At the film's end, she is willfully refusing to lose this love, to become the "caged animal" that prison's unfreedom, including the unfreedom of feelings, wills for her. Her Black feminist love politics are such that she cannot focus solely on getting out—the sort of neoliberal freedom prison conditions prisoners to anticipate—but must think of those unjustly imprisoned every day and pursue the fugitive freedom of liberation movements whether inside or out. Whereas the carceral regime would have us see her as criminal, she sees her incarceration as part of a long tradition of which she is proud. Pride here—her describing herself as a "very proud Black woman"—is not a personality trait; it is historical agency, a practice of Black feminist love politics, and evidence of fugitive freedom found. In celebrating this pride through the final freeze frame of her visage, *Inside Women Inside* conserves and extends prideful, loving freedom outward to audiences.

We're Alive diegetically connects those inside and outside, making the case that imprisoned women and their causes are integral to the women's movement and social movements more broadly. It also issues a freedom dream of what could follow if this argument were taken seriously. In the final black-and-white video section of the documentary, a Black woman articulates her and her imprisoned peers' struggles as not just one of the past but of the future: "You're going to go home sooner or later, but what about your son or your daughter that might be coming in? You have to try to have some kind of prison alternative, because this is not it." As for herself, she says: "Because I have a number behind me I feel that that's going to hold me back, you know. Because I'm Black, because I'm a woman, it's going to hold me back." However, like the Black woman at the end of *Inside Women Inside*, she declares, "But I'm going to keep on pushing." A white woman follows her, underscoring the economic basis for most imprisonment and the need to change society at large to abolish prisons:

> You have to realize that prisons exist. You have to realize that there's a lot of people out there with no education, that have not had the opportunities to better themselves, that want to eat, who don't want to stand in welfare lines, because that's been down for so long, who thinks that it's a matter of pride, that they can't take anything from anybody else, because that's part of the bullshit they've brainwashed into us. . . . There are people who go to prison because of economic reasons—like 95 percent. So if you want to get rid of prisons, you've got to start organizing in your own community and change the society.

The documentary has taken viewers, many previously unfamiliar with and unknowledgeable about the prison experiences of those imprisoned at "women's prisons," into one such institution and introduced them to those incarcerated there. Their circumstances, these final interview subjects underscore, are not separate from or unrelated to those on the outside. With the films' transition from this black-and-white video footage to its bookending color film, *We're Alive* issues a call for the recognition of the centrality of prisoners to liberation movements—and of imprisoned Black women to the women's movement, in particular—and a dream of what may result from this.

As in *Songs*, the freedom dreaming of *We're Alive* is facilitated by the potentiality of a musician, singer, and songwriter who, in turn, consigns to the project the potentiality of imprisoned women to make change writ large. After its last interview, *We're Alive* cuts to black, and an unsourced voice-over comes in, introducing the song she wrote from her maximum security cell before playing it on the guitar. As she sings, "Warmer than warmest/ deeper than deepest/Colors of crimson/We're here in prison," images return. They are no longer fuzzy, flat black-and-white video images but clear and in color. Tracking shots from a car window of the brick and wire of CIW's barracks and yards are crosscut with footage of protests and organizing. In one shot, as the singer croons the song's titular chorus, "We're alive, we're alive, we're alive," the film cuts to a shot of people marching past with signs. They are of many ages, genders, races, and ethnicities, and they crowd the frame so that their signs can be read only in part (see figure 2.15). One says, "Rich people cause poverty, poor people live it," and another says, "Stop Racist Health Care." In a later shot we see a group of Black women dressed in white around a table holding a meeting. A sign behind the woman speaking at the head of the table reads, "Recognize our Union." After the next tracking shot of CIW (see figure 2.16), two shots that could have appeared in the opening montage, as they present women at work, are cut in. One zooms in on an Asian woman at work as a doctor with a patient, and another zooms in on a white woman parking a work truck, as the singer moves from a revised version of the chorus—"I'm alive, I'm alive, I'm alive, I'm alive, I'm alive /I didn't die"—to a new, more confrontational section of the song: "Yeah, whatcha gonna do about me, sir?/Whatcha gonna do about me?" Whether formerly imprisoned women or simply comrades, these two working women are activated as feminist agents of prison abolition. The third shot in the series extends this activation to the documentary at hand. An Indigenous woman holds a video camera, while a white woman, presumably teaching her how to film, whispers in her ear, then steps back to give her space (see figure 2.17). On the soundtrack, the singer asks, "Whatcha gonna do about someone who sees you, sir?/Whatcha gonna do about me?" The documentary has not only given voice to imprisoned women and made their plight visible; it has made the economic, social, and political structures that enable such injustice visible, too. The final moments of *We're Alive* return us to black-and-white single shots of the women inside CIW. In a more traditional documentary, their names would appear below their smiling faces. Here we are denied that much. Their individual identities are protected. Sutured into the social movement montage, the singer affirms their centrality to social justice and future freedom: "We'll be comin' from prison/We'll be comin', watch us, we'll be comin' from prison."

While *Songs* circulated through the constellations of the International Videoletters project, meeting feminist media workers and their local audiences, and *Inside Women Inside* circulated as the latest entry in the popular social movement documentary distributor Third World Newsreel's catalog, *We're Alive* played an active role in women's prison activism across California. *We're Alive* traveled with the "Women on Wheels" tour, initiating post-concert conversations about the racism of the prison-industrial complex and neoliberal carceral state and the sexism, misogyny, and homophobia that affected those incarcerated at "women's prisons" differently from those at "men's prisons." After the "Women on Wheels" concert tour, those involved in the tour's

Producing Freedom

2.15–2.17 "We're alive"/"Whatcha gonna do about someone who sees you, sir?/Whatcha gonna do about me?" in *We're Alive* (CIW Video Workshop with the Women's Film Workshop of UCLA/Joint Productions, 1974). Screen grabs. Images courtesy of UCLA Film and Television Archive.

organization—including Frances Reid (of Iris Films/NWFC), who taught video workshops at CIW, as well as the trans scholar and artist Sandy Stone—partnered with the Women's Prison Coalition to take the concerns of prisoners at CIW to the California State Capitol.[81] Together they planned a demonstration in Sacramento following a public hearing with representatives of the Department of Corrections regarding the treatment of prisoners at CIW, including the prison's creation of a behavior modification unit for women who defied authority "by exercising political leadership, openly defining [themselves] as a lesbian, or refusing in any way to passively conform to the conventional and authoritarian standards of the prison."[82] At the rally, held on March 19, 1976, in Sacramento, Holly Near, Meg Christian, Cris Williamson, and Margie Adams all performed (just as they had on tour), and Norma Stafford and Sin Soracco, both of whom had recently been released from CIW, spoke to the crowd of one thousand people, many of whom had heard about the rally as a result of having attended one of the original concerts or one of the *We're Alive* workshops afterward. Not long after the hearing and

135

the rally, which concluded with women linking arms and singing Cris Williamson's "Song of the Soul" while occupying Governor Jerry Brown's office, the Department of Corrections announced it would be closing the behavior modification unit. Leaders of the rally checked with their contacts inside CIW, who confirmed that the unit, where some of the worst abuses of power had been enacted, had been terminated and those imprisoned there had been returned to general population.[83]

This instance provides a clear example of the interconnectedness of creative cultural production and on-the-ground activism. Considering how little attention prison abolition and prisoner rights activists paid to those imprisoned at "women's prisons" even when they led rebellions like the one at Attica—as those imprisoned at CIW, Bedford Hills, and NCCCW all did around this very time—these feminist prison documentaries could themselves been seen as important activist texts, a means of circulating Black feminist knowledge production. They modeled intersectional thought, analyzing women's "rehabilitation" through incarceration as racialized and gendered violence. Many of the points made in these documentaries either had been made or would soon be made by the few famous women political prisoners or in the women's prison newsletters. But *Songs, We're Alive,* and *Inside Women Inside* circulated their ideas among a wide women's movement audience and did so through the uniquely affective qualities of 16 mm film and black-and-white video. In their exhibition, the lesbian potentiality of their fugitive freedom found met that of feminist audiences outside, and anticarceral feminism and lesbian feminism became bound in the lesbian feminist affectivity of Black feminist love politics reception.

These are not the films profiled in chapters on feminist and lesbian cinema of the 1970s. Scholarship about Newsreel largely focuses on the organization's films of the 1960s before Choy, Robeson, Maurizio, and other women of color took over the organization and made films such as *Inside Women Inside.*[84] (For another powerful film, see *To Love, Honor, and Obey,* directed by Choy and Marlene Dann in 1980; it takes on domestic violence and centralizes a Black woman imprisoned, much like Little, García, Wanrow, and Woods, for killing her abuser.) *We're Alive,* once exemplary of feminist ethnographic documentary filmmaking, was believed by feminist documentary film scholars to have been lost for decades.[85] Recently, two prints were discovered at the British Film Institute (BFI). Months after I viewed it on a flatbed in the BFI's Stephen Street basement, the UCLA Film and Television Archive printed a copy for US researchers.[86] My hope is that this chapter marks but the beginning of a return to such media's study. Nearly lost in such cases of nearly nonextant media is a history that affirms the centrality of women of color in the women's movement and its documentary media. Exhuming these documentaries, studying their production history, and taking seriously their use of form means seeing and hearing Black feminists', including Black lesbians' and Black lesbian feminists', long history of producing freedom.

raising fannish consciousness
the formation of feminist
science fiction fandom

Those of us who loved SF in spite of the fact that we never found ourselves in it loved not the achievement of the field but its potentiality.
—SUZY MCKEE CHARNAS, "Women in Science Fiction"

What do I want? That community, truly. Fandom pays too much lip
service to the idea of being a tribe of equals, friends. SF pays too much
lip service to the idea of being a literature of new ideas, soaring visions
of human potential. Let's make it true. —SUSAN WOOD, "People's
Programming"

In the first batch of letters to come in to the *Khatru* fanzine's 1975 symposium
on "Women in Science Fiction," the participating feminist science fiction
(SF) authors spoke to what drew them to the genre—namely, its potentiality. Readers long before they were writers, Suzy McKee Charnas, Vonda
McIntyre, Joanna Russ, and Kate Wilhelm wrote that, growing up in the
United States in the 1940s and '50s, they found science fiction to be "wondrous, free of the dullness and limitations [of their everyday lives]."[1] And

yet, as they aged, either the genre did not seem to mature alongside them or the glaring gaps in the exploration of "human feeling, human sexuality, and patterns of power among people" became more apparent.[2] They each took it upon themselves to, as Charnas put it, "write the SF books that they wanted so badly to read."[3] Independent of one another, each of these SF readers-turned-writers identified within the genre the potential for oppressed people to explore their realities anew or "illuminated with the brilliance of the strange."[4] Furthermore, as McIntyre wrote, they "realized its potentials for exploring the kinds of changes that [their] society [was] going through and [would] continue to go through, sociological, technological, etc."[5] In writing these stories, they converted what, following Giorgio Agamben, we might identify as the genre's generic potentiality into an existing potentiality.[6] Reading science fiction for decades had provided them with the ability to write in the genre, and their experiences living as girls and women under patriarchy offered the impetus. In writing novels such as *The Female Man* (Russ, 1975) and *Motherlines* (Charnas, 1978) and editing collections such as *Aurora: Beyond Equality* (McIntyre and Susan Janice Anderson, 1976), which included, unknown to the editors, two Alice B. Sheldon stories (James Tiptree, Jr.'s "Houston, Houston, Do You Read?" and the less well-known Raccoona Sheldon's "Your Faces, O My Sisters! Your Faces Full of Light!")—these readers-turned-writers uttered their own "I can" and collectively ushered contemporary feminist science fiction into being. Ultimately, they did so not just for themselves but for all those passionate about making life as wondrous as science fiction had led them to believe it could be.

It would seem likely that these feminist authors would find their own readership in the US women's movement.[7] Their genre stimulated unique imaginations of lesbian (im)potentiality, transporting readers to entirely other times and places, envisioning what life might be like under different societal conditions and, without promising or committing to a certain future, making the limitations of the heteropatriarchal here and now ever more apparent. However, while women's bookstores began to carry more of these authors' titles as the decade progressed and the demand grew,[8] acceptance by the feminist press and movement at large was neither organic nor immediate, due to the initial strangeness of the genre, its low cultural status, and its common affiliations with boyhood. In the *Khatru* symposium, McIntyre and Russ shared the resistance they faced from editors when trying to publish SF in the liberal feminist magazine *Ms.*, the genre being deemed "a bit too heavy-handed" and categorically of little interest to *Ms.*'s readers.[9] Many of these women's titles featured female protagonists and poignantly explored women's oppression, lesbian sexualities, and alternative social structures to patriarchy such that male-dominated SF fandom was similarly resistant, declaring titles such as Russ's *The Female Man* to be anti-male propaganda rather than science fiction.[10]

Unable to find a home in either the broader feminist culture or fandom "proper," feminist SF authors and their early readers' shared sense of potentiality led to the formation of their own counterpublic: feminist SF fandom. At this same time, feminist media workers were building a feminist media network among local feminist communities, wherein individual spectators' felt sense that gendered and sexual life would someday be substantially different gained force and momentum. In feminist SF fandom, the potential of a future beyond compulsory heterosexuality in which society would be entirely reconfigured took a more concrete shape as a result of feminist fans reading and congregating around the same work. Significantly, the connections forged among feminist SF fans of disparate geographies, backgrounds, and politics were largely neither virtual nor fleeting. Certainly, individuals dipped in and out of feminist SF fandom, but the counterpublic was sustained through the regular circulation of fanzines (which was soon supplemented by feminist SF conventions and feminist spaces at more general conventions and, eventually, online activity). In the pages of these fanzines, as well as those of the science fiction literature they discussed, lesbian potentiality fused with that of the genre as a whole, collective visions of feminist futures often centering lesbian existence. Much like the lesbian impotentiality of "Houston, Houston, Do You Read?" in which, over the generations, Earth's humans as lesbian clones come to resemble 1970s lesbians less and less, feminist SF fandom itself evolved, renewing and revising itself time and again so that now it both is and is not what it once was.

In this chapter I offer a history of the formation of feminist SF fandom in the second half of the 1970s and argue that its unusual development has enabled the counterpublic to adapt over the years. I begin by detailing the unique form of feminist consciousness-raising (CR) that materialized across and between the letters of comment, book reviews, and fan art that appeared in *Khatru*, *The Witch and the Chameleon*, and *Janus* fanzines. Most of the chapter then focuses on how feminist SF fans, quite unlike many SF fans before them, did not presume a community but instead questioned, critiqued, and parodied the processes of community formation to allow, ironically, feminist SF fandom's institutionalization, which came in 1977 with the foundation of the first feminist SF convention, WisCon. Integral here were feminist authors' openness to accountability and vulnerability when thinking through differences and fans' self-reflexive and citational sense of humor. This self-activity of the counterpublic is still very much underway. Feminist SF fandom is likely here to stay, but its institutions (including, as we see in the next chapter, its accolades) could disappear. For now they do not, instead adapting through the activities of its multigenerational participants. I conclude with an analysis of policies and programming at recent WisCons to demonstrate how feminist fan practices have evolved, making WisCon a rare 1970s feminist cultural institution to navigate decades of financial and ideological struggles and feminist SF fandom a precious site of continued intergenerational feminist collaboration and comradery.[11]

Feminist SF Fandom as Counterpublic and Fannish Consciousness-raising

The authors and fans that formed feminist SF fandom in the mid-1970s brought together the knowledges and skills they had gained from their varied experiences with science fiction fandom, feminist activism, and feminist theory. Like other fans, they produced fanzines, held club meetings, and organized their own convention. However, within these spaces they also asked questions about the desirability of various futures or technologies for women, why women's well-being in these futures so often got sacrificed for that of the humanity as a whole, and what feminist science fiction might offer in return. In their fanzines and at WisCon, then, feminist fans read intertextually across the early entries in feminist SF and the genre more generally, as well as between these bodies of literature, feminist theory, and contemporary political events. They drew on their growing familiarity with various forms of feminist critique to revisit their favorite novels from childhood and write retrospective feminist reviews.[12] In their fanzine editorials they theorized the kind of philosophical investigation the genre itself offered various political subjects.[13] And they illustrated the covers of their fanzines with fantastical drawings of fairies, women embracing, and their own imaginations rising from their bodies as they drew at their desks (see figures 3.1–3.4). In 1978, when Harlan Ellison was invited to Arizona as the World Science Fiction Convention (or WorldCon) Guest of Honor, it was to a number of these feminist fans and authors that the esteemed author turned for advice as to whether he should attend, the state having yet to ratify the equal rights amendment.[14] In the end, he did, but he camped, brought his own food, and encouraged others to "walk the walk [of SF] and not just talk the talk" and join him in this partial boycott.[15]

3.1 Amanda Bankier, cover illustration, *The Witch and the Chameleon* 1, 1974.

the WITCH and the CHAMELEON

2
november
1974

3.2 Elizabeth Mordue, cover illustration, *The Witch and the Chameleon* 2, 1974.

3.3 Jeanne Gomoll, cover illustration, *Janus* 6, 1976.

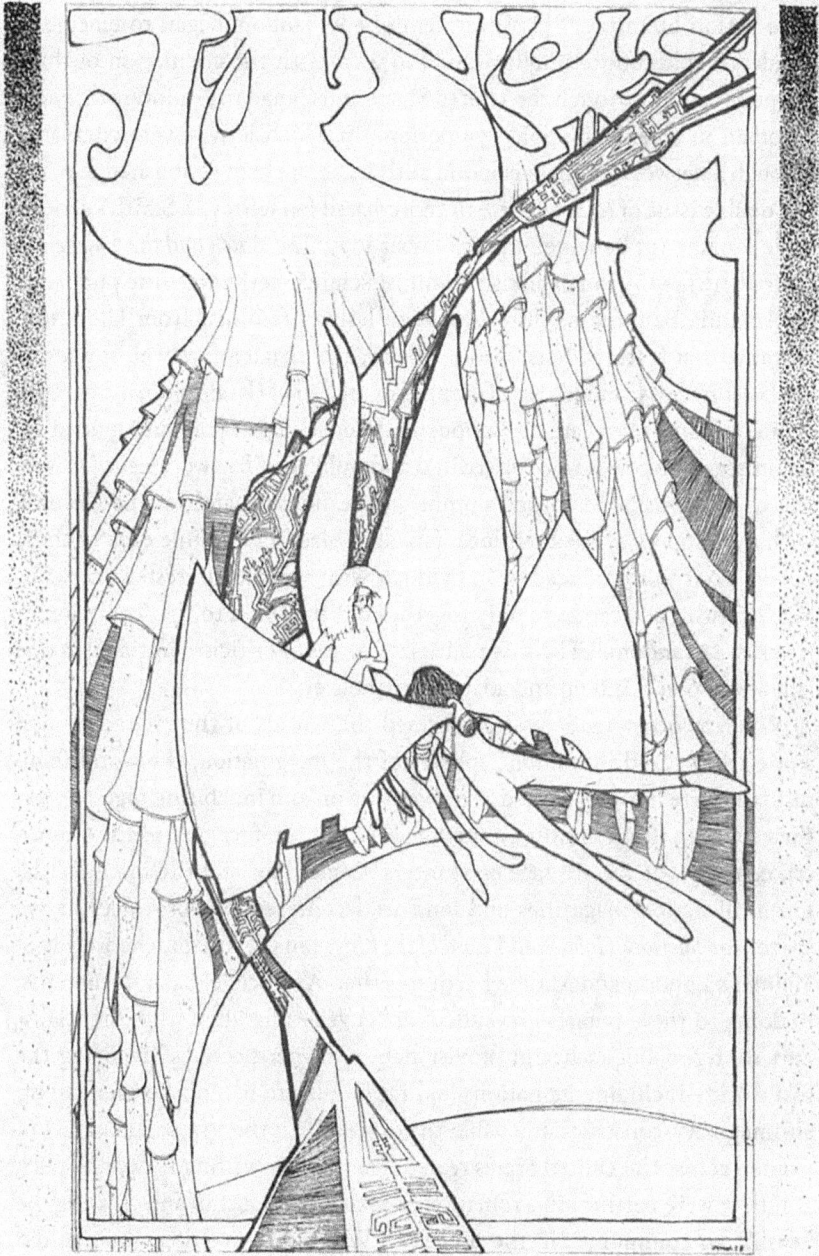

3.4 Olav Martin Kvern, cover illustration, *Janus* 14, 1978–79.

Feminism has a long history as an ideology or philosophy within science fiction literature.[16] However, feminist SF fandom began to emerge as an identifiable counterpublic around 1974-75 with the circulation of three fan publications through the United States and Canada: the aforementioned "Women in Science Fiction" symposium, in which letters were circulated through a network of science fiction authors before being published in a special double issue of *Khatru*, the Baltimore-based fan Jeffrey D. Smith's general topic fanzine (or genzine), in November 1975; *The Witch and the Chameleon* (*WatCh* [1974–76]), an explicitly feminist science fiction fanzine published by Amanda Bankier, a white Canadian lesbian feminist from Hamilton, Ontario, that featured fans' stories, poems, and visual art, as well as editorials, book reviews, and letters of comment; and *Janus* (later *Aurora* [1975-90]), a genzine and semi-sercon (serious and constructive) fanzine guided by feminist perspectives that was edited and published by two recent University of Wisconsin, Madison, alumni, Janice Bogstad and Jeanne Gomoll, with the support of the their local fan club, MadSTF.[17] While each of these publications was produced by individuals with specific interests in conjoining feminism and fandom, only together did they lead to the formation of feminist SF fandom.[18] The new politicized forms of criticism initiated in one zine were soon taken up and adapted by another.

Whereas other fandoms transformed the worlds of the characters and stories they loved into public spheres of the imagination, the world feminist fans were most interested in elaborating on and inhabiting together was their own: that of feminist SF fandom. During the first half of the twentieth century, the face-to-face encounters of fan clubs and the more textual forum of fiction magazines and fanzines letters sections provided playful spaces for *Sherlock Holmes* and *Lord of the Rings* fans to inhabit the worlds of Holmes's London and Middle Earth together. As Michael Saler documents, in doing so these publics grew adept at "envisioning life not in essentialist 'just so' terms but rather in provisional, 'as if' perspectives," realizing the real world—including its nations and races—also to be, to a certain extent, an imaginary construct amenable to revision.[19] In the 1970s, thousands of women across the United States revised *Star Trek* by writing Kirk and Spock as if they were partners in a romantic or sexual relationship and creating the "slash" fan community in the process.[20] While many of these women did not identify as feminists, Constance Penley and Henry Jenkins's early fan studies accounts of Kirk/Spock (K/S) draw on the comments of feminist SF authors to support their claims for the necessity of these women's alternative spaces; describe feminist SF authors as having opened up the genre for more feminine forms of writing; and lift up media fans' writing by suggesting that one of these feminist SF authors "dabbled in slash writing."[21] However, there is little room in Penley and Jenkins's K/S studies for these feminist SF authors' own fandom. Feminist SF fanzines, by contrast, carved out the space to celebrate and analyze the worlds of feminist science fiction, and through the public circulation of their fanzines they also envisioned and created the world of feminist SF fandom. Each of their reviews, editorials, letters of comment, and works of fan art contributed to the collective building of a counterpublic—"a multigeneric lifeworld organized not just by a relational axis of utterance and response but by potentially infinite axes of citation and characterization."[22] This world was not just that of a concrete or quantifiable audience (say, the few hundred fans who subscribed to their fanzines), but that of the partially imaginary world of feminist SF fandom, which addressing these feminist fans and authors brought into being.[23]

Feminist SF fandom marked itself off from not only the general public of the "mundane world," as other fandoms did, but also the dominant public of mainstream literary science fiction fandom.[24] As the SF fan Susan Wood pointed out in a guest editorial for *Janus* published 1978, in the 1960s the best a "femme fan" could do was be deemed an "honorary man."[25] Otherwise, she was considered a "sex object" and thought to have little to contribute on the subject at hand.[26] This was expressed in spaces in which participants, as she put it, more often than not considered themselves "enlightened and aware."[27] Male fans' self-identified progressiveness was undoubtedly a result of socialist and antiracist traditions in US fandom.[28] Readers of American science fiction pulp magazines in the 1940s were "male and female, professional and working class, old and young, well off and impoverished," and the diverse perspectives of these readers, Saler writes, "forced [public-sphere] participants to contend with unpalatable interpretations and to provide justifications for self-evident views."[29] Despite (or, perhaps, because of) this history and its security in 1960s and '70s fans' imaginations, mainstream literary SF fandom, like other dominant publics, misrecognized the universality of its address. Thus, when Smith chose to address the "Women in Science Fiction" participants as "Dear People," the Black science fiction author Samuel R. Delany called him out for obfuscating the dynamics of this unprecedented symposium on women in science fiction. (Delany, now well known as a queer author of nonfiction as well as fiction, at this time was still closeted to most in SF and married to the poet Marilyn Hacker, who would soon have a romance with Russ and come out as a lesbian.[30]) However well intended, Smith, as a male fan, was soliciting an education on feminism and science fiction (for himself but also, arguably, for the members of mainstream literary SF fandom who read his genzine) from the world's most esteemed female SF authors.[31] Writing from one man to another, Delany took this nominally inclusive address as an opportunity to outline sexism in the United States as he saw it, telling Smith, "Today, there simply is no happy reconciliation possible. We (who?) can't come on like one big happy family who for our (whose is that again?) purposes have solved it all already and face one another as 'people.' Even for this Symposium. We have to agree from the start that the situation is horrendous."[32]

As seen in moments such as these, feminist SF fandom, in contrast to mainstream literary SF fandom, became a space of circulation in which it was "hoped that the poesis of scene making [would] be transformative, not replicative merely."[33] Initially, the desired transformation for feminist SF fans and authors was the creation of fan spaces that were more hospitable to women. Symposiums such as Smith's and similar convention panels, such as the "Women and Science Fiction" panel organized by Susan Wood at the MidAmeriCon in Kansas City in 1976, which overflowed its room (causing *WatCh*'s editor, Amanda Bankier, and *Janus*'s editors, Janice Bogstad and Jeanne Gomoll, to meet), were among these early sites.[34] Before long, thanks to these feminist fans' reviews and critical essays, panels, and insistence on safe spaces for women at cons, feminist SF fandom began to challenge the genre and its writers to become as antisexist, antiracist, and antihomophobic as they already claimed to be. Ultimately, feminist SF fandom became a space in which to theorize social transformation. The feminist potentiality of science fiction, so coherently articulated by feminist SF authors in the 1975 *Khatru* symposium's opening pages, led to a reimagining not only of the genre but also of fandom. They developed a fannish form of feminist CR that brought together intertextual readings of science fiction and feminist theory; the idioms, styles, citations, and lexicons of fandom and feminism; and a critical approach to the social practices of each.

Inspired by the civil rights tradition of "telling it like it is," radical feminists developed consciousness-raising in the early 1970s to construct theories about gender and women's oppression and develop political action from personal experience.[35] By talking about their lives with one another, women in CR groups around the country began to discover that many of their problems were not solely their own. Other women had also experienced sexual assault, domestic violence, employment and legal discrimination, and everyday forms of sexism and misogyny, and these shared experiences would come to serve as the basis for demanding social change. For those imprisoned in "women's prisons" and cut off from the broader women's movement, as seen in chapter 2, feminist-led prison workshops provided rare opportunities to practice CR, and the films made in feminist media workshops often sought to connect the consciousness-raising being done inside and outside of prison. For feminist SF fans, the fanzines became a place in which they could do similar work. As Bogstad wrote in one of her editorials for *Janus*: "Fandom provides an outlet for developing ideas that I could not express in any other [fan] forum. As my co-editor, Jeanne Gomoll, so aptly put it when we [*Janus*] were criticized for militant feminism and political stances in some editorials, at this point we are not so much trying to change other people's minds with our writing as we are trying to develop our own consciousness."[36] Bogstad explained that fanzines, with their quick publishing cycle (*Janus* aimed for four issues each year), were great for developing one's consciousness, as "one must formulate ideas and one must deal with almost immediate feedback and criticism."[37] Both the authors who had their work reviewed and the fans who wrote reviews and other essays received this feedback, and together they explored their ideas for the genre, women's futures, and alternative societies. In discussing these subjects and how they got to their current formulations of them, they drew on their experiences and, like women in CR groups, often found that they had much in common. Rather than taking place in gatherings of ten or twenty and in the relative privacy of a women's center or "women's prison" workshop, this fannish CR developed across the pages of fanzines, each issue of which went out to hundreds of subscribers and then often circulated among their friends and local fan clubs.[38]

Consciousness-raising garnered criticism within the US women's movement from the start, including from those who questioned centralizing personal experience in the development of feminist theory.[39] And yet, CR had lasting effects on feminist, queer, and antiracist communities that lasted beyond the 1970s, as these communities' participants continued to insist on the impossibility of political action without personal interaction. As Black feminism and women of color feminism, more broadly, gained increasing prominence with a number of key publications in the early 1980s, their leaders championed CR as integral to confronting racism in the women's movement. In the essay "Face-to-Face, Day-to-Day—Racism CR," published in *All the Women Are White, All the Blacks Are Men, But Some of Us Are Brave: Black Women's Studies*, Tia Cross, Freada Klein, Barbara Smith, and Beverly Smith write, "The CR format encourages personal sharing, risk-taking, and involvement, which are essential for getting at how each of us is racist in a daily way; and it encourages the 'personal' change that makes political transformation and action possible."[40] Ten years later, after the sex wars of the 1980s, when butch and femme lesbians called for the working through of the lingering form of homophobia within feminist communities directed at those who for whom gendered desire was central to their experiences of lesbian sex, Amber Hollibaugh and Cherríe Moraga encouraged women to form CR groups:

> We believe that women must create sexual theory in the same way we created feminist theory. We need to simply get together in places where people agree to suspend their sexual values, so that all of us can feel free to say what we do sexually or want to do or have done to us. We do have fear of using feelings as theory. We do not mean to imply that feelings are everything. They can, however, be used as the beginning to form a movement which can *politically* deal with sexuality in a broad-based, cross-cultural way.[41]

For these women of color and butch and femme lesbians in the 1980s (all of whom were active participants in 1970s feminist communities), CR was an integral part of an ongoing process of navigating relations within feminism. Similarly, as feminist SF fandom began to theorize social transformation through science fiction, its fans and authors had to move beyond their shared experiences of oppression and work through their differences. How authors approached the writing of women in science fiction and how readers engaged with their choices depended in large part on their gender, age, race, class, and sexuality, as well as their varied relations to SF publishing and fandom. These cultural factors needed to be acknowledged so that the ideas developed in their approaches to the genre and its fandom's feminist theorizing could be explored as more than a matter of personal preference.

Accountability in Early Feminist SF Fandom

The centrality of accountability in feminist SF fandom is in many ways indebted to the fact that it was never completely separatist. While, like lesbian separatists, feminist SF fans were invested in creating spaces, physically and in print, where women were safe to explore ideas and practices counter to those of mainstream fandom, men (and likely people of many genders) were part of the fandom from the start. As a result, the fandom had to negotiate male comrades' participation, often demanding self-reflection that got them thinking beyond their good intentions. This is perhaps best exemplified by the "Women in Science Fiction" symposium, organized by Smith. Between October 1974 and May 1975, Smith organized a symposium in which twelve US-based science fiction writers and fans corresponded about women characters, authors, and fans through letters. Smith then published an edited collection of the symposium's 168 pages in November 1975 in a special double issue of his fanzine *Khatru*. The symposium included nine women (Suzy McKee Charnas, Virginia Kidd, Ursula K. Le Guin, Vonda N. McIntyre, Raylyn Moore, Joanna Russ, Luise White, Kate Wilhelm, and Chelsea Quinn Yarbro) and three men (Samuel R. Delany, Jeffrey D. Smith, and James Tiptree, Jr., who had yet to be outed as Alice B. Sheldon and very much presented through writing as a man). The symposium soon became divided along gender lines. More specifically, many of the women quickly became tired of the men's tendency to dominate the conversation, as they often wrote long and presumptuous letters about matters that they arguably knew less about than the women did. Eventually, the symposium became a reflection on its own processes, tackling the very topic of one's accountability to others in fandom and how this might vary based on identity and its attendant forms of knowledge and experience. Importantly, these conflicts and their resolutions were not voiced by and for just a few passionate individuals; they were enacted for circulation among a broader public. Tracking the flow of the symposium's negotiations reveals an early contestation of what feminist SF fandom as a counterpublic might become—the range of topics up for conversation, who would participate, how they ought to do so, and how the goals of such an enterprise could evolve.

The event that prompted the first substantial conflict was the arrival of James Tiptree, Jr.'s first letter, which offers up theories of what constitutes sexual difference, how sexual difference is gendered by a society invested in hierarchies, and how we might rethink "men" and "women" and reorganize society according to the patterns they actually present. Tiptree himself says he sees one pattern as pathological and ultimately destructive and a second as empathic and mothering. Tiptree initially asks, "What the hell are 'sexes' and how many and which are there?"[42] He then answers himself, "As a starter, let's clear away one dire fallacy. DOWN WITH YIN-AND-YANG THINKING!"[43] However, before long he replaces "women" with "mothers," by which he sometimes means those who attend to child raising and at other times those who provide other kinds of caregiving or leadership, arguing that it is these people who provide the answers to the aggression and violence of others. In so doing, Tiptree makes the now pointed claim that "individual women can quite easily be, in effect, males" and asks, "How soon, O Lord, can men learn to be mothers?"[44] The answer to this, he concludes rather dramatically, could determine the fate of humanity. He writes this very much as the SF author he is, telling the others that these are the thoughts that he is

151

currently working through in his story for McIntyre's *Aurora: Beyond Equality* anthology (i.e., "Houston, Houston, Do You Read?").[45]

Despite making a clear attempt to reframe gender in a feminist fashion and open up the meaning of the sign "mother," Tiptree quickly became a target of critique for the other symposium participants; his ideas were read less as a feminist resignification of gender than as a man's idealized, biologically deterministic account of present-day genders.[46] Responding, McIntyre exclaims, "Ah, Tip, you are the last person in the world I would expect to hand me the Baboon Theory of Human Behavior."[47] Russ challenges Tiptree to think beyond his new but nonetheless binary view of gender, writing that she believes science fiction ought to be a genre in which such dichotomies can disappear: "Out in space there is no up or down, no day or night, and in the point of view space can give us, I think there is no 'opposite' sex—what a word! Opposite what? The Eternal Feminine and Masculine become the poetic fancies of a weakly dimorphic species trying to imitate every other species in a vain search for what is 'natural.'"[48] Russ tells the symposium that she has already "rebutted Tiptree for this (oh, Tip, really! *Really!*) in private."[49] Turning to symposium readers, Russ recommends that any others similarly inclined to naturalize gendered differences read her attached feminist reading list, which included Shulamith Firestone's *The Dialectic of Sex*, Kate Millett's *Sexual Politics*, and Jill Johnston's *Lesbian Nation*.[50] Russ makes the important point that well-intentioned men would better support women if they saved such pontifications of gender theory until after they have read the feminist literature on the subject. The private correspondence between Tiptree and Russ from this time suggests that Tiptree took Russ up on her recommendations, as he would often write to Russ about feminist theory he was reading,[51] but for the rest of the symposium Tiptree publicly played the part of the deferring male, exclaiming at one point, "I feel about as relevant as a cuckoo-clock in eternity."[52]

While Delany would receive praise for his proposed parameters for writing women, his letters, too, soon incurred criticism. Across his letters, Delany models a kind of male feminist comradery for the other male contributors and male readers, reflecting on his own relationship to the subject matter at hand and sharing insights into the steps he has taken to write women differently.[53] In one long letter, Delany outlines the four parameters he and Marilyn Hacker came up with for writing female characters in literature. First, female characters must be shown performing purposeful actions that further the plot, that define them, and that imply a life beyond the limit of the fiction. Second, the characters must be shown having strong economic anchors to the world. Third, developing strong positive relations with other female characters must be central to the plot. And, fourth, whether or not they have romantic interests, female characters must also have a non-romantic problem that they try to solve. Despite having marked such useful parameters for himself, Delany concludes by writing that he is perpetually slipping up on them, often veering toward the inadequate "super-woman" solution, which "allows the emblems of success to women characters, at the price of those fictional necessities, change and growth."[54] In offering this impressive synthesis of genre and gender and reflecting on his own practices as a male author, Delany attests to the fact that feminist comradery does not begin and end with declarations of good intentions but is instead a matter of sustained self-critique and practice.

As many of his fellow symposium participants comment, letters such as this one were brilliant, insightful, and much appreciated. However, they were also frequent and many times longer than anyone else's and soon came to overwhelm the first half of the symposium, again centering a man's voice in the discussion of feminism. As Russ points out, Delany was able to write so intensely at great length precisely because sexism did not impede him—"He [did] not have to live the problem all the time and [could] therefore gather his energies for one great analytic attack."[55] Furthermore, his letters are made up of stories in which he relates learning about gender inequality by way of Hacker and her struggles. Thus, Delany's letters share an affinity with Smith's own, which are also full of "my wife" stories. After a number of such letters, Russ, McIntyre, and the others asked Delany and Smith to stop filling the symposium with tales of their commendable acts as romantic male partners of women so the "Women in Science Fiction" symposium could take up the concerns of women in science fiction.[56]

The discussion deepened substantially after this confrontation. With Tiptree, Delany, and Smith participating in a more supportive capacity, the group was able to discuss such topics as how to get one's feminist SF to women's communities around the globe; the importance of expressing and then working through one's anger and rage; the desirability of a utopian fiction in which not one woman but all women could be superhuman; the importance of empowering one another in order to survive; the difference between power and authority and their relevance to freedom; and whether women should be fighting for freedom, not just from men, but also from corporations and governments, making revolution and complete social transformation the actual goal of feminism. With this refocusing of the conversation away from men's experiences of women's oppression, conflict did not

153

dissipate but became more productive. The discussion of the role of violence in revolution (whether it signifies a failed revolution; whether it is the right of those who have experienced centuries of violence themselves; or whether its expression in art and literature is a necessary expression of anger) became especially heated among Russ, Yarbro, and White. In such cases, the women often also commented on their different attitudes toward these issues and reflect on whether or not they might be the results of generational or sexuality- or class-based differences.[57] When Yarbro expresses seeing sexuality as something more personal and less relevant to such discussions, Russ explains, "Who you sleep with matters and does significantly change your public behavior . . . because you are treated differently by most people on account of who you sleep with and sometimes (cross my heart) in what position. . . . It's the usual reverse-curse; it would not matter to you if it did not matter to them but because it matters to them it does matter to you."[58] In these cases, conversation builds, drawing on personal insights in the positing of actual theories of oppression, resistance, and their imagination in literature.

Any possible insights Delany might have had about empowerment, freedom, and fiction as a Black queer man, however, were nearly completely overlooked. At one point, Delany dismisses racism as a less pressing concern in everyday life than sexism: "As a black American, I would say that once a month on the average I have to endure some situation of overt racism. . . . As an owner of a radio and enjoyer of pop music, as a stroller in the streets, as a married man with a daughter, I cannot go for an hour without observing some emblem of overt and rampant sexism—mine or someone else's."[59] Delany offers a comparative perspective on manifestations of sexism and racism that only he, as the sole Black man and father in the symposium, can. But his comment also suggests an acceptance of the unspoken demarcation of the topic of discussion at hand—feminism, as a women's cause—such that a more thorough discussion of race on his part, as a Black male feminist, would be inappropriate. The potential for cross-coalitional or intersectional theorizing was lost.

In fact, whenever race and racism were discussed across the symposium, they were brought forward to draw analogies between racism and sexism. For example, Russ at one point discusses her own racism and how it (and that of any white person) differs from the reactive racism of, say, Muhammad Ali, essentially debunking claims of what conservatives today call "reverse racism."[60] She also references both the Black Power Movement and Black South Africans as influential to her consideration of the necessity of violence in rebellions.[61] In doing so, she briefly models antiracist comradery for feminist SF fandom and offers Black radicalism as a potential referent for the counterpublic. Ultimately, however, her references are intended to support the larger point she is making about systemic sexism and the difference between women's and men's killing fantasies in science fiction, the latter of which are motivated by the desire for control and the former by the desire for freedom.[62] Her analysis of race supports her analysis of gender. In cases such as this, the symposium participants demonstrated a defining characteristic of white 1970s feminisms, as articulated by bell hooks in *Ain't I a Woman* (1981): a view of the world as made up of Black people and women but never Black women.[63]

This early symposium on women in science fiction thus delineated a wide range of topics that might be suitable for discussion in feminist SF fandom and, in doing so, began to enact the feminist SF fan world. The topics these authors and fans discussed expanded those typical of mainstream fandom, which was more likely to keep its discussion to literature itself rather than any given novel's or short story's ramifications for society. The symposium also offered its readers an improvised model of a fannish CR process through which one might challenge presumptions of male authority in fan discourse. Unlike many other 1970s feminist publics, feminist SF fandom was open to male feminists' participation and thus was able to incorporate the insights of men while also demanding accountability from well-intentioned men. Male feminists were asked to recognize the limits of their knowledge in relation to others, to educate themselves on subjects that they did not know much about, and to acknowledge their own sexism and strategize as to what to do about it, because actions were declared more important than intentions. It was a large project not implemented without its own limitations. Still, the underlying principle of accountability would adapt with feminist SF fandom over time. Feminist fandom could not change, however, without addressing its participants' feelings of vulnerability.

Vulnerability in Early Feminist SF Fandom

Just before the start of the *Khatru* symposium, Canadian lesbian feminist Amanda Bankier began publishing *The Witch and the Chameleon*. The inaugural issue, published in August 1974, was only eighteen pages long, and Bankier wrote all but one of the entries. Soon the fanzine offered a number of substantial contributions from other fans and authors, including major feminist SF authors, who wrote in both as authors of certain texts and as

155

feminist fans in this burgeoning feminist SF counterpublic. Bankier's article "Women in the Fiction of Andre Norton," in the first issue, provoked a letter of comment from the senior author, and Vonda McIntyre's review of Marion Zimmer Bradley's *Darkover Landfall*, in the second issue, would, in turn, solicit a response from Bradley. Together, these two contributions generated a discourse about authorship and politics that would go on to dominate much of the zine's short run. In these series of reviews and letters of comment (LOCs) across *WatCh*, science fiction authors and fans together theorized authors' accountability both to their fans and to the historical context in which they write. Fans raised the consciousness of the established SF authors they addressed (as well as that of fanzine readers), challenging them to examine their assumptions about gender, sexuality, race, and publishing practices. For Norton and Bradley, two rare women of an older generation who had been writing successfully in the industry for decades,[64] self-reflection on a public scale came with a great sense of vulnerability, as they exposed their logics and reasoning to the critique of their readers and risked further appraisal. This sort of engagement with one's reading public was not a totally foreign experience in fandom.[65] But here, such contentious encounters provided invaluable opportunities for feminist fans and authors to think together about what futures they write and read and why.

Bankier began *WatCh* with a long essay on Norton's fiction because of the author's great influence on her (and, likely, other girls who read her young adult science fiction and fantasy [SF&F]) growing up. "For a long time before concern over sexism in SF became wide-spread," Bankier writes, "Andre Norton had been quietly providing us with strong female characters, and exploring the woman's side of sexist societies."[66] In particular, Bankier praises Norton's unique adeptness at writing female friendships. However, looking back on these formative texts, Bankier is critical of how often these women give up their friendships for male partners with whom they have little in common. Bankier argues, "The friendships are all actually or potentially romantic in character," and elaborates, "I can't help feeling that [Norton] could if she wished deal effectively with women who are forced to choose their integrity over companionship or who find friendship from several people or from another woman. At the least I think the stories would benefit if the true difficulty of finding and maintaining a relationship of equals was at least hinted at."[67] In reading these friendships as ostensibly, or "potentially," lesbian and making the argument that this would make more sense and be of greater emotional fulfillment for the characters, Bankier performs a retrospective lesbian feminist reading of a cherished girlhood oeuvre.

In writing such an essay, she offered *WatCh* readers an example of how feminist SF fan criticism might celebrate women's contributions to the genre while also advocating for female fans' desires and offering suggestions for more capacious visions for women and their futures.

The primary function of Norton's response, published in the second issue, is to quell the possibility of such a lesbian reading. In the letter, Norton writes that, as an author, she is not trying to "prove any sort of point, but rather to amuse the reader."[68] Neglecting the fact that Bankier wrote her essays as an ardent reader and fan, Norton insists that she writes endings in which the female protagonists find male partners because "the reader wants them."[69] In making such an argument, Norton tries to render the possibility that Bankier has suggested an impossibility while demonstrating that it is a possibility that must nonetheless be refuted. The second argument she makes is that such possibilities are delineated by a culture for which she cannot be held responsible but to which she must answer. Vaguely alluding to the women's movement and the growing perception of lesbian feminists as a threat to patriarchy, Norton explains that considering "conditions as they are nowadays," she "would not dare write a story with strong friendship between two women of this type."[70] She explains that she is financially dependent on selling her hardcover editions to libraries, so she "must be most careful that no one read into any book of [hers] a suggestion which [she] did not in least intend, but which could be inferred."[71] Excusing herself of any responsibility to write women's relationships otherwise, Norton concludes, "I must work within a certain frame of reference and there are limits laid upon plotting under those circumstances."[72] In less than one page, then, Norton rejects the possibility that readers might want more than what she gives them in terms of romance, suggesting that lesbian fans are no fans at all, while also absolving herself of the responsibility to even entertain such possibilities by blaming the conservative institutions that publish and circulate her work to a general public, implying that lesbians may be fans, but they are not the fans with power, so she cannot afford to think of them. Doing so reveals how vulnerable such a lesbian review (even in a new, small feminist fanzine) could make an established female SF author feel at this time. Considering this, Norton's letter reads as indicative of a desire on her part to engage but also her inability to think beyond the threat of what a more meaningful engagement might mean for her fiction's continued circulation.

Norton's letter opened the doors for readers and contributors to discuss homophobia, sexism, and SF publishing. Russ, in a letter anticipating Adrienne Rich's "Compulsory Heterosexuality and Lesbian Existence" (1980), wrote in to offer the thesis that the taboo is less about homosexuality per se, as Norton implies, than friendship between women.[73] Russ claims that in literature women can never be friends, only rivals, and they instead usually exist only in relation to male friends, colleagues, and romantic interests. She elaborates, "In fact, the taboo makes sure not that homosexuality will be absent from fiction, but that solidarity will never be shown. . . . Somebody is afraid we will get together and—perhaps?—start actually talking to each other."[74] To this, Bankier offers an editorial comment, which she published immediately after Russ's letter, affirming Russ's point: "Anyone who still doubts that societal sanctions against lesbianism are a form of social control over all women might consider just what forms of behavior are considered 'tainted': independence, aggressiveness, competence, free association with other women."[75] However, Bankier also amends Russ to challenge what she considers explicitly homophobic concerns suggested by Norton's letter, anticipating another of Rich's arguments about straight feminists' persistent naturalizing of heterosexuality in the face of conflicting evidence of its enforcement: "The absurdity of the usual rationale for keeping children's books 'pure' is monumental: apparently, although homosexuality is 'unnatural' and 'sick' in the eyes of the censors, it is also attractive that the slightest hint of its possibility will immediately 'pervert' children in the face of all their years of programming for (and of the supposed naturalness of) heterosexuality."[76] Norton did not publicly respond to these critiques. Still, this brief encounter reveals the threat feminist SF fan criticism and its close consort, lesbian potentiality, posed, including to those few women SF authors who had made it in the male world of science fiction publishing.

McIntyre's review of Bradley's *Darkover Landfall* initiated a similar intergenerational conflict, but it ended up being more acrimonious, much longer, and inspiring of a surprise lesbian reveal. In her review, McIntyre takes issue with Bradley's treatment of her female characters—most notably, forcing her protagonist, Camilla del Rey, to get pregnant and preventing her from having an abortion, despite her clear wish to do so. In so doing, McIntyre claims, the novel is a polemic directed at the women's movement.[77] It is not just that Bradley "shows that she deeply distrusts and dislikes the feminist movement" but that she "shows that her distrust and hatred are based on profound misunderstandings and misinterpretation."[78] McIntyre explains her conclusions through an analysis of the novel that highlights its claims to be set in a future in which men and women have achieved equality while nonetheless representing men dictating women's lives and bodies and the two sexes' grossly uneven expectations when it comes to parenting. In one of her examples, McIntyre quotes the male physician, who dismisses Camilla's request for an abortion by saying such measures were originated by the Women's Liberation Movement of the twentieth century, which he describes as "a pathological reaction to overpopulation and overcrowding."[79] He tells her that, for this reason, there is no need to worry and by the time her baby comes she will "probably have normal hormones too, and make a good mother."[80] Responding to these gross mischaracterizations of the women's movement, McIntyre uses her review of the novel to foster a more accurate knowledge of feminism within fandom.

Bradley, unaccustomed to this form of feminist SF criticism, took McIntyre's critique as a "personal attack" and, like Norton, wrote WatCh an LOC in defense of herself and her novel.[81] Bradley writes that if she could not be objective about a book, as McIntyre claimed about her own, she would not have reviewed it. Her main contention, however, is that any feminist or antifeminist statements made by characters were the characters' own and not necessarily hers, too. She explains, "If I had the time, I could go through my copy of Darkover Landfall and pick out statements made by the various characters which would telegraph to other readers, sensitive on other points, that I am homosexual, an anarchist, a technocrat . . . or any number of other things which I am not. I attempted deliberately to give the book some counterweight by having the nicer people in the book committed to a view I found repugnant."[82] She claims to be especially surprised by feminist fans' attacks on Darkover Landfall, as it has been celebrated by feminist groups for handling women as "individuals," rather than as "sex objects."[83] She concludes by naming Dorothy L. Sayers's "Are Women Human?" as a guiding influence on her "private opinions about feminism and women in science fiction."[84] Rather than engaging with McIntyre's critique, which was less about the words of a single character than the sexist ideology of her supposedly equal society, Bradley tried to debunk what she perceived as a personal attack.

Continuing her practice of candid critical feminist commentary, Bankier published Bradley's letter with an editorial response that questioned the author's self-proclaimed innocence and challenged her to think more critically about her knowledge of feminism. Bankier quotes Bradley quite contradictorily describing Darkover Landfall in another zine as taking "a few scathing snarls at Women's Lib."[85] She also points out that the Sayers essay Bradley cited was written in 1940 and had been out of print for years, making it very much out of date with the contemporary women's movement.[86] In so doing,

Bankier, as fan editor, linked her knowledge of fandom with her knowledge of feminism, performing a sort of belonging to both camps, connecting their discursive practices, and validating McIntyre's hybrid critique.

Readers joined the conversation in their LOCs, and in the next issue Russ wrote a long letter, demonstrating for Bradley and *WatCh* readers exactly how the novel iterates some of patriarchy's greatest lies about women, their desires, and their capabilities in contrast to men. Drawing on the fan tradition of demanding that authors "uphold the principles of rational analysis and extrapolation from known scientific fact" when writing their imaginary worlds,[87] Russ points out that Darkover's higher gravitational pull would in reality not only adversely affect the female population (leading to low birthrates and thus the overly precious treatment of the women who do get pregnant) but the male circulatory system and everyone's spines, as well, consequences left unexplored by Bradley. She explains that what makes *Darkover Landfall* antifeminist is that it is "yet another story of Woman-as-loser (because of her biology)," a story that many feminists are sick of reading.[88] This is particularly relevant, considering that Bradley denies her protagonist agency over her own uterus when a primary point of advocacy for the women's movement is women's reproductive rights. Russ contends that Bradley's argument that a critic ought to be objective is a common line used in science fiction criticism to dismiss authors' social and political commentary. Anticipating the critical reception *The Female Man* would receive the following year, Russ concludes by stating that if she had written a novel like *Darkover Landfall*, but with the sexes switched, it would undoubtedly be considered a polemic, making the case that science fiction is political not only when it is written by feminists but whenever it is written, as it engages with contemporary issues, whether intentionally political or not.

In this same issue, Bankier published a second letter from Bradley that is very different from the first in terms of both tone and content and includes the author's coming out as a "bisexual, and probably, more honestly, an offbeat lesbian who simply manages to form occasional strong attachments to men."[89] The letter reads as almost apologetic, as the author comes clean about her relative lack of experience with the women's movement. Woven between defensive statements appear intensely autobiographical reflections that, much in the vein of feminist consciousness-raising, attest to the contradictions she is currently working through as a rare established female author in science fiction, as well as a bisexual/lesbian and politically isolated woman in a heterosexual marriage. Bradley regularly uses "private" and "personal" to describe authorial sentiments or beliefs while also recognizing that her fiction, which correlates to these more private ideas, has significant public ramifications. In direct contrast to Norton's engagement with the issue of lesbian representation, Bradley, unprovoked, admits to holding back when it came to writing a romantic relationship between two female protagonists: "In my most recent [Darkover] book [*The Shattered Chain*] . . . I discovered while I was writing it that it would have seemed logical for two of the women protagonists, Magda and Jaelle, to fall at least briefly in love. And I chickened out on it, though I might possible have gotten away with it."[90] Her reasoning, she explains, was that she was already tackling one big theme in the book—the chains women wear in society, both visibly and invisibly (or consciously and unconsciously)—and bringing in lesbian existence "might blunt the impact."[91] Without referencing McIntyre's review, Bradley admits she came to this theme in realizing that the society she had created through her Darkover series was one in which women were not free.[92] In writing as much, she admits that her growing feminist consciousness informs her writing and models how an author might come around to believing in the validity and value of self-reflection.

Despite making such a dramatic shift, however, Bradley concludes this second letter by expressing exasperation at what she misperceives as her feminist readers' desire for her fiction to solve women's problems. Some social problems, she writes, have no answers in real life and thus cannot in fiction, either. She thus returns to her defensive idiom, writing, "There are always going to be bigots and racists . . . and since they will not be wiped out in my lifetime, all I can do is resolve not to be one myself."[93] She elaborates, "One can remove the symptoms of sexism by making laws about equal pay for equal work, by passing the Equal Rights Amendment, by consciousness-raising and by getting rid of sexism in schoolbooks, but it's not going to be wiped out in my lifetime. Or yours. Or my nine-year old daughter's. Or probably the lifetime of HER daughters. . . . We can't do it all this week. . . . So at my age all I can do is to take the steps I can, and not worry too hard about the rest."[94] In writing as much, Bradley placed limits on what she saw as the genre's potentiality for feminism, lesbian existence, and radical politics writ large. Nonetheless, in engaging with her feminist fans/critics, she demonstrated that, if one is willing to open one's self and one's work to critique in the face of vulnerability, change might be possible.

In the final letter on the subject, Russ responds generously to Bradley's opening up and counters, contending that such resignation might be overcome by a commitment to building alternative worlds. She begins by kindly arguing that Bradley's understanding of racism and sexism do not account for the many ways people are oppressed in contemporary society. It is not merely a matter of conscious and direct degradation, she explains, but institutionalized and systematized exploitation: "The system that pays [men] and feeds them, houses them and clothes them, exploits women. It also exploits black men. *I* exploit black men. There's hardly any way I can stop exploiting black men except by trying to change things so that nobody will exploit anybody. The only way men can stop exploiting women is by trying to change the system."[95] Thus, going back to Bradley's first letter, while Bradley might never have intended to write antifeminist propaganda, Russ writes, "Being feminist or anti-feminist isn't something you do in a neutral situation; the situation is already anti-feminist . . . and in order to avoid being anti-feminist, one must make an effort and be conscious of wanting to avoid being anti-feminist."[96] Bradley's sense of individualism is not going to get her far in this regard. Rather than neglecting her own complicity in such structures, Russ charges Bradley to continue to develop her consciousness. Doing as much is "very painful," Russ acknowledges, but the process also provides optimism, as opposed to the pessimism of resignation. Russ concludes her letter by stating, "I hope we can all take one step and one step and one step and then one day look up and say 'Hey! I've really gotten somewhere.'"[97] This could happen, she suggests, faster than we might imagine.

Uncharacteristically undogmatic, Russ's letter recognized Bradley's vulnerability in choosing to engage with *WatCh*'s feminist critique of her work and extend it to her own analysis of her most recent novel. It modeled for the fanzine's feminist readers another way to engage those who see the world differently. All of these reviews and LOCs, written and published for budding feminist SF fandom, were also about more than these individual authors and their novels' strengths and shortcomings. These reviews performed new forms of SF criticism that prioritize feminist concerns while also showing fan appreciation and investment in such writing. In the back and forth that developed through the LOCs, these fans and authors together developed a feminist ethics of relation—how one might listen to critique, reflect, and respond in an attempt to understand those different from one's self. As the awkwardness of these letters attest, the process was not easy, straightforward, or especially satisfying in the moment, but it was productive, as it moved uncomfortable but necessary conversations about differences forward.

Many of these threads about accountability and vulnerability in SF publishing and criticism would carry over into the publication of *Janus*. They reappear perhaps most prominently in the fanzine's sixth issue, in which Bogstad and Gomoll published the transcription of a conversation they had with Bankier and Charnas over lunch at the MidAmeriCon in Kansas City in November 1976.[98] Bogstad and Gomoll printed the conversation in their zine, with Gomoll providing its narrativization, including describing the mise-en-scène of the Sirloin Room across the street from the convention hotel where they dined, served by waitresses in hideous uniforms, complete with ribbons and many-layered ruffled skirts. Gomoll and Bogstad also published, alongside the transcript of the conversation, Bankier's and Charnas's reflections on and critiques of their own attitudes and behavior, developing for themselves something akin to Bankier's editorial practice from *WatCh*. There is a notable difference between how these feminist fans and authors respond to one another and how they and others like them did in *WatCh* just a year or two prior, as they had already delineated the range of topics and sorts of knowledge most relevant to feminist SF fandom in the earlier fanzines.

In this lunch conversation, Bradley's *The Shattered Chain* (and Bankier's decision to dress as a Free Amazon from the novel at a party the night before) sparks a conversation about lesbian characters in science fiction and the varying vulnerability of straight, gay, and bisexual authors in writing such characters. Without making a direct reference to *WatCh* and instead presuming a common knowledge, Bankier references Bradley having admitted to "chickening out" when it came to the lesbian romance and says she read the dissolution of an otherwise radical novel with an unbelievable heterosexual pairing as the result of fear. Charnas disagrees, saying she thought it indicative of a broader failure of the imagination to write a female society (the Free Amazons) from the inside. While Bankier argues that Bradley's bisexuality makes her vulnerable when writing such societies and relationships, Charnas counters that Bradley's marriage ought to provide protection from such a fear. She supports this by speaking to her own experience as a married woman writing women-only societies in her novel in progress, *Motherlines*. Furthermore, Charnas claims, science fiction as a genre offers freedom with regard to subject matters such as women's sexuality. One could even argue that the women she is writing cannot really even be considered lesbians, as they live in a totally different society and face different stresses than lesbians today. Bankier concurs that Bradley's marriage provides some protection, as people can use it to dismiss her coming out; however, she also implies that the risk of being perceived as a "lesbian man-hater" may still weigh heavily on a bisexual author. Charnas then slips in her analysis of this man-hater myth and implies—through a contrast of "women" and "lesbians"—that lesbians are not women (iterating the hegemonic misogynist logic, as explicated by Radicalesbians in "The Woman Identified Woman" (1970), that "women" are those who "get fucked by men").[99] When Bankier points this out, Charnas responds by saying it was a slip and telling Bankier she can "read into it what [she] like[s]."[100] However, when printed in *Janus*, Charnas's defensive comment in the moment is accompanied by an extensive reflection on her defensiveness and later letter of apology to Bankier, which was followed up by a phone call from an understanding Bankier. Charnas and Bankier thus build on their experiences with *WatCh* and *Khatru* and expand feminist SF fandom's practice of accountability and vulnerability in their discussions of difference.

In her supplemental commentary, Charnas acknowledges the fact that there are varying levels of risk for herself, as opposed to someone who is lesbian or bisexual, in writing women who love women. Bankier's criticism has pushed her to realize that she is at an immense advantage in writing such stories, as she is not "carrying any heavy emotional freight about such styles or modes of action drawn from living them."[101] Yet this does not mean that lesbian potentiality is not also hers to explore in her writing. In fact, perhaps, she is freer to do so. And it is her task, as a feminist author, to connect real women, who may or may not engage in sexual or romantic relations with other women, and lesbian feminist futures. "What I think I'm doing, you see, is writing from some kind of dream level that's available to all women in one degree or another, a level of imaginary experience that can nourish us all," she says. "That's where our visions of a decent future have to come from, I think, tempered with tough and realistic analysis of how to get there and cope with a whole new set of problems when we do."[102] Like Tiptree's "Houston, Houston, Do You Read?," Charnas's *Motherlines* (1978), which is about the conflicts between two lesbian communities as they build a women's world together after escaping the enslavement of men, maintains the defining characteristic of lesbian potentiality: lesbian impotentiality, in which all that is affiliated with lesbian potentiality might be rethought with further social change. And like Chick Strand, another publicly straight-identified artist who claimed her lesbian film *Fever Dream* came from "a dream [she] once had," Charnas invokes a lesbian "dream level," pointing to lesbian potentiality's broad appeal.[103] Still, Charnas does this while also modeling accountability to her lesbian and bisexual peers.

Although each of these negotiations of difference initially occurred between known individuals (established authors, younger authors, and fans), they were not a matter of private correspondence but, instead, performed for and as a part of a public: feminist SF fandom. The lunch conversation solicited dozens of LOCs, a selection of which *Janus* then published in its eighth and ninth issues. They included letters from the original participants, as well as a letter from Bradley written in the "white heat of—not anger but defensiveness, dismay," largely at having been "talked about behind her back."[104] Regardless of what others think of the choices she has made as a bisexual woman and author, Bradley writes, "I am out here on the firing lines, fighting with all the truth I can, making compromises with such grace, as I must. . . . If I can open little cracks here and there in the hard shell of the world men have made, fine. If I can't, I'll die trying."[105] *Janus* readers, unaffiliated with the original "Lunch Talk," also wrote in and offered their thoughts and opinions on *The Shattered Chain*, Bankier and Charnas's analyses of the novel, and Bradley's response. Ann Weiser of Chicago wrote to say that she found Bradley's writing about herself to be "very moving," and she read it with "great gratitude that she is sharing so much."[106] Gregory G. H. Rihn of Wisconsin Dells, meanwhile, pushed back on Bradley's surprise at having been written about in this personal way, as it bridged feminist and fan practices: "If you are going to write about things that are important to yourself and others, you have to open up. . . . And you have to be prepared for 'them', the <u>other</u> people who care about such things, to pick over your revelations and criticize them."[107] These LOCs acknowledged that the feminist self-reflection and criticism of *WatCh* and *Janus* contributors were not private reading practices transposed to a public platform. It was not simply that Bankier and Charnas were expressing disappointment at an individual author. Instead, their analyses were written for others, such as Weiser and Rihn, with whom they were building the world of feminist SF fandom.

Humor and the Institutionalization of Feminist SF Fandom

Perhaps the most curious LOC printed in *Janus 8*, however, is one from James Tiptree, Jr. Not really an LOC at all, in fact, but appearing like one is an illustration with a quotation of Tiptree's from the *Khatru* symposium. Printed in the top left-hand corner of a page in the middle of the eighth issue's LOC section is an illustration of a door that opens up to darkness. Out of the darkness appears a speech bubble in which Tiptree is quoted as saying, "Now what I have said here implies that individual women can quite easily be, in effect, males." This, in turn, is cited in the speech bubble as "a quote, quite out of context, from *Khatru* 3/4, 1975, pg. 21" (see figure 3.5). Credited in the issue to Gomoll, the illustration does not make its commentary on the matter at

3.5 Jeanne Gomoll, illustration, "Now what I have said here implies that individual women can quite easily be, in effect, males," *Janus* 8, 1977.

hand explicit. Instead, its meaning is dependent on one's prior knowledge of the *Khatru* symposium and one's interpretation of its attribution as "quite out of context" here. Published only months after Alice B. Sheldon's outing by the SF trade journal *Locus*, this is *Janus*'s nod to this historical event. But it also draws on Sheldon's earlier, now apparently less essentialist (or at least less straightforwardly so) theories as Tiptree. The illustration's placement alongside LOCs on the Bradley bisexuality debate could imply that Bradley is acting "male," by which Tiptree would have meant assertive to the point of being lethal to the counterpublic. This recalls similar debates that happened in early radical feminist CR groups, in which some women's aggressive behavior led to them being asked to leave, as they were taking time and attention away from others and interfering with the process by acting male.[108]

At the same time, the cuteness of this commentary suggests a more humorous critique. It can be read as pointing to a certain ridiculousness of this fan discourse with so many commentators yelling from the sidelines (or darkened doorways, as it may be). Only a little over two years after Bankier published the first issue of *WatCh* and Smith began organizing the *Khatru* symposium, feminist SF fandom and its part-and-parcel potentiality had spawned an impressive social body through these fanzines. According to the queer theorist Michael Warner, "Public discourse says not only 'Let a public exist' but 'Let it have this character, speak this way, see the world in this way.' It then goes in search of confirmation that such a public exists, with greater or lesser success—success being further attempts to cite, circulate, and realize the world understanding it articulates."[109] Success for feminist SF fandom meant the generation of an overwhelming number of feminist perspectives and opinions, lesbian and otherwise. *Janus*'s editors, then, in crafting and publishing this illustration as a fictional LOC, could be seen as deploying a little self-reflexive humor on the part of feminist SF fandom itself. Feminist fans, they hint, at times take themselves a little too seriously. However, they also know as much and can joke about it.

The archetype of the humorless second-wave feminist, and specifically the humorless lesbian feminist, saw a resurgence in queer studies of the 1990s and 2000s, shaping it into a myth to be repeated by scholars and activists alike in more casual accounts of feminist and queer histories.[110] What many do not know is that the archetype was already a stereotype and the subject of feminist commentary as early as the early 1970s. As the psychologist Naomi Weisstein contended in "Why We Aren't Laughing . . . Any More," published in *Ms.* in 1973, feminists were charged by men with lacking a sense of humor precisely because they refused to continue to laugh at their own degradation. She explains that much humor "serves to put whoever it is in their place by showing that they can't be taken seriously, that they're too stupid or dumb or ugly or childlike or smelly or mean to count as human. . . . So when we hear jokes against women and we are asked why we don't laugh at them, the answer is easy, simple, and short. Of course, we're not laughing, you asshole. Nobody laughs at the sight of their own blood."[111] In the *Khatru* symposium, McIntyre similarly remarked: "Misogynist jokes are supposed to be funny; where do we get off not laughing? (Feminists have no sense of humor, remember? We can't possibly have one, we don't think rape jokes, ugly teenage girl jokes, 'Take my wife—please!' jokes are funny)."[112] Meanwhile, at the same time feminists were developing their own forms of humor, which "would make clear that it is not women who are ridiculous, but the culture that has subjugated them" and "[laugh] at the very idea of gender inequality in an attempt to render such inequality absurd and powerless."[113] This overtly feminist humor, Nancy Walker claims, is "analogous to what [Umberto] Eco speaks of as the purely comic, which involves a perception of the opposite of what is normal or acceptable" and thus does not just break the rules but "imagines a different set of rules."[114] Walker argues that this is why feminist humor often involves fantasy and can be found so prominently in works of feminist science fiction, such as Russ's *The Female Man*.[115] Not unsurprisingly, the humor in these feminist SF fanzines often followed feminist science fiction's lead, and to enjoy it, as in the case of *The Female Man*, one had to be open to the idea that much of life for many people was far from laughable. After all, it was the acknowledgment of male privilege that led Tiptree, Smith, and Delany to take a back seat in *Khatru* and Tiptree to declare himself "about as relevant as a cuckoo-clock in eternity."[116]

While clearly neither the *Khatru* symposium nor *WatCh* had been devoid of art or humor, *Janus*'s Tiptree illustration/citation is exemplary of the questioning, critiquing, and parodying of the process of community formation that would ironically mark feminist SF fandom's approaching institutionalization. In 1976, MadSTF, the fan club in Madison, Wisconsin, that published *Janus*, incorporated as the Society for the Furtherance and Study of Fantasy and Science Fiction (SF³), and in 1977 SF³ organized the first feminist SF fan convention in Madison: WisCon. Early on, *Janus* issues would double as WisCon programs, granting subscribers unable to attend the convention a sense of its colorful feminist programming in black and white. WisCon 2 included a panel titled "Feminism: To Grasp the Power to Name Ourselves; Science Fiction: To Grasp the Power to Name Our Future," and its description in *Janus 11* was accompanied by a whimsical drawing of a femme figure, eyes closed, as if dreaming. WisCon 2 also featured "The Madison Parade of Cats," which *Janus 11* describes as "tak[ing] you to the homes of Madison fans, to acquaint you with their very fannish cats."[117] The panel description contends that "cats have made significant contributions in the field of science fiction" that are unknown to many, "as cats tend to write under pseudonyms."[118] And the program included short biographies for Chuck, Lottie, Maya, Wiserlan, and Muffin, those typically reclusive cat authors whom feminist SF fans taking the tour as a part of their WisCon 2 experience would get to meet. Now in addition to, or instead of, attending WorldCon and other general conventions each year, which might or might not feature minimal feminist programming, feminist fans could make their way to WisCon, where feminist SF panels were plentiful and the convention itself was organized around feminist principles and with comical and color-ful feminist flare.

This humorous self-activity in and through the founding of WisCon is anticipated in the pages of *Janus*, where often more obviously fannish fare is published alongside the more explicitly feminist, the juxtaposition no longer reading like the contrast it once had to many. This included the small and simple cartoons, sketches, portraits, graphs, and decorative patterns that littered *Janus*'s pages. In the early issues, Gomoll drew most of the illustrations. At the top of each of her first eight news editorials, she included a self-portrait of herself at a typewriter, an alien creature balanced on her right shoulder, watching her type. Pretty soon, however, she was able to include the artwork of two or more other artists in each issue, and by the sixth issue, few, if any, of the zine's pages did not include one, if not two or three, such illustrations. Much of the art holds no relation to the essays, LOCs, or interviews alongside which it was published. Instead, the illustrations were intended as autonomous contributions. Though they had nothing to do with what they were each published next to, they nonetheless drew on inter-textual and intergenerational fan knowledge to be understood. For example, the propeller beanie, a symbol for SF fandom since the 1940s, was put to new iconographic purposes in Rihn's beanie cartoon series, which across eight issues envisioned beanies for all of the characters of *The Rocky Horror Picture Show*; gave the propeller beanie an alternate history, beginning with Leonardo da Vinci; and designed beanies that could do such things as convert excess body heat into electricity and keep drunken fans on their feet.

On occasion, illustrations that gave image to local feminist science fiction events visualized feminist SF fandom for itself. *Janus 12–13* printed the transcript of a talk Delany gave in Madison in December 1977 on how science fiction creates dialogue with the present world to make another world possible. The back cover of the issue was a large, handsome portrait of the author in mid-speech drawn by Virginia Galko. The printed talk includes two additional images of Delany: a photograph by Sarah Prince and an illustration by Gomoll. All three depict Delany in his visit to the group, donning the same square glasses, plaid shirt, and sweater, as he expounds his philosophies of the genre for the fan group. Most of the contributions to the WisCon I issue of *Janus* include illustrations. Many are relatively straightforward, such as those of Nosferatu, Frank N. Furter, and Dr. Caligari and his somnambulist that adorn the WisCon Film Notes, but one rather mysteriously collages a canister of Philip K. Dick's titular reality-altering substance Ubik and Popeye into the convention committee photo.[119]

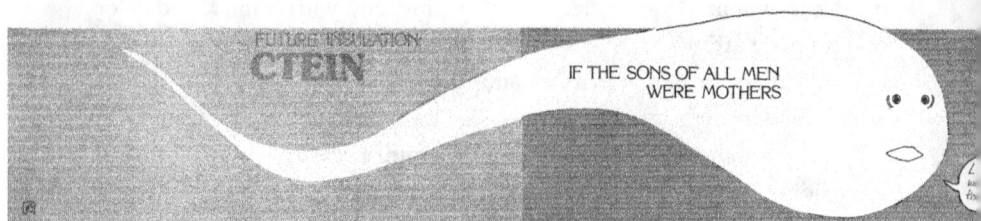

3.6 Jeanne Gomoll, illustration, "Let one who is without kin cast the first clone" in *Janus* 12–13, 1978.

Occasionally, as in the case with the Tiptree door piece, the art itself provided reflexive and humorous commentary on the subject at hand. Ctein, *Janus*'s speculative science columnist, published a series on cloning. In one of these articles, titled "If the Sons of All Men Were Mothers," Ctein worries, having recently read Marge Piercy's *Woman on the Edge of Time* (1976), that when women are "freed" from reproduction, they will nonetheless retain the "chains" of patriarchy. The article includes a header with a cartoon of a giant, friendly, smiley sperm, drawn by Gomoll, saying, "Let one who is without kin cast the first clone" (see figure 3.6). While Ctein is pessimistic, Gomoll's sperm stands in for those who would like to hold open the possibility of freedom with, if not through, cloning. And the sperm slyly names for whom the stakes of cloning are highest—those "ones" who are "without kin," those who have been cut off from birth family ties or denied support and access to reproduction: in short, queer and trans people. Through this goofy and charming illustration, Gomoll pushes back on what was often a super-straight and -cis discourse around reproductive freedom. In cases such as this, humor does not simply counterbalance, but paradoxically underscores, the very stakes of feminist fan discourse.

Often *Janus*'s multimodal sense of humor was directed at the process of publishing the fanzine or organizing WisCon itself. Gomoll, Bogstad, and other members of MadSTF were recurring characters in Gomoll's cartoons. In their first few editorials for *Janus*, Gomoll and Bogstad disagreed on the function of science fiction as a literature, Bogstad believing SF to be a unique literature with its own potential for thinking futures, and Gomoll arguing, quite contrarily and a tad polemically, that discussing SF as its own genre created false demarcations between it and literature as a whole. They then poked fun at how quickly such a disagreement escalated by printing the cartoon of the two of them "at war," throwing paper and ducking behind desks in the *Janus* office. In attempts to encourage readers to remember to send in change-of-address notices, Gomoll illustrated the perils of not doing so with great hyperbole. In one such cartoon, a nineteenth-century "rogue" is depicted being accosted in his bed by jailers in top hats, and in another, the gloomy castle of "the Lord of Yon Gloomy Castle" is seen being charged by knights on horseback, one commenting, "A pity too—This would make a great place for a con."[120] Snarky and passive aggressive, but delightfully so, the editors of *Janus* are asking their readers to keep their labor of love in mind and do what they can to help get issues out to where they need to go. They were not above cruder forms of humor, as long as they were directing that humor at themselves. The back cover of *Janus 8* depicts two aliens dressed in business attire reading the zine at a bus stop; one of them asks why the zine is named *Janus*, to which the other replies, "Because you nerd, *JASSHOLE* would have been a little rude."[121]

Janus's fan art also provided commentary on how feminism and science fiction fit together. In one cartoon by Teddy Harvia, an alien and a woman meet, pointing and smiling at each other in mutual recognition. This recognition is cemented by their thought bubbles, the woman's depicting the Venus symbol, so well associated by this time with the women's movement, and the alien's showing the same symbol but upside down, as if in an alien language.[122] Women—or, at least, those feminists attached to this symbol—are drawn to SF because they see themselves in the alien. In a cartoon by Gomoll, one woman declares exasperatedly to a friend seated with her at a bar, "It's hard enough explaining feminism to a traditional shrink . . . but explaining fandom too!?"[123] The double sense of being outsiders that feminist SF fans felt as both feminists and fans shines with tongue-in-cheek feminist humor.

Janus's artwork also coupled with written content at times to offer critiques of mainstream fandom. In *Janus 9*, Hank Luttrell published a review of the first *Star Wars* film, which sarcastically declared itself "the last *Star Wars* review," acknowledging the obscene amount of attention the film was receiving not just inside but outside of fandom. In his review, Luttrell assigns *Star Wars* to a growing body of pulpy comic book SF films that actually bear greater resemblance to westerns, which helps them "get away with a general lack of social or political meaning," as well as a "casual attitude toward scientific accuracy."[124] And while Luttrell finds Princess Leia to be a "surprising departure from the movie-serial mold" in that she is smart and adept, he also muses, "You can't help but wonder why [otherwise] it was that only white, blue-eyed, male Flash Gordons ventured into space."[125] Gomoll made a collage to accompany the review, which had the characters of the film echoing

3.7 Jeanne Gomoll, collage, "This is the <u>last</u> Star Wars review," *Janus* 9, 1977.

the review's sentiments (see figure 3.7). Obi-Wan Kenobi is pictured saying, "But it's so redundant!" Luke Skywalker declares, "I'm gonna be sick," and Chewbacca perhaps puts it best: "Grrrrrrr!" On its own, this collage would hold little meaning. However, in the context of this review and from the perspective of those who share Luttrell's reservations about the film's limited feminism, it offers a hilarious critique. While antifeminist mainstream fandom and the sexist "mundane" world—both of which largely loved the film—might be no fun, that need not be the case, these feminist fans insist, for their fan world.

Other 1970s feminist media cultures did not lack senses of humor. Spectra Media's flier picturing International Videoletters as one long embrace and inviting women to attend in order to "meet some interesting women" hinted at the erotics of the project with more than a dash of humor (see chapter 1). Laughter was central to the modes of solidarity and survival pictured in *Songs, Skits, Poetry, and Prison Life* (1974), and sarcasm was integral to a number of the critiques made in the prison documentaries of the previous chapter. This self-directed humor through fan art across *Janus*'s pages in the late 1970s was indicative of feminist SF fandom's successful constitution as a coherent and self-aware counterpublic. Though feminism would continue to be central to its approaches to science fiction fandom, a fact it would always insist on in the face of pressures from within fandom, Mad-STF/SF³'s statement of purpose in its application for incorporation as a nonprofit made no mention of feminism.[126] The intent was largely to leave room for the wide range of SF³'s fan activities, which included book groups, video production, outreach to area high schools, and guest lecturing in University of Wisconsin courses, not all of which were explicitly feminist.[127] It was also easier, when appealing to perhaps the most mundane of the mundane world, government bureaucracy, to appear legitimate, focused, and organized according to these outside standards.[128] And the fiscal opportunities of incorporation meant that SF³ was able to improve and expand its feminist fan activities. *Janus 6*, the first issue published after incorporating as SF³, was also its first printed using an offset press, a technological shift that allowed for easier, faster, and more attractive publishing. It also made founding a feminist SF convention possible. In *Janus 3*, Bogstad joked:

> Rumors about a Madcon appear to have been exaggerated. I do hear tell of plans for a one day Mad-Micro-Con, but who can tell what basis these rumors have in reality? One must always be suspicious of street-talk one picks up in Madcity. There could be many and mysterious motives behind the creation of such rumors. Nevertheless, I shall report the full contents of them to you. It is said that there may be a one-day extravaganza complete with female sf writers, panels on women in sf, movies, lectures on writing technique. It sounds like something no one would want to say they'd missed, if indeed it occurs.[129]

In her column in *Janus 4*, Gomoll referenced these rumors and wrote that the plans for such a convention were "still very much alive and squirming."[130] *Janus 6* put an end to this sly and silly form of anticipation building, announcing that WisCon I would be held in February 1977, and SF³'s first grant would cover the travel expenses of the convention's first guests of honor : the author Katherine MacLean and the fan Amanda Bankier.[131]

The founding of WisCon was a result of feminist SF fandom's successful constitution as a coherent and self-aware counterpublic through its fans' creative, intellectual, and material labor. Warner cautions that counterpublics are no longer "counter," becoming simply "publics," once they appeal to the

173

state. Miranda Joseph, meanwhile, writes that one must become a legitimate community before being recognized as a potential recipient of state goodies.[132] As Richard S. Russell put it in a *Janus* article on SF³'s incorporation, dealing with the "red tape" of "real-world governmental agencies" allowed for "blue-sky" fan activities.[133] Joseph's argument is not intended as a judgment or dismissal. Instead, Joseph considers the critique of communities' self-inscription into subjects of the nation-state and capital as central to the "ethical practice of community" under capitalism.[134] With its institutionalization, feminist SF fandom became something that Madison, as a city, could boast about. Arguably, it was in fact boasted about because it took place in a small midwestern city in Wisconsin and not in Los Angeles or New York. That WisCon brought commerce to the city was valued by others outside fandom, and Mayor Paul Soglin declared February 11–19, 1978, the week leading up to WisCon 2, science fiction week in Madison.[135] In founding this feminist convention while simultaneously neglecting its politicized self-identification in the incorporation process, SF³ and its feminist fans ambivalently recognized the contradictions necessary to growing feminist SF fandom.

Organized and run by the editors and regular contributors to *Janus*, WisCon continued feminist SF fandom's fannish CR, including its difficult discussions of difference and self-reflexive and citational sense of humor. Much of WisCon 1's programming came out of MadSTF club discussions, such as the panel "Politics and Science Fiction," which sprang from a debate Bogstad and Phil Kaveny had recently had at a MadSTF meeting about Le Guin's *The Dispossessed* and Ernest Callenbach's *Ecotopia*.[136] Keeping with the Tiptree-centric sense of humor, WisCon 2 included an event called "Will the Real James Tiptree, Jr. Please Stand Up!" It was a rerun of a similar production done at a MadSTF meeting, in which four contestants (two women, a man, and a cardboard cutout of a cat) were tested on their knowledge of Tiptree's oeuvre. Since the first production, Alice B. Sheldon's identity had been uncovered. It was with hopeful anticipation that the WisCon 2 program suggested attendees "keep [their] eyes on the audience rather than the fakers on stage, just in case."[137] Although Gomoll sent Sheldon an invitation to WisCon and included the flier for the earlier version of the event, Sheldon did not show.[138] Instead, the author chose to maintain a nearly purely epistolary relationship with feminist SF fandom and, post-reveal, signed letters "Tip/ Alli." Thus, not every practice or person from feminist SF fanzines transferred over to WisCon.

WisCon became its own entity. Because cons draw people together in person, they are often where, as Jenkins writes, "the sense of fandom as an alternative social community is most keenly felt."[139] Recognizing as much, SF³ had unique goals for its newest creation: "We're going to dispense with raising consciousness as a primary goal (though if that happens too, fine). We want to raise energy levels."[140] This did not mean that CR disappeared. If anything, it became, in obvious ways, more present than ever in face-to-face conversations about feminism. However, being face to face meant that the ways feminists went about CR changed dramatically. It got energized, as the excitement of being with other feminist fans radiated and reflected across the convention space. Among the WisCon 1 reports, Gomoll included a cartoon labeled "Sercon Silliness." Captioned with slightly altered *Rocky Horror* lyrics ("With a bit of a mind flip; You're into the time slip; Let's go to WisCon again"), it not only alluded to the popular programming of the *Rocky Horror Picture Show* at WisCon 1 but also suggested that the experience of WisCon might itself resemble attending the Annual Transylvanian convention held at Dr. Frank N. Furter's house.[141] Bogstad wrote in her report, "The flow of new ideas, or new ways of organizing ideas is what I prized most highly about my convention experience."[142]

WisCon enabled particular opportunities and presented new challenges to feminist SF fandom. To navigate them, its organizers, as well as its attendees and guests of honor, continued to draw on their double knowledge as feminists and fans. In addition to panels and activities typical of fandom, they learned from other women's communities and created safe spaces for women to congregate and share their experiences away from sexist men, who, despite many of their good intentions, nevertheless always seemed to make themselves heard as such.[143] In their programming, which again brought together feminist and fannish social practices, WisCon organizers insisted that feminist SF fandom was a necessary space. Gathering annually at WisCon allowed feminist fans to feel safe in travelling together to other conventions, at which they brought feminist programming to mainstream fandom. After attending the thirty-fifth WorldCon in Florida in 1977, where she discovered feminist and gay programming aplenty (the latter largely in response to statements by Anita Bryant, a local resident), Gomoll wrote: "Rather than seeing feminist activity within fandom as something that has grown from within fandom and is pulling it apart, however, I conceive of the growing awareness as a part of fandom that has at last opened up, a roadblock that has at last been cleared—that is not pulling fandom apart, but in fact is drawing people into fandom, revitalizing fandom!"[144] The potentiality so many feminist readers-turned-authors had attributed to the genre had come to fruition, but the process did not stop there. With WisCon, the

175

(im)potentiality of feminist SF fandom, including the lesbian potentiality central to its formation as a counterpublic, renewed itself in actuality, with hundreds of feminist fans finding their way to WisCon each year and valuing its specificity as a feminist con.

Future Comrades

As Janice Radway charges those interested in reception studies, including fan studies, "In learning how others actively make their own social worlds differently from the way we make our own perhaps it might also be possible to identify together those points where articulations and alliances could be forged across the borders in the service of a future not yet envisioned and therefore neither necessarily lost nor secured."[145] It is in this spirit that I have pursued this research. As I elaborate in the next chapter on transfeminist historiography, the writing of feminist histories too often is divided along generational lines. When one attends women's studies conferences, it often seems as if feminist generations cannot even speak to one another or listen when the other speaks. In March 2014, for example, transphobic feminists who had been active in the 1970s women's movement took Boston University's A Revolutionary Moment: Women's Liberation in the Late 1960s and Early 1970s conference as an opportunity to insist to younger presenters, myself included, that their conception of sisterhood cannot and should not be extended to trans women or men. This conflict especially upset me because of the high expectations set by my own WisCon attendance. I first attended WisCon in 2011, where I discovered a multigenerational feminist space where people of many genders, including children and elders, were not only welcome but also collaborators in the organization and leadership of events. At stake for many, if not all, was a feminist future in which folks of all genders might be free, and in the interim, spaces of greater freedom, accessibility, and accountability were taking shape. Quite simply, WisCon 35 modeled for me what intergenerational comradery might look like.

It was at WisCon 35 that I met Gomoll. Later that summer, she lent me her complete run of *Janus* and put me in touch with Bankier. From the scanner in the basement of my graduate school library, I helped digitize *Janus* so that issues like those I analyze here would be available to the public for browsing or downloading on the SF[3] website.[146] I did this not because I agreed with everything written within the zine's pages (obviously, the many voices within them often do not agree with each other), but because I believed that the negotiations therein ought to be widely available, as they document the exciting attempts of 1970s feminists to imagine a world in which life may one day be substantially different. *Janus*'s pages contain early forms of the fannish consciousness-raising—including the accountability, vulnerability, and senses of humor—feminist fans still practice at WisCon and online.

Feminist SF fandom has evolved greatly since 1975. The distinctions between literary and media fandom have broken down. With the diversification of participation, the need for concerted coalition has only expanded. Feminist SF fandom in the 1970s recognized and accommodated those, such as Bradley, who were invariably more secure within established fandom because of the newness of their endeavor and desire to reach out to and include successful women SF writers. However, since then it has become clear how important it is to recognize the vulnerabilities of those who—by virtue not only of their speaking out and speaking up but of their mere existence as trans, queer, Black, Indigenous, and disabled others—face a far greater risk. In 1999, feminist of color fans established the Carl Brandon Society at WisCon to advocate for fans of color and support the work of speculative fiction by and about people of color.[147] At a time when scholarly and professional institutions too often seem profoundly confused about how to meet trans participants' needs, it has been a relief to attend WisCon each year and see an institution work through these, and similar, concerns with care and understanding. For years, WisCon has provided attendees with multiple centralized all-gender bathrooms. Every room that hosts panels provides well-marked access lanes for people in wheelchairs and microphones so that all speakers can be heard. At the WisCon Vid Party, where my media fandom and love of editing and remix has landed me each year, physically or virtually, organizers subtitle all videos for hard-of-hearing viewers and provide guides to which videos include flashing lights, which can be physically difficult for some, or sexual or graphic violence, which can be difficult emotionally for others. Early feminist SF fans created "rooms of one's own" for women at various conventions. Fans organized an unofficial "Safer Space for People of Color" at WisCon in 2008 that was formally instituted in 2009, with a "Safer Space for Trans/Genderqueer People" and a "Safer Space for People with Disabilities" following in the 2010s. Importantly, each of these measures is not presumed to be a comprehensive or set solution. Instead, every year the convention ends with a "Post-Mortem" at which folks are invited to share what made the convention work, what did not, and how the convention can be improved for the next year.

Anyone interested in attending WisCon can organize a panel, and sometimes participants offer the con—meaning not just the convention committee

177

(concom) but also fellow attendees—feedback through their own creative takes on programming. One of WisCon 37's most popular panels was "Cousin of Return of Sibling of Revenge of Not Another F*cking Race Panel," the annual iteration of a game-show-format panel, complete with a giant die, in which six SF&F authors of color "get their geek on about any number of pop culture topics—none of them related to race."[148] The first of such panels was organized at WisCon 33 as a response to the experience of SF&F authors of color at WisCon, who found they were always expected to talk about race and race alone, a pattern that prevented them from interacting at the convention as full people with other experiences, passions, and interests related to the subjects at hand. Much like Gomoll and Bogstad, who deployed self-reflexive and self-critical humor through *Janus*'s art and editing, such programming raises white feminist fans' consciousness in simultaneously hilarious and exacting ways.

In *The Secret Feminist Cabal*, her history of feminist science fiction, Helen Merrick reminds readers how unusual it is for a feminist community forged in the 1970s to have "survived the coming of new generations." She contends that feminist SF authors and fans "have found a 'home,'" despite disagreements and differences, including much "antagonistic conflict," within the community across the years.[149] For her, the hope in this lies in the fact that "perhaps this once, our recent feminist histories will not be forgotten."[150] In writing this history of fannish CR, my hope has been slightly different. Rather than fetishize feminist SF fandom as a community, as Joseph would put it, I have focused on the self-activity of a counterpublic still very much underway.[151] Many feminist fans would describe feminist SF fandom as a "home," finding it to be a rare and special space in which, online and in person at conventions, they are able to connect with people with whom they share genuine interests and passions. However, this is so not *despite* past conflicts around differences but *because of* them. Substantial labor, on the parts of fanzine editors, LOC writers, and convention organizers, went into building this world many of us call home. I find hope in the fact that, as a counterpublic, feminist SF fandom is a scene of "self-activity, of historical rather than timeless belonging, and of active participation rather than ascriptive belonging."[152] Feminist SF fandom has not survived new generations but adapted with them. Its uniqueness as a counterpublic lies in its impotentiality—the genre, its authors, and its fans, very much in the spirit of lesbian potentiality, constantly renegotiating and renewing their commitment to thinking together what is, what was, and what could come to be.

tip/alli
cutting a transfeminist
genealogy of siblinghood

Since the 1970s, a primary imperative of feminist historiography has been to guarantee the survival of women through self-knowledge. In 1972, Adrienne Rich described her feminist peers as a generation of sleepwalkers collectively awakening to see the sexist world around them for what it was for the first time. Unlike awakened sleepwalkers before them, they were not alone in this process and together began to look back at women's history and women's writing. Rich named this collective activity of seeing the past anew "re-vision." She considered re-vision to be no less than "an act of survival" and wrote, "Until we can understand the assumptions in which we are drenched we cannot know ourselves. And this drive to self-knowledge, for woman, is more than a search for identity: it is part of her refusal of the self-destructiveness of male-dominated society."[1] In the following decade, feminist scholars, as well as feminist filmmakers and feminist artists working across media, took up this call for re-vision.[2] While the resulting projects varied greatly in both content and form, the underlying premise of women's survival went unchallenged until women of color historiographers in the 1980s and '90s began asking, "Survival for whom?" and deconstructive feminists in the 1990s began destabilizing the presumed ahistorical category of woman.[3] Despite the exigent contributions of this scholarship, self-knowledge and survival persist as the clarions for feminist historiography, which in recent years has shifted its attention to the 1970s themselves as the period in need of re-vision, as Rich's peers, her fellow sleepwalkers, enter their later years and donate their collections to institutional archives for preservation.[4] Concerned feminists of older generations often bemoan younger feminists' lack of interest in their histories.[5] Rather than addressing concerns about whose histories count and engaging with how feminism has changed over the decades, older feminists instead spurn neglectful daughters, and the failure to sustain sisterhood gets written as a family drama. And yet, contrary to such narratives of neglect, since the archival turn of the 1990s and early 2000s, more and more feminist historians of younger generations have found their ways into 1970s collections, hatching their own queer and trans re-visions of lesbian feminist pasts.[6]

The question of what to do with my archives has guided this entire project, and each chapter has offered a slightly different approach to their reception. I have thus far largely avoided genealogy, the historiographic methodology most commonly figured as the mapping of a family tree. Genealogy constitutes an increasingly complicated knot at the center of feminist historical studies, along with the feminist press and a number of feminist digital archives.[7] In 2010, Susan Faludi, writing for *Harper's Magazine*, succinctly rearticulated the call for re-vision as a genealogical matter: "With each go-round, women make gains, but the movement never seems able to establish an enduring birthright, a secure line of descent—to reproduce itself as a strong and sturdy force."[8] This is a knot that this chapter does not attempt to untangle. Instead, in revising re-vision, it is the knot I cut. If re-vision is also going to be an effective and affective history, it will need to see the discontinuities in the continuity, the queer reproduction alongside the more familiar.[9] Even as I continue to argue for the relevance of lesbian potentiality to twenty-first-century lesbians and non-lesbians alike and advocate for intergenerational relationality, my analysis of descent "disturbs what was previously considered immobile and fragments what was thought unified."[10] The feminist future need not be mapped out of a singular and static origin. Like any utopia, the feminist future ought to remain unknowable, itself open to re-vision.[11]

More specifically, my genealogy is a transfeminist genealogy. It is undertaken with both the certainty that trans people were there all along, if often difficult to spot in the archives,[12] and the conviction that trans people continue to augment the forms of imagination that lesbian existence in the

1970s made possible. In writing such a transfeminist genealogy, the sedentary line of descent drawn between radical and lesbian 1970s feminists and transphobic feminists of the twenty-first century is disrupted. Embracing trans women as sisters and all trans people as siblings is in fact very much in line with 1970s feminisms. It is a matter of where you cut the lines and how you conjoin them afterward. The stakes for doing such cutting are high, as the ever more frequent and public skirmishes between transfeminists (feminists who view the liberation of trans people as linked to the liberation of women and femmes) and transphobic feminists have made the question of trans women's sisterly belonging a pressing issue for envisioning feminist futures.[13] While the small but growing body of scholarship on queer and trans futures from which this project takes inspiration and hopes to contribute is transfeminist, the popular press too often give transphobic feminists the microphone.[14] This naturalizes their narratives of trans men and women invading cisgender women's spaces and erases transfeminist histories.

The dramatization of debates as to who constitutes the subject of feminism and who is included in LGBT communities as well as how such subjects relate to one another are not new. During the first decade of the twenty-first century, the popular press frequently mischaracterized conflicts between lesbians and trans men. Gayle Salamon chronicles how articles such as the *New York Times*'s "The Trouble When Jane Becomes Jack," published in 2006, tended to enact two distinct kinds of violence: a preemptive violence against trans men, who appeared deserving of lesbians' rejections, and a second disfiguring violence to butch lesbians, who became feminized to make them categorically distinct from trans men.[15] Salamon points out that this false and simplified contrast, which suggests that trans men want male privilege, while butches reject it, in turn recalls earlier lesbian feminist debates around butch-femme identities and sex roles. In the 1981 *Heresies* sex issue, Joan Nestle, founder of the Lesbian Herstory Archives, chronicled her experience coming of age in 1950s lesbian bar culture and contended, "As a way of ignoring what butch-fem meant and means, feminism is often viewed as the validating starting point of healthy Lesbian culture. I believe, however, that many Lesbians, pre-Stonewall, were feminists, but the primary way this feminism, this autonomy of sexual and social identities, was expressed was precisely in the form of sexual adventuring that now appears so oppressive. If butch-fem represented an erotically autonomous world, it also symbolized many other forms of independence."[16] Where she saw working-class women supporting themselves and their loved ones, creating a life and world outside of heteropatriarchy, many younger lesbian feminists instead simply saw the replication of heterosexuality. Reflecting on this history, Salamon writes about the *New York Times* article, "The argument is exactly the same, save only that trans men are now cast in the role of the villain previously played by butches."[17] As both lesbian existence and feminism change over time, their gendered boundaries oscillate, and nothing less than kinship and history is at stake.

Across the second decade of the twenty-first century the popular press has continued to support cissexist and transphobic feminism in its stories about the threat trans students pose to women's college campuses or its coverage of celebrities who transition after coming into notoriety with an earlier gender.[18] This privileging of transphobic feminist voices is itself not new. Narratives of the excommunications of the musician Beth Elliot and the recording engineer Sandy Stone from lesbian feminist organizations in the 1970s have been central to the production of women's liberation as a cisgender women's movement. Recently trans historians have studied the archival evidence of what led to these decisions, revealing that they were far from unanimous. Instead, big-name transphobic feminists abused their power in the feminist community and popularized their version of this history through their substantial access to the press.[19] What is new in the case of twenty-first-century debates about whether trans people constitute feminist subjects is the fact that the debates themselves are taking place in the broader public sphere—in the pages of the *New York Times*, on CNN, and on Facebook and Twitter—rather than within the confines of feminist counterpublics. This mainstreaming of transphobic discourse, often in the name of feminism, has been met with devastating consequences, especially for trans women of color.[20]

Yet more often than not, the *New York Times* and other news sources cast the conflict between transphobic feminists and trans people as a battle between evenly matched opponents, with equal ramifications for each or, even worse, a battle in which cisgender women are powerless victims. In a 2014 article in the *New Yorker*, Michelle Goldberg narrates the conflict between transphobic feminists and transfeminists as a full-out war in which senior cisgender women (tenured and retired faculty and forty-year organizers of the now canceled Michigan Womyn's Music Festival) appear to risk violence at every turn.[21] Goldberg chronicles threats these cisgender women receive on Twitter whenever they travel to speak without mentioning the many personal attacks they and others like them make daily against trans women online. She mentions neither the Twitter handles devoted to anonymous transphobic harassment in the name of radical feminism nor the threats to their lives and livelihoods that trans people face.[22] While the J. K. Rowlings of the world constitute a highly empowered and vocal transphobic extreme, more general cissexist feminist neglect of trans experiences has resulted in the undertheorizing of misogyny's manifold dimensions.[23] And as Julia Serano points out in her response to Goldberg's article, such characterizations of this often intergenerational conflict misconstrue the actual setting of debate, which is within feminism and within the LGBTQ community, not between radical feminists and trans people on the periphery.[24] Put in feminist historians' terms, transfeminism is a family issue.

In this chapter, feminist genealogy goes through a form of genre bending, as I rewrite this family drama and its intergenerational conflict as science fiction (SF). One goal is to reveal the fiction behind the conflict as it has been written thus far. As Susan Stryker notes in *Transgender History*, "There was nothing monolithic about second wave feminist attitudes toward trans issues."[25] While some women's movement leaders ostracized Elliot and Stone, others responded to such public attacks by writing articles that welcomed trans women as sisters and argued that feminism should not re-create gender oppression but offer safety from it.[26] Relatedly, while some radical and lesbian feminists were transmisogynist at the time, not all remain so today.[27] In speaking to those who participated in 1970s feminist media cultures, my research has revealed that those who remain actively involved in supporting the work of young feminist artists and writers are quite often transfeminist, many having witnessed friends, family members, and feminist comrades transition and educated themselves. Unfortunately, those who continue to carry cissexism, transmisogyny, and transphobia as beacons of their feminism forward are, like other conservatives in the digital age, skilled at making their opinions heard.[28] And, ironically, in their dogmatic commitment to stagnation, these feminists risk missing their generation's broader contributions to feminist thought, including the sometimes profound influence their peers have had on queer, nonbinary, and transgender feminists.

Here I focus on one branch of this genealogy: that of the science fiction author and feminist SF fandom participant James Tiptree, Jr. (a.k.a. Alice B. Sheldon). Tip/Alli has had a great influence on science fiction and fandom, as well as on broader and farther-reaching conversations about gender and sexuality. In studying how Tip/Alli did gender across Sheldon's life; Tiptree's epistolary relationships; and Tip/Alli's reckoning with feminism, queerness, and fandom after coming out, Tip/Alli teaches us that the story of gender in the 1970s was not so simple or straightforward as earlier feminist histories and queer theory might have us think. This transfeminist search for descent,

183

like that called for in Michel Foucault's classic essay on genealogy, "shows the heterogeneity of what was imagined consistent with itself."[29] Essentializing understandings of womanhood and androgyny were not the only options for feminists in the 1970s. Those who did not conform to normative sexual and gender identities, just as they do now, were working to find the language that fit. Often that was *lesbian*. Other times, including for Sheldon, it was a more amorphous constellation of concepts and identifications that orbited *lesbian*. Delving into the Alice B. Sheldon, Pen Name James Tiptree, Jr., Papers, recently opened for research at the University of Oregon's Special Collections, and culling from secondary literature on Tiptree, as well as from the history of the two prizes created in the author's name and their subsequent renaming, I show how, in working and living, Tip/Alli begot sisters, brothers, and siblings of great variety, who in turn through their own work and lives are continuing to shift how we think about gender. In doing as much, re-vision is revised.

Ultimately, the genealogy I initiate in this chapter privileges the survival of my trans siblings while also moving feminism toward a future in which, if we are lucky, "we" will not "survive." Rich and her cohort sought to guarantee the survival of women through self-knowledge. Surviving male-dominated, cissexist society is vital. However, in proposing revising re-vision, I am contending that what ought to be passed down from one generation to the next is not our sense of self, however we as gendered subjects currently identify, but a capacious commitment to the unknowability of the feminist future. Again I take inspiration from Foucault, who writes, "It is no longer a question of judging the past in the name of a truth that only we can possess in the present; but risking the destruction of the subject who seeks knowledge in the endless deployment of the will to knowledge."[30] In writing this transfeminist genealogy, I look to the past not for myself or my trans siblings but for a history of the reimagination of gender and sexual existence, which we might in turn pass along.

Lesbian potentiality landed me in the Tip/Alli archive. In the late 1970s, Sheldon would claim *lesbian* for herself. She wrote to other lesbians of her lifelong love of and desire for women and did so at the same time as she explored masculine and male gender identities alongside female ones, simultaneously reaching out for "sisterhood" and mourning the loss of Tiptree. All the while, Tip/Alli would craft stories of what could be, publishing in 1981 a lesbian alien romance set on a lavender-clouded planet where one chooses one's own gender as one comes of age. It is with this many-gendered lesbian potentiality that Tip/Alli spawned trans and nonbinary siblings, and it is just such an origin story that points to the need not only to revise re-vision but also to revise our own fixed sense of the Lesbian. Transphobic feminists do not own this sign or its history. It is all of ours to take up, hold close, roll around with, or let go as we see fit.

Tip/Alli

It may seem strange for a book dedicated to the study of feminist media cultures and lesbian existence to devote an entire chapter to a single author, and a male-presenting author at that. I have chosen to do this both because of Tiptree's formidable presence in US SF fandom in the 1970s and because of the author's unique contribution to this counterpublic, which extended beyond his published fiction to his unusual epistolary doing of gender. For eight years, Alice B. Sheldon passed as James Tiptree, Jr. Or, more specifically, Alice B. Sheldon passed as a cisgender man who took James Tiptree, Jr., as his pseudonym. Curious editors and fans could find no records of a James Tiptree, Jr., and thus knew the name to be a pseudonym. As pseudonyms were quite common in science fiction, Tiptree's fans initially had no reason to believe that, other than his name, he was not just as he presented himself to be. While Tiptree never attended SF conventions or met with editors in person, he was a voracious correspondent and developed dozens of friendships in SF fandom. Tiptree's outing in 1977 thus had profound immediate consequences. Among other things, it caused many cisgender male authors and fans to rethink their gendered presumptions about men's and women's writing and the varied subjects and styles authors of different genders may take up. Decades later, Tiptree's story continues to move SF readers and writers, many of whom identify elements of their own experiences as lesbian, bisexual, queer, nonbinary, and transgender people in the author's life and fiction. I write this history, paying attention to how Tip/Alli did gender differently across particular contexts. As Tiptree, Tip/Alli embraced the role of male feminist within feminist SF fandom and SF fandom more broadly. Tip/Alli also wrote and participated in feminist SF fandom as the female author Raccoona Sheldon.[31] While Tip/Alli would later claim to have had plans all along to kill off Tiptree and embrace either Raccoona or an entirely new female pseudonym, when outed, Tip/Alli grieved the loss of Tiptree, regularly referring to Tiptree's death.[32] And all the while, Alice B. Sheldon journaled avidly about her sexual desire for women—and specifically about being the doer rather than the one done to—and crafted a personal male persona, Alex, who did not live or act in fear in the way she did.[33]

While much of this history is already known (and has influenced young authors, artists, and fans for decades), some details, uncovered in Sheldon's papers, are being presented for the first time. I have been very deliberate in how and when I use pronouns. When referring to Tip/Alli I avoid pronouns, acknowledging that this very deliberately "slashed" signature signaled for the author a combination of male and female selves. Compelling cases have been made for either minimizing commonly gendered pronouns or using the gender-neutral *they* in recent projects of trans history.[34] Here, however, I do not find it fitting to avoid gendered pronouns altogether, considering that Tip/Alli wrote in highly gendered ways. Tip/Alli once bemoaned to an editor with regard to the alien genders of "With Delicate Mad Hands" (1981), "Oh, how we need a second neuter gender in English [in addition to "it/its"]! In ordinary speech and writing I'm getting to the sweating-point with She-and/or-he-and/or-?-if-any-and-where-applicable excrescences."[35] But "Tip/Alli," as a signature and self-naming, more often than not marked not an absence of gender but an abundance. I therefore protect the very binary language of the author, using "she/her/hers" when writing about Sheldon (Alice and Raccoona) and "he/him/his" when writing about Tiptree, gendering each as Tip/Alli in fact did. In doing this work, I hope to model a form of transfeminist historiography that is receptive to both its subject and its readers.

James Tiptree, Jr., began publishing in 1968 and was soon considered—alongside Ursula K. Le Guin, Joanna Russ, Samuel R. Delany, Philip K. Dick, Harlan Ellison, Thomas Disch, and others—an arbiter of a new wave of science fiction.[36] This new writing was socially conscious and sexually explicit, and seemingly overnight it had acquired realistic characters, complete with flaws and foibles recognizable to the times. Unlike his peers who published novels as well as short stories, Tiptree exclusively wrote short stories.[37] The stories' venomous, if also tongue-in-cheek, critiques of contemporary US culture and colonialism quickly caught the attention of editors in the field, including the influential Frederick Pohl. As they were published in *Analog, Galaxy, Amazing Stories,* and the *Magazine of Fantasy and Science Fiction* across the late 1960s and early 1970s, each seemed more intense than the last. Tiptree's biographer Julie Phillips describes these early stories this way: "Their narrators grab you by the lapels and blurt out wild tales; what stays with you afterward is the juice and energy, the sexy humor and defiance of the telling."[38] In his introduction to *Warm Worlds and Otherwise* (1975), a collection of many of these stories, the SF author Robert Silverberg describes Tiptree's fiction as "lean, muscular, supple, relying heavily on dialog broken by bursts of stripped-down exposition."[39] In his introduction to *10,000 Light Years from*

Home (1976), the author Gardner Dozois reflects on Tiptree's earliest stories: "Later, Tiptree would learn to compromise between the stripped down exposition and headlong narrative drive of stories like 'Dr. Ain' and the richer introspective mood and lusher stylistic details of stories like 'The Snows Are Melted, the Snows Are Gone' to produce fiction that combines the best of both modes."[40] Whether about the horror of love and sexuality, as told by a large insect searching for his mate; the tragic appeal of living as another and the cybernetic technology and capital that makes it possible; or capitalist heteropatriarchy's egotistical self-destruction of the planet and the cloned women who have a second chance to heal it, Tiptree's stories of the 1960s and '70s fascinated and awed readers. He took home a Nebula Award for "Love Is the Plan, the Plan Is Death" in 1973, a Hugo Award for "The Girl Who Was Plugged In" in 1974, and one of each for "Houston, Houston, Do You Read?" in 1976.

Tiptree never accepted his prizes in person. A self-declared recluse and a world traveler, he conducted all his business through written correspondence and, apologizing for his inability to attend awards ceremonies, often asked that the awards be sent to his agent. When in 1973 the Nebula Awards' Chairman Alan Dean Foster, anticipating Tiptree's reluctance to attend the banquet, offered to deliver Tiptree's Nebula to him personally when next in Washington, DC, Tiptree deflected in his typical jovial manner: "Many thanks for holding the beautiful object. . . . I'd like nothing better than to meet you in Sept. but am almost sure to be away at that time, a pity because it's nice here then. Tell you what: could you ship it to Bob Mills for me? I'll get it off him when I know where I'll be at."[41] A few times Tiptree had Jeffrey D. Smith, editor of the *Khatru* fanzine, accept awards on his behalf.[42] At a time when the new wave was revitalizing both science fiction and its fandom, this was odd. Dozois wrote about Tiptree's unusual anonymity: "Everyone knows everyone else, or knows *of* them at least, and even those people who generally avoid science fiction conventions and professional meetings are known to be known: someone, somewhere, knows them, has had them pointed out to him in passing, has spoken to them on the telephone, or at least knows someone who has. Not so with James Tiptree, Jr."[43]

Tiptree did develop epistolary friendships with other authors, fans, and editors. With other authors, he was usually the first of the two to reach out, sending eloquent fan letters of his own and then acting surprised when they returned an interest in his work. In 1970, when Philip K. Dick came across Tiptree's name on a Nebula nomination list and realized the guy who had been sending him fan letters for a year was an author himself, he asked, "Why didn't you tell me? Your story is damn good."[44] Tiptree promptly dismissed his writerly talents in his response: "My personal feeling is that as a writer I come on like a ninety-year-old sex fiend. Endless false starts, wriggling, doing everything but what's needful. A natural gift for the cliché, the horridly cute phrase. I cling onto limp ideas like a paranoid slug."[45] Despite (or perhaps because of) such endearing self-effacement (which, of course, was often quite exquisitely put through the awful metaphors of highly gendered sexual bodies), many of these epistolary friendships grew as deep as any "real life" relationship, lasting years, developing across hundreds of pages of correspondence, and fast exceeding professional decorum. In the early 1970s, Tiptree flirted with Le Guin, bashfully turned down an invitation to collaborate from Dick, and fervidly debated feminist matters with Russ.[46] It was through these friendships with Le Guin and Russ that, a few years later, Tiptree was brought into the *Khatru* symposium, and Sheldon helped shape feminist SF fandom in Tiptree's and Raccoona's contributions to the earliest feminist SF fanzines (see chapter 3). Still, no one ever met Tiptree in person or spoke to him on the phone. Tiptree grew so notorious for his elusiveness that, in 1975, one convention organizer even offered "glasses with the funny nose and mustache if [he] decide[d] to come but wish[ed] to remain unknown."[47] When fans began knocking on the door at the address in McLean, Virginia, included in Tiptree's early fanzine correspondence, Sheldon quickly secured a Post Office box.[48]

By the mid-1970s, rumors were circulating through SF fandom that Tiptree was an agent with the Central Intelligence Agency (CIA), a homosexual, or a woman.[49] Appropriately, Silverberg titled his introduction to Tiptree's *Warm Worlds and Otherwise* collection "Who Is Tiptree? What Is He?" To many, Tiptree's privacy, residence in the Washington, DC, area, and thorough knowledge of world affairs made the government official theory compelling. To most, the theories that he was either gay or female seemed far-fetched. Tiptree flirted not only with Le Guin (though their relationship was special) but with most women who wrote to him.[50] Plus, there was the clear virility of his protagonists and his prose. Silverberg insisted that the "ineluctably masculine" quality of Tiptree's writing made such rumors absurd.[51] Silverberg's statements are now notorious because he made them in a popular publication, but he was not alone in his beliefs. Dozois similarly wrote, "Tiptree is definitely his own man, a maverick individual even in our maverick and individualistic field."[52] In fact, a point of contention between Dozois and Silverberg was the comparability of Tiptree's masculine style to that of Ernest Hemingway. Whereas Silverberg thought the two authors shared a directness, Dozois considered Tiptree's voice "jazzy, irreverent, exuberant, colloquial" next to Hemingway's "deceptively 'natural' style."[53] For many who also corresponded with Tiptree, as Silverberg and Dozois both did, "Uncle Tip," as he often referred to himself, was clearly the older bachelor he claimed to be. Years later, Smith explained that, for most of Tiptree's fans and colleagues, asking questions such as "What if Tiptree were a woman? What if Tiptree were a spy?" was merely a fun game.[54]

As it turns out, none of these rumors was far-fetched. In November 1976, people began learning that Tiptree (always known to be a pseudonym) was the pen name of sixty-one-year-old Alice B. Sheldon, who earlier in life had worked in photo intelligence for the CIA and, though married, would soon come out to her SF friends as a lesbian. Tiptree always shared incredible details about his life, and in late 1976, when Tiptree wrote to friends about his mother's recent death, including a public letter to be published in the next issue of *Khatru*, he had finally shared too much. There were enough details in the *Khatru* letter for Smith, after a quick perusal of obituaries out of Chicago, to determine that Tiptree's mother was the explorer and author Mary Hastings Bradley.[55] According to the obituary, Bradley was survived by her only child, Alice Bradley Sheldon. Smith intended to let Sheldon know she would be divulging too much if Tiptree's letter was published in the fanzine, but before he could notify her, letters arrived from others who had made the same deduction.[56] Smith instead wrote to Sheldon to pass along the news of her inevitable outing.

The news of Tiptree's "true" identity became public in January 1977 when the SF trade journal *Locus* ran a column titled "Tiptree Revealed." The column, short but prominently placed at the top of the publication's front page, concluded, "In a recent speech, Ted Sturgeon commented that nearly all of the top newer writers, with the exception of James Tiptree, Jr., were women. The exception is now gone."[57] Worried that Tiptree's dearest friends might hear the news through such an announcement and feel betrayed, Sheldon spent much of November and December 1976 writing to them to explain in her own words and according to the nature of their relationship. Sheldon first wrote to Smith, "Yeah. Alice Sheldon. Five-feet-eight, sixty-one years, remains of a good-looking girl vaguely visible, grins a lot in a depressed way, very active in spurts. Also, Raccoona."[58] To Dozois, Sheldon expressed fearing that "a valued friendship is trembling in the balance."[59] Dozois wrote back that Sheldon had nothing to fear; he hoped Sheldon would continue to write and stay in touch. For the time being, Dozois said, he preferred to keep addressing his letters to Tip, "'Alli' still feel[ing] like a stranger in [his] mouth." While

189

largely supportive and encouraging, Dozois describes being disoriented by Sheldon's coming out, using a vernacular not unlike that of many cisgender people when processing the news of a close friend's gender transition: "But it's strange, like talking to somebody who keeps turning into somebody else before your eyes and then instantly flicking back again. . . . At the moment you're this vauge [*sic*] churning chimera shape, half man and half woman, and when I re-read your last letter I 'hear' it in two different 'voices,' one the usual 'Tiptree voice' I've developed over the years, and the other a new voice my subconscious instantly whipped up to cope with the fact of your being female."[60]

Dozois was not alone in his disorientation. Susan Janice Anderson, who had served as both Tiptree's and Raccoona's editor in the feminist SF anthology *Aurora: Beyond Equality* (1976), wrote to "Tip, Raccoona, Alice": "I've spent the past few days working through <u>emotionally</u> how I felt about Tiptree changing from male to female. It's one thing to explore themes of sexual equality intellectually, fictionally, and another to experience them as an emotional reality. One disappointment was losing such a wonderfully humane non-sexist male as Tiptree (may others appear in his place!). But my disappointment has been more than balanced by the knowledge that such a broad-minded, empathetic *human being* as yourself exists."[61] Anderson's co-editor, Vonda McIntyre, similarly wrote, "You, Raccoona Sheldon, Alli, have your own place in my heart; it's very near Tip's but it will take me a little time to push them close enough to combine them."[62] Contrary to Sheldon's fear, in coming out Sheldon lost few friends. Still, many, such as Dozois, Anderson, and McIntyre, admitted that it would take them a while to reconcile the man they knew with the woman who now stood figuratively before them.

Over the coming year, as Sheldon corresponded further with these and other friends to whom Tiptree had grown close, she would continually insist that "everything" she had written them "other than the signature" was true.[63] Sometimes this sounded like an excuse: "I was very careful about pronouns, things like 'child' instead of 'boy,' etc., etc."[64] Sheldon could not help the fact that the oddities of her life (parents who were explorers and thus childhood trips to the Congo, Nairobi, India, and Shanghai; military service during World War II; a doctorate in behavioral psychology; and work for the CIA) were more typical of a twentieth-century man than a woman. In these letters, Sheldon also describes playing off people's gendered assumptions as a feminist strategy. Sheldon tells Smith, for example, that during *Khatru*'s "Women in Science Fiction" symposium she realized that she could do a lot for younger women as an esteemed male comrade, "whereas just another woman coming in with sympathy and admiration tends to dissolve in a mutual embrace of woe."[65] It was at this same time that Tiptree withdrew "The Women Men Don't See" from the 1974 Nebula Award finals so as to not steal votes as a male feminist. Sheldon retrospectively explained to Silverberg, "That was why I pulled THE WOMEN MEN DON'T SEE out of the Nebula, I was afraid too many women—maybe men too—would vote for it as approbation for a male having that much insight."[66] At the time, Tiptree's female friends chastised him for the decision. McIntyre addressed the envelope containing her letter on the matter to "James Tiptree Dumbdumb Jr." and sternly wrote, as his editor, that Tiptree had better not pull such antics when "Houston, Houston" got nominated.[67] Thus, while early impressions that the person behind the pseudonym "Tiptree" was male might owe much to his readers' sexist assumptions about men's writing and lives, by 1974 Sheldon was feeding such presumptions by actively playing the part of the male feminist.

Feminist fun may have been behind such strategies, but in Sheldon's coming out letters of late 1976 and early 1977 she also often describes a feeling of truthfulness to Tiptree's masculinity. Sheldon insists that she did not lie. Instead, "What started as a prank dreamed its way into reality."[68] As Tiptree began making epistolary friends, he became not just a projection or veil but his own person, who was both part of Sheldon and not her at the same time. "Tiptree kept taking on a stronger and stronger life of his own," Sheldon told Smith. "This voice would speak up from behind my pancreas somewhere. *He* insisted on the nickname ['Tip'], he would not be 'Jim.'"[69] Sheldon elaborated, "And his persona wasn't too constricting; I wrote as me."[70] This persona was not purely literary or intellectual. Tiptree discussed his sexuality and physicality with friends (and not just through the unflattering metaphors such as those Tiptree used with Dick). Responding to an early inquiry from Russ, for example, Tiptree wrote, "No, I'm not gay so far as I know," and, elaborating in his next letter, "All right, I'll confess. What sends me is what I can't have because it isn't there. . . . Aliens. . . . I don't think they'll save me or save civilisation [*sic*], or do anything in particular—I just WANT 'EM. . . . Silicone flesh, green blood—tender six-legged girls."[71] On another occasion, when he angered Russ, Tiptree described his blunder: "It was just like a crass, presumptuous, raucous-mouthed old man."[72] Later still, when Russ made guesses about his appearance, Tiptree responded, "I'm not a 'new man,' whatever else. . . . But your radar is uncanny, 'middle-size, slight, sandy-hair' would be just right before the grey came in. Also to be known by a scar on the (unmustached) upper lip where a house fell on me, giving me a vaguely cynical right profile."[73] Tip/Alli never fully let go of this masculine physicality of Tiptree. In the feminist SF tradition of humorous self-reflexivity (see chapter 3), Tip/Alli wrote to Smith about anxiety regarding meeting readers' expectations for women's writing: "If there is something which is going to burst forth from my liberated gonads, it hasn't peeped yet. In fact, I may be written out for a while."[74] Of course, as Sheldon was well aware, "gonads" scientifically name testes and ovaries. However, under patriarchy, one rarely speaks of the latter, liberated or not, "bursting forth" (though I myself like to tease my younger sibling that my egg swam faster).

While at times Tip/Alli called on this masculine physicality humorously, Sheldon also recounted Tiptree's masculinity and maleness at equally sober moments of epistolary friendship. One example of this is in Tiptree's correspondence with the fantasy writer Jessica Amanda Salmonson, who began publishing fantastical works of poetry and fiction in the late 1970s. Between 1977 and 1979 she edited the feminist fantasy fanzine *Windhaven*.[75] Around this same time, Salmonson attended WisCon and contributed art, fiction, reviews, and letters of comment to *Janus*.[76] Salmonson is a trans woman, and in the 1970s she wrote mass letters to friends and acquaintances chronicling her experiences transitioning and how they informed her lesbian feminist politics.[77] Tiptree was on Salmonson's mailing list, and on November 13, 1975, just over a year before Tiptree's reveal, Tiptree wrote to Salmonson, praising her for her courage in "stepping across the sex-role barriers" before vaguely articulating his ability to relate and asking a series of probing questions that reads as overinvestment. Important in such substantive matters, Tiptree pedantically explains, is "honesty," which he has "fought to maintain . . . at least within [him]self, all [his] life." Articulating a cissexist confusion that reads as extremely bizarre coming from Tiptree, the author expresses his surprise to have "[found] a man who will exchange all the social advantages of the male role . . . for being what [Salmonson] correctly calls 'a game animal.' A target. A member of an oppressed class." Yet again playing the 1970s male feminist, but with an earnestness and quizzicality honest to this personal correspondence, Tiptree elaborates: "The hassles of sexism my female friends tell me of, which I'm just beginning to see in their full extent. Why? What makes it worth it?" He also wonders whether Salmonson is considering surgery as well as hormones; whether she would secretly want to be able to "change back"; and whether she has any desire to raise children. As for himself, Tiptree tells Salmonson that he is "making a long-sustained effort to live in non-material ways, to bloom under the suns of imagination. It seems like there might be some new ways to feel, waiting out there." While this turn to psychic processes of imagination, as opposed to material practices of hormones and surgery, might "remove [Tiptree] from [Salmonson's] lively circle," to Salmonson in 1975 the connections Tiptree appears dedicated to drawing between their experiences may have read like the confessions of another trans woman.[78] Knowing what we know now about Sheldon, one wonders whether instead, in corresponding with Salmonson as Tiptree, Sheldon was working through feelings around transmasculinity.

Tiptree, and Sheldon's masculinity more broadly, was not confined to SF publications and correspondence. Although a pseudonym, Tiptree also enjoyed an epistolary life as a US citizen and Virginia resident. In January 1974, Tiptree wrote to Joel T. Broyhill, one of Sheldon's Republican representatives, asking him not to support any constitutional amendment that would impede women's access to abortion. In 1973, Sheldon had corresponded back and forth with Broyhill, making an impassioned plea for him to see women's right to choose from the perspective of women dying during illegal abortions.[79] In 1974, Tiptree added his two cents but made the case from an entirely different perspective. Whereas Sheldon appealed to Broyhill's emotions, asking for empathy, Tiptree appealed to Broyhill's fiscal conservatism and argued, as a local businessman, that abortion should be supported because unwanted children were expensive for all taxpayers.[80] Sheldon emphasized the two's differences visually, as she did in all her correspondence, using one typewriter for her legal identity and another for Tiptree.

The earnestness of Sheldon's masculinity, evidenced in Tiptree's non- or beyond nom de plume correspondence, is corroborated in Sheldon's journals. In the 1970s, at the height of Tiptree's career, Sheldon journaled avidly. The entries include both personal reflections on her day and notes for potential story ideas or characters. Intermixed among these writings Sheldon chronicled the speculative experiences of Alex, a male alter ego free of her sexual hang-ups and proactive in finding solutions to situations that paralyzed her. Across 1976 and 1977, as Sheldon corresponded with Tiptree's friends and the SF community reckoned with the news of her identity, Sheldon, who had struggled with depression for much of her life, experienced extensive bouts of listlessness, anxiety, and depression. Alex would emerge in such moments as her stronger, calmer self. Sheldon would frequently describe her depression or anxiety at great length before "appeal[ing] to Alex" or asking, "What would Alex do?" On February 14, 1977, Sheldon bemoaned her inability to come up with a new plot for a story before wondering to herself, "My god, am I really going to be able to produce again?" Sheldon then asks herself, "If Alex felt as cheesy as I do, what would he do? Go for a walk? But it's raining, and threatening more." Sheldon, having gone for such a walk, writes upon her return, "I did, and got soaked . . . headache still with me. Took 2 codeine."[81]

Still, Alex was not just a less depressed, more productive professional male alter ego. Alex also provided Sheldon with a means to express sexual desires and masculine and male senses of self. With a doctorate in behavioral psychology and decades of therapy, Sheldon made a frequent habit of analyzing herself in her diaries. That the loss of her mother led to the loss of Tiptree was significant to her. Just as she was freed from an overbearing (and on at least one occasion during adolescence, sexually abusive) parent,[82] she lost the freedom Tiptree had provided. Alex, whom Sheldon refers to in her journal as "Tiptree's forerunner," served as a mitigating foil during this time.[83] In a journal entry written days after Tiptree's outing, Sheldon describes turning to masturbation for comfort and then, reflecting on this choice, bemoans finding herself in her accompanying fantasy "not a man," "not the doer, the penetrator."[84] Sheldon attributes this to the loss of Tiptree, "my 'magical' manhood, his pen my prick."[85]

The startling social and psychic castration Sheldon experienced with Tiptree's outing reveals the gravity behind queer patronymic appropriation. Judith Butler argues that the durability of patronymic names is dependent on the changeableness of feminine names and, in their analysis of Willa Cather's fiction, champions the appropriation of patronyms as a method of destabilizing social law.[86] In their attention to fictional characters, however, Butler neglects the devastating effect the failure of queer patronymic appropriation—or, perhaps more specifically in some cases, trans self-naming—might have on a historical subject such as Sheldon. As Sheldon elaborates in her journal entry dated February 2, 1977, "I had through [Tiptree] all the power & prestige of masculinity. I was—though an aging intellectual—<u>of</u> those who own the world." Now, she "loathe[s] being a woman. Wanting to be <u>done to</u>."[87] In being outed to SF fandom, Sheldon's gendered and sexual sense of self was undone. Through this difficult period, Alex remained above such perils. In her journal, Sheldon acknowledges that "some men have masochistic fantasies" before castigating "the hell with them. (Alex doesn't)." While Sheldon was "never to have known the simple power & pleasure of the penis" and Tiptree got "the prestige, the acceptance" of the phallus, Alex knew both. Tiptree's "death" was devastating because it meant never being able to participate in a public (if not the social law proper) as a man. It also caused Sheldon to confront the fact that "I'll never have it. I'm stuck with this perverse, second rate body; my life."[88] Through this experience Alex traveled alongside Alice, the man Sheldon could be, the person as whom Sheldon often wished to live.

Sheldon did, however, also at times identify, including positively, as a woman. While playfully participating in feminist SF fandom as the staunch and at times ignorant male feminist, Sheldon occasionally longed to be a part of the sisterhood of Russ, Le Guin, Suzy McKee Charnas, McIntyre, and the others. Sheldon sometimes got the urge, as she later explained, "to write as me, or at least a woman." Thus, she created the second public persona of Raccoona Sheldon.[89] As previously mentioned, Raccoona published alongside Tiptree in the collection *Aurora: Beyond Equality*. In fact, Raccoona's "Your Faces, O My Sisters! Your Faces Filled of Light!" immediately precedes Tiptree's award-winning "Houston, Houston, Do You Read?"[90] While Raccoona did not have the same robust epistolary life as Tiptree, she did participate actively in her own way. In 1975, when Tiptree was getting intellectually clobbered by Russ, McIntyre, and Delany in the *Khatru* symposium (see chapter 3), Raccoona was corresponding at length with the editor of *The Witch and the Chameleon*, Amanda Bankier. In July 1975, she wrote to Bankier about a seemingly "gay-oriented" fanzine, hoping it was for gay women. Appealing to the minoritizing view of lesbian feminism, she elaborates, "Some of my best friends are male gays, but women they are not. And our thing is not theirs, pleasant though many may be." As for herself, she writes, "I'm so old nobody including me would care if I'm gay or straight or queer for typewriters."[91] However, Bankier did care, and she published Raccoona's poems, letters, and drawings, including a romantic sketch of two women staring into each other's eyes (see figure 4.1). Still, Raccoona was never as successful in publishing or in garnering fans as Tiptree. When Salmonson heard the news that Tiptree and Raccoona were the machinations of the same person, she wrote to Sheldon that she thought it "marvelous." Unlike others in feminist SF fandom, Salmonson did not presume Raccoona was any more Sheldon than Tiptree was. She told Sheldon she found herself "lamenting somewhat the 'loss' of Racoona [*sic*]," having found her a "remarkable, loving, radical woman," compared with Tiptree, who "annoyed [her] at times."[92] Such glowing reviews of Raccoona were rare. While Sheldon later complained about editors' sexism when it came to Raccoona, she also admitted to giving Raccoona some of her weaker stories.[93] Nevertheless, Raccoona's "The Screwfly Solution"—a short story composed of letters between a husband and wife as men destroy society, misogyny having been caught like a virus—won a Nebula in 1977.

195

4.1 Raccoona Sheldon, illustration, *The Witch and the Chameleon* 5–6, 1976.

Sheldon's outing in 1977 brought an end to Raccoona. When Sheldon published science fiction, it was under Tiptree's name. However, Sheldon did
begin participating in SF fandom as a woman without the Raccoona pseudonym. In November 1975, Tiptree had written a self-described "disturbing
query" to Russ: "Am I looking in the womens' [*sic*] movement for my missing
daughter, or sister?"[94] A year later, when Sheldon revealed herself to Russ,
she proclaimed: "God, the number of times I've wanted to cry out, dear
Sister, how well I know, how well I know what you mean."[95] Meanwhile, the
second iteration of WisCon was fast approaching, and while Jeanne Gomoll
had sent both Raccoona and Tiptree invitations the year before, this year
she wrote to Sheldon directly. Upon receiving a standard declination due to

travel, this time from Sheldon rather than Tiptree, Gomoll sent a poster for the "Will the Real James Tiptree, Jr. Please Stand Up!" skit she and others were preparing for the convention (see figure 4.2). Three panelists dominate the poster, each seated behind a podium like a game show contestant. One is a mustached man shielded by dark aviators and wearing a fedora and trench coat, a paper with "[to]p secret" jutting out of one pocket. Another is a be-spectacled, well-accessorized older academic woman waving welcomingly to an unseen audience. And the third is a casually reclining young woman in safari gear, holding a rifle and accompanied by an African guide. While two of these recalled Tiptree's and Raccoona's personalities, another represented the unmasked Alice B. Sheldon, an independent, masculine white woman and daughter of the famous explorer Mary Hastings Bradley.

News of Sheldon's identity soon spread through the women's movement at large. In 1977 Sheldon was invited—alongside Russ, Le Guin, Charnas, McIntyre, Marge Piercy, Pamela Sargent, Elizabeth A. Lynn, Chelsea Quinn Yarbro, and Kate Wilhelm—to contribute a letter on her writing to an academic dossier on women's fiction in *Frontiers: A Journal of Women's Studies*.[96] In the letter, Tip/Alli names "Houston, Houston" and "The Women Men Don't See" as Tiptree's "really feminist tales" and recommends "'The Screw-fly Solution' . . . , another heavy feminist story by me, writing as Raccoona Sheldon."[97] A few years later, when "Houston, Houston" was solicited for a collection of lesbian and gay science fiction, Sheldon wrote to the editors about the real-world inspiration for the novella's "woman's world"—her time in the Women's Army Corps (WAC). As a member of the WAC, Sheldon began a relationship with an Army nurse, Ava "Dilly" Dilworth. The two maintained their romantic and sexual relationship for many years after their time together during the war, and it was with Dilly that Sheldon, like Alex, got to be the doer, not the done to.[98] While Sheldon kept this relationship quite private, she described to the editors of the gay and lesbian SF anthology *Worlds Apart* living among twelve thousand women at Fort Des Moines as "the most exciting experience of [her] life." It was there that Sheldon "*did* see a real 'women's world' not too unlike the one hinted at in 'Houston.'"[99]

Despite her newly found freedom to speak publicly as a lesbian, Sheldon never fully joined fandom, the women's movement, or gay liberation. Sheldon started speaking on the phone with a number of formerly purely epistolary friends and even had Smith, who would eventually become the executor of Sheldon's literary estate, over for lunch.[100] However, Sheldon never attended WisCon or any other convention. At first, Sheldon continued to dodge invitations from Gomoll and others, much as Tiptree had, claiming

4.2 Jeanne Gomoll, flyer, "Will the REAL James Tiptree, Jr. Please Stand Up!" (1977).

to be traveling (which the author often was). But before long, Sheldon was sending brutally honest declinations, explaining that while quite gregarious in print, she was unfortunately painfully agoraphobic.[101] She joined two chapters of the National Organization for Women but spent much of her day-to-day life among women "untouched by [feminism], who d[id]n't even care about—or <u>know</u> about—ERA (Which Virginia has failed to ratify)."[102]

Le Guin ended her flirtation with Tiptree when she learned of Sheldon's identity.[103] But such epistolary exchanges were soon taken up with Russ, with whom Sheldon could speak about her sexuality and sexual history. In July 1977, Sheldon described herself to Russ as a "frustrated gay," writing that "gays were always throwing themselves at my once-handsome feet, and I hadn't a clue how to pick them up. Still don't really."[104] Three years later, Sheldon wrote that she, too, was a Lesbian (with a capital L) "or at least as close as one can come to being one never having had a successful love with any of the women I've loved." She bemoaned to the other author, "Oh, had 65 years been different! I like some men a lot, but from the start, before I knew anything, it was always girls & women who lit me up."[105] Upon receiving the first such complaint, Russ propositioned Sheldon, "Your very description of your 'aging body' turns me on," elaborating, "I was in love with you when you were 'James Tiptree, Jr' and have been able to transfer the infatuation to Allie [sic] Sheldon, who is, after all, the same person."[106] Russ and Sheldon never met in person, despite repeated requests by Russ. Nonetheless, over the coming years they spoke on the phone; wrote to each other about their sexual fantasies; sent each other erotic postcards; and declared their love for each other many times over. They discussed Adrienne Rich; *The Coming Out Stories*, edited by Julia Penelope Stanley and Susan J. Wolfe; and Tiptree's newest "Lesbian 'I love aliens' sf yarn." [107] "With Delicate Mad Hands" (1981) ends with a coda revealing that the aliens of the far-off lavender planet on which the human protagonist has crash-landed choose their genders when they come of age. Sheldon writes Russ that the reason the story is "indirectly a Lesbian 'I love aliens' sf yarn'" is that "neither lover knows or cares what sex the other is, heroine (human) ends calling alien 'he' because she doesn't feel 'sisterly.'" [108] *Lesbian* outpaces the present. It transcends pronouns. It names sex and romance that exceed anything either human or alien has ever known. Sheldon describes "the sexiest bit" as the scene where the two lovers are "divided by a window, holding palms up together, and the alien by mental commo 'forces' the knowledge of their mutual love on heroine's recognition." Sheldon then asks Russ, "Have you ever noticed what palm-to-palm contact can do if it <u>has</u> to?"[109] Fandom, feminism, and gay liberation were eager and ready for the female Tiptree, but Sheldon—though eager and open with Russ—was still shy of ready for them.

If everything about Tiptree except his signature had been Sheldon, it is important to note that, on coming out as female, Sheldon did not switch to signing letters with her legal name. Instead, Sheldon signed her November 23, 1976, letter to Smith as "Tip/Alli," and it is this signature that Sheldon would continue to use in SF correspondence for the rest of her life. Sometimes Sheldon would abbreviate it to "T/A," as she did in the 1980 "With Delicate Mad Hands" letter to Russ.[110] In the *Frontiers* table of contents, despite being a dossier of "Letters from Women Fantasy and Science Fiction Writers," Tiptree, not Sheldon, is listed as one of the contributors and signed the letter "Tip/Alli (James Tiptree, Jr.)."[111] With acquaintances, Tip/Alli would often split in two. This is seen in instances where Sheldon held on to Tiptree as an entity who was both part of her and his own person. When speaking with an interviewer about writing, for example, Sheldon answered, "Now James Tiptree—I'm not trying to be cute here, I mean the voice that murmurs in the darkness when all else is silence and you're alone—Tiptree may know something more about writing, but if so he hasn't told Alice B. Sheldon, and I'm afraid that's whom you're talking with today."[112] With the friends Tiptree had made over the preceding decade within feminist SF fandom, however, Tip/Alli found a kind of equilibrium. While Sheldon's news had been disorienting to many of Tiptree's friends, including Dozois and Anderson, the masculine Tip was never replaced by a feminine Alli. Instead, they got Tip/Alli, someone who was never consistently female or particularly feminine. This included additionally cute nicknames that proliferated between Tip/Alli and close SF friends. Le Guin, who had often addressed Tiptree as simply "Tree," sometimes even drawing a tilted pine, now often wrote to "Allitree." And in a playful acknowledgment of her friend's rich identity, Le Guin addressed one 1977 letter to "Allicampane Raccoona Gerbilia Tippo Sempervirens."[113]

In saying Tip/Alli was neither consistently female nor particularly feminine, I am not making the presentist argument that Sheldon was nonbinary. Nor is my transfeminist reading of Tiptree's genealogy intended to claim Sheldon as a transgender man. To me, the archives reveal a genderqueerness or transness to Tip/Alli's story that exceeds any singular identity, as they are currently thought, a genderqueerness that the writing of women's liberation as a cisgender women's movement and lesbian feminism as a gender-conforming and essentialist political formation obfuscates. That Sheldon would claim *Lesbian* late in life, after Tiptree's 1977 reveal and in conversation with both cisgender and transgender lesbian feminists, such as Russ and Salmonson, supports my argument that in the late 1970s the word *Lesbian* signified something far more nebulous and dynamic than it has come to signify following queer movements and queer studies of the 1990s. Lesbian potentiality, for Sheldon and many of Sheldon's peers, included exploring gender in ways that may look nonbinary or transmasculine to us today (and that may read entirely differently as something else yet unnamed years after the "today" of this writing/reading).

Next Generation: Siblings in the Tip/Alli Archive

Tiptree's story not only demands a rethinking of gender during the height of lesbian feminism; it also inspires a transfeminist revision of feminist genealogy. I see the signature "Tip/Alli" as symbolic of the transitive (if not always transgender) work engendered by Sheldon's outing. In *Shimmering Images: Trans Cinema, Embodiment, and the Aesthetics of Change*, Eliza Steinbock explores the logics of the "cine-typographic technology" of the slash (/) as seen in self-representations of before/after (transitioning, surgery, identities, etc.).[114] Whereas cis authors often use a slash to mark the subject made possible through the cut of surgery and cis filmmakers frequently make cinematic cuts to construct prototypical trans subjects, trans authors and artists often use these and other methods of montage to account for nonbinary shimmering over and through the cuts of perceived sex.[115] In Tip/Alli's case, such a slash carried with it a very particular cultural meaning. Beginning in the 1970s, "Kirk/Spock" (K/S) romantic and pornographic writing by female *Star Trek* fans circulated through a particular subset of fandom via the publication and distribution of "slash" fanzines.[116] Sheldon was a *Star Trek* fan and, like Russ and many others of their time, loved Spock especially and read K/S avidly.[117] Considering that the slash between the characters' names signified the characters' romantic and sexual relation to each other, Sheldon's choice of Tip/Alli as a post-Tiptree SF correspondence moniker is rather suggestive of masturbation and self-love. The author's two past selves coupled to produce a new self and beget siblings of great variety.

During the last few years of the 1970s, Tip/Alli's story circulated through SF fandom and, in cases such as the *Frontiers* dossier, the women's movement. Now when people discover Tiptree's fiction, depending on where they read it (whether in an original SF magazine, short story collection of the era, or reprinted collection or post-reveal novel), they may or may not discover Sheldon's biography simultaneously or in quick succession. While not as famous in the mainstream as other new wave authors, Tip/Alli's fiction and life have had an immeasurable influence on many queer, nonbinary, and transgender readers. Sheldon was roughly twenty years older than Russ, Le Guin, and Dick, and just as Sheldon corresponded with them as peers (or even, as Tiptree so often did at first, with the great reverence of a subordinate), Tiptree's and Raccoona's fans have found in the author and the author's life story not a parent but an intergenerational sibling more akin to (if differently gendered from) a feminist "sister."

Sheldon was far from the first author to write what was perceived to be masculine fiction under a male or gender-neutral pseudonym and later inspire feminist readings of her work. Like Willa Cather, who began writing under pseudonyms and later went by "Will," Sheldon for the most part articulated her queer desire through heterosexual representations, and her use of a male pseudonym enabled the movement of this desire's articulation through a wider readership than her own name would have. One might therefore argue, much as Butler does in the case of Cather's fiction, that Sheldon, in appropriating a patronym as a part of her masculine writing practice, displaced the social basis of its identity-conferring function and opened up the referent to gendered and sexual epistemological contestation.[118] As Phillips notes, "With the 'Junior' in her name, she took a place in the hierarchy of fathers and sons," the author's queer appropriation containing from the start a hint of the genealogical done anew.[119]

Tip/Alli's story is exceptional in a few regards. Significantly, Sheldon did not do this work of contesting the function of gendered language and expanding the possibilities of gender alone. Tip/Alli was a part of a counterpublic—a rare 1970s feminist counterpublic that, as I argue in chapter 3, has been able to adapt and grow into the twenty-first century. Furthermore, Tip/Alli left this counterpublic abundant language about Tiptree, Raccoona, Sheldon, Alex, and Tip/Alli. This language, quoted extensively across this chapter, is archived in Sheldon's papers at the University of Oregon. As early as the 1970s, Sheldon began imagining an audience for even her most personal writing—her journals and correspondence. When attempting to dissuade a concerned correspondent about these archival plans, the author wrote, "So relent; think of that far-off PhD candidate, reverently fingering your yellowed pages with green furry fingers, and feeling you live again in the facets of her huge nocturnal eyes."[120] But before my fellow furry-fingered colleagues and I could get our hands on Sheldon's papers, Sheldon's accounts of living as Tiptree became accessible to feminist SF fans due to a posthumously published volume of largely autobiographical work edited by Smith,

Meet Me at Infinity (2000), and a biography by Phillips, *James Tiptree, Jr.: The Double Life of Alice B. Sheldon* (2006).

This self-writing, when coupled with Tiptree's and Raccoona's fiction, has generated a great volume of discourse about gender and sexuality. As a result, Tip/Alli's names have only proliferated, among other things becoming attached to not one but two annual prizes: the James Tiptree, Jr. Literary Award (Tiptree Award; 1991–2019) and the Tiptree Fellowship (2014–2019). In 2015, Australia's independent speculative fiction publishing house Twelfth Planet Press published *Letters to Tiptree* in celebration of what would have been Sheldon's one-hundredth birthday.[121] The volume is a collection of forty letters from feminist, lesbian, bisexual, and transgender fans and authors written to Tip/Alli, explaining how the author's life and work affected them personally and professionally. While Tiptree's letters in the *Khatru* symposium shaped feminist SF fandom as a counterpublic, distinct from both mainstream fandom and the women's movement more broadly conceived, and Raccoona's drawings in *The Witch and the Chameleon* gave image to the forms of intimacy this counterpublic enabled, in addressing these letters to "Alice," "Tiptree," "Alice Sheldon," "Dr. Sheldon," "Mr. Tiptree," "Mr. James A. Tiptree, Jr.," "Alice," "Tip," "Alli," "James Tiptree & Alice Sheldon," "James/Alice (and sometimes Raccoona)," and "James Tiptree/Raccoona Sheldon/Alice Bradley/Alice Sheldon/others," the authors of these letters sustain the growth and transformation of feminist SF fandom through their own appropriation and repurposing of the author's many names, patronymic and otherwise.

An initial glance at these letters would reveal Tip/Alli to be a very site of the kinds of feminist contestation described at the start of this chapter. Among the diverse addresses and their nearly equally diverse authors, you could sort out those, such as the contemporary lesbian SF author Nicola Griffith, who wish to shore up a more contained, gender-normative understanding of *lesbian* for Sheldon and carry this conception of Sheldon into the present, and those, such as Lee Mandelo, Cheryl Morgan, and Bogi Takács, who find elements of their trans experiences wrapped up in Tip/Alli and take this as a reason to speculate about how Sheldon might identify were the author to have been born in a different era, such as their own. Both pursuits draw on what we might, following queer studies, name the Tip/Alli archive, like the Brandon archive, which Jack Halberstam describes as having taken shape following Brandon Teena's murder. Exceeding Brandon Teena, the twenty-one-year-old who died in 1993 at the hands of transphobic white supremacists, the Brandon archive constitutes the multimedia discourse that emerged in the years that followed. The Brandon archive, Halberstam argues, "is simultaneously a resource, a productive narrative, a set of representations, a history, a memorial, and a time capsule."[122] As such, it sheds light on the many lives and social formations Brandon came to symbolize.

The Tip/Alli archive, which took shape across the 1990s and 2000s, after Sheldon's death by suicide in 1987, opened a range of queer and trans fannish returns to the lesbian 1970s. In her letter addressed to "Alice Sheldon" in *Letters to Tiptree*, Griffith references both Tip/Alli's letter to Russ about identifying as a lesbian and Sheldon's writing about her time in the WAC before claiming, "I suspect that if wanting to be a man was a thing of the body rather than the spirit, if you wanted physically to have been born a man—as opposed to yearning to be treated with the respect usually reserved to men—being among women would not have made you feel free or proud."[123] Mandelo, Morgan, and Takács, meanwhile, describe reading Phillips's biography as integral to their relationships with the author. Having heard Tip/Alli's story in all its richness, Mandelo, Morgan, and Takács share their own stories with Tip/Alli, building on the author's epistolary practices. Mandelo tells "James/Alice (and sometimes Raccoona)" that, in reading Tiptree's and Raccoona's stories that dealt with "that sense of not-quite-right-ness" and exploring "the space of one's love and one's body [as] an in-between or contested space," nonbinary and transmasculine people such as themself have been made to "feel less alone, or less marked out as different."[124] Morgan, meanwhile, fills "Alli" in about how she and others like her have to see psychiatrists and conform to gender stereotypes to receive gender-affirming hormones or surgery. "Old men—doctors—telling us how to be women," she writes. "You would have laughed. Joanna [Russ] would have burst a few blood vessels."[125] Takács asks "Tip," speculatively, "Could we . . . tackle vagaries of gender, how I am situated in the neither-land between male and female while you yourself seemingly occupied both?" One way to think about the compilation of Griffith's, Mandelo's, Morgan's, and Takács's letters in a Tiptree volume such as this is to take them as exemplary of the transfeminist debate getting played out within the family, as it were. In his introduction to *Meet Me at Infinity*, Smith tells readers, "I still 'hear' the male Tiptree voice when I reread the early letters, whereas you probably hear a female voice throughout."[126] The letters written *to* Tip/Alli (in all the author's manifestations) in that volume attest to the fact that, over the decades, the author has actually been heard across a great number of gender registers. Early feminist SF fanzines' letters of comment, including Tiptree's, addressed not simply an individual but a counterpublic that was marked off from both the general public of the mundane world and the dominant public of mainstream fandom. Well into the twenty-first century the authors in *Letters to Tiptree* continue feminist SF fandom's self-activity through the performative address of a multitude of Tip/Alli's. Thus, another way to think about the location of such conflicts around identity and feminist history is to take them as evidence of Tip/Alli's continuing older-sibling support of the still transformative process of potentiality. Even as the Lesbian sign's hold on potentiality as its primary radical feminist modifier relaxes, potentiality is not itself dispelled. Instead, it mutates and regenerates.

For many of the book's contributors, Tip/Alli's influence, much like the author's chosen genre, was transformative. Discovering Tip/Alli did not merely affirm what they already knew (about themselves, about gender, about feminism) but shifted each contributor's sense of possibility. The book opens with a letter by the author Jo Walton, written in the form of a poem, in which she describes Tip/Alli's effect on feminist SF fandom. Science fiction renders the present the history of the future.[127] Tip/Alli, Walton explains through SF metaphors of her own, rendered binary gender and the conflation of sex and gender a thing of our future's past:

> You rocked our spaceport,
> left it changed, wider,
> more solid, more open,
> stranger, expanded,
> containing doors undreamed of,
> marked "men," "women," "other."
> Now, each reaching out,
> shall we walk forward
> step into 'other'
> to see where it takes us?[128]

Knowing the present is nearly impossible, Fredric Jameson explains, because of "the sheer quantitative immensity of objects and individual lives it comprises . . . and also because it is occluded by the density of our private fantasies as well as the proliferating stereotypes of media culture that penetrates every remote zone of our existence."[129] However, science fiction shifts this sense of impossibility, providing the necessary perspective. "Upon our return from the imaginary constructs of SF," Jameson writes, the present "is offered to us in the form of some future world's remote past, as if posthumous and as though collectively remembered."[130] Likewise, for many 1970s SF fans, as well as those who have discovered Tip/Alli's fiction and life story since, the gender binary now appears quaint, a thing of the past. Many institutions, including much of academia, have yet to acclimate to the fact that "genders beyond the binary of male and female are neither fictive nor futural."[131] There are many gendered ways to move through the world, including a range of nonbinary modes. But what constitutes "men" and "women" also has changed profusely. Walton's poem describes all three doors—"men," "women," and "other"—as "undreamed of." One can no longer presume that being assigned male at birth leads to either "man" or masculinity; being assigned female at birth leads to "woman" or femininity; or that any of these will look, sound, or feel like they do for others. While transgender and gender-nonconforming people know this because of their lived experiences, and some cisgender people have learned as much from trans people and texts, others still have either discovered this or had such knowledge affirmed through encounters with the Tip/Alli archive.

Since 1992, the Tip/Alli archive has grown to include the authors and titles nominated for the James Tiptree, Jr. Literary Award. Each year for nearly thirty years the prize was awarded to a work of science fiction or fantasy that "expands or explores our understanding of gender."[132] The authors Pat Murphy and Karen Joy Fowler, two self-described "troublemakers," initially conceived of the Tiptree Award as a joke on the genre-writing community.[133] In February 1991, Murphy announced its creation at WisCon. She and Fowler intended "to shake things up. To make people examine the fiction they read a little more carefully. And to honor the woman who startled the science fiction world by making people suddenly rethink their assumptions about what women and men could do."[134] As Murphy tells the author in her *Letters to Tiptree* letter, she also wanted to "piss some people off"—namely, those involved in the feminist backlash of the 1980s, "those people who kept complaining that women's writing was ruining science fiction."[135] Unlike the somber sincerity of most awards ceremonies, Murphy and Fowler brought a sense of humor, apropos of Tip/Alli and feminist SF fandom, funding the prize through bake sales; crowning each year's winner with a sparkly tiara; and awarding winners with original works of art, a song about their story, and chocolate as well as money.[136] Funding for the prize expanded to include cookbooks with Tiptree puns for titles (*The Bakery Men Don't See* and *Her Smoke Rose up from Supper*), fan art T-shirts, and a humorously emceed WisCon auction. Before long, each year the prize was receiving hundreds of submissions from around the world. Thus, while the persona James Tiptree, Jr., was a "prank" that, according to Alice B. Sheldon, "dreamed its way into reality," the James Tiptree, Jr. Award became an institution, which, as Murphy for a number of years liked to joke, made it a prank on its own whimsical creators.[137]

Significantly, the Tiptree Award's institutionalization within feminist SF fandom built change into its process from the start. It was never meant to be a liberal celebration of representations of gender "equality"; thus, each jury has had to define for itself what exploring and expanding gender through science fiction means for its members that year. As the Tiptree Award's website read for a number of years, "The aim of the award is not to look for work that falls into some narrow definition of political correctness, but rather to seek out work that is thought-provoking, imaginative, and perhaps even infuriating. The Tiptree Award is intended to reward those writers and other artists who are bold enough to contemplate shifts and changes in gender roles, a fundamental aspect of any society."[138] Charnas, who served on the first jury, writes that among the many questions she and the other jury members discussed were: "What *did* James Tiptree, Jr. stand for, literally speaking? And, assuming we could figure that out, was that how we want to define the standards of this award, years after her death? Would she approve?. . . . What do *we* want this award to *do*?"[139] After winning the Tiptree Award in 1999 for *The Conqueror's Child*, Charnas was asked to serve on the jury for a second time. By then, she writes, the jury "no longer concerned themselves with what James Tiptree/Alice Sheldon would have thought, considering it sufficient for [their] purposes that in her working life she had personally blurred the line between male and female writers in her own authorial identity, to great and lasting effect."[140] And, writing in 2005 with what now strikes one as remarkable prescience, Charnas claimed that she would not be surprised if the Tiptree Award no longer existed in 2021. Part of the process each year, she explained, includes addressing the question of the award's longevity and purpose. Acknowledging the award's own impotentiality, Charnas argued that it would only last as long as it seemed a necessary cause. Should the award still exist in 2021, and should she still be around and able to judge again, however, Charnas wrote, she would jump at the chance. Yet again, "The first question raised among the judges would be familiar, and rightly so: 'What are we looking for, exactly, in our winner? What do we think this award should be doing now?'"[141] Named after Tip/Alli, the Tiptree Award, like any progeny, had a life of its own, but as markers of feminist SF fandom's thinking of gender across three decades, spanning the millennia, its winners, short list entries, and honor list entries are a part of the Tip/Alli genealogy.

As a member of the 2016 Tiptree Award jury and the chair of the Tiptree Fellowship Committee the year both the award and its younger sibling, the

207

fellowship, took new names, I count myself a part of this genealogy, too. My 2016 jury, which was chaired by Jeanne Gomoll and included Aimee S. Bahng, James Fox, and Deb Taber, waited to formulate our vision for such a prize's winner until we had a long list. Ultimately, we selected Anna-Marie McLemore's *When the Moon Was Ours*, a young adult magical realism novel that tells the story of Sam, a transgender teenage Pakistani American boy growing up in rural California, and Miel, his Latina cisgender friend-turned-girlfriend. The novel is based on the adolescent experiences of the author and their husband, but these experiences are transfigured through fantasy. While science fiction must be neither impossible nor possible, thus allowing its readers to judge the science fiction-ness of any story according to their own knowledge of the actual world, fantasy is framed by actuality, telling impossible stories of that which can never happen.[142] For many, both Miel and Sam would be considered impossible, fantastical creatures. Miel is a girl who appeared as a child out of nowhere, the town finding her one night in the outpouring of a demolished water tower, crying for the loss of the moon and sprouting roses from her wrist. Sam is a boy who has been living as "Sam" since he and his Pakistani mother relocated to the same town but was once named Samira, a secret that, if discovered, would render him impossible to many. What sets Miel and Sam apart brings them together. It is for her that he lights the town with his bright hand-painted moons, and it is in response to his touch that Miel's roses change color. The novel's fantasy elements thus serve both to mark these characters' racialized queerness to distrusting outsiders and to construct the queer magical setting of their romance. We chose the novel as the 2016 James Tiptree, Jr. Literary Award winner because it gives trans and queer kids the language and imagery of possibility. I taught *When the Moon Was Ours* in my Sexuality and Science Fiction seminar, and, as I told the WisCon 41 audience before McLemore gave their acceptance speech and got crowned with the Tiptree tiara:

> Too often rendered impossible by those who would wish them so, my queer and trans students found in the magic of Sam and Miel's love (and that of Miel's sister and Sam's mother and even the Bonner sisters who learn to let go) the magic they experience every day. In speaking [their] and [their] husband's truths, Anna-Marie McLemore shattered the frame that tells queer youth that their love could not or ought not to exist. [They] created imagery that made the forms of intimacy and kinship so familiar to me, my students, and thousands of others like us as palpable as a pollination brush on a flower petal. [They] gave us the moon and made it ours.[143]

In the time since McLemore won the Tiptree and I had the opportunity to award the author with it, we have both arrived at new public articulations of our own genders. What at the time read to many as an exchange between two cisgender queer women has retrospectively taken the shape of a gracious acknowledgment between two trans nonbinary folks. McLemore has come to their own nonbinary identity through the process of writing fantastical fiction, their trans characters in *Moon* and their other titles expressing a shifting and complex sense of self that is not totally unfamiliar to—though still very different from—Tip/Alli's own.

In 2014, the Tip/Alli archive and its work of supporting the examination and reimagination of gender through fantasy and science fiction expanded to include yet another accolade in the author's name. The Tiptree Fellowship was designed to supplement the Literary Award by supporting speculative work in development by historically underrepresented communities across media.[144] In their *Letters to Tiptree* contribution, the Black bisexual gender-fluid writer Nisi Shawl, winner of the 2009 Tiptree Award, tells Tip/Alli/feminist SF fandom about the fellowship, for which, as they were writing their letter, they were serving on the first jury. Acknowledging Tiptree's own reticence about awards and awards politics, Shawl tells "Tip" that unlike most awards, which recognize accomplishments, the fellowship is "a sort of buoy indicating that these are waters to watch."[145] Furthermore, they write, it recognizes those working "outside traditional literary modes . . . because that's how storytelling is done these days: in various and multiplex ways."[146] Finally, the Tiptree Fellowship makes the importance of intersectionality explicit, which, Shawl tells Tip, "I think you'd like."[147] Sounding very much the younger sibling, Shawl beams, "We will make you so proud!" In the second half of their letter, Shawl tells Tip about how gender has changed since the author's passing, writing, "In the near thirty years since you left us, Tip, a serious effort has gotten underway to think and speak and act as if gender, sexuality, and self-identity were fluctuating and non-binary." They elaborate, "We're treating them like the nuanced expressions they actually appear to be. Which is a wonder to me and would be a wonder to you if you were here to experience it."[148] Since this letter was written, Shawl's familial labor has led to the inaugural Tiptree Fellowship's being awarded to the Columbian American trans speculative media artist and scholar micha cárdenas, who, in turn, helped craft the language for the fellowship's description. Between 2014 and 2019, Walidah Imarisha, Elizabeth LaPensée, Mia Sereno, Porpentine Charity Heartscape, H. Pueyo, Ineke Chen-Meyer, Ana Hurtado, and Vida Cruz were all named Tiptree Fellows. The unusual directive of the fellowship's support for those speculative thinkers of feminism who are most vulnerable is perhaps most apparent in the fellows' own frank writing on the Tiptree website about how the fellowship supported their living—helping them pay rent, get health care, or make workspace improvements—and thus their creative work.[149] In this frankness, the fellowship wears its legacy in 1970s feminisms' negotiations with and within capitalism on its sleeve.

In September 2019, the Tiptree Award became the Otherwise Award, and the Tiptree Fellowship became the Otherwise Fellowship. Many people involved with the award and fellowship—like those in other corners of the SF world—felt the weight of being attached to a single, historical personage in their recognition of new and remarkable work.[150] Over the decades, Tip/Alli had chaperoned so many into feminist SF fandom; yet because of the nature of the author's death and the uncertainty of key details, many expressed concern that Tip/Alli would keep others out. At the time, I was serving as the chair of the fellowship committee, which eventually selected the science fiction and fantasy (SF&F) drag king Devonix and the sound and media artist and writer Martha Riva Palacio Obón as its two winners. One morning that August, I woke up to a Twitter feed with tweets reading "Alice Sheldon was a murderer" and "James Tiptree, Jr. was a caretaker murderer." My initial thought was that new evidence regarding the deaths of the author and her husband had been uncovered. Alice and Huntington "Ting" Sheldon had long had a suicide pact that their friends and family members, including Ting's adult children from his earlier marriage, knew about. When police found the two shot dead in their bed at their home in McLean, Virginia, on May 19, 1987, those near to them believed they had fulfilled that pact. However, neither of the Sheldons had written notes that evening. The note Alice left was dated September 13, 1979. Alice did make three phone calls that evening, sharing her plan to shoot Ting and then herself and referencing their pact—two to a family friend and lawyer and one to Ting's son Peter. When the police stopped by the house after the friend called out of concern, Alice and Ting assured the officers that nothing was awry. The two were found dead a few hours later. The Sheldons had been living a relatively solitary life. Huntington was partially deaf and was going blind. Alice's mental health had never stabilized following her mother's death in 1976, and she had had her fair share of medical scares in the previous decade. At earlier times in their marriage, both had expressed the desire to leave the world together, neither wanting to outlive the other. No one knows for certain why they chose to die the night they did or whether the decision was definitively consensual or mutual, and this is disconcerting.[151]

In August 2019, feminist SF fans new to Julie Phillips's biography of Alice Sheldon raised concerns about this uncertainty and the unevenness of the documentation: Alice, the writer, kept a diary and shared more emotionally in correspondence than did Ting, a retired senior CIA analyst. They raised the question about whether the Sheldons' deaths were the fulfillment of their long-standing suicide pact or whether there was a chance that it was a murder-suicide, Alice Sheldon wishing to pass and taking Ting with her against his will. Were the Tiptree Award and Tiptree Fellowship named after an author who had murdered a disabled loved one? We will likely never know for certain. Phillips, who spoke to many of the Sheldons' friends and family members in researching her book, has since tweeted and emailed the Motherboard, responsible for the Tiptree Award and Fellowship, apologizing for the lack of clarity in her chapter on the Sheldons' deaths that enabled such questions to be raised and sharing the evidence gathered during her research, all of which points to a mutual and consensual double suicide.[152] But a growing body of concerned feminist SF fans, who recognized in the uncertainty the possibility of a caregiver murder—Alice being thirteen years younger and more physically fit in 1987 than Ting—pressed the Tiptree Motherboard to change the name of the prize and fellowship.

In a process very much made possible by the same counterpublic discourse that led to the foundation of WisCon and the creation of the prize to begin with, the Motherboard, which included Murphy, Fowler, Gomoll, Smith, and three younger feminist SF fans (Alexis Lothian, Sumana Harihareswara, and Gretchen Treu), debated and discussed the possibilities moving forward. On September 2, 2019, the Motherboard made a blog post announcing no intention to immediately change the name of the prize and fellowship and quoting Phillips on the subject of the Sheldons' deaths at length. However, on October 13, 2019, after further deliberation and in conversation with members of feminist SF fandom, myself included, they announced the decision to change the names. As the Motherboard stated in a second blog post, and again during a WisCon panel the following May (which, because of COVID-19, was held online), the decision to change the names of the award and fellowship was ultimately less about what may or may not have happened in 1987 than about looking to the future of feminist SF fandom.[153] The Motherboard wanted disabled fans to feel like the welcomed and valued members of the community that they are. The Motherboard also wanted to think beyond what any individual author's name could signify. While Tiptree is deeply important to each of the members of the Motherboard personally as the figure who ushered many of them into feminist SF fandom, the name

211

could prevent the entrance of others. As Treu stated on the WisCon panel, "[The award is] no longer doing the service that it did for me. . . . We can still remember Alice, we can still remember this important figure, but the award doesn't need to be the space that memorializes her and valorizes her life. . . . Tiptree brought me in[to the community], but if it shuts others out, that's not what we're looking for." Murphy likewise reflected, "We wanted an award that gave people ownership of the imagined future who were being shut out of that ownership. We all get to imagine the future, not some sub-set of everyone. . . . This is an award that came out of the community. . . . It only happened because of and for the community. So when the commu-nity speaks, if you're being a good steward, you have to listen." As one of the founders of the award, Murphy acknowledged the loss she and others felt in letting go of the name Tiptree. Gomoll and Smith did not attend the panel, having chosen to step down from the board following the award's name change.[154] For Murphy, as the remaining senior member, the feeling of loss was reconciled in a commitment to remembering Tiptree and the history of women and others once shut out of science fiction and the community of feminist SF they built as a result. Ultimately, "the name is not the award, the community is the award."[155]

Rather than letting go of the accolade and starting anew, the Motherboard decided to rename the award to encourage the exploration and expansion of gender, holding on to Tiptree as integral to its formation while opening itself to feminist SF fandom of the future. Together the members of the Mother-board landed on the Otherwise Award. "Otherwise" does not name a person. It is not tied to a particular place or time. "Otherwise," the Motherboard writes on the award's website, "means finding different directions to move in—toward newly possible places, by means of emergent and multiple path-ways and methods. It is a moving target, since to imagine otherwise is to divert from the ways of a norm that is itself always changing."[156] In short, it is a naming of potentiality—a potentiality that is constantly renewing itself. As a pun, "Otherwise" holds on to the sense of humor and play that have always been central to the Tiptree Award and feminist SF fandom in its honoring of SF&F that celebrates the wisdom of those often deemed "other." For Tiptree fans, it also holds on to kinship ties, as the author's best-known collection, which included the notorious Silverberg introduction, is *Warm Worlds and Otherwise*. However, just as Charnas could imagine the Tiptree Award no longer existing in 2021, the Motherboard acknowledges that the Otherwise Award may itself be renamed someday, its potentiality taking on a different title fitting for the future yet unknown.[157] Since James Tiptree, Jr.'s first publication in 1968, Tip/Alli's many-gendered lesbian potentiality has spawned hundreds, if not thousands, of queer, trans, and nonbinary siblings. Who knows what the otherwise progeny may produce.

Conclusion

The Tip/Alli archive and the transfeminist genealogy it reveals is but one example of the myriad stories to be told about twenty-first-century feminists' loving relations with 1970s feminists. Its writing here joins a growing body of scholarship on transfeminism and the second wave.[158] Writing this genealogy was not merely a matter of cutting and conjoining 1970s feminisms and twenty-first-century transfeminisms; it also meant coupling approaches from queer studies and transgender studies and pairing them with the philosophies and sensibilities of feminist SF fandom itself. Often seen as at odds with each other when it comes to issues of discourse and embodiment and the lives and works of gender-nonconforming queers and those of transgender subjects, and further confused by the trickiness of historical writing in particular, queer studies and trans studies, as I hope to have shown here, need not be opposed or, alternatively, collapsed.[159] If we must take Sheldon at her word, understanding Sheldon as a lesbian and reading same-sex love metamorphosed in her stories, we can also identify in these stories characters whose gendered selves do not fit with the two options they are given or the option they were assigned at birth and appreciate their journeys as irreducible to sexuality. In "Houston, Houston," this includes not just Andy but also Lorimer, the 1970s scientist astronaut who has never felt comfortable around his hypermasculine male peers and gets along best with Gloria's Judys while identifying as neither female nor gay. In Sheldon's life story, including the author's outing and subsequent inability to "pass" as a cisgender male author in SF fandom, we can also recognize an experience familiar to many transgender people. While Sheldon would continue to publish under Tiptree's name, including two novels, there is much evidence that being outed had devastating effects on the author's ability to write and, arguably, the author's life. Sheldon wrote extensively about the loss and pain that came with being stripped of Tiptree's masculine voice.[160] To Sheldon, it quite often felt like nothing less than death.[161] And while the entirety of the reasoning and circumstances that led to the deaths of Alice and Huntington Sheldon ten years later cannot be known, the turn to suicide on Alice B. Sheldon's part rings all too familiar to both queer and transgender people.[162] In allowing for, and holding on to, such complexity, queer and trans scholars might re-vision lesbian feminist historiography and kinship.

Alice B. Sheldon did not survive. James Tiptree, Jr., became otherwise. Tip/Alli, meanwhile, has not so much survived as mutated or morphed. Tip/Alli reappears across history, in each instance always the same and yet different, helping others to survive not just "male-dominated society"—as Rich would have it—but our homophobic, transphobic, cissexist, and racist late-capitalist society. Tip/Alli does this work emotionally, as many of the *Letters to Tiptree* attest, and financially, as the prizes once named after the author support the work of those often overlooked by major cultural institutions. If the durability of patriarchal subjectivity is dependent on the changeability of the feminine name, as Butler contends, then what remains durable throughout the Tip/Alli archive's genealogy is not the subject (James Tiptree, Jr., or Alice B. Sheldon) but Tip/Alli's ever-renewed commitment to the difficult negotiations of gender necessary for the continued re-vision of feminist futures. Like the clones of "Houston, Houston" (who, interestingly, shed all patronyms, choosing instead their cities of birth as last names—for example, "Judy Paris" and "Judy Dakar"), each iteration of Tip/Alli resembles a mid-twentieth-century subject less and less, adapting according to their personal and historical context. The inaugural Tiptree Fellow and one of Tip/Alli's many sisters, micha cárdenas, writes that mutability is "the specialty of trans women of color who face multiple forms of violence on a daily basis, shifting their body and appearance as necessary for survival." To live, a trans woman of color might "at one moment [pass] invisibly as a cisgender woman and at another [stand] on stage speaking out against racist, transphobic violence."[163] Such moments of shifting are moments of great uncertainty. They exist in spaces of multiple possible futures, and in these possible futures a trans woman of color may live or may die.[164] cárdenas reminds us that this is true because passing is a poetics of relation; it depends on both a person's modulation of their visibility and the reception of their modulated image by another. For this reason, the shape-shifting of trans women of color is necessary for their survival in the present. However, it is also enacted with the hope that the future will be different. It has to be. Tip/Alli, too, plays a part in building toward the possibility of such a disruption. As Dozois wrote about Tiptree in 1976: "Of all the new SF writers, Tiptree is perhaps the most aware that everything changes, that the future will be wildly different from either the present or the past, and that our descendants will not be ourselves in crome [*sic*] helmets and plastic tights—they will be creatures of their own times, shaped by those times in what they desire as well as what they fear, in their dreams and in their nightmares."[165] Thus, while lesbians, queers, nonbinary people, trans men, trans women, and others might all identify with moments in Sheldon's life and fiction, the Tip/Alli archive ultimately frees us from feminist genealogical commitments to self-survival. Our feminist progeny will not be you or me. They will be feminist creatures of their own times. In the science fiction and autobiographical writing inspired by Tip/Alli, the prizes awarded in the author's name, and feminist SF fandom—which outgrows and exceeds the author's name even as it owes that author's fiction, self-narration, and own fan practices so much—what was and what is, both of which are historically contingent, think together what might come to be. In this process's renewal in the face of enduring sexism, homophobia, and transphobia, as well as gender and sexual struggles unnamed and otherwise—potentiality, no longer lesbian but still oriented toward freedom, regenerates.

epilogue
potentiality born in flames

When Lizzie Borden's science fiction (SF) indie feature *Born in Flames* (1983) was first screened for art-house and feminist film festival audiences, reactions were mixed. The film is set in New York City ten years after a socialist democratic revolution. When clashes break out between police and Black men protesting the unfair hiring practices of the "Workfare Program," the government promises to privilege male heads of households, and working-class lesbians, and single straight women find themselves without jobs or even spousal support. To add insult to injury, childcare remains inadequate, and women are still regularly being sexually harassed and raped. As a result, a group consisting largely of Black women who call themselves the Women's Army organizes to provide childcare for poor communities across the city and respond to rape threats, chasing away attackers in teams on bikes with whistles. Many not in the Women's Army consider the group's tactics separatist, as they distract from working toward income equality for all, or downright silly. However, the further layoffs of working-class women, agitation of middle-class women stuck in secretarial positions without the possibility of advancement, and eventual murder of the Women's Army's leader,

Adelaide Norris, by police spark a second women's liberation movement aimed first and foremost at the dissemination of antifeminist nationalist propaganda through the media. "This film about militant black lesbians and revolutionary consciousness," reported *off our backs*, won the top prize at the International Women's Film Festival in Sceaux, France, after "[bringing] the audience to its feet."[1]

But at its run at the Film Forum in downtown Manhattan, not far from where much of the film was shot, *Born in Flames* did not impress the *New York Times* film critic Janet Maslin. She found nothing "particularly cinematic" about the film and described it as "more like a manifesto than anything else." Thus, "Only those who already share Miss Borden's ideas [we]re apt to find her film persuasive."[2] When the film was rereleased three years later on WNET, New York City's PBS affiliate, as a part of the station's "Independent Focus" series, John Corry, the *New York Times* TV critic, was even less forgiving. Whereas Maslin had praised the film's "brash and very natural performers," noting especially the basketball player Jeanne Satterfield's performance as Norris and the Black feminist activist and civil rights lawyer Florynce Kennedy's performance as Norris's mentor Zella Wiley, Corry thought *Born in Flames* looked "very much like a home movie," with "friends, colleagues and relatives ham[ming] it up."[3] Even worse, the film had "a narrow-minded piety at its core," Corry wrote. "Its values are set in cement. Government, in whatever shape or form, is oppressive. Goodness is measured by the distance that separates us from the power structure. 'Progressive' politicians may have taken over, but once in office they are just like all the rest. They calm the huddled masses with free heroin and also run 'fascist' prisons. Only armed lesbians can set us free."[4]

Feminist critics were themselves torn. In particular, a number of feminist film critics expressed skepticism when it came to the film's apparent advocacy for violence. Corry felt a need to remind readers that "bombs, after all, do kill and maim."[5] And even those less thrown by the film's leading lesbians were wary when it came to its ending. In the final minutes, the Women's Army teams up with the white feminist journalists of the *Socialist Youth Review* and the members of the two radical feminist radio stations, Radio Regazza and Phoenix Radio, to blow up the transmission tower atop the World Trade Center. As Alexis Lothian notes, this very particular fictional turn to violence raises a new set of questions for post-2001 scholars and fans of the film.[6] But in 1983, it already troubled film reviewers. Amy Taubin and Marcia Pally, both writing for the *Village Voice*, concluded that they could not support a film that seemingly prescribed such an extreme form of feminism.[7]

217

Pally cites and then dismisses Borden's claims that she was exploring a "What if?," writing, "One is left, in the absence of approbation, with a sense of endorsement, with the notion that Borden finds appropriate the actions taken at the end of her film."[8] For Taubin, the film terrifyingly harked back to the era of radicalism; she writes, "Does [Borden] seriously believe the future of the feminist movement is to repeat (and not as farce) the militant positions of the black and white underground during the late '60s and early '70s?"[9] Taubin attributes the film's success at film festivals and support within New York's independent film community to its accessible populist style, which, she worries, overshadows "its political and conceptual weaknesses."[10] In the year of *Return of the Jedi* (1983), the violent end of *Born in Flames* served as a metonym for the potential return of a radical, lesbian feminism. And in each of these reviews, *New York Times* and *Village Voice* alike, the film's revelation that liberal feminism and gay liberalism's successes might not be enough affronts.

Two years later, in her classic essay "Rethinking Women's Cinema" (1985), the feminist film scholar Teresa de Lauretis would describe the tenuous reception of *Born in Flames* as having an "unusual intensity."[11] This intensity, I argue, is a testament to the film's blending of narrative structures common to 1970s feminist SF literature with filmmaking styles typical of much feminist experimental and documentary film and video from the same period. Put another way, the film's reception reveals that lesbian potentiality was not for all. Explored by filmmakers, video activists, and SF authors; put into circulation by feminist media workers and fans; and sparking the imaginations of thousands in these counterpublic spaces, lesbian potentiality was stopped short in the 1980s when it ventured before broader audiences. A certain acceptance of lesbian existence may have been becoming increasingly common in both liberal feminist circles and popular culture (see, for example, New Hollywood's *Personal Best* of the year before), but that this existence for many carried with it the potential that gendered and sexual life could and would someday be substantially different, that heteropatriarchy may topple, and that women would be the ones to topple it was going too far.

I have followed lesbian potentiality as it circulated through media in movement. While lesbian potentiality did similar things in feminist experimental and documentary film and video and feminist SF literature—engendering the vast imagination of what might follow the Lesbian in her wake—rarely did the two media cultures meet. As detailed in the preceding chapters, feminist SF fandom took shape as a counterpublic through the fannish consciousness-raising of those who had grown up reading science fiction, while the network built by feminist media workers enabled intimate, if sometimes fleeting, exchanges among US feminist communities curious about the potential of feminist film and video. Over the course of my research I found little evidence of the two media cultures overlapping, of someone actively participating in both. One exception, which I want to tease out here in my analysis of the reception of *Born in Flames* and the stakes of this reception for the future of lesbian potentiality, is de Lauretis's essay. In "Rethinking Women's Cinema," de Lauretis argues that *Born in Flames* is indicative of a new feminist aesthetic—a feminist aesthetic of reception. This aesthetic of reception takes the spectator as the film's primary concern and, in the case of *Born in Flames*, conceives of its audience as heterogeneous from the start. This can be seen, de Lauretis claims, in the film's "unusual handling of the function of address," including its use of many forms of music and modes of speech.[12] But it is also to be found in the manner in which *Born in Flames* combines "the look of a documentary (after Chris Marker)" and "the feel of contemporary science-fiction writing (the post-new-wave s-f of Samuel Delany, Joanna Russ, Alice Sheldon, or Thomas Disch)."[13]

Much like Tiptree and the Tiptree Award, queer theory began as a joke that dreamed its way into reality,[14] and in her 1985 essay, de Lauretis, the future founding prankster of queer theory, appears as a rare feminist film scholar or critic to read (or admit to reading) science fiction literature.[15] She addresses a film theory audience, largely analyzing aspects unique to film, including the film's use of music and spoken word, but her analysis also demonstrates an understanding of SF absent from the film's reviews. Pally's claim that *Born in Flames* "boasts no space suits or anti-gravity gadgets," so the film cannot be understood as "fantasy or allegory" but must instead be taken as an imagined likely near-future anchored in reality where "we might need to do what these women do," reveals her unfamiliarity with the genre's thought experiment heuristic.[16] Familiar only with the big-budget, special-effects-driven science fiction of New Hollywood, with its space suits and antigravity gadgets, Pally cannot fathom a science fiction more about the ideas enabled by a shift to a not-so-unfamiliar future. A decade prior, as feminist SF fandom was taking shape, Samuel R. Delany and Joanna Russ both argued that science fiction, more than a delineable body of texts, was a way of reading.[17] As Russ writes, "A science fiction story that succeeds in being altogether strange is not comprehensible. One that succeeds in being altogether familiar is not science fiction. That is, without any points of reference that connect straightforwardly with actuality, the work falls apart. But with every point of reference clearly and directly related to actuality, the work loses its science-fictionalness. . . . To put it another way: science fiction must neither be impossible nor possible."[18] To read or understand SF requires intellectual athleticism.[19] Russ's novel *The Female Man* (1975), with its many iterations of its protagonist "J" across time—including the 1970s Joanna who kisses Laur—does this, as does Tiptree's "Houston, Houston, Do You Read?" (1976), introducing the 1970s present and a feminist future aboard the spaceship *Gloria*. And, as each of these stories feature violent actions taken against men by women or those of future genders, Russ and Tiptree themselves faced antifeminist outrage.[20]

De Lauretis, meanwhile, appears not only up for the challenge of reading science fiction but curious enough also to follow the news of feminist SF fandom, so that she knows Tiptree as Sheldon.[21] Even after the 1977 reveal, Sheldon continued to publish as Tiptree, so de Lauretis could not have known Sheldon's name merely from looking at the cover of the SF magazines on her nightstand. To this day, people continue to pick up stories by James Tiptree, Jr., without knowing the author's own story. Considering the centrality of Tiptree to Sheldon's writerly identity, I cringe at the use of "Alice Sheldon" in de Lauretis's essay. My immediate concern is for the imagined 1985 feminist film scholar who might want to follow de Lauretis's thinking here but, lacking the online research tools of today, might have had trouble hunting down Tiptree's fiction based on such a reference. I also understand de Lauretis's use of "Sheldon" as indicative of the author's commitment to "re-vision," à la Adrienne Rich: "And something of this process of reformulation—revision, rewriting, rereading, rethinking, 'looking back at *ourselves*'—is what I see inscribed in the texts of women's cinema but not yet sufficiently focused on in feminist film theory or feminist critical practice in general."[22] *Born in Flames* can be said to practice some form of cinematic "re-vision" of gendered subject formation for its contemporary audiences (a contention central to de Lauretis's "aesthetic of reception" argument). However, the film theorist's suggestion that this methodology get taken up by other feminist critics and scholars continues to neglect the historian's location-in-time quandary—namely, that an "ourselves" both past and present might be impossible to delineate while holding on to terms such as *women, the female social subject*, or even *women's writing* or *women's cinema*.[23] And, in the case of de Lauretis's referencing of Tiptree's writing, re-vision's "refusal of the self-destructiveness of male-dominated society" translates all too easily into a cisnormative naming of a gender-nonconforming individual.[24] That said, de Lauretis is correct to name feminist SF as a formal precursor. *Born in Flames* does more than "feel like" a Delany, Russ, or Tiptree tale. By setting the story in a fictional future that does not appear so different from our present, *Born in Flames* enacts the kind of thought experiment so common to feminist SF of the decade prior, allowing its 1980s viewers to cast an askew glance at their own post-liberation movement present.

In both the socialist-democracy future of *Born in Flames* and its early 1980s present, rhetoric about how conditions for women had improved, making ongoing resistance passé or even counterproductive, predominates. It is there in Pally's and Taubin's reviews. In the film, it is repeatedly voiced by the three young, white, female reporters for *Socialist Youth Review*—played by Kathryn Bigelow, Becky Johnston, and Pat Murphy (an Irish feminist filmmaker and different from the Pat Murphy who founded the Tiptree Award)—who refuse Norris's appeals for collaboration by making the argument that things are much better for women than they once were. Achieving true equality, the three tell Norris, is merely a matter of patience. Appearing on a TV show in which the host asks the three reporters about criticisms coming from the burgeoning feminist movement that rape still exists, the reporter played by Becky Johnston says, "I think the statistics will show you that the percentage of rape and prostitution at this point is significantly lower than it was in pre-revolutionary society and that obviously this is an advancement, it's a step forward. It's impossible to talk about the complete abolition [of rape], because that is not the nature of this government. They don't abolish. It's a question of a gradual movement toward something." Depending on one's political persuasion, as well as one's vulnerability to such violence, this could be a compelling argument. Pally begins her review by admitting she very quickly realized she was "on the wrong side of the fence." Sounding not unlike the SF author Marion Zimmer Bradley when confronted with the limits of her own feminism in the rich and varied criticism of feminist SF fanzines, Pally explains, "Wordly, gutless, and a little ridiculous, those ladies are me. Not only because I'm a white girl writing for the *Voice*, crossover paper in mode, but because, at bottom, I buy their line. I believe they're right, and the film is telling me I'm full of shit."[25] However, *Born in Flames*, like the works of feminist SF literature and fandom accused of propaganda before it, is not simply enacting ridicule; it is not telling Pally or anyone like her they are "full of shit." Written, directed, and edited by arguably another such "white girl," *Born in Flames* confronts post-social-movement liberalism, taking on its comforts and their limits in the US political climate of the early 1980s.

Drawing on feminist SF traditions of feminist futures where differences still reside, the film does not simply tell those who can relate to the white women reporters that they are wrong or foolish in their beliefs. Instead, like Lorimer in "Houston, Houston, Do You Read?," their familiarity (and, one might as easily say, their middle-class whiteness) draws viewers in, only to trouble their presumptions that things must be the way they are. Like Suzy McKee Charnas's *Motherlines*, *Born in Flames* narrativizes such negotiations of difference, presenting collaboration around shared values (such as honest, forthright media) as a temporary site of potential. The film also puts forward not simply two feminist positions but many overlapping feminist positions and, like both 1970s feminist SF literature and 1970s feminist documentary film and video, enables viewers to engage intellectually and affectively with each.

While a fiction film, *Born in Flames* is edited in many ways like the feminist documentaries and experimental films that preceded it. As they are in feminist prison documentaries of the 1970s, viewers' consciousnesses are raised through the crosscutting of characters' many perspectives. Norris and the reporters speak. But the reporters also speak to their male boss at the party newspaper, and Norris speaks to fellow members of the Women's Army; her mentor, Wiley; and DJ Honey of Phoenix Radio. Honey then speaks to her friends and, after Norris has been murdered, to the more music-focused and organizing-averse DJ Isabel (Adele Bertei) of Radio Regazza and to the other members of the Women's Army. In each of these spaces, different perspectives, including as to whether taking violent actions is wise or ethical, are heard. As another member of the Women's Army cautions, "The reality of having to deal with taking up arms, Adelaide, is really heavy—whether we can accept or be responsible for the potential violence thrust upon us from our own violence thrust out." To this Norris presciently responds, "It's already happening." The government and society at large already routinely enact violence against feminists, against women, and against poor people and people of color. But here the real conflict, unlike in *Like a Rose* or *Inside Women Inside*, is no longer between feminist activists and those seeking to curtail or contain their freedom through "rehabilitation." It is inside feminism itself. Rather than say one party is right and the others are not, the film's quick cutting of many feminisms together allows the perspectives and arguments of each to bump up against each other in the viewer's mind. And as in much lesbian feminist media of the 1970s, sex is kept off-screen, yet, again, the film's erotic charge is "powerful" and "unmistakable."[26]

While liberal rhetoric of the 1980s suggested that major achievements had been made by the social movements of the 1960s and '70s, rendering any ongoing radical efforts unnecessary, the insidious economic theory, praxis, and cultural ideology of neoliberalism took hold. Through its "deregulation, privatization, and withdrawal of the state from many areas of social provision,"

222

neoliberalization in the late 1970s and '80s creatively and effectively destroyed prior institutional frameworks, as well as common senses.[27] One of neoliberalism's many contradictions meant that, while the government was supposed to withdraw itself from citizens' daily lives, granting them the freedom to manage their own well-being, the prison-industrial complex expanded, capturing Black and Brown lives for state and corporate profit.[28] The freedom those imprisoned in "women's prisons" had produced, through their documentaries and care for one another, was of an entirely different sort from the "freedom" of the free market that kept them in chains.[29] Despite anticarceral and prison-abolition activists' efforts, the state's "war on drugs" led to millions being put behind bars for nonviolent drug crimes and rendered women of color the fastest-growing US prison population of the 1970s, '80s, and '90s.[30]

Neoliberalism took its toll on the arts communities that might, in turn, shed light on such matters. With President Ronald Reagan's defunding of the arts and the strains neoliberal policies exerted on small businesses, alternative media companies and producers were forced to approach audiences differently if they were to stay in business. Many of the feminist media organizations written about throughout this book closed their doors. The few that remained open struggled, relying even more heavily on volunteer labor, as WisCon did, or, as was the case with Women Make Movies, becoming more financially savvy.[31] In the early 1970s, Women Make Movies had focused on local efforts, prioritizing providing women in New York City, especially those of their Chelsea neighborhood, with film equipment access and instruction, before reaching out to build a translocal network with other, similar organizations across the United States and Canada through the Conference of Feminist Film and Video Organizations and projects such as International Videoletters.[32] By the 1980s, the organization's focus had shifted to building a robust transnational catalog of feminist films for a predominantly academic rental market.[33] While the feminist organizations that would rent from Women Make Movies were struggling to keep programming running, the institutionalization of cinema and media studies and feminist film theory's centrality to that institutionalization created a demand in the academy for feminist film rentals, and Women Make Movies built its collection accordingly. By 1987, the organization could boast of being "the only national non-profit media organization in the United States devoted to the distribution of media by and about women."[34]

Festivals in cities such as New York, Los Angeles, Chicago, and San Francisco, with the capacity to build structural support for seasonal feminist and

223

queer film programming, developed as the independent film and video exhibition standard. In the late 1970s, the Gay Film Festival of Super 8 Films and the Gay and Lesbian Media Conference made their debuts in San Francisco and Los Angeles, respectively. Within a few years they would become the Frameline Film Festival and Out on Screen (renamed Outfest in 1994), both of which are still in operation.[35] Such spaces enabled collaborations among previously isolated queer communities. However, these cultural changes were not merely a matter of a more enlightened intersectional politics, as queer historiographies cordoning off the 1970s from the pre-Stonewall past and queer 1980s–'90s future would have one believe.[36] They were also the result of material financial strains put on alternative media and were accompanied by the loss of explicitly feminist public spaces throughout the United States.

While public television had provided an expansive site for independent media exhibition in the early 1970s (and gave a number of feminist media workers their first firsthand experience in production and programming), by the mid-1970s slashes in the Corporation for Public Broadcasting (CPB) budget under President Richard Nixon meant an increasing turn to corporate funding and therefore more mainstream fare. As Amy Villarejo contends, TV—and public television in particular, with programs such as *An American Family* (1973)—was central to the American public's reshaping of gayness.[37] This public programming was carried on in the Mariposa Film Group's talking-heads documentary *Word Is Out: Stories of Some of Our Lives* (1978), which broadcast on PBS stations in October 1978, delivering to broad US audiences an unprecedentedly generous slice of gay and lesbian life. The film was partially funded by a $50,000 grant from WNET, and while, after a community screening of a rough cut, Thomas Waugh would pan its "soft-peddling" of politics as a work of "establishment TV," Greg Youmans reports that the archives contain no evidence that the film caused any controversy at the station or that the station demanded any changes to its form or content.[38] The film's traditional talking heads and carefully selected subjects, Youmans claims, were more likely the result of the producer Peter Adair's experience in getting gay content onto public television.[39] *An American Family* had privileged the gay eldest son Lance Loud's queer epistemology, providing a pragmatic pedagogy of queer life for American families.[40] *Word Is Out*, meanwhile, normalized queerness while also queering the normal, "stag[ing] a takeover of the categories of the private and the domestic and us[ing] them to launch a resolutely public assault on heteronormativity."[41]

224

By the late 1980s, the effects of PBS's mid-'70s swerve toward corporate sponsors, exacerbated by the Reagan administration's further budget cuts, were acutely felt by media makers and media scholars alike. In 1991, PBS announced a new season of its POV series, which was set to including Adair's *Absolutely Positive* (1991), about eleven people living with HIV, and Marlon Riggs's *Tongues Untied* (1989), about Black gay life—including HIV-positive Black gay life. However, two-thirds of the country's PBS stations cancelled *Tongues Untied.*[42] As Ronald Gregg chronicles in *Jump Cut*, this cancellation was consistent with PBS's past responses to threats to its mandate to offer a diverse set of political and social viewpoints. Nixon ordered that "all funds for public broadcasting be cut immediately," only to be persuaded to appoint people of his persuasion to the CPB's board, and subsequently used his veto power to force Congress to "pass budgets with less funding devoted to public affairs programming." Congress under Reagan's influence would continue to substantively chip away at the CPB budget, making the courting of corporate and public support necessary for survival.[43] Important queer and feminist films, including *Longtime Companion* (Norman René, dir., 1990) and *Daughters of the Dust* (Julie Dash, dir., 1991), both of which were partially funded by PBS's American Playhouse, received public television distribution. But in such a charged climate, an explicitly political film like *Tongues Untied*, critical not only of homophobia but also of white supremacy and the devastating and deadly effects overlapping forms of oppression have on those who are most marginalized, was easily and quickly censored. In 1986, *Born in Flames*, while broadcast, served as a harbinger for *Tongues Untied*'s censorship. Too radical for white liberal feminists, and therefore far too radical for the broader US public, *Born in Flames* was perceived by liberals as threatening the increasingly tenuous government support for public television. In his review of the film's WNET broadcast in CPB, Corry cautions, "Conservative political critics of public television dote on programs like 'Born in Flames.' Productions like this provide a useful argument for the abolition of Federal financing."[44] The film's failure to garner widespread support, like lesbian feminism's supposed "failure" to radically alter society's basic structures, was a result of social movement backlash initiated and spurred by the New Right and the accompanying transformation of the global economy under the leadership of Reagan and Britain's Margaret Thatcher.

But, while the initial reception of *Born in Flames* may have been "intense," with many critics resistant to the film's implication that liberalism is not enough, the film has lately—apropos of its titular metaphor—witnessed a rebirth of critical and scholarly attention.[45] For Sara Ahmed, "*Born in Flames* teaches us how impatience can be a feminist virtue. . . . We must not wait. We must demand justice and equality now."[46] For Alexis Lothian, *Born in Flames* and Derek Jarman's *Jubilee* (1978) "teach viewers to inhabit a temporality whose futuristic orientation is marked not by technology but by an alternative mediation and reproduction of political and social life."[47] That both these scholars argue for the film's pedagogical value is indicative of its history's bearing on our present and, in particular, on our present forms of thinking and imagining futures. This is also how I would understand the film's prevalence in contemporary university syllabi and its showcasing at queer film festivals such as Outfest, where in 2015 it was featured as part of the festival's legacy project.[48] In these academic and cultural spaces, people often express surprise at the existence of such an early radical Black lesbian feminist film. "It is quite uncanny," Ahmed writes, "to watch this film, to witness your own struggles potently formed into words uttered by characters you can relate to, from a film about the future made in the past."[49] Craig Willse and Dean Spade, who edited a *Women and Performance* dossier on the film in 2013, recount leaving a Queer/Film/Art screening of the film held in New York City in 2010 in a state of "awe and confusion." Walking the West Village thirty years after Borden and her cast and crew, they asked each other, *"How does this film exist?"*[50] In 2010—nine years into the "war on terror," which, like the "war on drugs" before it, led to an increase in criminalization and police force domestically—the film struck Spade and Willse as especially prescient. "Most surprising" to the two was "the willingness of the film to portray political differences and debates among activists and its refusal to neatly resolve conflict."[51]

My hope is that you, having made your way through this book, will find *Born in Flames'* 1983 appearance less of a shock. It is a film very much of its time. The stamp of lesbian potentiality and 1970s feminist media cultures on it is quite clear. Its comrades are the novels, novellas, and short stories of Joanna Russ, James Tiptree, Jr./Raccoona Sheldon, and Suzy McKee Charnas; the films of Chick Strand, Barbara Hammer, and Jan Oxenberg and of countless feminist documentary film and video collectives; and the discourse— verbal and written, taped, mailed, and filed—of thousands of unnameable but not forgotten feminist SF fans, National Women's Film Circuit audiences, and International Videoletter and women's prison media producers. *Born in Flames* did not need to wait for queer and queer of color politics and temporalities of the 1990s and 2000s "for its aesthetics and practices of open-ended speculation to become legible as a politics," as Lothian argues.[52] De Lauretis's essay, the work of a 1970s–'80s film theorist and feminist SF fan, is early evidence of this. While Lothian acknowledges that *Born in Flames* "resonates powerfully with the work of other feminist thinkers active in the 1970s and 80s," including the women of color feminists of Kitchen Table Press, such contentions about the film's political legibility naturalize queer genealogies that ahistorically excise Black and Brown lesbians from the context of lesbian feminism and produce women's liberation as a white women's movement.[53] Audre Lorde's essay "The Master's Tools Will Never Dismantle the Master's House" (1979), meanwhile, is central to de Lauretis's 1985 argument about the aesthetic of reception of *Born in Flames* and seeing difference differently, and de Lauretis cites the version of Lorde's essay published in Cherríe Moraga and Gloria Anzaldúa's *This Bridge Called My Back: Writings by Radical Women of Color*, which was originally published by the lesbian feminist Persephone Press in 1981 and reissued in 1983 by Kitchen Table.[54]

This epilogue corroborates and expands de Lauretis's analysis. Like the feminist film and video and the feminist SF literature that preceded it, including the Black feminist consciousness-raising of 1970s feminist prison documentaries, *Born in Flames* juxtaposes heterosexual presents (including those of the original viewers' world and of the film) with potential lesbian futures (those of the film and that might follow the film's) and does so to provoke questions about the desirability of each. And yet, that scholars such as Spade and Willse, both of whom contribute to activism and critical theory beyond or against equality politics, understand this in a way that initial reviewers at the *New York Times* and the *Village Voice* could not also makes sense to me. As Spade and Willse write about the film's ending, "Instead of providing a pat narrative of a unified movement advocating for a single clear demand, *Born in Flames* leaves us with the unexploded bomb—the possibility that we do not know, cannot know, where we are in the history of the transformations we seek, what impact our varying actions will have, and whether our divisions and splits will expand or dampen different forms of momentum."[55] Potentiality—including impotentiality, which, in the case of *Born in Flames*, means not knowing what will come of the actions taken at its end and includes the possibility of expanding or dampening momentum—is integral to the ongoing work of activists, scholars, and artists committed to social change. The imagination of resistance, of alternative worlds and alternative ways to structure the social, is necessary to sustaining the work of creating such worlds. The results may not look as we imagine they will; and if they do, this, too, may need reimagination. The animating force of this perpetual reimagination may no longer fittingly be named *lesbian potentiality*. What was once an electric form of naming no longer excites in the same way. But this force—however or whatever we name it or refuse to name it—can become a potentiality for us to think with. And such transference of potentiality is accomplished only as long as the location-in-time quandary is acknowledged. Not only is how we affectively relate to former presents, now past, constantly changing (as is the "we" invoked and the "former presents," which include "our" present), but potentiality is also only contingently "ours." With it, "we" open ourselves to futures that we hope will want to think and imagine with "us," in turn.

In this light, de Lauretis's theory of *Born in Flames*' aesthetic of reception can be updated. Not cancelled but renewed, de Lauretis's argument that *Born in Flames* allows her "'to see difference differently,' . . . inscrib[ing] the differences among women as *differences within women*" can be regenerated, transformed, as it has also allowed so many to see feminism, including its radical, lesbian histories, differently. What people have taken away after seeing the film appears not only to be "the image of a heterogeneity in the female social subject," as de Lauretis claims, but also the heterogeneity of feminism in a given historical moment. Extending or expanding de Lauretis's theory models how transfeminism and lesbian feminism might think together what could be. And it acknowledges that this transfeminism may not be of the present and this lesbian feminism of the past. Instead, in the minds of *Born in Flames* viewers, they become coexisting, coconstituted temporalities imagining a future when our present is past.

Much has been made of the film's final scene, in which of a member of a new feminist movement in formation—led by the Women's Army and the now merged Phoenix-Regazza radio station—plants a bomb atop one of the World Trade Center towers. In the minutes leading up to the scene, the philosophy of this future feminist movement, now past, is outlined on the film's soundtrack. The buildings that hosted Phoenix Radio and Radio Regazza have both been destroyed in fires, which the media report as being "possibly related" and say "may have been the work of vandalism." The two stations' teams join forces, climbing the chain link fence of a U-Haul parking lot to steal vehicles that will then serve as their new joint radio station "on the move." As viewers witness this tongue-in-cheek spectacle of Robin Hoodery, they hear, cut together on the soundtrack, not one but three calls to arms. The first is made by Pat Murphy, one of the journalists-turned-Women's Army member, who, much as Zella Wiley had done before, disrupts a public TV broadcast to share a message from the Women's Army. The second and third are made by Honey and Isabel of Phoenix-Regazza, now on the road and on the move. Murphy's direct address to the fictional socialist future

228

that is socialist "in name only" also speaks to the film's neoliberal 1980s present: "We are surrounded by the very images our mothers fought to destroy. Decades of women's work for socialism, for freedom of choice, for equality of opportunity is being swept away." Honey declares that Phoenix-Regazza, a metonym for this former future's vision of feminist futures, is "dedicated not only to the liberation of women . . . but dedicated to deconstruct[ing] and reconstruct[ing] all the laws that suppress and oppress all of us." And, finally, Isabel announces, "[This fight] begins in celebration of the rights of alchemy, the transformation of shit into gold—the illumination of dark clouded night into light. This is the time of sweet, sweet change for us all." This is the time. Potentiality is born in flames.

notes

Introduction

1 Rich, "Compulsory Heterosexuality and Lesbian Existence," 648.
2 Katie King similarly refers to lesbianism as a "magical sign to feminists." In the late 1960s and early 1970s, according to King, feminism and lesbianism rubbed off on each other as a result of contiguity, lesbianism offering new senses of change or possibility for lesbians and non-lesbians alike. While King's primary cases in point are the theories of radical feminists, she quickly acknowledges women's music and writing as "offer[ing] lesbianism as a sign in a way that non-lesbians are certainly able to enjoy": King, *Theory in Its Feminist Travels*, 135. This book takes seriously the cultural work of cultural feminism and looks to two media cultures in which this signifying power of the lesbian did its most creative work.
3 See, e.g., Abbott and Love, *Sappho Was a Right-On Woman*; Faderman, *Surpassing the Love of Men*, 377–91; Julia Penelope Stanley and Susan J. Wolfe, "Introduction," in Stanley and Wolfe, *The Coming Out Stories*, xv–xxiv.
4 Faderman, *Surpassing the Love of Men*, 314–31. See also Abbott and Love, *Sappho Was a Right-On Woman*, 185–239.
5 Abbott and Love, *Sappho Was a Right-On Woman*, dedication.
6 Abbott and Love, *Sappho Was a Right-On Woman*, 217–39.
7 Abbott and Love, *Sappho Was a Right-On Woman*, 16.
8 Abbott and Love, *Sappho Was a Right-On Woman*, 16.
9 Butler, "Imitation and Gender Insubordination," 19.

10 Warner, *The Trouble with Normal.*

11 Sender, *Business, Not Politics*, 174–99.

12 Butler, "Imitation and Gender Insubordination," 14.

13 Butler, *Bodies That Matter*, 226–30; de Lauretis, "Queer Theory"; Warner, *The Trouble with Normal*, 33–40.

14 Faderman, *Surpassing the Love of Men*, 386–88.

15 Rosen, *The World Split Open*, 164–66.

16 Kesselman, "Coming Out, Coming In and 'Be-Coming.'"

17 Kesselman, "Coming Out, Coming In and 'Be-Coming.'"

18 Rich, "Compulsory Heterosexuality and Lesbian Existence," 648.

19 Agamben, *Potentialities*, 177.

20 Agamben, *Potentialities*, 177.

21 Agamben, *Potentialities*, 178.

22 Russ, *The Female Man*, 208.

23 Russ, *The Female Man*, 208.

24 Agamben, *Potentialities*, 270.

25 Echols, *Daring to Be Bad*, 243–86.

26 Hogan, *The Feminist Bookstore Movement*; McKinney, *Information Activism*; Youmans, *Word Is Out.*

27 I am especially thinking of Alice Echols and her grouping together of feminist presses, bookstores, music labels, and credit unions as examples of cultural feminism: Echols, *Daring to Be Bad*, 269–81.

28 A rare example of the two being even being mentioned in the same piece is Teresa de Lauretis, "Rethinking Women's Cinema: Aesthetics and Feminist Theory" (1985), in de Lauretis, *Technologies of Gender*, 127–48, which I study at length in the epilogue.

29 See, e.g., de Bruin-Molé, "Space Bitches, Witches, and Kick-Ass Princesses"; Sobchack, *Screening Space*, 223–305; Wood, "Feminist Icons Wanted." Meanwhile, Judith Newton has argued that, despite its strong female hero, *Alien* (Ridley Scott, dir., 1979) is best read as an anxious response to the rise of feminism as a collective force disruptive of traditional gender roles, the sexual division of labor, and late capitalism: Newton, "Feminism and Anxiety in *Alien.*"

30 Coppa, "An Editing Room of One's Own"; Henry Jenkins, "'Layers of Meaning': Fan Music Video and the Poetics of Poaching," in Jenkins, *Textual Poachers*, 223–49; Penley, NASA/*Trek*, 113–16.

31 Muñoz, *Cruising Utopia*, 1.

32 Rich, "Compulsory Heterosexuality and Lesbian Existence," 648–49.

33 Amin, *Disturbing Attachments*, 183.

34 Sedgwick, *Epistemology of the Closet.*

35 See, e.g., Dinshaw, *Getting Medieval*; Freccero, *Queer/Early/Modern*; Halperin, "Forgetting Foucault"; Love, *Feeling Backward*; Nealon, *Foundlings.*

36 Foucault, *The History of Sexuality*, 101.

37 Halberstam, *Female Masculinity*, 117.

232

38 Muñoz, *Cruising Utopia*, 3.

39 Ahmed, *Living a Feminist Life*, 22.

40 Ahmed, *Living a Feminist Life*, 222.

41 Freeman, *Time Binds*, 62.

42 Freeman, *Time Binds*, 65.

43 Hesford, *Feeling Women's Liberation*, 230–31.

44 Hesford, *Feeling Women's Liberation*, 6.

45 Hesford, *Feeling Women's Liberation*, 2.

46 Castle, *The Apparitional Lesbian*. See also Patricia White, "Female Spectator, Lesbian Spector," in White, *Uninvited*, 61–93. Hesford, *Feeling Women's Liberation*, 15.

47 Hesford, *Feeling Women's Liberation*, 14–15, 23–24.

48 Hesford, *Feeling Women's Liberation*, 16.

49 Hesford, *Feeling Women's Liberation*, 248.

50 "Cisgender" demarcates a person whose gender has remained consistent with that assigned at birth. I add it here for specificity. Anne Koedt did not herself use it. It was not a term available to her for use at the time.

51 Koedt, "The Myth of the Vaginal Orgasm," 199–202.

52 Koedt, "The Myth of the Vaginal Orgasm," 206.

53 Koedt recognizes the importance of fantasy to sexual pleasure as well as many women's enjoyment of vaginal penetration, but their significance gets downplayed in her emphasis on physical climax.

54 Koedt, "The Myth of the Vaginal Orgasm," 206.

55 Agamben, *Potentialities*, 182.

56 Hesford, *Feeling Women's Liberation*, 132.

57 While Abbott and Love are not commonly credited as authors of "The Woman Identified Woman," Artemis March, who is, has credited Abbott with its perhaps most famous line: "A lesbian is the rage of all women condensed to the point of explosion": Humm, "Sidney Was a Right-on Woman."

58 Echols, *Daring to Be Bad*, 215–19; Shugar, *Separatism and Women's Community*, 26.

59 Radicalesbians, "The Woman Identified Woman," 241.

60 Radicalesbians, "The Woman Identified Woman," 242.

61 Radicalesbians, "The Woman Identified Woman," 245.

62 Audre Lorde, "Uses of the Erotic: The Erotic as Power" (1978), in Lorde, *Sister Outsider*, 59.

63 Rich, "Compulsory Heterosexuality and Lesbian Existence," 657.

64 Atkinson, *Amazon Odyssey*, 132.

65 Atkinson, *Amazon Odyssey*, 134.

66 Agamben, *Potentialities*, 178–79.

67 Hesford, *Feeling Women's Liberation*, 145.

68 Rich, "Compulsory Heterosexuality and Lesbian Existence," 637.

69 Shugar, *Separatism and Women's Community*, 57–58.

70 Shugar, *Separatism and Women's Community*, 90–91.

71 Douglas, "A Feminist Nation," 22.

72 Shugar, *Separatism and Women's Community*, 91.

73 Killer Dykes, "Sexist Pig Oppressors . . . Beware!," 3.

74 Ginny Berson, untitled editorial, *The Furies*, vol. 1, no. 1, January 1972, 1. For further details of the collective's founding, see Beemyn, *A Queer Capital*, 193-204; Valk, *Radical Sisters*, 135-57.

75 Valk, *Radical Sisters*, 139.

76 Berson, untitled editorial, 1; Valk, *Radical Sisters*, 139.

77 Coletta Reid, "Ideology: Guide to Action," *The Furies*, vol. 1, no. 3, March–April 1972, 6.

78 Charlotte Bunch, "Notes for the Cell Meeting, January, 1972," Joan E. Biren Papers, box 1.

79 Berson, untitled editorial, 1.

80 Valk, *Radical Sisters*, 150.

81 Valk, *Radical Sisters*, 150-51.

82 Coletta Reid, "Details," *The Furies*, vol. 1, no. 5, June–July 1972, 7.

83 Reid, "Details," 7.

84 Valk, *Radical Sisters*, 136-49.

85 JEB, "Come Outside," *The Furies*, vol. 1, no. 5, June–July 1972, 10-11.

86 Muñoz, *Cruising Utopia*.

87 Muñoz, *Cruising Utopia*, 1.

88 Aristotle, quoted in Agamben, *Potentialities*, 183.

89 Agamben, *Potentialities*, 183.

90 Agamben, *Potentialities*, 184.

91 Agamben, *Potentialities*, 183-84.

92 Le Guin, "Is Gender Necessary?," 132.

93 Tiptree, "Houston, Houston, Do You Read?," 79.

94 Tiptree, "Houston, Houston, Do You Read?," 98.

95 Phillips, *James Tiptree, Jr.*, 312. Examples of Sheldon's assuaging letters to male fans and critics can be found in Alice B. Sheldon, Pen Name James Tiptree, Jr., Papers (hereafter, Sheldon Papers), boxes 61-83. However, on October 23, 1976, Tiptree (before being outed as Alice B. Sheldon) privately wrote to Joanna Russ, "I'm not afraid of male irrelevancy; I believe in it. It was the *point* of my HOUSTON story": Joanna Russ Papers, box 10.

96 James Tiptree, Jr., in Smith, *Symposium*, 22. For more on the *Khatru* symposium, including the chastising of Tiptree by Russ and others for his binary thinking, see chapter 3. For letters from male fans and critics, see Sheldon Papers, boxes 61-83.

97 Rich, "When We Dead Awaken," 18.

98 Rich, "When We Dead Awaken," 19.

99 Rich, "When We Dead Awaken," 19.

100 Even as I critique the essay elsewhere in this manuscript, my analysis here is indebted to Claire Johnston's writing on Woman as a sign and myth of Classical Hollywood: Claire Johnston, "Women's Cinema as Counter-Cinema," in Johnston, *Notes on Women's Cinema*, 24-31.

101 Agamben, *Potentialities*, 180–81.

102 Leimbacher and Strand, "An Introduction to the Films of Chick Strand," 131.

103 Muñoz, *Cruising Utopia*, 49.

104 Perhaps due to avant-garde film studies' indebtedness to art history and literary studies, biography plays an integral role in much of avant-garde film scholarship. When combined with traditional understandings of feminist and gay and lesbian politics, whereby declaring allegiance and identification with such causes (or, at least, knowledge of filmmaker's sexual practices, despite any disavowal, as in the case of Kenneth Anger) is given precedence, many women's experimental films that might otherwise be read as "lesbian" have not been. David E. James has done work to contextualize Chick Strand's feminism: James, *The Most Typical Avant-Garde*, 357–67.

105 See, e.g., Keeling, "Joining the Lesbians"; White, *Uninvited*.

106 Leimbacher and Strand, "An Introduction to the Films of Chick Strand," 148.

107 Kesselman, "Coming Out, Coming In and 'Be-Coming.'"

108 See, e.g., Cvetkovich, *An Archive of Feelings*; Halberstam, *In a Queer Time and Place*.

109 In addition to *An Archive of Feeling*, see Cvetkovich, "In the Archives of Lesbian Feelings."

110 Regina Kunzel, in Arondekar et al., "Queer Archives," 229; Corbman, "Does Queer Studies Have an Anti-empiricism Problem?"

111 Eichhorn, *The Archival Turn in Feminism*, 31.

112 Faludi, "American Electra." I also owe much here to Eichhorn's critique of Faludi: Eichhorn, *The Archival Turn in Feminism*, 21–27.

113 Eichhorn, *The Archival Turn in Feminism*, 60.

114 "The Three Faces of Sylvester Mule" (Sheldon) to Charles Brown, letter, March 23, 1979, Sheldon Papers, box 63.

115 Eichhorn, *The Archival Turn in Feminism*, 60–61. See, e.g., Cifor, "Presence, Absence, and Victoria's Hair"; McKinney, *Information Activism*.

116 I am currently in production on *Tip/Alli*, a documentary about the life, work, and influence of James Tiptree, Jr./Alice B. Sheldon.

117 Hesford, *Feeling Women's Liberation*, 17–19.

118 Blackwell, *¡Chicana Power!*, 20; Thompson, "Multiracial Feminism," 337–60.

119 Enke, "Collective Memory and the Transfeminist 1970s"; Heaney, "Women-Identified Women"; Williams, "Radical Inclusion."

120 Enke, "Collective Memory and the Transfeminist 1970s," 12–13.

121 Enke, "Collective Memory and the Transfeminist 1970s," 18; Heaney, "Women-Identified Women," 139.

122 Rawson, "Introduction."

123 "An Ongoing Manifesto," February 2, 1975, Ariel Dougherty Papers, box 15; Biren Papers, box 64.

124 Thuma, *All Our Trials*, 112–13.

125 Hesford, *Feeling Women's Liberation*, 247.

126 Heaney, "Women-Identified Women," 137–45.

127 Bassichis et al., "Building an Abolitionist Trans and Queer Movement with Everything We've Got," 25.

128 Gaines, *Pink-Slipped*, 43–44, 95–131.

129 Keeling, *Queer Times, Black Futures*, 1–13.

130 Agamben, *Potentialities*, 243–71.

131 Agamben, *Potentialities*, 261–64.

132 Agamben, *Potentialities*, 267–68.

133 Keeling, *Queer Times, Black Futures*, 84.

Chapter One. Feminist Media in Movement

Epigraphs: Villarejo, *Lesbian Rule*, 6–7; Joan E. Biren, "Moonforce Media Interview," Feminist Radio Network, May 1978, Biren Papers, cassette 225.

1 A few of the feminist media organizations that contributed to this range of work were the Just Us Video Collective, Berkeley, California; the Feminist Videotape Collective, New York City; Lesbians Organized for Video Experience (LOVE), New York City; the Rochester Women's Video Collective; the Santa Cruz Women's Media Collective; the Tucson Feminist Media Collective; and the Spectra Feminist Media Project, Washington, DC.

2 The Women's Film Co-op of Northampton, one such early distributor, described its work by saying, "Our priority is for feminist films to get seen and made. We are non-competitive and therefore more than willing to refer women/community groups to other sources, and suggest ways in which films can be combined in order to present different facets or historical developments of issues. Many of the groups that rent our films are poor (unless they're universities)—and we often waive the rentals in this case. Filmmakers, therefore, don't get a huge return on being distributed by us, though we do think it's important for people to get paid for their labor. But women filmmakers have had a hard time getting their films distributed (and often when they have been accepted by a distribution company, their films are buried)—we get the films to women's audiences while the films are relevant—and we are also committed to relaying criticism/support from our own and audience reactions back to the filmmaker, many of whom say that they've rarely had that feedback and concern": Women's Film Co-op catalog, Joan E. Biren Papers (hereafter, Biren Papers), box 64.

3 Fallica, "More than 'Just Talk.'"

4 "The relationship between the Feminist Eye Conference and the Conference of Feminist Film and Video Organizations marked the beginnings of a national feminist film and video network. We sprang up independently, and then discovered also that we had the same goals and shared values": Frances Reid and Cathy Zheutlin, "Statement of Relation," March 14, 1975, Biren Papers, box 64.

5 Reid and Zheutlin, "Statement of Relation."

6 Representatives from more than forty media organizations (including a few from Canada and Australia) attended the New York conference: "Report on the New York Conference of Feminist Film and Video Organizations," Biren Papers, box 64. Twenty-two of these women wrote and signed the manifesto: Tracy Ward, Barbara Halpern Martineau, Sharon Karp, Joan Robins, Lorna Rassmussen, Marge Smilow, Ariel Dougherty, Taylor Ross, Joan E. Biren, Marion Hunter, Gretchen Bruskewicz, Vasiliki Stidiotis, Rena Hanson, Cathy Zheutlin, Alice Skinicke, Joan E. Nixon, Frances Reid, Carol Clement, Rebecca High, Phyllis Gomperts, Laurel Siebert, and Sheila Page, "An Ongoing Manifesto," February 2, 1975, Ariel Dougherty Papers (hereafter, Dougherty Papers), box 15; Biren Papers, box 64.

7 Ward et al., "An Ongoing Manifesto."

8 "Womanifesto," *Women and Film* 2, no. 7 (1975): 11.

9 Biren Papers, box 64.

10 International Videoletters flier for a New York City screening on August 8, 1975, Dougherty Papers, box 17. In an earlier set of notes on the conception of International Videoletters at the Conference of Feminist Film and Video Organizations in New York on February 2, 1975, the project is described as having as its intention "to produce a loose format of exchange of news/information among feminists throughout the world," and exchanges with participants in Sydney, Australia, and Edmonton, Alberta, Canada, are listed as expected to happen every six months "due to distance, changes in standards, and limited facilities": Dougherty Papers, box 17.

11 See later sections of this chapter for further cities and towns to which these projects traveled. Here I name New York City; Los Angeles; Tucson, Arizona; and Rochester, New York, as they are examples of places to which both of these projects journeyed.

12 Kuhn, *Women's Pictures*, 4.

13 Camera Obscura Collective, "Chronology"; Camera Obscura Collective, "Feminism and Film"; Doane, "Woman's Stake."

14 Again, see Camera Obscura Collective, "Chronology"; Camera Obscura Collective, "Feminism and Film"; Doane, "Woman's Stake."

15 Johnston, *Notes on Women's Cinema*, 25; Camera Obscura Collective, "Feminism and Film," 10.

16 Camera Obscura Collective, "Chronology," 8.

17 Most notable among these feminist scholarly advocates for realist documentary was Julia Lesage; see Lesage, "The Political Aesthetics of Feminist Documentary Film." For further critical studies of documentary film in the 1970s, see early issues of *Jump Cut*, which Lesage edited with Chuck Kleinhans and John Hess, available online at https://www.ejumpcut.org/archive. Shilyh Warren makes a similar argument and engages with Alexandra Juhasz's writing on this subject (cited at the end of this chapter) in her recent book on women's realist documentary; see Warren, *Subject to Reality*, 2–4, 7–9.

237

18 See Barker, *The Tactile Eye*; Marks, *Touch*; Sobchack, *The Address of the Eye*.

19 Marks, *Touch*, 18.

20 Bergstrom, "*Jeanne Dielman, 23 Quai du Commerce, 1080 Bruxelles*," 116.

21 Becker et al., "Lesbians and Film"; Straayer, *Deviant Eyes, Deviant Bodies*; White, *Uninvited*.

22 Villarejo, *Lesbian Rule*, 86, 97–98.

23 Frances Reid, interview by Rox Samer, October 28, 2014.

24 For more on the Furies, see Beemyn, *A Queer Capital*, 193–204; Valk, *Radical Sisters*, 135–57. See also the introduction to this book.

25 Joan E. Biren and Mary Farmer, interview by Rox Samer, November 7, 2014.

26 Biren Papers, cassette 210. About two-thirds of these tapes from Iris's first six months are in the Biren Papers at Smith. Because this is Biren's collection, more of these are the West Coast tapes, which she received rather than sent. Unless noted otherwise, the information summarized in the following pages was gleaned from these tapes.

27 Reid interview (October 28, 2014).

28 Iris Films to "Dear Sister Filmmaker," letter, May 25, 1975, Biren Papers, box 57.

29 Iris Films to "Dear Sister Filmmaker."

30 To avoid as much awkwardness as possible, for their June 21, 1975, tape on the subject of their personal finances, the West Coast group interviewed one another and then presented their finances on the tape, Zheutlin describing Reid and Stevens's combined finances and Stevens describing Zheutlin's. Unfortunately, according to the July 14, 1975, West Coast tape, the East Coast personal finance tape was stolen in a burglary of Reid and Stevens's house, but they were able to listen to it once: Biren Papers, cassettes 218–19.

31 Cathy Zheutlin, interview by Rox Samer, December 5, 2014.

32 Biren and Farmer interview.

33 Correspondence between Cathy Zheutlin and Joan Biren and Mary Lee Farmer after dissolution of Iris East in Biren Papers, box 57, as well as correspondence between Cathy Zheutlin and Ariel Dougherty, in Dougherty Papers, box 9; Zheutlin interview.

34 National Women's Film Circuit DC Festival flier and Iris Films press release, Biren Papers, box 61.

35 Iris Films press release, Biren Papers, box 61.

36 Festival Schedule, Biren Papers, box 61.

37 Stone, "Nat. Women's Film Circuit Makes Powerful One Hundred-Movie Debut," 15.

38 Stone, "Nat. Women's Film Circuit Makes Powerful One Hundred-Movie Debut," 15.

39 Dowell, "Iris Film Festival," 14.

40 Dowell, "Iris Film Festival," 14.

41 Stone, "Nat. Women's Film Circuit Makes Powerful One Hundred-Movie Debut," 16.

42 Dowell, "Iris Film Festival," 4.

43 Dowell, "Iris Film Festival," 5.

44 Dowell, "Iris Film Festival," 5.

45 Dowell, "Iris Film Festival," 15.

46 Correspondence between members of Iris West and Iris East, September 1975, Biren Papers, box 57.

47 Iris Feminist Collective, catalog, Biren Papers, box 57.

48 Zheutlin and Dougherty correspondence.

49 Camera Obscura Collective, "*Camera Obscura* Questionnaire on Alternative Film Distribution," 157.

50 Camera Obscura Collective, "*Camera Obscura* Questionnaire on Alternative Film Distribution," 157.

51 The cities and towns outside DC where the NWFC traveled were Tucson (twice); Los Angeles (twice); Santa Barbara, California; Santa Cruz, California; San Diego; Denver/Boulder (twice); Gainesville, Florida; Bloomington, Indiana; Fort Wayne, Indiana (twice); Minneapolis (twice); St. Louis; Omaha (twice); Albuquerque (twice); Durham, North Carolina (twice); Albany, New York; Huntington, New York; New York City; Stonybrook, New York; Cleveland (twice); Columbus, Ohio (three times); Norman, Oklahoma (twice); Dayton, Ohio; Portland, Oregon; Seattle; Athens, Georgia; Atlanta (twice); Makawao, Hawaii; Chicago; Normal, Illinois; Milwaukee (twice); Lexington, Kentucky; New Orleans; Boston; Lynn/Salem, Massachusetts; College Park, Maryland; Blacksburg, Virginia; Lansing, Michigan; Greensboro, North Carolina; Tulsa, Oklahoma; Philadelphia; Memphis; Amarillo, Texas; Houston; Dallas; and Kingston, Rhode Island: Producer contracts, questionnaires, and accounting information, Biren Papers, boxes 62–64.

52 Producer contracts, questionnaires, and accounting information.

53 Knight and Thomas, *Reaching Audiences*, 84–93.

54 The topic of producers' capabilities when it came to producing a screening independent of Iris Films' oversight was an ongoing debate between Iris West and Iris East during the spring of 1975: Biren Papers, audio cassettes 214–16.

55 "Producer Notes," Biren Papers, box 62.

56 In fact, Moonforce was one of the first organizations with "lesbian" in its mission statement to apply for tax exemption and had to appeal an Internal Revenue Service rejection to get approved: Biren and Farmer interview.

57 Reid recently said of Iris Films, "I feel at that point, lesbians in particular were really hungry for images of themselves. . . . We were very explicitly a lesbian collective. . . . We wanted to have a visibility in that way. That didn't mean all the films we were distributing were lesbian films, but the highest profile ones definitely were lesbian films": Reid interview (October 28, 2014).

58 Citron, "The Films of Jan Oxenberg," 31–32; Dyer, *Now You See It*, 169–201.

59 Biren, "Moonforce Media Interview."

60 NWFC pamphlets, Biren Papers, boxes 61–64.

61 Discussion leader notes, Biren Papers, box 62.

62 One package consisted of the Women's Film Project's *Emerging Woman* (1974), Linda Klosky's *And Then There Were* (1973), Barbara Hammer's *Dyketactics* (1974), Sally Barret-Page's *Like a Rose* (1975), Jean Shaw's *Fear* (1973), and Doe Mayer's *A Foot in the Clouds* (1975). The other included Donna Deitch's *Woman to Woman* (1975), Women Make Movies' *Livia Makes Some Changes* (1974), Lois Tupper's *Our Little Munchkin Here* (1975), Jan Oxenberg's *Home Movie* (1972), Barbara Hammer's *Menses* (1974), and Cambridge Documentary Films' *Taking Our Bodies Back* (1974): NWFC pamphlets and fliers, Biren Papers, boxes 57–64.

63 NWFC fliers, Biren Papers, boxes 57–64.

64 Freude, "Notes on Distribution," 151.

65 Freude, "Notes on Distribution," 151.

66 Contracts and quarterly financial reports, Biren Papers, boxes 59–61.

67 Biren and Farmer interview.

68 One of these was made up of the Twin Cities Women's Film Collective's *My People* (1977), Barbara Jabaily's *On a Cold Afternoon* (1977), Kathleen Laughlin's *Madsong* (1976), Christine Mohana's *Ninja* (1977), and Elizabeth Barret's *Quilting Women* (1976). The other included Jane Meyers's *Getting Ready* (1977), Sharon Madden's *Friends* (1976), Kathleen Shannon's *Would I Ever Like to Work* (1974), Barbara Hammer's *Women I Love* (1976), and Women Make Movies' *Healthcaring: From Our End of the Speculum* (1976): NWFC pamphlets and fliers.

69 "Discussion Leader Guide," Biren Papers, box 62.

70 "Discussion Leader Guide."

71 Kuhn, *Women's Pictures*, 186–90; Kaplan, *Women and Film*, 196–200.

72 Kaplan, *Women and Film*, 196.

73 Bartlett, "Notes on Distribution," 151.

74 Thompson, "Multiracial Feminism," 344.

75 Roth, *Separate Roads to Feminism*.

76 Sandoval, *Methodology of the Oppressed*, 57.

77 Bartlett, "Notes on Distribution," 151.

78 Muñoz, "Ephemera as Evidence."

79 Keeling, *The Witch's Flight*, 26.

80 Keeling, *The Witch's Flight*, 25.

81 Casey, the local producer, speculates that the low attendance at the lesbian event was partially due to the Daughters of Bilitis organizing a Halloween dance the same night: Producer questionnaire, Biren Papers, box 63.

82 Producer questionnaire, Biren Papers, box 63.

83 Producer questionnaire, Biren Papers, box 59.

84 Producer questionnaire, Biren Papers, box 63.

85 Producer questionnaire, Biren Papers, box 62.

86 Producer questionnaire, Biren Papers, box 62.

87 Producer questionnaire, Biren Papers, box 62.

88 Producer questionnaire, Biren Papers, box 59.

89 Producer questionnaire, Biren Papers, box 62.

90 Producer questionnaires and correspondence, Biren Papers, box 59.

91 My findings thus support those of Michelle Citron, who writes, "Oxenberg's films have had an enthusiastic reception by lesbian and feminist audiences. . . . The films have been programmed over and over again and have achieved a feminist and lesbian cult reputation": Citron, "The Films of Jan Oxenberg," 31.

92 Producer questionnaire, Biren Papers, box 63.

93 Producer questionnaire, Biren Papers, box 62.

94 Goddess Films sales and rentals brochure, Biren Papers, box 60.

95 Producer questionnaire, Biren Papers, box 62.

96 Producer questionnaire, Biren Papers, box 64.

97 Audience survey, Biren Papers, box 64.

98 For a history of the "gay-straight split" in the US women's movement in the 1970s, including the National Organization for Women's resistance to discussing (never mind affiliating itself with) lesbians, see Echols, *Daring to Be Bad*, 203-41.

99 Producer questionnaire, Biren Papers, box 64.

100 Producer questionnaire, Biren Papers, box 63.

101 Most notably, Dyer, *Now You See It*; Weiss, "*Women I Love* and *Double Strength*," 30. For a synthesis of these early critiques and critical analysis of their historical and theoretical repercussions, see Youmans, "Performing Essentialism."

102 Youmans, "Performing Essentialism."

103 Youmans, "Performing Essentialism," 113.

104 Biren and Farmer interview.

105 Producer questionnaire, Biren Papers, box 62.

106 Producer questionnaire, Biren Papers, box 59.

107 Producer questionnaire, Biren Papers, box 59.

108 Producer questionnaire, Biren Papers, box 63.

109 Producer questionnaire, Biren Papers, box 59.

110 Audre Lorde, "Transformation of Silence into Language and Action" (1977), in Lorde, *Sister Outsider*, 40-44.

111 Muñoz, "Ephemera as Evidence," 9.

112 Zimmermann, *Reel Families*, 113.

113 Producer questionnaire, Biren Papers, box 62.

114 Biren, "Moonforce Media Interview."

115 JoAnn DiLorenzo to Moonforce Media, letter, August 10, 1977, and Joan Biren's September 11, 1977 letter in response; Norma Bahia to Moonforce Media, letter, August 15, 1977 (among others), all in Biren Papers, box 61.

116 K. K. Ho to Moonforce Media, letter, October 8, 1977, Biren Papers, box 59.

117 Mary Farmer for Moonforce Media to K. K. Ho, letter, November 1, 1977, Biren Papers, box 59.

118 Biren and Farmer interview.

119 For more on the history of Women Make Movies, see Fallica, "Sustaining Feminist Film Cultures."

120 International Videoletter fliers, Dougherty Papers, box 17.

121 Carol Clement had previously designed the T-shirt for the Conference of Feminist Film and Video Organizations in New York, which featured a similar handheld camera: Ariel Dougherty, interview with Rox Samer, November 21, 2014.

122 Interestingly, the geographer Jack Gieseking recently has offered "constellations" as a theoretical concept to help make sense of how lesbians and queers imagined and produced urban space in New York City of the 1980s and '90s: Gieseking, *A Queer New York*.

123 Dougherty interview; Sharon Karp, interview with Rox Samer, December 11, 2014; Zheutlin interview.

124 Karp interview.

125 International Videoletters flier, n.d., Dougherty Papers, box 17.

126 Hilderbrand, *Inherent Vice*, 12–13.

127 Hilderbrand, *Inherent Vice*, 36.

128 Hilderbrand, *Inherent Vice*, 8. See also Hilderbrand's brief description of International Videoletters: Hilderbrand, *Inherent Vice*, 204–5.

129 Feminist Eye Conference program, Dougherty Papers, box 17; Biren Papers, box 64; Frances Reid, interview by Rox Samer, December 4, 2014.

130 Dougherty interview.

131 Ariel Dougherty, e-mail message to Rox Samer, November 21, 2014.

132 For example, in a 1976 *off our backs* article, Deborah George of the Spectra Feminist Media Project in DC describes her group's constellation as having grown to include "DC, Portland, San Francisco, Boston, Women's House of Detention in Frontera, California, and sometimes San Diego": Cheng et al., "Spectra," 23.

133 Although representatives from the United Kingdom and Australia were present when the idea was conceived at the New York conference, Canada appears to have been the only country outside the United States to have contributed videoletters and held International Videoletter screenings. In the description of International Videoletters to come out of the conference, the project is described as a "six month experimental video exchange between six cities in Australia, Canada, and the United States." The document goes on to detail the structure of this international exchange this way: "Four US cities will participate on a monthly basis. The exchange with sister organizations in Sydney, Australia and Edmonton, Alberta will happen once in the six month period due to distance, changes in standards, and limited facilities." However, correspondence suggests that the challenges of long distances and the challenges of communicating about them limited non–North American involvement: Dougherty Papers, box 17.

134 Spectra Feminist Media Project International Videoletters flier, Dougherty Papers, box 17.

135 Dougherty interview.

136 Ariel Dougherty to Sue Scott, Just Us Video Collective, letter, November 15, 1975, Dougherty Papers, box 9.

137 Just Us Video Collective to Ariel Dougherty and others, letter, August 1, 1975, Dougherty Papers, box 9.

138 Reid interview (December 4, 2014).

139 Milano, "Women's Media," 4.

140 Lesage, "The Political Aesthetics of Feminist Documentary Film," 507.

141 Feminist Studio Workshop Videoletter, Long Beach Museum of Art Video Archive, Getty Research Institute, Los Angeles.

142 On an undated postcard sent with the tape to New York City, Deborah George notes, "P.S. The statue on top of the Capitol Building is a woman": Dougherty Papers, box 17.

143 George to Dougherty, undated postcard.

144 Marks, *Touch*, 2–4.

145 Marks, *Touch*, 4.

146 Marks, *Touch*, 13–14.

147 Barker, *The Tactile Eye*, 36.

148 Villarejo, *Lesbian Rule*, 13–14.

149 Villarejo, *Lesbian Rule*, 7.

150 In American Sign Language, the signs for "free" and "safe" are exactly the same. In the videoletter, Timothy signs each with initialized hands, meaning she signs "free" with an "F" and "safe" with an "S," to distinguish the two for fellow singers and make her case for a largely hearing audience. I thank Melanie Dabbs for her help here.

151 Creative signing is a common strategy for signers when signing songs. I thank Melanie Dabbs for her help here.

152 Davis, "The Face Is a Politics," 153.

153 In using the term "compulsory able-bodiedness," I am, of course, indebted to Robert McRuer's work on queerness and disability: McRuer, *Crip Theory*.

154 Two are located in the Long Beach Museum of Art Video Archive, Getty Research Institute, Los Angeles, having been donated by Susan Mogul, an artist and filmmaker and videoletter participant in Los Angeles; two are in the Ariel Dougherty Audiovisual Collection at the Arthur and Elizabeth Schlesinger Library on the History of Women in America at Harvard University; two are available to screen on the Media Burn Independent Video Archive website, which were acquired as a part of Kartemquin Films' collection; and another six have been located in the last few years due to Ariel Dougherty's tireless search, after donating her materials to the Schlesinger Library, to find other videoletters and get them digitized and archived. These processes are still underway: Media Burn Independent Video Archive, "International Videoletters, 1975: Recently Discovered Rare Tapes from Feminist Video Network," accessed August 12, 2020, https://mediaburn.org/blog/international-videoletters-1975-recently-discovered-rare-tapes-from-feminist-video-network.

155 Women Make Movies correspondence, board minutes, and grant applications, Dougherty Papers, boxes 14–15.

156 Juhasz, "They Said We Were Trying to Show Reality," 192.

157 Juhasz, "They Said We Were Trying to Show Reality," 199.

158 Eichhorn, *The Archival Turn in Feminism*, 6.

Chapter Two. Producing Freedom

Epigraph: Lesage, "The Political Aesthetics of Feminist Documentary Film," 507.

1 Faith and Women's Prison Project Los Angeles, *Inside/Outside*. (Found at the Lesbian Herstory Archives, prison subject files, New York City, New York.)

2 Audre Lorde, "Uses of the Erotic: The Erotic as Power" (1978), in Lorde, *Sister Outsider*, 56.

3 Rich, "Compulsory Heterosexuality and Lesbian Existence," 648–51. For more on how I am drawing on and engaging with Rich in this project, please see the book's introduction.

4 Kunzel, *Criminal Intimacy*, 122–25.

5 Juhasz, "No Woman Is an Object," 71.

6 Combahee River Collective, "A Black Feminist Statement," 8.

7 Díaz-Cotto, *Gender, Ethnicity, and the State*, 63–64.

8 Baunach and Murton, "Women in Prison," 12.

9 Díaz-Cotto, *Gender, Ethnicity, and the State*, 28.

10 Bernstein, *America Is the Prison*, 15–16.

11 Díaz-Cotto, *Gender, Ethnicity, and the State*, 277; Law, *Resistance behind Bars*, 9; Thuma, *All Our Trials*, 3.

12 Díaz-Cotto, *Gender, Ethnicity, and the State*, 277.

13 Griffiths, *Carceral Fantasies*, 211–22.

14 Griffiths, *Carceral Fantasies*, 216.

15 Faith, *Unruly Women*, 64.

16 Adler, *Sisters in Crime*, 1.

17 Adler, *Sisters in Crime*, 13.

18 Faith, *Unruly Women*, 64–66.

19 Faith, *Unruly Women*, 64–66; Law, *Resistance behind Bars*, 164–65.

20 Adler, *Sisters in Crime*, 179–80.

21 "Repression at Bedford Hills," *off our backs*, vol. 4, no. 12, December 1974, 4; "Women Inmates Battle Guards in North Carolina," *New York Times*, June 17, 1975, 18; "Officers Charge Women Inmates Staging North Carolina Protest," *New York Times*, June 20, 1975, 32; Díaz-Cotto, *Gender, Ethnicity, and the State*, 324–27; Law, *Resistance behind Bars*, 12–13; Thuma, *All Our Trials*, 59–60, 115.

22 Law, *Resistance behind Bars*, 3–4.

23 Díaz-Cotto, *Gender, Ethnicity, and the State*, 4–5; Law, *Resistance behind Bars*, 6–10.

24 Michele Wallace, "A Women's Prison and the Movement" (1972), in Wallace, *Invisibility Blues*, 44.

25 Wallace, "A Women's Prison and the Movement," 44.

26 Thuma, *All Our Trials*, 16.

27 "Freedom for Inez García," *Through the Looking Glass*, vol. 2, no. 4, April 1977, 11; Thuma, *All Our Trials*, 34–38. In researching this chapter, I accessed partial runs of *Through the Looking Glass* at the Arthur and Elizabeth Schlesinger Library on the History of Women in America at Harvard University and Archives and Special Collections at the University of Connecticut Library.

28 "Yvonne Is Free," *Through the Looking Glass*, vol. 4, no. 6, June 1979, 4; Yvonne (Swan) Wanrow, "To My Supporters," *Through the Looking Glass*, vol. 4, no. 6, June 1979, 5; "More about Yvonne," *Through the Looking Glass*, vol. 4, no. 6, June 1979, 6–7; Thuma, *All Our Trials*, 41–44.

29 Thuma, *All Our Trials*, 39–41.

30 Rashida [Dessie Woods], "Dessie Woods on Iran and the Draft," *No More Cages*, vol. 2, no. 1 (August 1980), 48; "International Demonstrations to Free Dessie Woods," *Through the Looking Glass*, vol. 4, no. 11, December 1979, 17–19; Thuma, *All Our Trials*, 40–41.

31 Thuma, *All Our Trials*, 17.

32 See, e.g., Resources for Community Change, *Women behind Bars: An Organizing Tool* (1975), 49, Lesbian Herstory Archives, prison subject files, New York, NY. *Through the Looking Glass* and *No More Cages* also often reprinted articles on "women's prisons" from *off our backs*. Interestingly, *off our backs* was also prohibited in many prisons. Regina Kunzel quotes an official at the women's federal prison in Alderson, West Virginia, as saying in 1977 that the journal was "detrimental to the security, good order and discipline of this institution because of its advocation or support of homosexuality": Kunzel, *Criminal Intimacy*, 206.

33 At the end of the August 1980 issue's "Statement of Purposes" (which was published in every issue of *No More Cages*), Women Free Women in Prison makes a note of clarification, stating, "In the past few months, the composition of our group has changed. For the time being, we are four lesbians—three Jewish and one Greek": "Statement of Purposes," *No More Cages*, vol. 2, no. 1, August 1980, 2. In a later issue, they write, "The Women Free Women In Prison Collective has been active for the past 8 years and we've published NO MORE CAGES for 4 years. Those of us who worked on this issue are 4 white, Jewish, working class lesbians. Some of us are anarchists, some socialists, some undefined, and we are all feminists. We welcome more participation from Women of Color, from Ex-Prisoners and Ex-Psychiatric Inmates": "Inside," *No More Cages*, vol. 4, no. 6, December 1983–January 1984, 1.

34 While I have done my own research in these newsletters' archives (see nn. 27, 35), I am indebted to Emily L. Thuma's published scholarship on the subject: Thuma, *All Our Trials*, 88–122.

35 A version of this statement is published at the front of each issue of *No More Cages*. I have quoted from the version published in the very first issue: "Statement of Purpose," *No More Cages*, vol. 1, no. 1, March–April 1979. Later issues replaced the line naming themselves as lesbian feminists with "feminists and

lesbians." Partial runs of *No More Cages* are at the ONE National Gay and Lesbian Archives at the University of Southern California Libraries; the Arthur and Elizabeth Schlesinger Library on the History of Women in America at Harvard University; Archives and Special Collections at the University of Connecticut Library; and the Lesbian Herstory Archives.

36 Julia Lesage first drew just such a connection between feminist documentary filmmaking and consciousness-raising in "The Political Aesthetics of Feminist Documentary Film," 507.

37 Thuma, *All Our Trials*, 90.

38 Kelley, *Freedom Dreams*, 6–9.

39 Davis, "Reflections on the Black Woman's Role in the Community of Slaves," 5.

40 Kelley, *Freedom Dreams*, 154.

41 Lesage, "The Political Aesthetics of Feminist Documentary Film," 508.

42 Ariel Dougherty, interview with Rox Samer, November 21, 2014.

43 Faith and Women's Prison Project Los Angeles, *Inside/Outside*, 15.

44 The video workshop at Bedford Hills was organized more around women acting out and improvising their experiences through performance for the camera, while others learned how to operate the camera and sound equipment. The resulting video is a compilation of a selection of these performances and interviews, edited, by necessity, by Ariel Dougherty: Ariel Dougherty, email correspondence with Rox Samer, August 2020.

45 Christine Choy, interview with Rox Samer, August 16, 2016.

46 Kunzel, *Criminal Intimacy*, 124.

47 Miller, *Camp TV*, 18.

48 Kelley, *Freedom Dreams*, 137.

49 Díaz-Cotto, *Gender, Ethnicity, and the State*, 284–85.

50 Lorde, "A Litany for Survival," 31–32.

51 "Racism from the Sky," *Through the Looking Glass*, vol. 1, no. 1, January 1976, 11–13; "Banning the Klan," *Through the Looking Glass*, vol. 5, no. 4, April 1980, 7–8; Díaz-Cotto, *Gender, Ethnicity, and the State*, 109–10.

52 Chion, *The Voice in Cinema*, 17–29.

53 Youmans, *Word Is Out*, 170–71.

54 Young, *Making Sex Public and Other Cinematic Fantasies*, 175.

55 Davis, "The Face Is a Politics" 151.

56 Faith, *Unruly Women*, 286–98.

57 Combahee River Collective, "A Black Feminist Statement," 6.

58 Schneider, "Like a Rose," 103.

59 Schneider, "Like a Rose," 107.

60 "Fear for Queers," *Through the Looking Glass*, vol. 2, no. 6, July 1977, 4; Thuma, *All Our Trials*, 103; Kunzel, *Criminal Intimacy*, 206.

61 Dillon, *Fugitive Life*, 12.

62 Dillon, *Fugitive Life*, 9.

63 See my engagement with Laura U. Marks's scholarship on haptic cinema in chapter 1; Marks, *Touch*.

Notes to Chapter Two

64 Villarejo, *Lesbian Rule*, 13–14.

65 Kelley, *Freedom Dreams*, 9.

66 Keeling, *Queer Times, Black Futures*, 84.

67 Dillon, *Fugitive Life*, 67.

68 Dillon, *Fugitive Life*, 67.

69 Ariel Dougherty names "wishful filming" as a term she and her cohort of feminist documentary filmmakers used to describe a filmmaking process in which one filmed what one wanted to happen in reality: Dougherty, email correspondence. In 1973, Cathy Zheutlin and the Santa Cruz Women's Media Collective made a documentary with this very title: see *Wishfulfilming*, posted January 15, 2015, YouTube, accessed September 29, 2020, https://www.youtube .com/watch?v=xE-xpa7Z5lc.

70 Nash, "Practicing Love."

71 Nash, "Practicing Love," 18–19.

72 Lorde, "Uses of the Erotic," 56.

73 These terms of endearment ring in a similarly gender-ambiguous fashion as "man" and "daddy" in the blues tradition. As Angela Davis notes in her studies of blues women, "African American working-class argot refers to both husbands and male lovers—and even in some cases female lovers—as 'my man' or 'my daddy'": Davis, *Blues Legacies and Black Feminism*, 13.

74 Agamben, *Potentialities*, 182.

75 Williams, "Porn Studies." See also Young, *Making Sex Public and Other Cinematic Fantasies*, 3.

76 Kunzel, *Criminal Intimacy*, 138.

77 Halberstam, *Female Masculinity*, 200–202; Holmlund, "Wham Bam! Pam!"; Mayne, *Framed*, 115–48.

78 Rangan et al., "Humanitarian Ethics and Documentary Politics," 200.

79 Producer questionnaire, Joan E. Biren Papers (hereafter, Biren Papers), box 62.

80 I am using "anchorage" and "relay" in the Barthesian sense: Barthes, *Image, Music, Text*, 39–41.

81 Faith and Women's Prison Project Los Angeles, *Inside/Outside*, 39.

82 Faith and Women's Prison Project Los Angeles, *Inside/Outside*, 27.

83 Faith and Women's Prison Project Los Angeles, *Inside/Outside*, 30–32.

84 Nichols, "Newsreel"; Renov, "Early Newsreel"; Renov, "Newsreel." For a relieving counterexample, see Young, "Third World Newsreel." For an account of the contributions of Choy, Robeson, Maurizio, and other women of color to Third World Newsreel, see Warren, *Subject to Reality*, 113–30.

85 Rich, *Chick Flicks*, 75.

86 According to correspondence with archivists, the BFI prints were donated by the feminist film distributor Cinema of Women (later Cinenova). I owe Beth Capper massive thanks for informing me of this discovery and to the Lesbian Herstory Archives for providing the perfect setting for our fortuitous meeting.

247

Epigraphs: Suzy McKee Charnas, in "Women in Science Fiction: A Symposium," *Khatru,* nos. 3-4, 1975, 8; Susan Wood, "People's Programming," *Janus 11,* vol. 4, no. 1, 1978, 7.

1   Joanna Russ, in Smith, *Symposium,* 6.

2   Suzy McKee Charnas, in Smith, *Symposium,* 8.

3   Charnas, in Smith, *Symposium,* 8. Kate Wilhelm similarly wrote, "When I started to write a few years later, it seemed quite natural for me to do those kinds of things I wanted to read, not the kinds of things others were doing that I didn't want to read any longer": Kate Wilhelm, in Smith, *Symposium,* 9.

4   Charnas, in Smith, *Symposium,* 9.

5   Vonda McIntyre, in Smith, *Symposium,* 5.

6   For greater clarification of what I mean by this, see the analysis of Agamben in the introduction.

7   Samuel R. Delany had begun publishing regularly in the early 1960s; Ursula K. LeGuin, Joanna Russ, and James Tiptree, Jr., publishing in the late 1960s; and Vonda McIntyre, Suzy McKee Charnas, and Octavia E. Butler publishing in the early 1970s.

8   According to handwritten inventory lists, for example, by 1977 science fiction had become a good portion (maybe one-fifth or one-sixth) of the stock of the women's bookstore New Words in Cambridge, Massachusetts, and was selling fast: New Words Records, box 13.

9   McIntyre, in Smith, *Symposium,* 56; Russ, in Smith, *Symposium,* 100. Russ's essay, initially 1,100 words, was eventually published in much-abbreviated fashion as Russ, "Outta Space," 109.

10   For example, Alexei Panshin and Cory Panshin claim that Russ's book is neither science fiction nor a novel but "a mediation or an exercise in self-revelation that uses some of the devices of science fiction." They elaborate, "It is not a novel. Nothing is visualized, nothing happens. If there is a conclusion to be drawn from the book, it is that the author feels that men are not altogether human, but that women without men are or might be. . . . If you share these feelings, *The Female Man* is a perfect emotional mirror. If you don't share these feelings, go fuck yourself": Panshin and Panshin, "Books," 51.

11   Another rare lesbian feminist cultural institution of the 1970s to navigate decades of financial and ideological struggles that continues to serve as a precious site of intergenerational feminist collaboration and comradery is the Lesbian Herstory Archives: see McKinney, *Information Activism,* 153–204.

12   Amanda Bankier, "Women in the Fiction of Andre Norton," *The Witch and the Chameleon,* no. 1, August 1974, 3–5.

13   Janice Bogstad, "Editorial: The Future of Future Histories," *Janus 5,* vol. 2, no. 3, 1976, 4–5; Janice Bogstad, "Editorial: Prescription and Proscription," *Janus 7,* vol. 3, no. 1, 1977, 4; Janice Bogstad and Jeanne Gomoll, "Politics and Science Fiction: A Discussion, a Panel, a Philosophy," *Janus 8,* vol. 3,

no. 2, 1977, 4–5; Janice Bogstad, "Editorial: Samurai of Space," *Janus 9*, vol. 3, no. 3, 1977, 5.

14 The equal rights amendment was a proposed constitutional amendment designed to guarantee legal equality for all US citizens, regardless of sex. Despite substantive organizing and bipartisan support, it did not receive the necessary state ratifications in the 1970s to be entered into law.

15 In particular, Ellison names Le Guin, Russ, Greg Brown, McIntyre, Bradley, and Wood as his advisers. Ellison elaborates, "Can we permit the gap between what we <u>say</u> we are and what we <u>really</u> are to exist? OR is this, perhaps, a moment when we can make a brave statement with our fiction, our literary love, our bodies, and our annual world gathering?": Harlan Ellison, "A Statement of Ethical Position by the WorldCon Guest of Honor," *Janus 10*, vol. 3, no. 4, 1977, 32–33.

16 See Lefanu, *Feminism and Science Fiction*; Merrick, *The Secret Feminist Cabal*.

17 In her "News Nurds" column in the zine's eighth edition, Gomoll writes, "*Janus* began and has clung steadfastly to its semi-sercon, most emphatically genzine image": Jeanne Gomoll, "News Nurds," *Janus 8*, vol. 3, no. 2, 1977, 2. In the tenth edition, Bogstad situates *Janus* among other SF fanzines by writing, "There are fanzines that deal with everything from the personal lives of their editors, to general magazines (such as *Janus*) which mix fan communication and critical articles, to specialized publications which focus only on book reviews (*SF Review*) or fantasy (*Orcrist*) or feminist issues in science fiction (*The Witch and the Chameleon*, a relatively new publication)": Janice Bogstad, "The Science Fiction Connection: Readers and Writers in the SF Community," *Janus 10*, vol. 3, no. 4, 1977, 6. As early as the second edition of *Janus*, Bogstad felt a need to issue a statement on "the feminist perspectives presented in *Janus*," in which she concludes that "JANUS is not entirely a feminist sf magazine, but the Editor and Managing Editor are longstanding sf readers. You can therefore expect us to respond to and print sf which presents women as the many-faceted beings that they are in real life. Be heartened Ye who seek to change the status quo. Be warned Ye who perpetuate its faults": Janice Bogstad, "Editorial," *Janus 2*, vol. 1, no. 2, 1975, 39–40.

18 Bankier was an active member of a number of lesbian/feminist groups in the Toronto area, including CR groups, and she volunteered at a domestic violence center. Bogstad and Gomoll had recently begun familiarizing themselves with feminist theory, and both had written feminist criticism in college: Samer, "Reflections on Queer Feminist Fandom Then, Now and in the Future." Meanwhile, Smith would soon admit that at first "the idea of Women in Science Fiction was an intellectual concept," having since learned how provocative a subject it could be: Jeffrey D. Smith, in Smith, *Symposium*, 61.

As Michael Warner reminds us, no author or text can be responsible for the formation of a public. Instead, a public can be created only through the concatenation of texts through time: Warner, *Publics and Counterpublics*, 90.

19 Saler, *As If*, 7.

20 Bacon-Smith, *Enterprising Women*, 228–54; Jenkins, *Textual Poachers*, 185–222; Penley, "Feminism, Psychoanalysis, and the Study of Popular Culture"; Penley, NASA/*Trek*.

21 Penley, NASA/*Trek*, 112. See also Jenkins, *Fans, Bloggers, and Gamers*, 50.

22 Warner, *Publics and Counterpublics*, 91.

23 Warner, *Publics and Counterpublics*, 73, 113–14.

24 For more on the "mundane world" or "mundania," see Jenkins, *Fans, Bloggers, and Gamers*, 41–42; Jenkins, *Textual Poachers*, 262–64. According to Warner, the poetic function of public address is something of which counterpublics are acutely aware. It becomes salient to consciousness in the process of marking themselves off not just from a more general public (as Nancy Fraser, expanding on Habermas, first characterized counterpublics) but from a dominant public: Warner, *Publics and Counterpublics*, 119–20. See also Fraser, "Rethinking the Public Sphere."

25 Susan Wood, "People's Programming," *Janus 11*, vol. 4, no. 1, 1978, 4.

26 Wood, "People's Programming," 4.

27 Wood, "People's Programming," 4.

28 On the socialist and populist history of early SF pulps, see Ross, *Strange Weather*, 102–35.

29 Saler, *As If*, 100.

30 Correspondence between Russ and Hacker and Russ and Delany, Joanna Russ Papers, boxes 3–5.

31 Samuel R. Delany, in Smith, *Symposium*, 22–37. Although he did not address race here, I think many of his claims can retrospectively be thought of in terms of racism, as well, and recommend reading this letter with Delany, "Racism and Science Fiction."

32 Delany, in Smith, *Symposium*, 24.

33 Warner, *Publics and Counterpublics*, 122.

34 Samer, "Reflections on Queer Feminist Fandom Then, Now and in the Future," 12.

35 Echols, *Daring to Be Bad*, 83–84.

36 Bogstad, "The Science Fiction Connection," 7.

37 Bogstad, "The Science Fiction Connection," 7.

38 Jeanne Gomoll, interview by Rox Samer, July 16, 2011. Excerpts of this interview were published in Rox Samer, "Reflections on Queer Feminist Fandom Then, Now and in the Future."

39 Echols, *Daring to Be Bad*, 84.

40 Cross et al., "Face-to-Face, Day-to-Day," 52.

41 Hollibaugh and Moraga, "What We're Rollin' around in Bed With," 252–53, italics in the original.

42 James Tiptree, Jr., in Smith, *Symposium*, 17.

43 Tiptree, in Smith, *Symposium*, 17.

44 Tiptree, in Smith, *Symposium*, 21.

45 The *Aurora* anthology would not be published until 1976, so the rest of the symposium participants—other than, perhaps, McIntyre—would not have yet read Tiptree's "Houston, Houston, Do You Read?"

46 For the zine's second printing in 1993, reflections from original symposium participants were solicited, as were responses from new readers. Here, both Russ and Le Guin comment on how their understanding of Tiptree's gender guided their responses to what he said and how they read Sheldon's contribution, as Tiptree, differently now: Russ and Ursula K. Le Guin, in Smith, *Symposium*, 110–11.

47 McIntyre, in Smith, *Symposium*, 56.

48 Russ, in Smith, *Symposium*, 47.

49 Russ, in Smith, *Symposium*, 47.

50 Titles Russ included in her "Partial List: Feminist Reading" (in the order in which she listed them, which she described as "the order in which they should probably be read by the semi-knowledgeable") were Michael Korda, *Male Chauvinism! How It Works*; Betty Friedan, *The Feminine Mystique*; Eva Figes, *Patriarchal Attitudes*; Elizabeth Janeway, *Man's World, Woman's Place*; Ruth Herschberger, *Adam's Rib*; Simone de Beauvoir, *The Second Sex*; Shulamith Firestone, *The Dialectic of Sex*; Vivian Gornick and Barbara K. Moran, eds., *Woman in Sexist Society*; Leslie Tanner, ed., *Voices from Women's Liberation*; Phyllis Chesler, *Women and Madness*; Germaine Greer, *The Female Eunuch*; Kate Millett, *Sexual Politics*; Mary Ellmann, *Thinking about Women*; and Jill Johnston, *Lesbian Nation*: Russ, in Smith, *Symposium*, 47–48.

51 Joanna Russ Papers, box 10.

52 Tiptree, in Smith, *Symposium*, 101.

53 Delany, in Smith, *Symposium*, 22–37.

54 Delany, in Smith, *Symposium*, 37.

55 Russ, in Smith, *Symposium*, 46.

56 Russ, in Smith, *Symposium*, 96–101.

57 As Merrick comments on this symposium, "One of the most intriguing and valuable aspects of this document of feminist social history is the chronicling of the tensions and struggles over the meaning of feminism between women of different generations, different backgrounds and positionings (for example, middle-class liberal, socialist feminist, radical lesbian), and [in its 1993 republication] the contemporary reflections by women like Le Guin, Russ, and Charnas on their 'previous selves' and also their treatment of others": Merrick, *The Secret Feminist Cabal*, 116.

58 Russ, in Smith, *Symposium*, 83.

59 Delany, in Smith, *Symposium*, 26.

60 Russ, in Smith, *Symposium*, 117.

61 Russ, in Smith, *Symposium*, 115–16.

62 Russ, in Smith, *Symposium*, 111–18.

63 hooks, *Ain't I a Woman*.

64 In taking up this exchange here, I hope to help remedy the neglect of Bradley and other established female SF authors' potential feminism that Merrick

points out: Merrick, *The Secret Feminist Cabal*, 9. At the same time, however, I do not find their peripheral status in the feminist SF canon to be such a problem as Camille Bacon-Smith claims, writing, "Foremothers with the science fiction community such as Andre Norton, Marion Zimmer Bradley, and even C. L. Moore were often 'disappeared' from the feminist record or anachronistically criticized for their sensibilities [in the 1970s and '80s]": Bacon-Smith, *Science Fiction Culture*, 95–96. In fact, these critical fan engagements in early feminist SF fanzines attest to feminist SF fans' and critics' attempts to engage their work.

65 Saler, *As If*, 135–36, 176–79.
66 Bankier, "Women in the Fiction of Andre Norton," 3.
67 Bankier, "Women in the Fiction of Andre Norton," 5.
68 Andre Norton, letter of comment, *The Witch and the Chameleon*, no. 2, November 1974, 4.
69 Norton, letter of comment, 4.
70 Norton, letter of comment, 4.
71 Norton, letter of comment, 4.
72 Norton, letter of comment, 4.
73 Rich, "Compulsory Heterosexuality and Lesbian Existence."
74 Joanna Russ, letter of comment, *The Witch and the Chameleon*, no. 3, April 1975, 27.
75 Amanda Bankier, editorial comment, *The Witch and the Chameleon*, no. 3, April 1975, 27.
76 Bankier, editorial comment, 27–28.
77 Vonda McIntyre, "Review: *Darkover Landfall*," *The Witch and the Chameleon*, no. 2, November 1974, 20.
78 McIntyre, "Review," 20.
79 Marion Zimmer Bradley, quoted in McIntyre, "Review," 23.
80 Bradley, quoted in McIntyre, "Review," 23.
81 Marion Zimmer Bradley, letter of comment, *The Witch and the Chameleon*, no. 3, April 1975, 28–31.
82 Bradley, letter of comment, 29.
83 Bradley, letter of comment, 30.
84 Bradley, letter of comment, 30.
85 Bradley, quoted in Bankier, editorial comment, 31.
86 Bankier, editorial comment, 31.
87 Saler, *As If*, 87–89.
88 Joanna Russ, letter of comment, *The Witch and the Chameleon*, no. 4, September 1975, 17.
89 Marion Zimmer Bradley, letter of comment, *The Witch and the Chameleon*, no. 4, September 1975, 22.
90 Bradley, letter of comment, 23.
91 Bradley, letter of comment, 23.
92 Bradley, letter of comment, 23.

93 Bradley, letter of comment, 24.

94 Bradley, letter of comment, 24.

95 Joanna Russ, "A Letter to Marion Zimmer Bradley," *The Witch and the Chameleon*, nos. 5–6, 1976, 11.

96 Russ, "A Letter to Marion Zimmer Bradley," 11.

97 Russ, "A Letter to Marion Zimmer Bradley," 12.

98 Janice Bogstad and Jeanne Gomoll, "Interview: Lunch Talk with Suzy McKee Charnas, Amanda Bankier, Janice Bogstad, and Jeanne Gomoll," *Janus 6*, vol. 2, no. 4, 1976, 23–27.

99 Radicalesbians, "The Woman Identified Woman," 242. The idea that lesbians are not women was later given a positive constructivist spin by the French lesbian feminist Monique Wittig: Wittig, "One Is Not Born a Woman.".

100 Charnas, quoted in Bogstad and Gomoll, "Interview," 26.

101 Charnas, quoted in Bogstad and Gomoll, "Interview," 26.

102 Charnas, quoted in Bogstad and Gomoll, "Interview," 26.

103 Leimbacher and Strand, "An Introduction to the Films of Chick Strand," 131. For my analysis of "Houston, Houston, Do You Read?" and *Fever Dream*, see this book's introduction.

104 Marion Zimmer Bradley, "Letters: Round 2: Reactions to 'Lunch and Talk,'" *Janus 8*, vol. 3, no. 2, 1977, 32; Bradley, "Letters," 30.

105 Bradley, "Letters," 32.

106 Ann Weiser, letter, *Janus 9*, vol. 3, no. 3, 1977, 8.

107 Gregory G. H. Rihn, letter, *Janus 9*, vol. 3, no. 3, 1977, 11.

108 Echols, *Daring to Be Bad*, 150–58.

109 Warner, *Publics and Counterpublics*, 114.

110 For example, Jack Halberstam has recently described cultural feminism's humorlessness as partially responsible for the movement's "disintegrat[ing] into a messy, unappealing morass of weepy, hypo-allergic, psychosomatic, anti-sex, anti-fun, anti-porn, pro-drama, pro-processing post-political subjects." The queerer 1990s would then usher in "a multi-racial, poststructuralist, intersectional feminism of much longer provenance [in which] people began to laugh, loosened up, people got over themselves and began to talk and recognize that the enemy was not among us but embedded within new, rapacious economic systems." Halberstam, "You Are Triggering Me!" Fortunately, I am not alone in my reconsideration of humor in 1970s feminisms: see, e.g., Leng, "Pleasure and Pedagogy."

111 Weisstein, "Why We Aren't Laughing . . . Any More," 51, 88.

112 McIntyre, in Smith, *Symposium*, 119.

113 Walker, *A Very Serious Thing*, 143, 145.

114 Walker, *A Very Serious Thing*, 151.

115 Walker, *A Very Serious Thing*, 151.

116 Tiptree, in Smith, *Symposium*, 101.

117 Jeanne Gomoll, "Feminism: To Grasp the Power to Name Ourselves; Science Fiction: To Grasp the Power to Name Our Future," *Janus 11*, vol. 4, no. 1, 1978, 20.

253

118 Gomoll, "Feminism," 20.

119 See *Janus 7*, vol. 3, no. 1, 1977, 3, 26–28.

120 Jeanne Gomoll, "A Lesson," *Janus 8*, vol. 3, no. 2, 1977, 39; Jeanne Gomoll, "A Great Place for a Con," *Janus 9*, vol. 3, no. 3, 1977, 25.

121 Dan Steffan, back cover art, *Janus 8*, vol. 3, no. 2, 1977.

122 Teddy Harvia, "Alien and Woman Recognition Sketch," *Janus 17*, vol. 6, no. 1, 1979, 25.

123 Jeanne Gomoll, "Explaining Fandom Too," *Janus 16*, vol. 5, no. 2, 1979, 19.

124 Hank Luttrell, "The Last *Star Wars* Review," *Janus 9*, vol. 3, no. 3, 1977, 17–18.

125 Luttrell, "The Last *Star Wars* Review," 18.

126 See the WisCon 2 reports in *Janus 12–13*, vol. 4, nos. 2–3, 1978, 47–53. For its article of purpose, SF³ wrote, "The purposes shall be to foster interest in, appreciation for, and criticism of fantasy and science fiction in literature, art, film, drama, and other forms of communication": Russell, "Blue Sky and Red Tape, Part 2," *Janus 15*, vol. 5, no. 1, 1979, 38.

127 Email correspondence with Jeanne Gomoll and Richard S. Russell.

128 Richard S. Russell, "Blue Sky and Red Tape," *Janus 15*, vol. 5, no. 1, 1979, 43.

129 Janice Bogstad, "News," *Janus 3*, vol. 2, no. 1, 1976, 2.

130 Jeanne Gomoll, "The What's-Going-On-Dept," *Janus 4*, vol. 2, no. 2, 1976, 2.

131 Jeanne Gomoll, "News Nose," *Janus 6*, vol. 2, no. 4, 1976, 2–3.

132 Joseph, *Against the Romance of Community*, 28.

133 Russell, "Blue Sky and Red Tape," 42.

134 Joseph, *Against the Romance of Community*, ix.

135 Mayor Paul Soglin, letter, *Janus 11*, vol. 4, no. 1, 1978, 61.

136 Bogstad and Gomoll, "Politics and Science Fiction," 4–5, 29.

137 Jeanne Gomoll, "Will the REAL James Tiptree, Jr. Please Stand Up!" *Janus 11*, vol. 4, no. 1, 1978, 15.

138 Correspondence between Gomoll and Sheldon, Alice B. Sheldon, Pen Name James Tiptree, Jr., Papers, box 61.

139 Jenkins, *Textual Poachers*, 254.

140 Jeanne Gomoll, "Alice through the Looking Glass of SF," *Janus 7*, vol. 3, no. 1, 1977, 9.

141 Jeanne Gomoll, "Sercon Silliness," *Janus 8*, vol. 3, no. 2, 1977, 21.

142 Janice Bogstad, "Confessions of a Co-chairperson as a Panelist," *Janus 8*, vol. 3, no. 2, 1977, 27.

143 Reports from WisCons 1–3 make note of male con-goers complaining about the feminist slant of the convention as well as explaining that they are good feminists and thus do not need a con to talk about feminism. Fortunately, con reports also occasionally reflect male allies' changing perspectives on feminism and how to be a good ally. One great example is Jon Singer's report from WisCon 3: see Jon Singer, "WisCon Report," and Bill Hoffman, "Wiscon Report," *Janus 15*, vol. 5, no. 1, 1979, 16–17.

144 Jeanne Gomoll, "Happy Gays Are Here Again," *Janus 9*, vol. 3, no. 3, 1977, 22.

145 Radway, "Reception Study," 374.

146 "Janus and Aurora," Society for the Furtherance and Study of Fantasy and Science Fiction website, n.d., accessed September 28, 2019, http://sf3.org/history/janus-aurora-covers.

147 For information about the Carl Brandon Society, see the organization's website at http://www.carlbrandon.org.

148 WisCon 37 Pocket Program Book, 55.

149 Merrick, *The Secret Feminist Cabal*, 178.

150 Merrick, *The Secret Feminist Cabal*, 179.

151 Joseph, *Against the Romance of Community*, 57.

152 Warner, *Publics and Counterpublics*, 88–89.

Chapter Four. Tip/Alli

1 Rich, "When We Dead Awaken," 18.

2 One example of this re-vision work in the visual arts is Judy Chicago's *The Dinner Party* (1979), a giant triangular dining table installation with thirty-nine vulva-like place settings, so that women from across time—from "the primordial goddess" to Sappho and Georgia O'Keeffe—might sit together in conversation. Viewers, including early audiences and visitors to its installation at the Brooklyn Museum (2007–present), become participants in this cross-temporal feminist communion. For more on *The Dinner Party*, see Gerhard, *The Dinner Party*. For additional examples, see Samer, "Revising 'Re-vision.'"

3 See Butler, *Gender Trouble*; hooks, *Ain't I a Woman*; Hull et al., *All the Women Are White, All the Blacks Are Men, but Some of Us Are Brave*; Moraga and Anzaldúa, *This Bridge Called My Back*; Haraway, "Situated Knowledges"; Riley, *"Am I That Name?"*; Sandoval, *Methodology of the Oppressed*.

4 Perhaps most notable among the institutions doing this preservation work are the Arthur and Elizabeth Schlesinger Library on the History of Women in America at Harvard University, the Sallie Bingham Center for Women's History and Culture at Duke University, the Sophia Smith Collection Women's History Archives at Smith College, and the Feminist History Archives at Stanford University, each of which includes notable and growing digital components. Some of these feminist collections, such as that at the Schlesinger Library, preceded the Women's Liberation Movement, while others, such as that at the Sallie Bingham Center, were a direct result of it. It should also be noted that while the majority of Rich's papers are housed at the Schlesinger Library, she donated a small collection to the noninstitutional Lesbian Herstory Archives (LHA) in the 1970s (collection 7901), because she wanted researchers to have to go to LHA to research her life: Rachel Corbman, email correspondence with Rox Samer, December 2020. Information on the LHA's digitizing practices are in McKinney, *Information Activism*, 153–204.

5 Feminist historians heard this time and again at feminist conferences in the 1970s. It is also a common rhetorical move in documentaries about the 1970s. See my early essay on revising re-vision, including the documentaries *!Women*

Art Revolution (2010), directed by Lynn Hershman Leeson, and *Makers: Women Who Make America* (2013), directed by Dyllan McGee, Betsy West, and Peter Kunhardt: Samer, "Revising 'Re-vision.'" Susan Faludi has articulated this concern most egregiously as "feminism's ritual matricide": Faludi, "American Electra." See Kate Eichhorn's sharp critique of Faludi on which this study builds: Eichhorn, *The Archival Turn in Feminism*, 25–32.

6 On the archival turn, see Eichhorn, *The Archival Turn in Feminism*. On the queer and trans re-visions, see Corbman, "Conferencing on the Edge"; Enke, "Collective Memory and the Transfeminist 1970s"; Gieseking, *A Queer New York*; Heaney, "Women-Identified Women"; McKinney, *Information Activism*; Strongman, "The Sisterhood"; Williams, "Radical Inclusion," 254–58.

7 Two such projects, which I explore in greater depth in "Revising 'Re-vision,'" are Leeson's *!Women Art Revolution* and McGee and colleagues' PBS documentary *Makers: Women Who Make America*. Leeson's film offers a history of the Feminist Art Movement in the United States, and she has made the raw footage and transcripts of the film's interviews available to the public as a part of Stanford University's online Feminist History Archives collection. The PBS film, meanwhile, tells the more general story of how "second-wave feminism" changed the lives of American citizens for the better. For the release of *Makers*, PBS partnered with AOL, and together they built a supplementary ongoing collection of thousands of interviews online, most of which are now part of the three-and-a-half-hour film itself: Samer, "Revising 'Re-vision,'" n.p.

8 Faludi, "American Electra," 29–30.

9 Foucault, "Nietzsche, Genealogy, History."

10 Foucault, "Nietzsche, Genealogy, History," 147.

11 Jameson, *Archaeologies of the Future*.

12 Rawson and Devor, "Archives and Archiving."

13 For an elaboration of this definition of transfeminism, see Koyama, "The Transfeminist Manifesto."

14 Among this body of scholarship I would include cárdenas, "Shifting Futures"; Keeling, "Looking for M—"; Lothian, *Old Futures*; Muñoz, *Cruising Utopia*.

15 Salamon, *Assuming a Body*, 105–8.

16 Nestle, "Butch-Fem Relationships," 23.

17 Salamon, *Assuming a Body*, 109.

18 See, e.g., Padawer, "When Women Become Men at Wellesley"; Burkett, "What Makes a Woman?"

19 Enke, "Collective Memory and the Transfeminist 1970s"; Heaney, "Women-Identified Women"; Williams, "Radical Inclusion."

20 Myriad sources cite this rise in violence against trans women of color: see, e.g., Cox and McDonald, "Black Trans Bodies Are under Attack"; Hauser, "Transgender Woman Shot Dead in Motel Is Seventh Killed in US This Year"; National Coalition of Anti-Violence Programs, "A Crisis of Hate"; National Coalition of Anti-violence Programs, "Lesbian, Gay, Bisexual, Transgender, Queer, and HIV-Affected Hate Violence in 2016."

21 Goldberg, "What Is a Woman?"

22 There are so many examples of this hateful behavior. One account of this extensive history and its movement online is Vasquez, "It's Time to End the Long History of Feminism Failing Transgender Women."

23 As Judith Butler points out in an interview conducted in September 2020, it is "worrisome that suddenly the trans-exclusionary radical feminist position is understood as commonly accepted or even mainstream," because "it is actually a fringe movement that is seeking to speak in the name of the mainstream." Here Butler likewise points out that their interviewer cites the harassment Rowling has received online but not that leveled at trans people: Ferber, "Judith Butler on the Culture Wars, J. K. Rowling and Living in 'Anti-intellectual Times.'" The transfeminist scholars and activists Kai M. Green and Emi Koyama teach us that misogyny affects not only cisgender women but all those assigned female at birth, as well as all women and femmes: see Green, "Navigating Masculinity as a Black Transman"; Koyama, "The Transfeminist Manifesto."

24 Serano, "Op-ed."

25 Stryker, *Transgender History*, 109.

26 See Enke, "Collective Memory and the Transfeminist 1970s," 13–23; Heaney, "Women-Identified Women," 138–39; Stryker, *Transgender History*, 109; Williams, "Radical Inclusion," 255–57.

27 Julia Serano coined the term "trans-misogyny" to describe the specific form of discrimination that trans women experience, wherein they are "ridiculed or dismissed not merely for failing to live up to gender norms, but for their expressions of femaleness or femininity." She elaborates: "When the majority of jokes made at the expense of trans people center on 'men wearing dresses' or 'men who want their penises cut off,' that is not transphobia—it is trans-misogyny. When the majority of violence and sexual assaults committed against trans people is directed at trans women, that is not transphobia—it is trans-misogyny. When it's okay for women to wear 'men's' clothing, but when men who wear 'women's' clothing can be diagnosed with the psychological disorder transvestic fetishism, that is not transphobia—it is trans-misogyny. When women's or lesbian organizations and events open their doors to trans men but not trans women, that is not transphobia—it is trans-misogyny": Serano, *Whipping Girl*, 14–15.

28 See, e.g., Ouellette and Banet-Weiser, "Media and the Extreme Right."

29 Foucault, "Nietzsche, Genealogy, History," 147.

30 Foucault, "Nietzsche, Genealogy, History," 164.

31 For the sake of clarity, I refer to Raccoona Sheldon as Raccoona and Alice B. Sheldon as Sheldon.

32 See, e.g., Sheldon's journals from late 1976 and 1977 (but also scattered throughout correspondence with SF friends and colleagues from this same time and shortly after), Alice B. Sheldon, Pen Name James Tiptree, Jr., Papers (hereafter, Sheldon Papers), boxes 11–12.

33 Sheldon Papers, boxes 11–12.

34 Manion, *Female Husbands*, 13–14; Miller, *Camp TV*, 17–21.

35 "With Delicate Mad Hands," ms., Sheldon Papers, box 59.

36 For a more thorough account of this New Wave of science fiction as it relates here, see Melzer, *Alien Constructions*, 5–7.

37 Sheldon would go on to publish two novels under the name James Tiptree, Jr.— *Up the Walls of the World* (1978) and *Brightness Falls from the Air* (1985)—but they were post-reveal, and neither garnered great acclaim the way her short fiction had and would continue to. Tiptree is considered by most a short story writer.

38 Phillips, *James Tiptree, Jr.*, 249.

39 Silverberg, "Introduction," xv.

40 Dozois, *The Fiction of James Tiptree, Jr.*, n.p. Originally published as the introduction to G. K. Hall's 1976 edition of *10,000 Light Years from Home*, which is now out of print.

41 Tiptree to Dean Foster, letter, April 26, 1974, Sheldon Papers, box 75.

42 Phillips, *James Tiptree, Jr.*, 324.

43 Dozois, *The Fiction of James Tiptree, Jr.*, n.p.

44 Dick to Tiptree, letter, February 27, 1970, Sheldon Papers, box 64.

45 Tiptree to Dick, letter, March 10, 1970, Sheldon Papers, box 64.

46 Sheldon Papers, box 74. See also Joanna Russ Papers (hereafter, Russ Papers), box 10.

47 Artemus to Tiptree, letter, February 15, 1975, Sheldon Papers, box 61.

48 Phillips, *James Tiptree, Jr.*, 243.

49 Dozois, *The Fiction of James Tiptree, Jr.*, n.p.; Silverberg, "Introduction," xi–xv.

50 For an account of Le Guin and Tiptree's special relationship, see Phillips, *James Tiptree, Jr.*, 266–70.

51 Silverberg, "Introduction," xii.

52 Dozois, *The Fiction of James Tiptree, Jr.*, n.p.

53 Silverberg, "Introduction," xv; Dozois, *The Fiction of James Tiptree, Jr.*, n.p.

54 Smith, *Meet Me at Infinity*, 305.

55 Smith, *Meet Me at Infinity*, 305–6. See also Phillips, *James Tiptree, Jr.*, 356–62.

56 Tiptree's letter to Smith was later published, embedded within an article by Jeffrey D. Smith titled "The Short, Happy Life of James Tiptree, Jr." in the Program Book of SunCon, the Thirty-fifth World Science Fiction Convention, 1997, and in *Khatru*, no. 7, February 1978, 8–11. It has since also been published for a broader public in Smith, *Meet Me at Infinity*, 302–4.

57 "Tiptree Revealed," *Locus 198*, vol. 10, no. 1, January 30, 1977, 1, Sheldon Papers, box 85.

58 Tip/Alli to Smith, November 23, 1976, Sheldon Papers, box 77. The letter was published in *Khatru* as James Tiptree, Jr., "Everything but the Signature Is Me," *Khatru*, no. 7, February 1978, 12–17, and reprinted in Smith, *Meet Me at Infinity*, 305–14. Original copies of *Khatru*, including no. 7, are in Sheldon Papers, box 98.

59 Tip/Alli to Dozois, letter, December 20, 1976, Sheldon Papers, box 65.

60 Dozois to Tip/Alli, letter, December 27, 1976, Sheldon Papers, box 65.

61 Anderson to Sheldon, letter, March 21, 1977, Sheldon Papers, box 62.

62 McIntyre to Sheldon, letter, December 7, 1976, Sheldon Papers, box 71.

63 Tiptree, "Everything but the Signature Is Me," 12. See also Tip/Alli to Le Guin, letter, November 24, 1976, Sheldon Papers, box 69, and "Tip, Alli, Raccoona" to Russ, letter, December 4, 1976, Russ Papers, box 10. Both letters are reprinted in Pierce and Krasnostein, *Letters to Tiptree*, 229, 260.

64 Tiptree, "Everything but the Signature Is Me," 15.

65 Tiptree, "Everything but the Signature Is Me," 17.

66 Sheldon to Silverberg, letter, December 28, 1976, Sheldon Papers, box 77. Earlier that month, Sheldon had written similarly to Smith, "[Ursula K. Le Guin] called it a marvelous 'ethical put-on.' . . . I guess what she meant was why I withdrew THE WOMEN MEN DON'T SEE when it looked like winning a Nebula. You see, I thought too many women—and men—would vote for it to 'reward' a man for having so much insight. And that would be taking advantage": Sheldon to Smith, letter, December 7, 1976, Sheldon Papers, box 78.

67 McIntyre to Tiptree, letter, March 13, 1975, Sheldon Papers, box 71.

68 Tiptree, "Everything but the Signature Is Me," 15.

69 Tiptree, "Everything but the Signature Is Me," 16. Sheldon wrote the same story to Le Guin in her letter to the author dated November 24, 1976, Sheldon Papers, box 69, which is also published in Pierce and Krasnostein, *Letters to Tiptree*, 230.

70 Tiptree, "Everything but the Signature Is Me," 16.

71 Tiptree to Russ, letter, September 25, 1973, and Tiptree to Russ, letter, n.d. (Fall 1973), Russ Papers, box 10.

72 Tiptree to Russ, letter, November 16, 1973, Russ Papers, box 10.

73 Tiptree to Russ, letter, May 9, 1974, Russ Papers, box 10.

74 Tiptree, "Everything but the Signature Is Me," 17.

75 Original copies of *Windhaven* are in Jessica Salmonson Papers, box 13.

76 See Jessica Amanda Salmonson, "Letter," *Janus 8*, vol. 3, no. 2, 1977, 19; Jessica Amanda Salmonson, "Round 2: Reactions to 'Lunch and Talk,'" *Janus 8*, vol. 3, no. 2, 1977, 36; Jessica Amanda Salmonson, "The Wisewomen and the Wonder," *Janus 8*, vol. 3, no. 2, 1977, 59; Jessica Amanda Salmonson, "Letter," *Janus 9*, vol. 3, no. 3, 1977, 9; Jessica Amanda Salmonson, artwork, *Janus 9*, vol. 3, no. 3, 1977, 13, 41; Jessica Amanda Salmonson, artwork, *Janus 10*, vol. 3, no. 4, 1977, 15; Jessica Amanda Salmonson, "Letter," *Janus 10*, vol. 3, no. 4, 1977, 27–28; Jessica Amanda Salmonson, "Anna and the Miserable Man," *Janus 11*, vol. 4, no. 1, 1978, 40–41; Jessica Amanda Salmonson, "Letter," *Janus 15*, vol. 5, no. 1, 1979, 10; Jessica Amanda Salmonson, "View from the Other Side: Reviews of the Feminist Small Press," *Janus 15*, vol. 5, no. 1, 1979, 46–48; Jessica Amanda Salmonson, "View from the Other Side: Reviews of the Feminist Small Press," *Janus 16*, vol. 5, no. 2, 1979, 26–28. Jeanne Gomoll and Greg G. H. Rihn also

reviewed Jessica Amanda Salmonson's edited collection *Amazons!* in *Janus 16*, vol. 5, no. 2, 1979, 20–24.

77 Examples of these letters are in Sheldon Papers, box 75.

78 Tiptree to Salmonson, letter, November 13, 1975, Sheldon Papers, box 75.

79 Sheldon Papers, box 114.

80 Tiptree to Broyhill, letter, January 12, 1974, Sheldon Papers, box 114.

81 Sheldon, journal entry, February 14, 1977, Sheldon Papers, box 12. The ellipses are Sheldon's.

82 Across Sheldon's journaling and correspondence occasional references appear to turning down a sexual advance from her mother when she was fourteen: see, e.g., Tip/Alli to Russ, letter, July 16, 1977, Russ Papers, box 10.

83 Sheldon, December 21, 1982, journal entry on yellow scrap paper, Sheldon Papers, box 12.

84 As Julie Phillips notes in her introduction of this same journal entry, the inciting incident that preceded masturbation is a report of childhood abuse, but in reading the entry myself, this is a detail in a larger story Sheldon is writing about herself and her depression in the face of losing her abusive mother, and this "loss" (which she questions as such in the same entry) leading to the loss of Tiptree and all that he offered her: Phillips, *James Tiptree, Jr.*, 363.

85 Sheldon, journal entry, February 2, 1977, Sheldon Papers, box 12.

86 Butler, *Bodies That Matter*, 143–66.

87 Sheldon, journal entry, February 2, 1977, Sheldon Papers, box 12.

88 Sheldon, journal entry, February 14, 1977, Sheldon Papers, box 12.

89 Tiptree, "Everything but the Signature Is Me," 16.

90 Anderson and McIntyre, *Aurora*, 16–35, 36–98.

91 Raccoona to Bankier, letter, July 19, 1975, Sheldon Papers, box 62.

92 Salmonson to Sheldon, letter, July 18, 1977, Sheldon Papers, box 75.

93 Tiptree, "Everything but the Signature Is Me," 16.

94 Tiptree to Russ, letter, November 17, 1975, Russ Papers, box 10.

95 "Tip, Alli, Raccoona" to Russ.

96 *Frontiers* Editors, "Dear Frontiers."

97 Tip/Alli (James Tiptree Jr.), "Dear Frontiers," in *Frontiers* Editors, "Dear Frontiers," 68–69.

98 Julie Phillips, interview with Rox Samer, October 14–15, 2019.

99 Tiptree/Sheldon, "Note on 'Houston, Houston, Do You Read?'" in Smith, *Meet Me at Infinity*, 374–75.

100 Phillips, *James Tiptree, Jr.*, 366–67.

101 See, e.g., Tiptree/Sheldon to Aly and Paul Parsons, letter, May 15, 1982, Sheldon Papers, box 61.

102 Tip/Alli to Russ, letter, January 15, 1977, Russ Papers, box 10, published in Pierce and Krasnostein, *Letters to Tiptree*, 267.

103 Le Guin to "Allitree" (Sheldon), letter, December 19, 1976, Sheldon Papers, box 69, published in Pierce and Krasnostein, *Letters to Tiptree*, 239–41.

104 Tip/Alli to Russ, letter, July 16, 1977, Russ Papers, box 10.

105 Alli/Tip to Russ, letter, September 25, 1980, Russ Papers, box 10.

106 Russ to Sheldon, letter, July 25, 1977, Sheldon Papers, box 74, published in Pierce and Krasnostein, *Letters to Tiptree*, 277–81.

107 "T/A" (Sheldon) to Russ, letter, November 29, 1980, Sheldon Papers, box 74, and Russ Papers, box 10.

108 "T/A" (Sheldon) to Russ, letter, November 29, 1980, Sheldon Papers, box 74, and Russ Papers, box 10.

109 "T/A" (Sheldon) to Russ, letter, November 29, 1980, Sheldon Papers, box 74, and Russ Papers, box 10.

110 Often, with her closest SF friends over the years, she abbreviated this to a scrolling "T/A": Sheldon Papers, boxes 62–78.

111 Tip/Alli (James Tiptree, Jr.), "Dear Frontiers," 69.

112 Alice Sheldon, "*Contemporary Authors* Interview," in Smith, *Meet Me at Infinity*, 367.

113 Le Guin to Tip/Alli, letter, February 7, 1977, Sheldon Papers, box 69.

114 Steinbock, *Shimmering Images*, 21.

115 Steinbock, *Shimmering Images*, 26–60.

116 For detailed accounts of early Kirk/Spock and its textual and social practices, see Bacon-Smith, *Enterprising Women*; Jenkins, *Textual Poachers*; Penley, "Feminism, Psychoanalysis, and the Study of Popular Culture."

117 See Russ, *Magic Mommas, Trembling Sisters, Puritans and Perverts*, 79–99.

118 Butler, *Bodies That Matter*, 152–56.

119 Phillips, *James Tiptree, Jr.*, 225.

120 "The Three Faces of Sylvester Mule" (Sheldon) to Charles Brown, letter, March 23, 1979, Sheldon Papers, box 63.

121 Pierce and Krasnostein, *Letters to Tiptree*.

122 Halberstam, *In a Queer Time and Place*, 23.

123 Nicola Griffith, "The Women You Didn't See," in Pierce and Krasnostein, *Letters to Tiptree*, 188–89.

124 Lee Mandelo, "Dear James/Alice (and Sometimes Raccoona)," in Pierce and Krasnostein, *Letters to Tiptree*, 26–27.

125 Cheryl Morgan, "Dear Alli," in Pierce and Krasnostein, *Letters to Tiptree*, 120.

126 Smith, introductory note to "Everything but the Signature Is Me," as reprinted in Smith, *Meet Me at Infinity*, 305.

127 Jameson, *Archaeologies of the Future*, 287–89.

128 Jo Walton, "Dear Tiptree," in Pierce and Krasnostein, *Letters to Tiptree*, 3.

129 Jameson, *Archaeologies of the Future*, 288.

130 Jameson, *Archaeologies of the Future*, 288.

131 Salamon, *Assuming a Body*, 95.

132 James Tiptree Literary Award Council, "James Tiptree, Jr. Literary Award," accessed June 19, 2019, https://tiptree.org. The prize was described earlier in its history as awarding a work that "explores and expands gender roles in speculative fiction": Pat Murphy and Karen Joy Fowler, "Introduction," in Fowler et al., *The James Tiptree Award Anthology 1*, ix.

133 Pat Murphy, "Illusion and Expectation," WisCon 15, March 2, 1991, http://www.wiscon.info/downloads/patmurphy.pdf, 3 (no longer available).

134 Murphy and Fowler, "Introduction" ix.

135 Pat Murphy, "Dear James Tiptree and Alice Sheldon," in Pierce and Krasnostein, *Letters to Tiptree*, 33.

136 Murphy, "Illusion and Expectation," 3.

137 Murphy, "Dear James Tiptree and Alice Sheldon," 34.

138 The statement is from the http://tiptree.org website, which became http://otherwiseaward.org in 2020 and details the renamed prize.

139 Suzy McKee Charnas, "Judging the Tiptree," in Fowler et al., *The James Tiptree Award Anthology 1*, 95.

140 Charnas, "Judging the Tiptree," 100.

141 Charnas, "Judging the Tiptree," 103.

142 Joanna Russ, "Speculations: The Subjunctivity of Science Fiction," *Extrapolation* 15, no. 1 (December 1973), 51–59, as reprinted in Russ, *To Write like a Woman*, 15–25.

143 The full speech is on my webpage, accessed June 19, 2018, https://roxsamer.com/2017/05/30/wiscon-41.

144 James Tiptree Literary Award Council, "Tiptree Fellowships," accessed June 19, 2018, https://tiptree.org/tiptree-fellowships.

145 Nisi Shawl, "Dearest Tip," in Pierce and Krasnostein, *Letters to Tiptree*, 71.

146 Shawl, "Dearest Tip," 71.

147 Shawl, "Dearest Tip," 71.

148 Shawl, "Dearest Tip," 71–72.

149 James Tiptree Literary Award Council, "Tiptree Fellowships."

150 In 2019, the John W. Campbell Award for Best New Writer became the Astounding Award for Best New Writer, following accusations that Campbell was a fascist: "A Statement from the Editor," *Astounding Analog Companion*, August 27, 2019, accessed September 15, 2020, https://theastoundinganalogcompanion.com/2019/08/27/a-statement-from-the-editor.

151 Phillips, *James Tiptree, Jr.*, 437–60; Phillips interview.

152 Julie Phillips, Twitter post dated September 1, 2019, https://twitter.com/jcfphillips/status/1168267581708546049; Alexis Lothian (on behalf of Motherboard), "Alice Sheldon and the Name of the Tiptree Award," September 2, 2019, https://otherwiseaward.org/2019/09/alice-sheldon-and-the-name-of-the-tiptree-award; Julie Phillips, "On Tiptree and Naming," *Julie Phillips* (blog), September 2019, https://www.julie-phillips.com/wp/?p=1052.

153 Alexis Lothian (on behalf of Motherboard), "From Tiptree to Otherwise," October 13, 2019, https://otherwiseaward.org/2019/10/from-tiptree-to-otherwise; Sumana Harihareswara, Alexis Lothian, Pat Murphy, and Gretchen Treu, "Renaming the Otherwise Award," WisCon virtual panel, May 24, 2020, https://www.youtube.com/watch?v=F-yw1uRldoU.

154 Jeanne Gomoll, email correspondence with Rox Samer, October 2020.

155 Harihareswara et al., "Renaming the Otherwise Award."

Notes to Chapter Four

156 Harihareswara et al., "Renaming the Otherwise Award." See also "Why 'Otherwise,'" accessed July 27, 2020, https://otherwiseaward.org/about-the -award/why-otherwise.

157 Harihareswara et al., "Renaming the Otherwise Award."

158 See, e.g., Heaney, "Women-Identified Women."

159 For a strong critique of queer theory along these lines, see Prosser, *Second Skins.* Butler's *Bodies That Matter,* which I cited earlier and still very much see this chapter as in conversation with, is central to Prosser's critique. I would note further that Butler's theory of performativity reveals its limits in the one paper thus far written on Tiptree and transness: Wendy Gay Pearson's "The Text of This Body: 'Reading' James Tiptree Jr. as a Transgender Writer," which she delivered at the International Conference on the Fantastic in the Arts, Ft. Lauderdale, March 1999, and published in Pierce and Krasnostein, *Letters to Tiptree,* 321–38. Pearson values Tiptree for being "(mis)taken for male for almost a decade" and thus "emphasiz[ing] not only the performative nature of gender itself, but the alien-ness of being the 'wrong' gender, or no gender": Pearson, "The Text of this Body," 332. According to Pearson, Tiptree's stories, in turn, generate "(mis)takes" and "invariably throw light on the artifice of our systems of thought, our attempts to know the alien, the other, even when it/she/he is us": Pearson, "The Text of This Body," 336. However, as M. W. Bychowski recently put it, "Transgender does more in society, history, and art than merely disturb cisgender people and norms." And for Pearson, working in this queer theory vein, questions such as "does the persona of Tiptree have a certain existence in its own right, separable from the persona of both Alice Sheldon and of her female writer creation, Raccoona Sheldon" remain purely rhetorical: Pearson, "The Text of this Body," 326. In fact, many of Bychowski and her colleagues' thoughts are imperative to my point here: see Bychowski et al., "Trans*historicities," 668.

160 See Sheldon, 1977 journal, Sheldon Papers, box 12.

161 Sheldon's journals from late 1976, 1977, and later regularly reference Tiptree's death, often providing an occasion for the author to elaborate on her own desire for, but also fear of, death: Sheldon Papers, boxes 11–12.

162 It should be noted, though, that in her biography Phillips does a good job of chronicling Sheldon's decades-long battle with depression: Phillips, *James Tiptree, Jr.*

163 cárdenas, "Shifting Futures."

164 cárdenas, "Shifting Futures."

165 Dozois, *The Fiction of James Tiptree, Jr.,* n.p.

Epilogue

1 Joanschild and Kaplan, "International Women's Film Festival."

2 Maslin, "*Born in Flames.*"

3 Maslin, "*Born in Flames*"; Corry, "*Born in Flames* Is Ninety Minutes of Fizzle."

4 Corry, *"Born in Flames* Is Ninety Minutes of Fizzle."

5 Corry, *"Born in Flames* Is Ninety Minutes of Fizzle."

6 Lothian, *Old Futures*, 250.

7 Pally, "Is There Revolution after the Revolution?"; Taubin, "Pale Fire."

8 Pally, "Is There Revolution after the Revolution?," 80.

9 Taubin, "Pale Fire," 81.

10 Taubin, "Pale Fire," 108.

11 De Lauretis, "Rethinking Women's Cinema," 139.

12 De Lauretis, "Rethinking Women's Cinema," 141.

13 De Lauretis, "Rethinking Women's Cinema," 136.

14 As David Halperin writes, "Queer theory originally came into being as a joke. Teresa de Lauretis coined the phrase 'queer theory' to serve as the title of a conference that she held in February 1990 at the University of California, Santa Cruz. . . . She had heard the word 'queer' being tossed about in a gay-affirmative sense by activists, street kids, and members of the art world in New York during the late 1980s. She had the courage, and the conviction, to pair that scurrilous term with the academic holy word, 'theory.' Her usage was scandalously offensive. Sympathetic faculty at UCSC asked, in wounded tones, 'Why do they have to call it that?' But the conjunction was more than merely mischievous: it was deliberately disruptive": Halperin, "The Normalization of Queer Theory," 339–40.

15 As noted, de Lauretis coined the term while titling the Queer Theory: Lesbian and Gay Sexualities Conference. She also edited a special issue of *differences* that came out of the conference: see de Lauretis, "Queer Theory." It includes an essay by the science fiction author Samuel R. Delany (the same Delany who had participated in *Khatru*'s "Women in Science Fiction" symposium in 1975), who was now writing about the differences between rhetoric and discourse and the control of AIDS rhetoric by its murderous discourse: see Delany, "Street Talk/Straight Talk."

16 Pally, "Is There Revolution after the Revolution?," 80.

17 Samuel R. Delay's "About Five Thousand One Hundred and Seventy-five Words" was an expansion of his talk on the subject to the Modern Language Association in 1968. It was printed in numerous SF fan and academic volumes: see Delany, "About Five Thousand One Hundred and Seventy-five Words."

18 Russ, *To Write like a Woman*, 24.

19 Russ, *To Write like a Woman*, 15, 23.

20 See, e.g., Panshin and Panshin, "Books," 46–51; Phillips, *James Tiptree, Jr.*, 312.

21 Tellingly, de Lauretis and Delany were both on temporary appointments at the University of Wisconsin, Milwaukee, in 1977, the year of Tiptree's reveal. In September 1977, Delany wrote to Russ that de Lauretis was a "champion" of Russ's work there: Delany to Russ, letter, September 23, 1977, Joanna Russ Papers, box 3.

22 De Lauretis, "Rethinking Women's Cinema," 139.

23 Gaines, *Pink-Slipped*, 43–44, 95–131.

24 De Lauretis, "Rethinking Women's Cinema," 139.

25 Pally, "Is There Revolution after the Revolution?," 80.

26 De Lauretis, "Rethinking Women's Cinema," 142.

27 Harvey, *A Brief History of Neoliberalism*, 3.

28 Davis, *Abolition Democracy*, 37–44; Dillon, *Fugitive Life*, 63–66; Law, *Resistance behind Bars*, 97–109.

29 For more on neoliberal freedom as a response to freedom dreams, see Dillon, *Fugitive Life*, 66–83.

30 Davis, *Abolition Democracy*, 41; Díaz-Cotto, *Gender, Ethnicity, and the State*, 274; Kunzel, *Criminal Intimacy*, 11–12, 112, 272; Law, *Resistance behind Bars*, 1–3; Thuma, *All Our Trials*, 4, 167.

31 Women Make Movies meeting minutes, retreat agendas, and intraoffice memos from the late 1970s and early 1980s regularly stress the need to think about cost-effectiveness and whether proposed programs anticipate generating revenue. This is a marked change from the organization's earlier internal correspondence: see Ariel Dougherty Papers (hereafter, Dougherty Papers), boxes 12–14.

32 Fallica, "More than 'Just Talk.'" Organization documents and correspondence make clear that these workshops were let go in favor of the more lucrative distribution wing, which disturbed, and led to the resignation of, a number of board members, staff, organization members, and volunteers: Dougherty Papers, box 14.

33 Promotional materials for the organization from the late 1970s and early 1980s stress the growing "international perspective" of both Women Make Movies' rental catalog and festival programming. One letter to "friends" of Women Make Movies, February 3, 1981, about the upcoming Independent Film Festival it was sponsoring states, "We plan to present films from a range of countries encompassing different approaches. . . . This international perspective will strive to illuminate the commonality and diversity of women's lives, while illustrating the influence of national origin, culture and politics on film form and content": Dougherty Papers, box 14. Distribution reports from the early 1980s, meanwhile, list universities as the organization's top "distribution market." There is also extensive internal correspondence about the need to extend Women Make Movies' "public relations" in academia, including women's studies, to increase this lucrative market: Dougherty Papers, box 14.

34 Women Make Movies, Inc., catalog, 1987, Dougherty Papers, box 13.

35 Ross, "Queering Identity in Early Outfest Documentaries." Ross is working on a dissertation on this subject.

36 Here I am referring to works in queer theory such as Freeman, *Time Binds*, and Muñoz, *Cruising Utopia*. But see also Sara Ahmed's writing on lesbian feminism as the miserable scene of much queer scholarship: Ahmed, *Living a Feminist Life*, 222–23.

37 Villarejo, *Ethereal Queer*, 95.

38 Waugh, "Films by Gays for Gays," 14–18.

39 Youmans, *Word Is Out*, 82–84.

40 Villarejo, *Ethereal Queer*, 107.
41 Young, *Making Sex Public and Other Cinematic Fantasies*, 173.
42 Gregg, "PBS and AIDS."
43 Gregg, "PBS and AIDS."
44 Corry, "*Born in Flames* Is Ninety Minutes of Fizzle."
45 B. Ruby Rich credits the film's rerelease and reconsideration to Jamie Babbit, who touted the film as an inspiration for *Itty Bitty Titty Committee* (2007): Rich, *New Queer Cinema*, 203.
46 Ahmed, *Living a Feminist Life*, 208.
47 Lothian, *Old Futures*, 176.
48 An informal survey of colleagues reveals that *Born in Flames* has been taught, among other places, by Caetlin Benson-Allot at Georgetown University; Krista Benson at Ohio State University; micha cárdenas at the University of Washington, Bothell; Nick Davis at Northwestern University; Kara Keeling at the University of Southern California; Alexis Lothian at the University of Maryland; Candace Moore at the University of Michigan; Teddy Pozzo at the University of California, Santa Barbara; Erica Rand at the University of Oregon; and Greg Youmans at Western Washington University (as well as in my courses at the University of Southern California and Clark University).
49 Ahmed, *Living a Feminist Life*, 207.
50 Willse and Spade, "Introduction," 1.
51 Willse and Spade, "Introduction," 3.
52 Lothian, *Old Futures*, 205.
53 Hesford, *Feeling Women's Liberation*, 17–19. For more information, see the introduction in this book.
54 De Lauretis, "Rethinking Women's Cinema," 131, 142.
55 Willse and Spade, "Introduction," 3.

bibliography

Archives

Academy Film Archive, Los Angeles, CA

Arthur and Elizabeth Schlesinger Library on the History of Women in America,
Radcliffe Institute for Advanced Study, Harvard University, Cambridge, MA.
  Ariel Dougherty Audiovisual Collection
  Ariel Dougherty Papers
  New Words Records

British Film Institute National Archive, London, UK

Lesbian Herstory Archives, Brooklyn, NY.

Long Beach Museum of Art Video Archive, Getty Research Institute, Los Angeles.

Sophia Smith Collection, Smith College Special Collections, Northampton, MA.
  Joan E. Biren Papers, SSC-MS-00587

Special Collections and University Archives, University of Oregon Libraries,
Eugene.
  Alice B. Sheldon, Pen Name James Tiptree, Jr., Papers, Coll. 455
  Jessica Salmonson Papers, Coll. 472
  Joanna Russ Papers, Coll. 261

Interviews

Bankier, Amanda. Interview by Rox Samer, June 12, 2019.

Bankier, Amanda. Interview by Rox Samer, June 18, 2011.

Biren, Joan E., and Mary Lee Farmer. Interview by Rox Samer, November 7, 2014.

Choy, Christine. Interview by Rox Samer, August 16, 2016.

Dougherty, Ariel. Interview by Rox Samer, November 21, 2014.

Gomoll, Jeanne. Interview by Rox Samer, May 25, 2019.

Gomoll, Jeanne. Interview by Rox Samer, July 16, 2011.

Karp, Sharon. Interview by Rox Samer, December 11, 2014.

Phillips, Julie. Interview by Rox Samer, October 14–15, 2019.

Reid, Frances. Interview by Rox Samer, December 4, 2014.

Reid, Frances. Interview by Rox Samer, October 28, 2014.

Smith, Jeff. Interview by Rox Samer, May 25, 2019.

Zheutlin, Cathy. Interview by Rox Samer, December 5, 2014.

Published Sources

Abbott, Sidney, and Barbara Love. *Sappho Was a Right-On Woman: A Liberated View of Lesbianism*. New York: Stein and Day, 1972.

Adler, Freda. *Sisters in Crime: The Rise of the New Female Criminal*. New York: McGraw-Hill, 1975.

Agamben, Giorgio. *Potentialities: Collected Essays in Philosophy*. Edited and translated by Daniel Heller-Roazen. Stanford, CA: Stanford University Press, 1999.

Ahmed, Sara. *Living a Feminist Life*. Durham, NC: Duke University Press, 2017.

Amin, Kadji. *Disturbing Attachments: Genet, Modern Pederasty, and Queer History*. Durham, NC: Duke University Press, 2017.

Anderson, Susan Janice and Vonda N. McIntyre, eds. *Aurora: Beyond Equality*. Greenwich, CT: Fawcett, 1976.

Arondekar, Anjali, Ann Cvetkovich, Christina B. Hanhardt, Regina Kunzel, Tavia Nyong'o, Juana María Rodríguez, and Susan Stryker. "Queer Archives: A Roundtable Discussion." Compiled by Daniel Marshall, Kevin P. Murphy, and Zeb Tortorici. *Radical History Review* 122 (May 2015): 211–31.

Atkinson, Ti-Grace. *Amazon Odyssey*. New York: Links, 1974.

Bacon-Smith, Camille. *Enterprising Women: Television Fandom and the Creation of Popular Myth*. Philadelphia: University of Pennsylvania Press, 1992.

Bacon-Smith, Camille. *Science Fiction Culture*. Philadelphia: University of Pennsylvania Press, 2000.

Barker, Jennifer M. *The Tactile Eye: Touch and the Cinematic Experience*. Berkeley: University of California Press, 2009.

Barthes, Roland. *Image, Music, Text*. Translated by Stephen Heath. New York: Hill and Wang, 1977.

Bassichis, Morgan, Alexander Lee, and Dean Spade. "Building an Abolitionist Trans and Queer Movement with Everything We've Got." In *Captive Genders: Trans Embodiment and the Prison Industrial Complex*, edited by Eric A. Stanley and Nat Smith, 21–46. Chico, CA: AK Press, 2015.

Baunach, Phyllis Jo, and Thomas Murton. "Women in Prison: An Awakening Minority." *Crime and Corrections* (Fall 1973): 4–12.

Becker, Edith, Michelle Citron, Julia Lesage, and B. Ruby Rich, eds. "Lesbians and Film." *Jump Cut* 24–25 (March 1981): 17–60.

Beemyn, Genny. *A Queer Capital: A History of Gay Life in Washington, D.C.* New York: Routledge, 2015.

Bergstrom, Janet. "*Jeanne Dielman, 23 Quai du Commerce, 1080 Bruxelles* (Chantal Akerman)." *Camera Obscura* 2 (Fall 1977): 115–21.

Bernstein, Lee. *America Is the Prison: Arts and Politics in Prison in the 1970s.* Chapel Hill: University of North Carolina Press, 2010.

Biren, Joan E. (JEB). "Come Outside." *The Furies* 1, no. 5 (June–July 1972): 10–11.

Blackwell, Maylei. *¡Chicana Power! Contested Histories of Feminism in the Chicano Movement.* Austin: University of Texas Press, 2011.

Bradley, Marion Zimmer. *The Shattered Chain.* New York: Daw, 1976.

Burkett, Elinor. "What Makes a Woman?" *New York Times*, June 6, 2015. http://www.nytimes.com/2015/06/07/opinion/sunday/what-makes-a-woman.html.

Butler, Judith. *Bodies That Matter: On the Discursive Limits of "Sex."* New York: Routledge, 1993.

Butler, Judith. *Gender Trouble: Feminism and the Subversion of Identity.* New York: Routledge, 1990.

Butler, Judith. "Imitation and Gender Insubordination." In *Inside/Out: Lesbian Theories, Gay Theories*, edited by Diana Fuss, 13–31. New York: Routledge, 1991.

Bychowski, M. W., Howard Chiang, Jack Halberstam, Jacob Lau, Kathleen P. Long, Marcia Ochoa, and C. Riley Snorton. "Trans*historicities: A Roundtable Discussion." Curated by Leah Devun and Zeb Tortorici. *TSQ: Transgender Studies Quarterly* 5, no. 4 (November 2018): 658–85.

Camera Obscura Collective. "*Camera Obscura* Questionnaire on Alternative Film Distribution." *Camera Obscura* 3–4 (Summer 1979): 157–75.

Camera Obscura Collective. "Chronology: The Camera Obscura Collective." *Camera Obscura* 3–4 (Summer 1979): 5–13.

Camera Obscura Collective. "Feminism and Film: Critical Approaches." *Camera Obscura* 1 (Fall 1976): 3–10.

cárdenas, micha. "Shifting Futures: Digital Trans of Color Praxis." *Ada*, no. 6 (2015). doi:10.7264/N3WH2N8D.

Castle, Terry. *The Apparitional Lesbian: Female Homosexuality and Modern Culture.* New York: Columbia University Press, 1993.

Charnas, Suzy McKee. *Motherlines.* New York: Berkley-Putnam, 1978.

Cheng, Scarlett, Margie Crow, Debbie George, Valle Jones, and Marian Sandmaier (The Women of Spectra Feminist Media Project). "Spectra: Feminists First." *off our backs* 5, no. 11 (January–February 1976): 22–23.

Chion, Michel. *The Voice in Cinema.* Translated and edited by Claudia Gorbman. New York: Columbia University Press, 1999.

Cifor, Marika. "Presence, Absence, and Victoria's Hair: Examining Affect and Embodiment in Trans Archives." *TSQ: Transgender Studies Quarterly* 2, no. 4 (November 2015): 645–49.

Citron, Michelle. "The Films of Jan Oxenberg: Comic Critique." *Jump Cut* 24–25 (March 1981): 31–32.

Combahee River Collective. "A Black Feminist Statement." *off our backs* 9, no. 6 (June 1979): 6–8.

Coppa, Francesca. "An Editing Room of One's Own: Vidding as Women's Work." *Camera Obscura* 77 (2011): 123–30.

Corbman, Rachel. "Conferencing on the Edge: A Queer History of Feminist Field Formation, 1969–89." PhD diss., Stony Brook University, 2019.

Corbman, Rachel. "Does Queer Studies Have an Anti-empiricism Problem?" *GLQ* 25, vol. 1 (2019): 57–62.

Corry, John. "*Born in Flames* Is Ninety Minutes of Fizzle." *New York Times*, August 24, 1986, H21.

Cox, Laverne, and CeCe McDonald. "'Black Trans Bodies Are Under Attack': Freed Activist CeCe McDonald, Actress Laverne Cox Speak Out." *Democracy Now!*, February 19, 2014. http://www.democracynow.org/2014/2/19/black_trans_bodies_are_under_attack.

Cross, Tia, Freada Klein, Barbara Smith, and Beverly Smith. "Face-to-Face, Day-to-Day—Racism CR." In *All the Women Are White, All the Blacks Are Men, But Some of Us Are Brave: Black Women's Studies*, edited by Gloria T. Hull, Patricia Bell Scott, and Barbara Smith, 52–56. Old Westbury, NY: Feminist Press, 1982.

Crow, Margie. "Keeping an Eye on Women: Videoletters." *off our backs* 5, no. 11 (January–February 1976): 22.

Cvetkovich, Ann. *An Archive of Feelings: Trauma, Sexuality, and Lesbian Public Cultures*. Durham, NC: Duke University Press, 2003.

Cvetkovich, Ann. "In the Archives of Lesbian Feelings: Documentary and Popular Culture." *Camera Obscura* 49 (2002): 107–47.

Davis, Angela Y. *Abolition Democracy: Beyond Empire, Prisons, and Torture*. New York: Seven Stories, 2005.

Davis, Angela Y. *Blues Legacies and Black Feminism: Gertrude "Ma" Rainey, Bessie Smith, and Billie Holiday*. New York: Pantheon, 1998.

Davis, Angela Y. "Reflections on the Black Woman's Role in the Community of Slaves." *The Black Scholar* 3, no. 4 (December 1971): 2–15.

Davis, Nick. "The Face Is a Politics: A Close-Up View of Julie Dash's *Illusions*." *Camera Obscura* 86 (2014): 149–83.

De Bruin-Molé, Megen. "Space Bitches, Witches, and Kick-Ass Princesses: *Star Wars* and Popular Feminism." In *Star Wars and the History of Transmedia Storytelling*, edited by Sean Guynes and Dan Hassler-Forest, 225–40. Amsterdam: Amsterdam University Press, 2018.

Delany, Samuel R. "About Five Thousand One Hundred and Seventy-five Words." In *The Jewel-Hinged Jaw: Notes on the Language of Science Fiction*, 1–16. New York: Berkley, 1978.

Delany, Samuel R. "Racism and Science Fiction." *New York Review of Science Fiction*, no. 120, August 1998. http://www.nyrsf.com/racism-and-science-fiction-.html.

Delany, Samuel R. "Street Talk/Straight Talk." *differences* 3, no. 2 (Summer 1991): 21–38.

De Lauretis, Teresa, ed. "Queer Theory: Lesbian and Gay Sexualities." Special issue of *differences* 3, no. 2 (Summer 1991).

De Lauretis, Teresa. "Rethinking Women's Cinema: Aesthetics and Feminist Theory" (1985). In *Technologies of Gender: Essays on Theory, Film, and Fiction*, 127–48. Bloomington: Indiana University Press, 1987.

Díaz-Cotto, Juanita. *Gender, Ethnicity, and the State: Latina and Latino Prison Politics*. Albany: State University of New York Press, 1996.

Dillon, Stephen. *Fugitive Life: The Queer Politics of the Prison State*. Durham, NC: Duke University Press, 2018.

Dinshaw, Carolyn. *Getting Medieval: Sexualities and Communities, Pre- and Postmodern*. Durham, NC: Duke University Press, 1999.

Doane, Mary Ann. "Woman's Stake: Filming the Female Body." *October* 17 (Summer 1981): 22–36.

Douglas, Carol Anne. "A Feminist Nation." *off our backs* 4, no. 4 (March 1974): 22–23.

Dowell, Pat. "Iris Film Festival." *Sibyl-Child* 2, no. 1 (1976): 4–17.

Dozois, Gardner. *The Fiction of James Tiptree, Jr.* New York: ALGOL, 1977.

Dyer, Richard. *Now You See It.* London: Routledge, 1990.

Echols, Alice. *Daring to Be Bad: Radical Feminism in America, 1967–1975*. Minneapolis: University of Minnesota Press, 1989.

Eichhorn, Kate. *The Archival Turn in Feminism: Outrage in Order*. Philadelphia: Temple University Press, 2013.

Enke, Finn. "Collective Memory and the Transfeminist 1970s: Toward a Less Plausible History." *TSQ: Transgender Studies Quarterly* 5, no. 1 (2018): 9–29.

Faderman, Lillian. *Surpassing the Love of Men: Romantic Friendship and Love between Women from the Renaissance to the Present*. New York: William Morrow, 1981.

Faith, Karlene. *Unruly Women: The Politics of Confinement and Resistance*. New ed. New York: Seven Stories, 2011.

Faith, Karlene, and Women's Prison Project Los Angeles. *Inside/Outside: An Account of the Women on Wheels 1976 Tour of California and Women's Struggle to Bring Their Culture to Sisters in Prison*. Culver City, CA: Peace, 1976.

Fallica, Kristen. "More than 'Just Talk': The Chelsea Picture Station in the 1970s." *Camera Obscura* 82 (2013): 125–33.

Fallica, Kristen. "Sustaining Feminist Film Cultures: An Institutional History of Women Make Movies." PhD diss., University of Pittsburgh, 2013.

Faludi, Susan. "American Electra: Feminism's Ritual Matricide." *Harper's Magazine*, October 2010, 29–42.

Ferber, Alona. "Judith Butler on the Culture Wars, J. K. Rowling and Living in 'Anti-intellectual Times': Interview." *New Statesman*, September 22, 2020. https://www.newstatesman.com/international/2020/09/judith-butler -culture-wars-jk-rowling-and-living-anti-intellectual-times.

Foucault, Michel. *The History of Sexuality, Volume 1: An Introduction*. Translated by Robert Hurley. New York: Vintage, 1978.

Foucault, Michel. "Nietzsche, Genealogy, History." In *Language, Counter-Memory, Practice: Selected Essays and Interviews*, edited by D. H. Bouchard, 141–64. Ithaca, NY: Cornell University Press, 1977.

271

Fowler, Karen, Pat Murphy, Debbie Notkin, and Jeffrey D. Smith, eds. *The James Tiptree Award Anthology 1*. San Francisco: Tachyon, 2005.

Fraser, Nancy. "Rethinking the Public Sphere: A Contribution to the Critique of Actually Existing Democracy." *Social Text*, nos. 25–26 (1990): 56–80.

Freccero, Carla. *Queer/Early/Modern*. Durham, NC: Duke University Press, 2006.

Freeman, Elizabeth. *Time Binds: Queer Temporalities, Queer Histories*. Durham, NC: Duke University Press, 2010.

Freude. "Notes on Distribution." *Camera Obscura* 3–4 (1979): 151–56.

Frontiers Editors. "'Dear Frontiers': Letters from Women Fantasy and Science Fiction Writers." *Frontiers: A Journal of Women Studies* 2, no. 3 (Autumn 1977): 62–78.

Gaines, Jane M. *Pink-Slipped: What Happened to Women in the Silent Film Industries?* Urbana: University of Illinois Press, 2018.

Gerhard, Jane F. *The Dinner Party: Judy Chicago and the Power of Popular Feminism, 1970–2007*. Athens: University of Georgia Press, 2013.

Gieseking, Jack. *A Queer New York: Geographies of Lesbians, Dykes, and Queers*. New York: New York University Press, 2020.

Goldberg, Michelle. "What Is a Woman? The Dispute between Radical Feminism and Transgenderism." *New Yorker*, August 4, 2014. http://www.newyorker.com/magazine /2014/08/04/woman-2.

Green, Kai M. "Navigating Masculinity as a Black Transman: 'I Will Never Straighten Out My Wrist.'" *Everyday Feminism*, April 5, 2013. http://everydayfeminism.com/2013/04/i -will-never-straighten-out-my-wrist.

Gregg, Ronald. "PBS and AIDS: *AIDS: Chapter One, Tongues Untied, Absolutely Positive. Jump Cut* 37 (July 1992): 64–71.

Griffiths, Alison. *Carceral Fantasies: Cinema and Prison in Early Twentieth-Century America*. New York: Columbia University Press, 2016.

Halberstam, Jack. *Female Masculinity*. Durham, NC: Duke University Press, 1998.

Halberstam, Jack. *In a Queer Time and Place: Transgender Bodies, Subcultural Lives*. New York: New York University Press, 2005.

Halberstam, Jack. "You Are Triggering Me! The Neo-liberal Rhetoric of Harm, Danger and Trauma." *Bully Bloggers* (blog), July 5, 2014. https://bullybloggers .wordpress.com/2014/07/05/you-are-triggering-me-the-neo-liberal-rhetoric -of-harm-danger-and-trauma.

Halperin, David. "Forgetting Foucault: Acts, Identities, and the History of Sexuality." *Representations* 63 (Summer 1998): 93–120.

Halperin, David. "The Normalization of Queer Theory." *Journal of Homosexuality* 45, nos. 2–4 (2003): 339–43.

Haraway, Donna. "Situated Knowledges: The Science Question in Feminism and the Privilege of Partial Perspective." *Feminist Studies* 14, no. 3 (Autumn 1988): 575–99.

Harvey, David. *A Brief History of Neoliberalism*. Oxford: Oxford University Press, 2005.

Hauser, Christine. "Transgender Woman Shot Dead in Motel Is Seventh Killed in US this Year." *New York Times.* Accessed June 19, 2018. https://www.nytimes.com/2018/03/30/us/transgender-woman-killed-baton-rouge.html.

Heaney, Emma. "Women-Identified Women: Trans Women in 1970s Lesbian Feminist Organizing." *TSQ: Transgender Studies Quarterly* 3, nos. 1–2 (May 2016): 137–45.

Hesford, Victoria. *Feeling Women's Liberation.* Durham, NC: Duke University Press, 2013.

Hilderbrand, Lucas. *Inherent Vice: Bootlegged Histories of Videotape and Copyright.* Durham, NC: Duke University Press, 2009.

Hogan, Kristen. *The Feminist Bookstore Movement: Lesbian Antiracism and Feminist Accountability.* Durham, NC: Duke University Press, 2016.

Hollibaugh, Amber, and Cherríe Moraga. "What We're Rollin' around in Bed With: Sexual Silences in Feminism: A Conversation toward Ending Them." In *The Persistent Desire: A Femme-Butch Reader,* edited by Joan Nestle, 243–53. Boston: Alyson, 1992.

Holmlund, Chris. "Wham Bam! Pam! Pam Grier as Hot Action Babe and Cool Action Mama." *Quarterly Review of Film and Video* 22, no. 2 (2005): 97–112.

hooks, bell. *Ain't I a Woman: Black Women and Feminism.* Cambridge, MA: South End, 1981.

Hull, Gloria T., Patricia Bell Scott, and Barbara Smith, eds. *All the Women Are White, All the Blacks Are Men, But Some of Us Are Brave: Black Women's Studies.* Old Westbury, NY: Feminist Press, 1982.

Humm, Andy. "Sidney Was a Right-on Woman." *Gay City News,* June 25, 2015. Accessed November 26, 2020. https://www.gaycitynews.com/sidney-was-a-right-on-woman.

James, David E. *The Most Typical Avant-Garde: History and Geography of Minor Cinemas in Los Angeles.* Berkeley: University of California Press, 2006.

Jameson, Fredric. *Archaeologies of the Future: The Desire Called Utopia and Other Science Fictions.* London: Verso, 2005.

Jenkins, Henry. *Fans, Bloggers, and Gamers: Exploring Participatory Culture.* New York: New York University Press, 2006.

Jenkins, Henry. *Textual Poachers: Television Fans and Participatory Culture.* New York: Routledge, 1992.

Joanschild, Aurora, and Caren Kaplan. "International Women's Film Festival." *off our backs* (July 14, 1983): 23.

Johnston, Claire. *Notes on Women's Cinema.* London: Society for Education in Film and Television, 1973.

Joseph, Miranda. *Against the Romance of Community.* Minneapolis: University of Minnesota Press, 2002.

Juhasz, Alexandra. "No Woman Is an Object: Realizing the Feminist Collaborative Video." *Camera Obscura* 54 (2003): 71–97.

Juhasz, Alexandra. "They Said We Were Trying to Show Reality—All I Want to Show Is My Video: The Politics of the Realist Feminist Documentary." In

273

Collecting Visible Evidence, edited by Jane Gaines and Michael Renov, 190–215. Minneapolis: University of Minnesota Press, 1999.

Kaplan, E. Ann. *Women and Film: Both Sides of the Camera*. New York: Routledge, 1983.

Keeling, Kara. "Joining the Lesbians: Cinematic Regimes of Black Lesbian Visibility." In *Black Queer Studies: A Critical Anthology*, edited by E. Patrick Johnson and Mae G. Henderson. Durham, NC: Duke University Press, 2005.

Keeling, Kara. "Looking for M—: Queer Temporality, Black Political Possibility, and Poetry from the Future." GLQ 15, no. 4 (2009): 565–82.

Keeling, Kara. *Queer Times, Black Futures*. New York: New York University Press, 2019.

Keeling, Kara. *The Witch's Flight: The Cinematic, the Black Femme, and the Image of Common Sense*. Durham, NC: Duke University Press, 2007.

Keller, Sarah. "Barbara Hammer: Lesbian Feminist Iconography and Queer Aesthetics." In *The Oxford Handbook of Queer Cinema*, edited by Amy Villarejo and Ronald Gregg, 361–79. Oxford: Oxford University Press, 2021.

Kelley, Robin D. G. *Freedom Dreams: The Black Radical Imagination*. Boston: Beacon, 2002.

Kesselman, Amy. "Coming Out, Coming In and 'Be-Coming': Lesbians and the Women's Liberation Movement in New Haven, Connecticut." Paper presented at A Revolutionary Moment: Women's Liberation in the Late 1960s and Early 1970s conference, Boston University, March 29, 2014.

Killer Dykes. "Sexist Pig Oppressors . . . Beware!" *Killer Dykes* 1, no. 1 (September 1971): 3.

King, Katie. *Theory in Its Feminist Travels: Conversations in U.S. Women's Movements*. Bloomington: Indiana University Press, 1994.

Knight, Julia, and Peter Thomas. *Reaching Audiences: Distribution and Promotion of Alternative Moving Image*. Bristol, UK: Intellect, 2011.

Koedt, Anne. "The Myth of the Vaginal Orgasm." In *Radical Feminism*, edited by Anne Koedt, Ellen Levine, and Anita Rapone, 198–207. New York: Quadrangle, 1973.

Koyama, Emi. "The Transfeminist Manifesto." In *Catching a Wave: Reclaiming Feminism for the Twenty-first Century*, edited by Rory Dicker and Alison Piepmeier, 141–62. Lebanon, NH: Northeastern University Press, 2003.

Kuhn, Annette. *Women's Pictures: Feminism and Cinema*. London: Routledge and Kegan Paul, 1982.

Kunzel, Regina. *Criminal Intimacy: Prison and the Uneven History of Modern American Sexuality*. Chicago: University of Chicago Press, 2008.

Law, Victoria. *Resistance behind Bars: The Struggles of Incarcerated Women*, 2d ed. Oakland, CA: PM, 2012.

Lefanu, Sarah. *Feminism and Science Fiction*. Bloomington: Indiana University Press, 1988.

Le Guin, Ursula K. "Is Gender Necessary?" In *Aurora: Beyond Equality*, edited by Susan Janice Anderson and Vonda N. McIntyre, 130–39. Greenwich, CT: Fawcett, 1976.

Leimbacher, Irina, and Chick Strand. "An Introduction to the Films of Chick Strand." *Discourse* 20, nos. 1–2 (Winter–Spring 1998): 127–52.

Leng, Kirsten. "Pleasure and Pedagogy: The Role of Humor in Florynce Kennedy's Political Praxis." *Feminist Formations* 31, no. 2 (2019): 205–28.

Lesage, Julia. "The Political Aesthetics of Feminist Documentary Film." *Quarterly Review of Film and Video* 3, no. 4 (Fall 1978): 507–23.

Lorde, Audre "A Litany for Survival." In *The Black Unicorn: Poems*, 31–32. New York: W. W. Norton, 1978.

Lorde, Audre. *Sister Outsider.* Freedom, CA: Crossing, 1984.

Lothian, Alexis. *Old Futures: Speculative Fiction and Queer Possibility.* New York: New York University Press, 2018.

Love, Heather. *Feeling Backward: Loss and the Politics of Queer History.* Cambridge, MA: Harvard University Press, 2007.

Manion, Jen. *Female Husbands: A Trans History.* Cambridge: Cambridge University Press, 2020.

Marks, Laura U. *Touch: Sensuous Theory and Multisensory Media.* Minneapolis: University of Minnesota Press, 2002.

Marshall, Daniel, Kevin P. Murphy, and Zeb Tortorici, eds. "Queering Archives: Historical Unravelings." Special issue of *Radical History Review* 120 (Fall 2014).

Maslin, Janet. "*Born in Flames*: Radical Feminist Ideas." *New York Times*, November 10, 1983, C17.

Mayne, Judith. *Framed: Lesbians, Feminists, and Media Culture.* Minneapolis: University of Minnesota Press, 2000.

McKinney, Cait. *Information Activism: A Queer History of Lesbian Media Technologies.* Durham, NC: Duke University Press, 2020.

McRuer, Robert. *Crip Theory: Cultural Signs of Queerness and Disability.* New York: New York University Press, 2006.

Melzer, Patricia. *Alien Constructions: Science Fiction and Feminist Thought.* Austin: University of Texas Press, 2006.

Merrick, Helen. *The Secret Feminist Cabal: A Cultural History of Science Fiction Feminisms.* Seattle: Aqueduct, 2009.

Milano, Susan. "Women's Media: 9 cities share videoletters." *TeleVISIONS Magazine*, vol. 3, no. 4 (October–November 1975): 4.

Miller, Quinlan. *Camp TV: Trans Gender Queer Sitcom History.* Durham, NC: Duke University Press, 2019.

Moraga, Cherríe, and Gloria Anzaldúa, eds. *This Bridge Called My Back: Writings by Radical Women of Color*, 2d ed. New York: Kitchen Table/Women of Color, 1983.

Muñoz, José Esteban. *Cruising Utopia: The Then and There of Queer Futurity.* New York: New York University Press, 2009.

Muñoz, José Esteban. "Ephemera as Evidence: Introductory Notes to Queer Acts." *Women and Performance* 8, no. 2 (1996): 5–16.

Nash, Jennifer C. "Practicing Love: Black Feminism, Love-Politics, and Post-Intersectionality." *Meridians* 11, no. 2 (2013): 1–24.

National Coalition of Anti-violence Programs. "A Crisis of Hate: A Mid-Year Report on Lesbian, Gay, Bisexual, Transgender and Queer Hate Violence Homicides." Accessed June 19, 2018. http://avp.org/wp-content/uploads/2017/08/NCAVP-A-Crisis-of-Hate-Final.pdf.

National Coalition of Anti-violence Programs. "Lesbian, Gay, Bisexual, Transgender, Queer, and HIV-Affected Hate Violence in 2016." Accessed June 19, 2018. http://avp.org/wp-content/uploads/2017/06/NCAVP_2016HateViolence_REPORT.pdf.

Nealon, Christopher. *Foundlings: Lesbian and Gay Historical Emotion before Stonewall.* Durham, NC: Duke University Press, 2001.

Nestle, Joan. "Butch-Fem Relationships: Sexual Courage in the 1950's." *Heresies* 12 (1981): 21–24.

Newton, Judith. "Feminism and Anxiety in *Alien*." In *Alien Zone: Cultural Theory and Contemporary Science Fiction Cinema*, edited by Annette Kuhn, 82–90. Brooklyn, NY: Verso, 1990.

Nichols, Bill. "Newsreel: Film and Revolution." *Cinéaste* 5, no, 4 (1973): 7–13.

Nuñez, Louis. "Rights of Spanish-speaking Minorities." *American Journal of Correction* 34 (November–December 1972): 24–26.

Ouellette, Laurie, and Sara Banet-Weiser, eds. "Media and the Extreme Right." Special issue of *Communication, Culture, and Critique* 11, no. 1 (March 2018).

Padawer, Ruth. "When Women Become Men at Wellesley." *New York Times Magazine*. October 15, 2014. http://www.nytimes.com/2014/10/19/magazine/when-women-become-men-at-wellesley-college.html.

Pally, Marcia. "Is There Revolution after the Revolution?" *Village Voice*, November 15, 1983, 80–81.

Panshin, Alexei, and Cory Panshin. "Books." *Magazine of Fantasy and Science Fiction*, vol. 49, no. 2, August 1975, 46–53, 162.

Penley, Constance. "Feminism, Psychoanalysis, and the Study of Popular Culture." In *Cultural Studies*, edited by Lawrence Grossberg, Cary Nelson, and Paula A. Treichler, 479–94. New York: Routledge, 1992.

Penley, Constance. *NASA/Trek: Popular Science and Sex in America.* New York: Verso, 1997.

Phillips, Julie. *James Tiptree, Jr.: The Double Life of Alice B. Sheldon.* New York: St. Martin's, 2006.

Pierce, Alexandra, and Alisa Krasnostein, eds. *Letters to Tiptree.* Australia: Twelfth Planet Place, 2015.

Prosser, Jay. *Second Skins: The Body Narratives of Transsexuality.* New York: Columbia University Press, 1998.

Radicalesbians. "The Woman Identified Woman." In *Radical Feminism*, edited by Anne Koedt, Ellen Levine, and Anita Rapone, 240–45. New York: Quadrangle, 1973.

Radway, Janice. "Reception Study: Ethnography and the Problems of Dispersed Audiences and Nomadic Subjects." *Cultural Studies* 2, no. 3 (1988): 359–76.

Rangan, Pooja, Brett Story, and Paige Sarlin. "Humanitarian Ethics and Documentary Politics" *Camera Obscura* 98 (2018): 197–207.

276

Rawson, K. J. "Introduction: An Inevitably Political Craft." *TSQ: Transgender Studies Quarterly* 2, no. 4 (November 2015): 544–52.

Rawson, K. J., and Aaron Devor, eds. "Archives and Archiving." Special issue of *TSQ: Transgender Studies Quarterly* 2, no. 1 (November 2015).

Reid, Coletta. "Ideology: Guide to Action." *The Furies* 1, no. 3 (March–April 1972): 6.

Renov, Michael. "Early Newsreel." *Afterimage* (February 1987): 12–15.

Renov, Michael. "Newsreel: Old and New—Towards an Historical Profile." *Film Quarterly* 41, no. 1 (Autumn 1987): 20–33.

Resources for Community Change. *Women behind Bars: An Organizing Tool*. Washington, DC: 1975.

Rich, Adrienne. "Compulsory Heterosexuality and Lesbian Existence." *Signs* 5, no. 4 (Summer 1980): 631–60.

Rich, Adrienne. "When We Dead Awaken: Writing as Re-vision." *College English* 34, no. 1 (October 1972): 18–30.

Rich, B. Ruby. *Chick Flicks: Theories and Memories of the Feminist Film Movement*. Durham, NC: Duke University Press, 1998.

Rich, B. Ruby. *New Queer Cinema: The Director's Cut*. Durham, NC: Duke University Press, 2013.

Riley, Denise. *"Am I That Name?": Feminism and the Category of "Women" in History*. Minneapolis: University of Minnesota Press, 1988.

Rochester Women's Video Collective. "International Videoletters: Rochester Women's Video Collective." Media Burn Independent Video Archive. http://mediaburn.org/video/videoletters-rochester-may-womans-video-collective.

Rosen, Ruth. *The World Split Open: How the Modern Women's Movement Changed America*. New York: Viking, 2000.

Ross, Allison. "Queering Identity in Early Outfest Documentaries." Paper presented at the Society of Cinema and Media Studies, Seattle, March 15, 2019.

Ross, Andrew. *Strange Weather: Culture, Science, and Technology in the Age of Limits*. London: Verso, 1991.

Roth, Benita. *Separate Roads to Feminism: Black, Chicana, and White Feminist Movements in America's Second Wave*. Cambridge: Cambridge University Press, 2004.

Russ, Joanna. *The Female Man*. New York: Bantam, 1975.

Russ, Joanna. *Magic Mommas, Trembling Sisters, Puritans and Perverts: Essays on Sex and Pornography*. Freedom, CA: Crossing, 1985.

Russ, Joanna. "Outta Space: Women Write Science Fiction." *Ms.*, vol. 4, no. 7, January 1976, 109–11.

Russ, Joanna. *To Write like a Woman: Essays in Feminism and Science Fiction*. Bloomington: Indiana University Press, 1995.

Salamon, Gayle. *Assuming a Body: Transgender and Rhetorics of Materiality*. New York: Columbia University Press, 2010.

Saler, Michael. *As If: Modern Enchantment and the Literary Prehistory of Virtual Reality*. New York: Oxford University Press, 2012.

Samer, Rox. "Reflections on Queer Feminist Fandom Then, Now and in the Future: Interviews with Amanda Bankier and Jeanne Gomoll." In *Futures of Feminism and Fandom: The WisCon Chronicles Volume 6*, edited by Alexis Lothian, 2–17. Seattle: Aqueduct, 2012.

Samer, Rox. "Revising 'Re-vision': Documenting 1970s Feminisms and the Queer Potentiality of Digital Feminist Archives." *Ada*, no. 5 (2014). doi:10.7264/N3FF3QMC.

Sandoval, Chela. *Methodology of the Oppressed*. Minneapolis: University of Minnesota Press, 2000.

Santa Cruz Women's Media Collective. "International Videoletters: Santa Cruz." Media Burn Independent Video Archive. http://mediaburn.org/video/international-videoletters-santa-cruz.

Schneider, Suzanne. "'Like a Rose': Review and Interview." *Frontiers* 1, no. 3 (Winter 1976): 103–12.

Sedgwick, Eve Kosofsky. *Epistemology of the Closet*. Berkeley: University of California Press, 1990.

Sender, Katherine. *Business, Not Politics: The Making of the Gay Market*. New York: Columbia University Press, 2004.

Serano, Julia. "Op-ed: An Open Letter to *The New Yorker*." *The Advocate*, August 5, 2014. http://www.advocate.com/commentary/2014/08/05/op-ed-open-letter-new-yorker.

Serano, Julia. *Whipping Girl: A Transsexual Woman on Sexism and the Scapegoating of Femininity*. Emeryville, CA: Seal, 2007.

Shugar, Dana R. *Separatism and Women's Community*. Lincoln: University of Nebraska Press, 1995.

Silverberg, Robert. "Introduction." In *Warm Worlds and Otherwise*, by James Tiptree, Jr., ix–xviii. New York: Ballantine, 1975.

Smith, Jeffrey D., ed. *Meet Me at Infinity: The Uncollected Tiptree: Fiction and Nonfiction*. New York: Tor, 2000.

Smith, Jeffrey D., ed. *Symposium: Women in Science Fiction, Khatru 3 and 4*, 3d ed. Oakland, CA: James Tiptree Award, 2009.

Sobchack, Vivian. *The Address of the Eye: A Phenomenology of Film Experience*. Princeton, NJ: Princeton University Press, 1992.

Sobchack, Vivian. *Screening Space: The American Science Fiction Film*, 2d ed. New Brunswick, NJ: Rutgers University Press, 1998.

Stanley, Julia Penelope, and Susan J. Wolfe, eds. *The Coming Out Stories*. Watertown, MA: Persephone, 1980.

Steinbock, Eliza. *Shimmering Images: Trans Cinema, Embodiment, and the Aesthetics of Change*. Durham, NC: Duke University Press, 2019.

Stone, Beth. "Nat. Women's Film Circuit Makes Powerful One Hundred-Movie Debut." *Grass Roots* 4, no. 9 (October–November 1975): 15–16.

Straayer, Chris. *Deviant Eyes, Deviant Bodies: Sexual Re-orientations in Film and Video*. New York: Columbia University Press, 1996.

Strongman, SaraEllen. "The Sisterhood: Black Women, Black Feminism, and the Women's Liberation Movement." PhD diss., University of Pennsylvania, 2018.

Stryker, Susan. *Transgender History*. Berkeley, CA: Seal Studies, 2008.

Taubin, Amy. "Pale Fire." *Village Voice*, November 15, 1983, 81, 108.

Thompson, Becky. "Multiracial Feminism: Recasting the Chronology of Second Wave Feminism." *Feminist Studies* 28, no. 2 (Summer 2002): 336–60.

Thuma, Emily L. *All Our Trials: Policing and the Feminist Fight to End Violence*. Urbana: University of Illinois Press, 2019.

Tiptree, James, Jr. "Houston, Houston, Do You Read?" In *Aurora: Beyond Equality*, edited by Susan Janice Anderson and Vonda N. McIntyre, 36–98. Greenwich, CT: Fawcett, 1976.

Valk, Anne M. *Radical Sisters: Second-Wave Feminism and Black Liberation in Washington, D.C.* Urbana: University of Illinois Press, 2008.

Vasquez, Tina. "It's Time to End the Long History of Feminism Failing Transgender Women." *Bitch Media*, February 17, 2014. https://bitchmedia.org/post/the-long-history-of-transgender-exclusion-from-feminism.

Villarejo, Amy. *Ethereal Queer: Television, Historicity, Desire*. Durham, NC: Duke University Press, 2013.

Villarejo, Amy. *Lesbian Rule: Cultural Criticism and the Value of Desire*. Durham, NC: Duke University Press, 2003.

Walker, Nancy A. *A Very Serious Thing: Women's Humor and American Culture*. Minneapolis: University of Minnesota Press, 1988.

Wallace, Michele. *Invisibility Blues: From Pop to Theory*. London: Verso, 1990.

Warner, Harry, Jr. *All Our Yesterdays: An Informal History of Science Fiction Fandom in the Forties*. Chicago: Advent, 1969.

Warner, Michael. *Publics and Counterpublics*. New York: Zone, 2002.

Warner, Michael. *The Trouble with Normal*. Cambridge, MA: Harvard University Press, 1999.

Warren, Shilyh. *Subject to Reality: Women and Documentary Film*. Urbana, Chicago, and Springfield: University of Illinois Press, 2019.

Waugh, Thomas. "Films by Gays for Gays: *Who Are We?*, *A Very Natural Thing*, *The Naked Civil Servant*." *Jump Cut* 16 (1977): 14–18.

Weiss, Andrea. "*Women I Love* and *Double Strength*: Lesbian Cinema and Romantic Love." *Jump Cut* 24–25 (March 1981): 30.

Weisstein, Naomi. "Why We Aren't Laughing . . . Any More." *Ms.*, 2, no. 5 (November 1973): 49–51, 88–90.

White, Patricia. *Uninvited: Classical Hollywood Cinema and Lesbian Representability*. Bloomington: Indiana University Press, 1999.

Williams, Cristan. "Radical Inclusion: Recounting the Trans Inclusive History of Radical Feminism." *TSQ: Transgender Studies Quarterly* 3, nos. 1–2 (2016): 254–58.

Williams, Linda. "Porn Studies: Proliferating Pornographies On/Scene: An Introduction." In *Porn Studies*, edited by Linda Williams, 1–23. Durham, NC: Duke University Press, 2004.

Willse, Craig, and Dean Spade. "Introduction: We Are *Born in Flames*." *Women and Performance: A Journal of Feminist Theory* 23, no. 1 (2013): 1–5.

Wittig, Monique. "One Is Not Born a Woman." *Feminist Issues* 2 (Winter 1981): 47–53.

Wood, Mara. "Feminist Icons Wanted: Damsels in Distress Need Not Apply." In *A Galaxy Here and Now: Historical and Cultural Readings of Star Wars*, edited by Peter W. Lee, 62–83. Jefferson, NC: McFarland, 2016.

Youmans, Greg. "Performing Essentialism: Reassessing Barbara Hammer's Films of the 1970s." *Camera Obscura* 81 (2012): 101–35.

Youmans, Greg. *Word Is Out: A Queer Film Classic*. Vancouver: Arsenal Pulp, 2011.

Young, Cynthia. "Third World Newsreel: Third Cinema Practice in the United States." In *Global Migration, Social Change, and Cultural Transformation*, edited by Emory Elliott, Jasmine Payne, and Patricia Ploesch, 77–99. New York: Palgrave Macmillan, 2007.

Young, Damon R. *Making Sex Public and Other Cinematic Fantasies*. Durham, NC: Duke University Press, 2018.

Zimmermann, Patricia. *Reel Families: A Social History of Amateur Film*. Bloomington: Indiana University Press, 1995.

Index

Index

285

288

289